THE STORY OF
CHRISTIANITY

THE STORY OF
CHRISTIANITY

AN ILLUSTRATED HISTORY OF 2000 YEARS OF THE CHRISTIAN FAITH

David Bentley Hart

Quercus

CONTENTS

Byzantine mosaic of Jesus Christ

Stained-glass window of Resurrection angel

Statue of Saint Patrick

Icon of the Virgin Mary

INTRODUCTION

Needless to say, no single volume can possibly contain the entire story of Christianity – a religion that spans 20 centuries of history, that has reached every quarter of the globe, that has assumed an incalculable variety of institutional and cultural forms, and that today is the faith (at least nominally) of one-third of the human race. What it is possible to do in a book of this sort, however, is to provide a broad picture of Christian history, with as much detail as space allows, without allowing any single aspect to overwhelm the narrative as a whole. This is not necessarily an easy ambition to realize. Most Christians, after all, are conscious of only a small portion of Christian tradition, belief and practice, and rarely have cause to investigate the many forms of their faith with which they are not immediately familiar. It is quite possible to be an Eastern Orthodox, Roman Catholic, Presbyterian, Evangelical, Anglican, Coptic, Chaldean, Ethiopian Orthodox, Armenian Orthodox or Malankaran Christian (to name a few of the many possibilities), perfectly aware of the tenets of one's own tradition, and still know very little indeed of the larger scope of Christian thought and piety. And it is always a temptation when writing a work like this to allow oneself to concentrate so exclusively on a single version of Christianity – say, the Western communions – that the sheer richness of Christian tradition and experience is hidden from view.

It is a temptation, though, that should be resisted, because the true story of Christianity – when told in something like its full breadth – is immeasurably fascinating. It is even, one might say, rather exotic. A faith that began in Roman-occupied Judaea, as a small and fugitive faction within Judaism, and that was legally proscribed for centuries, even at times on pain of death, persisted, grew, thrived and finally 'conquered' the empire that had sought to exterminate it. Then, over many centuries and in many lands, it became the vital source from which new civilizations sprang and developed and drew constant nourishment. At times, its geographical range expanded mightily, at others contracted perilously. At times, the church proved heroically true to its deepest moral principles; at others, inexcusably traitorous to them. But, at the end of the tale (at least to this point), this faith that began in such fragility, and that became so powerful – even though its temporal power has now receded in its historic homelands – is the most widespread and diverse of all religions, and is rapidly taking root in cultures very different from those in which it was born and in which it once flourished, and is assuming configurations that could not have been anticipated a century ago.

To tell this story in a way that does proper justice to its improbability and variety, one must consider not only its larger features, but its more minute as well; not only its most resplendent and historically successful expressions, but its most obscure and frequently forgotten; not only its most familiar forms, but its strangest. I have, at any rate, attempted in what follows to give something like equal time to the churches of the East and of the West, and to accord attention to the smaller, ancient Christian communities of Asia and Africa, and to take note of those contemporary communions (like the Chinese house churches) that exist somewhat at the margins of the Christian world. If I have failed in this in any respect, it is because certain requirements of space proved impossible to defy.

The story of Christianity is not merely the story of a religion indigenous to Western civilization; in a very real sense, it is the story of that civilization itself. One cannot really understand the values that inform those cultures that were originally conceived in the womb of Christendom without understanding the faith that created them. Even in nations where an explicit devotion to Christian faith is on the wane, the Christian understanding of what it is to be human continues to shape imaginations and desires at the profoundest levels, and to determine much of what we hold most dear and many of the moral expectations we have of ourselves and others. For this reason alone, the story of Christianity is one we should all wish to know better.

That said, perhaps one caution should be kept in mind. A written history of Christianity is concerned – of necessity – with history, which is to say with social and political matters: nations and rulers, states and institutions, compromises and wars. This being so, one might object that a book of this sort cannot really record the story of Christianity as such – of the beliefs, ideas and values that Christian faith instills in individual men and women – but can, at most, relate a series of episodes in the evolution of cultures and institutions that happen to have been populated by persons who happened to be baptized. This is a perfectly fair objection. Perhaps the only true story of Christianity is that which unfolds in the hearts and minds of believers. Even so, these hidden movements of the spirit have made themselves manifest, even if only fitfully, in the outward events of Christian history. Thus, a book like this perhaps still has the power to illuminate that other more secret and mysterious story, whose discrete moments occur everywhere and nowhere, and which cannot otherwise be told.

David Bentley Hart

THE ABIDING GLORY: THE PEOPLE OF ISRAEL

The books of the Hebrew Bible (the Christian Old Testament) come from many periods, are written in diverse styles and are the work of many authors. They do not, therefore, constitute a simple, continuous narrative. Yet, taken as a whole, they can be said to tell a single, great story – the epic of the Glory of God come to dwell on earth.

This stone relief carving from the ruins of a synagogue shows a wheeled cart bearing the Ark of the Covenant, the sacred chest containing the tablets of the law (Ten Commandments) that Moses brought down from Mount Sinai.

This Glory, which later Jewish tradition called the *Shekhinah* (meaning 'that which rests' or 'that which abides'), was conceived of as being nothing less than the real, mysterious and overwhelming presence of God himself. At times, the Glory would descend (often in a cloud of impenetrable darkness) upon the Ark of the Covenant, the sacred gold-plated chest in which the tablets of the law of Moses were kept. The Ark itself, as the throne of God, was initially housed within the Tabernacle (or 'tent of meeting') prepared for it by Moses, but was later transferred to the inner sanctuary of the Temple built for it in Jerusalem by King Solomon.

The Calling of Israel and the Age of the Patriarchs

The Bible also recounts God's election of a chosen people and describes how this choice inevitably becomes ever narrower. In other words, God initially creates all mankind for communion with him, but eventually, as a result of human sin, decides instead to fashion a particular people for himself, with whom he forges an unbreakable bond so as to establish his home on Earth among them. Israel thus becomes the object of special divine attention, which is likened in scripture to the love of a father for his child or of a husband for his wife. The story is marked by episodes of faithfulness and betrayal by Israel, and mercy and anger on God's part. The relationship is ruptured and restored; Israel is sometimes seduced by strange gods, only to return to God for forgiveness. God punishes and pardons, his Glory departs and returns – but he never abandons his people.

This is the sacred story of the Jews, in the light of which Hebrew scripture interprets all the concrete events of Israel's history. By the time of Jesus' birth, that story already spanned nearly two millennia, beginning in the age of the Patriarchs, when the ancestors of the Jews were merely a tribe of semi-nomads. The first tribal patriarch was Abraham (originally named Abram), whom God summoned from the Mesopotamian city of Ur, to journey to an unknown land where his descendants would become a great nation. This was God's special covenant with Abraham: one that was, so to speak, written in the very flesh of the community, through the circumcision of all the males of the tribe. Abraham was succeeded as patriarch by his son Isaac, whom Abraham's wife Sarah miraculously conceived and bore when she was well beyond child-bearing age. Isaac in turn

In a scene from a painting by the 17th-century Italian artist Giovanni Castiglione (1616–70), Moses strikes a rock in the wilderness to produce water as he leads his people out of captivity in Egypt – a sign that God had kept faith with the People of Israel.

was succeeded by his son Jacob. The patriarchal narratives end with the migration of Israel into Egypt, under the protection of Isaac's son Joseph, who had been sold into slavery as a youth by his jealous elder brothers, but who had risen to a position of immense authority in Pharaoh's court.

Prophets and Kings

The protection under which Israel sheltered, however, was withdrawn after the time of Joseph, and the people languished in slavery for many centuries, until around the 14th or 13th century BC, when the prophet and legislator Moses arose to lead them to freedom. It was to Moses that God for the first time revealed his 'proper' name, the mysterious 'tetragrammaton' YHWH, which the Book of Exodus claims derives from the even more mysterious phrase '*Eyeh asher Eyeh*': 'I will be as I will be'. It was under Moses that the Jewish priesthood and the rites of the Tabernacle were established, and through Moses that God gave Israel the law: the body of religious, moral and civil ordinances that was to guide the Israelites.

Subsequent narratives tell of Israel's settlement and conquest of Canaan, the 'Promised Land', after a delay of 40 years and the death of Moses. For nearly two centuries thereafter, Israel remained a loose federation of 12 distinct tribes, governed by judges, but before the beginning of the 10th century BC it became

c.1800–1700 BC
Life of Abraham (Abram), the first patriarch of the Jewish people

c.1300 BC
Moses leads the Israelites out of slavery in Egypt and crosses the Sinai Desert to Canaan, the 'Land of Milk and Honey'

c.1029–c.1007 BC
Reign of Saul in Israel sees many conquests over neighbouring peoples (e.g. Ammonites, Moabites), but Saul and three of his sons fall in battle against the Philistines

c.1007 BC
David becomes King of Israel, reigning for 40 years

c.965–928 BC
Solomon's reign; construction of the First Temple of Jerusalem commences in 965; death of Solomon brings division of his kingdom into Israel and Judah

587–586 BC
Babylonians conquer Judah and destroy the First Temple. Start of the Babylonian Captivity

539 BC
Conquest of Babylon by King Cyrus I of Assyria brings freedom and return to Israel

168 BC
Revolt of Judas Maccabeus against Antiochus IV leads to the establishment of an independent Jewish state

Roman general Pompey overruns Palestine

a monarchy, ruled first by King Saul (d. *c*.1007 BC), and then by King David (d. *c*.965 BC); the latter was a brilliant warrior and leader, who forged Israel into a united military and cultural power. It was he who brought the Ark of the Covenant to Jerusalem from the Tabernacle in Shiloh. Yet it fell to David's son, the legendarily wise and wealthy King Solomon (d. *c*.928 BC), to build the great Temple, in whose inner chamber – the Holy of Holies – the Ark was finally placed. Thereafter, no one but the High Priest was permitted to enter into the 'Presence' and he only once each year, on Yom Kippur, the Day of Atonement.

For all its grandeur, Solomon's reign was largely a failure. His tolerance of foreign cults – in order to indulge his many foreign wives – not only hastened his own demise, but also caused the schism of the Jews into two kingdoms: Israel in the north and Judah in the south. Israel endured for two centuries, but fell to the Assyrians in 722 BC and ultimately faded from history; and so it is from the latter that later Judaism descends.

This was also the age of the prophets, men called by God to proclaim justice for the poor and oppressed, to denounce idolatry, to warn of divine retribution, and to announce the approach of a day when the God of Israel would draw all the world under his merciful governance.

A Subject People

The kingdom of Judah was overrun by the Babylonians in 587–586 BC; the Temple was destroyed and stripped of its treasures (though, apparently, the Ark was no longer among them) and much of the population was led away into exile as captives. In 539 BC, however, Babylon fell to Persia, and the Persian king Cyrus permitted those Jews who wished to do so to return to Israel and rebuild the Temple – a task completed in 516–515 BC. In 332 BC, with Alexander the Great's conquest of Persia, the age of Hellenistic – or Late Greek – Judaism began.

Under the rule of the Greek-Egyptian dynasty of the Ptolemies, the Jews were granted freedom of worship, and for more than 150 years, Jewish culture, in Palestine and abroad, peacefully assimilated Hellenistic culture. In 198 BC, however, the Greek-Syrian Seleucid dynasty conquered Israel, and in 168 BC King Antiochus IV Epiphanes set about eradicating Judaism. He desecrated the Temple, instituted pagan sacrifices in Jerusalem, and mercilessly persecuted any Jews who resisted.

A Jewish revolt, initially led by Judas Maccabeus of the Hasmonean dynasty forced the Seleucid regime to recognize Judaism and permit reconsecration of the Temple in 164 BC. Thirty years later, the Hasmoneans even succeeded in winning independence for Judaea – a condition that lasted for a century, until the Roman conquest of 63 BC.

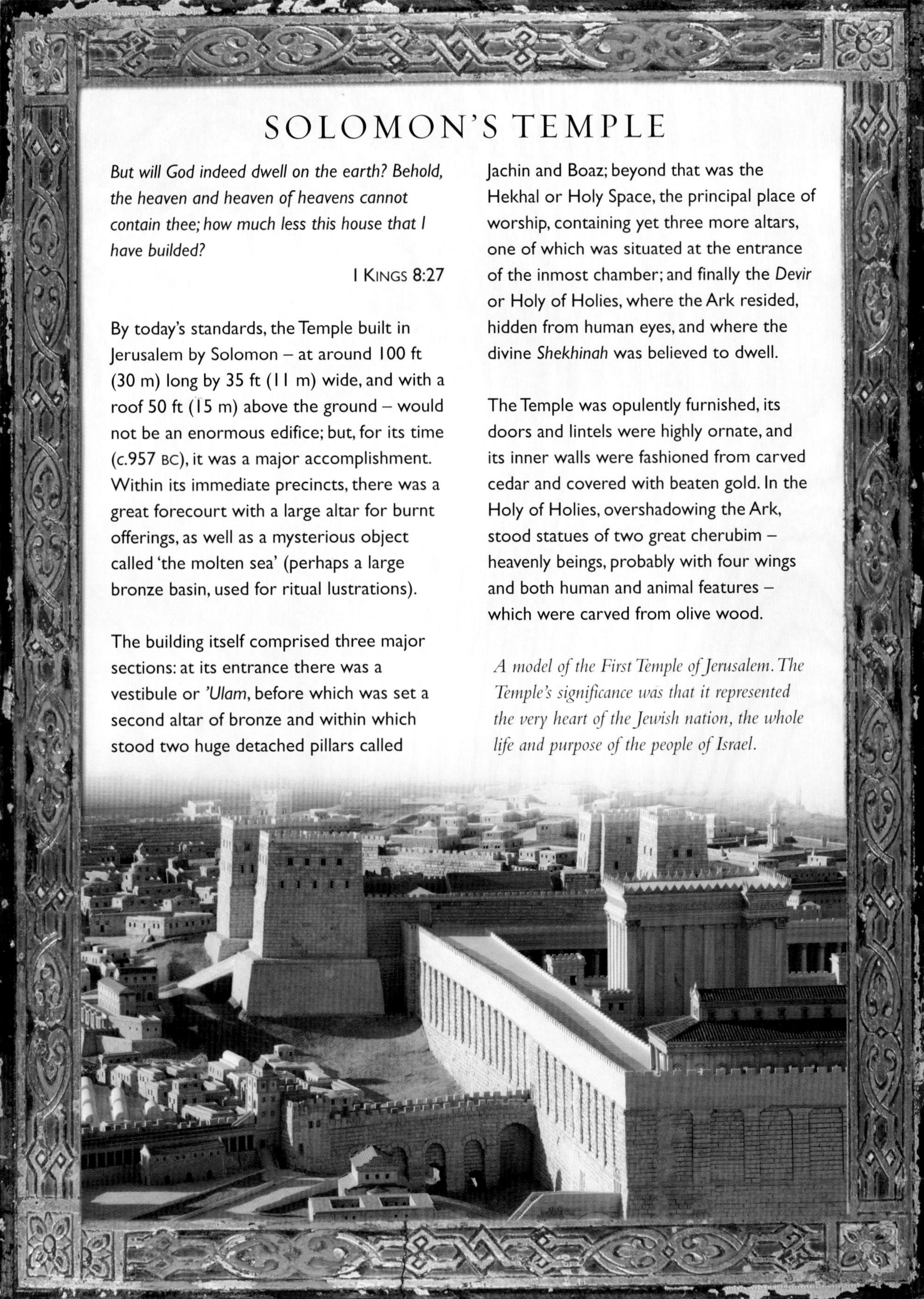

SOLOMON'S TEMPLE

But will God indeed dwell on the earth? Behold, the heaven and heaven of heavens cannot contain thee; how much less this house that I have builded?

I KINGS 8:27

By today's standards, the Temple built in Jerusalem by Solomon – at around 100 ft (30 m) long by 35 ft (11 m) wide, and with a roof 50 ft (15 m) above the ground – would not be an enormous edifice; but, for its time (c.957 BC), it was a major accomplishment. Within its immediate precincts, there was a great forecourt with a large altar for burnt offerings, as well as a mysterious object called 'the molten sea' (perhaps a large bronze basin, used for ritual lustrations).

The building itself comprised three major sections: at its entrance there was a vestibule or *'Ulam*, before which was set a second altar of bronze and within which stood two huge detached pillars called Jachin and Boaz; beyond that was the Hekhal or Holy Space, the principal place of worship, containing yet three more altars, one of which was situated at the entrance of the inmost chamber; and finally the *Devir* or Holy of Holies, where the Ark resided, hidden from human eyes, and where the divine *Shekhinah* was believed to dwell.

The Temple was opulently furnished, its doors and lintels were highly ornate, and its inner walls were fashioned from carved cedar and covered with beaten gold. In the Holy of Holies, overshadowing the Ark, stood statues of two great cherubim – heavenly beings, probably with four wings and both human and animal features – which were carved from olive wood.

A model of the First Temple of Jerusalem. The Temple's significance was that it represented the very heart of the Jewish nation, the whole life and purpose of the people of Israel.

JESUS CHRIST, BORN OF THE JEWS

In the New Testament, the theme of the descent of the divine Glory to earth continues, but in a radically different key; for, in Christian thought, God comes to dwell among human beings not merely in the awesome but intangible form of the *Shekhinah*, but as a concrete presence, a living man.

A terracotta bas-relief of the Virgin Mary in the Italian city of Milan. The fullest accounts of the mother of Christ are found in the gospels of Luke and Matthew.

Thus, in the Gospel of Luke, when the angel of the annunciation tells Mary of the conception of Jesus in her womb, his language clearly recalls the cloud of darkness that used to attend the Lord's entry into his house: 'The Holy Ghost shall come upon thee, and the power of the Highest shall overshadow thee … ' (Luke 1:35). The Gospel of John proclaims that, in becoming flesh, the divine Son literally 'tabernacled' among us – 'and we beheld his Glory, the Glory of the only begotten of the Father' (John 1:14). Jesus likens himself to the Temple. And all three of the Synoptic Gospels (Matthew, Mark and Luke) tell of Christ's Transfiguration, when the Glory of his divinity briefly became visible through the veil of his humanity.

The Centre of History

For the early Church, the entire history of God's indwelling had culminated in the coming of Christ, who was nothing less than the 'express image' of God's essence, the very 'brightness of his Glory' (Hebrews 1:3). Already in Hebrew scripture, God's Glory had at times been portrayed as a kind of heavenly person, resembling a man (most notably in the Book of Ezekiel); but, according to Christian belief, that Glory had now actually become a man, through whom the radiance of the divine had been brought into intimate contact with human nature. As a result, all human beings were now able to become vessels of the divine presence, and Christians looked forward to a day when God's Glory would be revealed in those who had been joined to Christ, and would transfigure the whole of creation (Romans 8:18-21). For Christians, Jesus of Nazareth was, then, the centre of all human and cosmic history, and the consummation of all God's purposes in creation.

To those outside the circle of faith, of course, the sheer extravagance of the claims made for Christ's significance by Christians could scarcely have seemed more absurd. Certainly, during the early centuries of the Church, pagan critics of the gospel never failed to point out how peculiar it was for God to have chosen so obscure and humble a form for his final revelation to humanity – an itinerant preacher born among a subject people, neither noble of birth nor great amid the councils of the mighty, who lived his brief life far from the centre of the empire, and who numbered no philosophers among his friends and associates. But Christians positively rejoiced in God's desire to confound the expectations of the powerful, and to reveal himself among the poor, the nameless, the despised and the forgotten.

The Synoptic Gospels recount the story of Christ's Transfiguration by the light of divine glory. It is depicted here by the Baroque artist Giovanni Lanfranco (1582–1647).

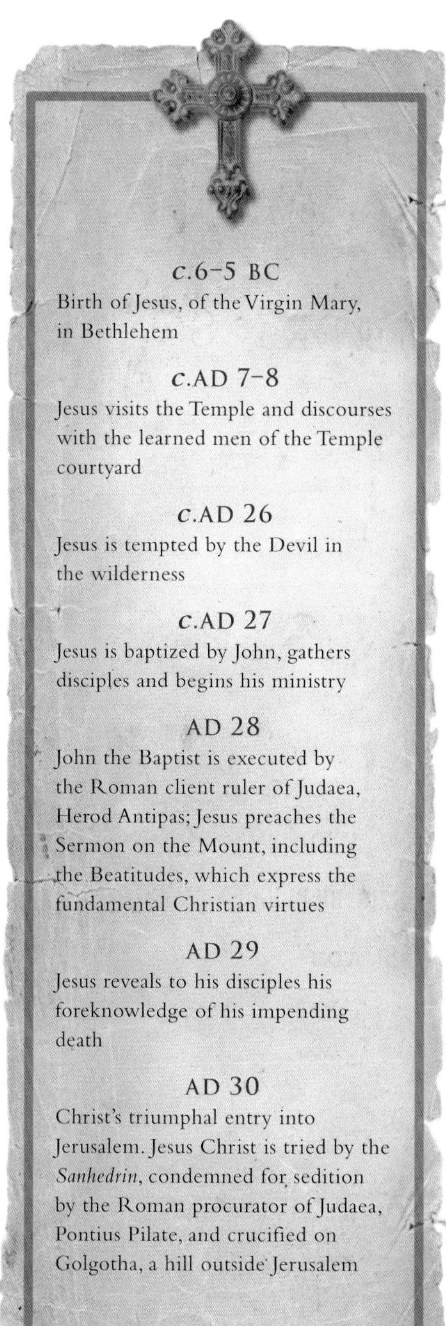

c.6–5 BC
Birth of Jesus, of the Virgin Mary, in Bethlehem

c.AD 7–8
Jesus visits the Temple and discourses with the learned men of the Temple courtyard

c.AD 26
Jesus is tempted by the Devil in the wilderness

c.AD 27
Jesus is baptized by John, gathers disciples and begins his ministry

AD 28
John the Baptist is executed by the Roman client ruler of Judaea, Herod Antipas; Jesus preaches the Sermon on the Mount, including the Beatitudes, which express the fundamental Christian virtues

AD 29
Jesus reveals to his disciples his foreknowledge of his impending death

AD 30
Christ's triumphal entry into Jerusalem. Jesus Christ is tried by the *Sanhedrin*, condemned for sedition by the Roman procurator of Judaea, Pontius Pilate, and crucified on Golgotha, a hill outside Jerusalem

Not that Judaea was a backwater. At the time of Christ's birth, the Jews had endured centuries of foreign subjugation – by Babylon, Persia, Greece and Rome – but had also, as a result, been profoundly influenced by foreign cultures, and had established communities throughout the wider Hellenistic and Roman world. Many aspects of the Judaism of the synagogues evolved during the Babylonian exile, when there was no Temple and no sacrifices to perform, and public prayer and study of the law and the prophets became Judaism's chief religious activities.

Moreover, various beliefs typical of Persian Zoroastrianism – life after death, resurrection, the Day of Judgment, the great cosmic struggle

THE SON OF MAN

In the Gospels, Jesus frequently speaks – somewhat enigmatically – of 'the Son of Man'. Occasionally, he uses this phrase to refer to a heavenly emissary of God who will be sent to earth on Judgement Day to judge the nations and gather the righteous into the Kingdom of God. At other times, however, he clearly applies it to himself in his earthly mission.

In Hebrew scripture, 'son of man' (ben Adam) is generally quite a mundane phrase. It often denotes little more than 'human being'. In the book of Job and in the Psalms, it is simply a poetic circumlocution for 'man': '... man, who is a maggot, and the son of man, who is a worm' (Job 25:6). It is also the name by which God (or God's messenger) addresses the prophet Ezekiel, in order constantly to remind the prophet that he is only mortal clay.

In the Book of Daniel, however, in a vision of the final judgment, Daniel describes the Ancient of Days upon his throne, and tells of 'one like a Son of Man' arriving amid the clouds of heaven and approaching the throne and being given everlasting dominion over all the nations of the earth.

In the New Testament, both meanings are present, in some cases simultaneously. There is something exquisitely appropriate in this. In the Christian understanding of Jesus, after all, exaltation and abasement – the heavenly and the earthly – are inseparable. Inasmuch as the phrase 'Son of Man' can serve to indicate both the humility of Christ in assuming mortal flesh and also the glory of Christ as the divine Lord of history, it elegantly comprises within itself what for Christians is the central mystery of the incarnation.

between good and evil – had been absorbed into the faith of most Jews, and that of the influential sect of the Pharisees (though other Jews, such as the Saducees, rejected such beliefs). For three centuries, moreover, Judaism – in Judaea and throughout the Jewish Diaspora (the dispersed Jewish community abroad) – had been shaped by Greek culture and thought. Jesus' older contemporary, Philo of Alexandria (*c.*15 BC–*c.*AD 50), for example, was a typical product of the Diaspora: he employed Greek methods of exegesis to interpret Hebrew scripture, borrowed freely from Greek metaphysics, and even elaborated a theory of the divine *Logos* – a secondary expression of God, or eternal 'Son', through whom God creates and communicates with the world. All of these 'foreign' influences were reflected either in the ministry of Christ or in the Church's understanding of his identity.

THE MINISTRY OF CHRIST

Little can be said of the early life of Jesus. The Gospels of Matthew and Luke tell of his miraculous conception and birth of the Virgin Mary; Matthew tells of the visit of the Magi, the flight of the holy family to Egypt, and their later return to Nazareth; Luke tells of Christ's birth in a stable, his adoration in the manger by shepherds, his presentation in the Temple and his dialogue – at the age of 12 – with the scholars of the Temple courtyard. Nothing else is known of his early years.

The Gospel accounts of Jesus himself all begin in earnest with his baptism in the Jordan by his cousin John, which inaugurated his ministry; this, in fact, is where the Gospels of Mark and John begin their narratives (though in the latter case,

Christ among the Doctors *(Jusepe de Ribera, 1635); early evidence of Christ's skill in disputation was provided by his learned discourse with the doctors of the Temple at the age of 12: 'And all who heard him were astonished at his understanding and answers'.*

only after a prologue 'in eternity'). According to the Synoptic Gospels, Christ first went into the wilderness for 40 days, to pray and fast, and to resist Satan's attempts to sway him from his mission; he then began gathering disciples – including the inner 12, the Apostles – and travelling through the Judaean countryside.

In the context of their time, Christ's teachings combined elements at once familar and strange. He was, in many ways, like any other rabbi: he expounded upon the scriptures, recalled men and women to the central precepts of the law, and proclaimed God's love for the poor, the oppressed and the forsaken. And he was, apparently, a master of 'dialectical' instruction, being especially adept at answering queries – whether sincere or hostile – by posing complementary questions that induced his questioners to answer the questions for themselves. Yet the main thrust of his mission was to proclaim the imminent approach of the Day of the Lord and the establishment of God's Kingdom on earth. As such, his message was one of drastic urgency.

These aspects of Christ's teachings are less remarkable than the manner in which he indicated the Kingdom's nature and scope – not only, that is, his frequent use of elliptical metaphors and evocative parables, but his absolutely uncompromising emphasis upon the renunciation of violence, the supremacy of charity over all other moral virtues and the limitless inclusiveness of divine love. Above all, Christ gave imaginative shape and dimensions to the Kingdom he proclaimed by requiring that his followers forego vengeance, bear the burdens of others, forgive debts, share their goods with the poor, and love their enemies, and by forbidding them from passing judgment on others for their sins. He also insisted that his disciples keep company with the most despised members of society, including even tax collectors, Samaritans and harlots.

THE DEATH OF THE MESSIAH

To judge from scripture, for many of Christ's contemporaries the principal questions raised by his ministry concerned the power with which he acted and the authority with which he spoke: not, that is, whether in fact his power and authority were real, but what their source was.

In the Gospels, Christ's enemies seldom doubt that he is able to work wonders, heal the sick, give sight to the blind, make the lame walk, perform exorcisms and so forth; what they doubt is that his works are of divine origin. Some even go so far as to suggest that he is actually using the power of the devil to cast demons out. By the same token, the Pharisees and scribes with whom Christ debates do not deny his charisma or the force of his teachings; but they still wish to know by what authority he presumes to teach, to proclaim God's will for men, to give moral instruction, or – most crucially – to declare sins forgiven (which, after all, only God can do).

In Roman times, crucifixion was an ignominious death (as witness the fact that Christ was placed between two common thieves at Golgotha). Yet the cross became Christianity's abiding symbol.

THE MYSTERY OF CHRIST'S POWER

In truth, Christ's reputed ability to perform miracles would have been less astonishing – or, at any rate, less provocative – than the liberty with which he interpreted the law of Israel. In the 1st century AD, it was taken for granted that some men were capable of exercising some degree of control over nature, or at least give the impression of doing so; but it was also assumed that such abilities might have an evil or merely magical provenance. In the Gospel of John, Christ's miracles are described not simply as *thaumata*, or 'wonders', as they are in the Synoptic Gospels, but as *semeia*, 'signs': clear demonstrations, that is, of the presence of the Kingdom in Christ's ministry. But, as John's Gospel also suggests, not everyone would have seen them as such: the last and greatest of these 'signs' is the raising of Lazarus from the dead, to which Christ's most adamant enemies respond not by putting aside their reservations and acknowledging him as the true harbinger of God's Kingdom, but by intriguing to put him to death.

Again, however, the chief scandal of Christ's ministry – and the cause, no doubt, of the enmity of certain scribes and Pharisees – was the rather lordly licence with which he approached the prescriptions of the Mosaic code. According to his own testimony, he had no desire to abolish the law; yet, by his actions, he clearly showed that he believed that the spirit of the law was too often violated by an excessively rigid adherence to its letter. He inveighed ceaselessly against legalism unattached to any concern for justice. When rebuked for healing a man on the Sabbath, he replied that the Sabbath was made for man, not man for the Sabbath. He consorted freely with sinners. He regarded ritual hygienes as unimportant compared to purity of heart. Perhaps no episode in the Gospels more vividly

Leonardo da Vinci's renowned portrayal of the Last Supper (c. 1497) – Judas Iscariot is seated to the left of Jesus, clutching a small bag containing the 30 pieces of silver for which he betrayed Christ. The period between this meal, at which Christ instituted the Communion by sharing bread and wine, and his death on the cross is known as the Passion.

illustrates his approach to the law than that of the woman taken in adultery: he does not deny the legality of her death sentence, but instead places the law on a far more radical moral basis – requiring that no man execute the sentence who is not himself free of all sin – and thereby, in essence, nullifies its verdict (or perhaps one should say, transforms justice into mercy).

The Messiah

Needless to say, those who followed Jesus firmly believed that the authority upon which he acted was no less than God's own: it was the authority, that is, of God's 'anointed' – God's 'Messiah' or 'Christ'. There is no evidence in the Gospels that Jesus ever used this title in reference to himself; but it is recorded that when, in Caesarea Philippi, Peter opined that his master was the Messiah, Jesus did not contradict him. More to the point, the crowds that gathered to acclaim Jesus on his final entry into Jerusalem were obviously animated by Messianic expectations. Admittedly, the Messiah for whom many Jews longed was not merely a religious leader, but a kind of national liberator, an inspired man of war in the mould of Judas Maccabeus, but even greater. Given his absolute rejection of violence, Jesus was wholly unsuited to such a role. No sooner, in fact, had Peter made his confession than Jesus began to predict not his imminent victory over the Romans, but his death at their hands.

Since Jesus excited hopes that Israel's promised deliverer had come, he must have appeared to the ruling powers as a serious threat to the political stability of Judaea. The peace of Jerusalem was principally the responsibility of the High Priest of Israel and the Temple guard, but ultimate power belonged to the Roman governor, and any hint of a popular uprising – or merely of popular unrest – could have had catastrophic consequences. When Jesus went so far as to drive the money-changers out of the Temple, he gave every appearance of being both dangerously uncompromising in his principles and utterly assured of his own authority to act upon them.

Betrayal in the Night

The Gospels do not entirely explain the motives that prompted Judas Iscariot to betray Christ; they merely recount that he approached the chief priests soon after Christ's triumphal arrival in Jerusalem and agreed to surrender his master to the Temple guard.

According to the Synoptic Gospels (though not the Gospel of John), Christ's final meal with his disciples was a Passover *seder*, during which he predicted his own imminent arrest and death (despite their protests), and then granted them a prophetic foretaste of his sacrifice by sharing bread and wine with them and identifying these as his body and blood.

'Then the soldiers of the governor took Jesus into the common hall, and gathered unto him the whole band of soldiers. And they stripped him, and put on him a scarlet robe. And when they had platted a crown of thorns, they put it upon his head, and a reed in his right hand: and they bowed the knee before him, and mocked him, saying, Hail, King of the Jews!

Gospel of St Matthew, 27: 27–29

That same night, Jesus went with all his disciples except Judas to the Garden of Gethsemane on the Mount of Olives. There his agony began, as he set himself apart from his disciples and prayed to God to spare him the suffering and death that awaited him. It was there that the Temple guards found him, guided there by Judas, who marked him out by giving him a kiss. One of the disciples (John's Gospel says it was Peter) drew a sword and cut off the ear of one of the High Priest's slaves, but Christ rebuked him for using violence (and, according to Luke, healed the wounded man). Then the disciples fled and Christ allowed himself to be led away.

Before dawn, Jesus was examined by the High Priest Caiaphas and the *Sanhedrin*, the governing council of priests and elders. Various accusers were called in against him, but their testimonies were at variance with one another. When, though, Caiaphas asked Jesus directly if he was the Messiah, and even the Son of the Most High, the latter replied that he was, and prophesied that his judges would see the Son of Man seated at the right hand of the Mighty One. This, argued Caiaphas, was sufficient grounds for condemnation.

Death on the Cross

In the morning, a delegation from the *Sanhedrin* took Jesus to the Roman governor Pontius Pilate and accused Christ of having seditiously styled himself 'King of the Jews'. According to Luke's Gospel, Pilate tried to sidestep the matter by referring it to King Herod, the 'native' ruler of Galilee, but Herod soon sent Jesus back. The Gospels also state that Pilate was unconvinced of the threat Jesus posed, and even offered to set him free in recognition of Passover. Ultimately, however, he bowed to the wishes of the assembled mob that the rebel Barabbas be released instead, and turned Jesus over to his soldiers, who whipped him, crowned him with thorns, mocked and beat him, and forced him to bear his own cross to a hill outside Jerusalem called Golgotha (meaning 'place of the skull'), where he was crucified.

THE TEARS OF PETER

All four Gospels report that, on the night he was betrayed, Christ prophesied that his disciples would abandon him in his hour of crisis; Peter protested, assuring Christ that, even if the courage of all the others failed, he, Peter, would remain loyal. To this, however, Christ responded by predicting that that very night, before the cock crowed, Peter would deny him three times.

Peter was originally a Galilean fisherman named Simon, whom Christ called to become a disciple. His remorse at his denial of Christ is depicted here by Francisco de Goya (1746–1828).

When Peter did indeed thrice deny Christ – having turned back from his flight and approached the High Priest's courtyard, only to arouse the suspicion of other persons there that he was one of Christ's followers – and when he did hear the cock crow, he went apart and (according to the synoptic accounts) wept bitterly at the knowledge of what he had done.

This may perhaps seem a rather unextraordinary episode, albeit a moving one, but therein lies its peculiar grandeur. To us today, it seems only natural that a narrator should pause to record such an incident, and treat it with a certain gravity; but, in the days when the Gospels were written, the tears of a common man were not deemed worthy of serious attention. They would have been treated by most writers as, at most, an occasion for mirth. Only the grief of the noble could be tragic, or sublime or even fully human.

The tears of Peter were therefore indicative of a profound shift in moral imagination and sensibility. Something had become visible that had formerly been hidden from sight. For Christian thought, God had chosen to reveal himself among the least of men and women, and to exalt them to the dignity of his own sons and daughters. And, as a consequence, a new vision of the dignity of every soul had entered the consciousness of the Gentile world.

The Roman world knew of no more humiliating or agonizing form of execution than crucifixion. It was reserved for the lowliest of criminals and killed its victim slowly, through unbearable pain, physical exhaustion and slow asphyxiation. All the Gospels concur that Christ spoke from the cross: Luke tells of his promise to one of the thieves crucified with him that 'this day you will be with me in paradise', and of his prayer 'Father forgive them, for they know not what they do'; Matthew and Mark record his cry of 'My God, My God, why have you forsaken me?'; Luke records him as saying 'Father, into your hands I commend my spirit'; while John notes, among other 'last words', the most tersely eloquent of them all: 'It is finished'.

When, after only a few hours, Christ died, those who had sought his death no doubt earnestly hoped and believed that the story of Jesus of Nazareth *was* indeed finished. But, of course, it was really only just beginning.

THE EASTER PROCLAMATION

The Gospels describe the portents that accompanied the death of Christ on the cross: the sky was darkened, the earth shook, blood and water flowed from a spear wound in his side, and so on. The Synoptic Gospels, in fact, state that the veil in the Temple, which covered the entrance to the Holy of Holies, was rent from top to bottom, as if somehow the abiding Glory of God had now been poured forth into the entire world.

A 19th-century stained-glass window showing the Resurrection. This portrayal follows the accounts of all the gospels that Christ first reappeared to the women among his followers.

Nevertheless, in purely historical terms, Christ's death appeared to signal the end of his mission and the defeat of the movement that had sprung up around him. All the hopes that had surrounded him had been shatteringly frustrated. The Messiah of God had died the death of a slave; his disciples were leaderless, scattered and in hiding; one of their own number had betrayed them and then (according to Matthew) committed suicide. Finally, only a handful of Christ's female followers remained to take away his body and give it a proper burial. Other Messianic sects had similarly perished, and there was no reason to expect that the cult of Jesus would not soon vanish as well.

And yet it was not long after Christ's death that his disciples were triumphantly proclaiming that he had risen from the tomb and was living once more. It was an incredible claim, obviously; but almost as incredible was the speed with which Jesus' followers recovered from the devastating loss of their leader, regrouped, and began to preach a common message – and that a message of victory.

The Empty Tomb

Each of the Gospels relates how certain women who had been followers of Christ (all mention Mary Magdalene by name, and John mentions her alone) went early in the morning on the Sunday after the crucifixion to visit the tomb where he had been laid. According to the earliest account, that of Mark, they found that the stone had been rolled away from the entrance to the tomb and, on entering, discovered a 'young man robed in white' who told them that Jesus had risen and who instructed them to tell the disciples that they would meet Christ in Galilee.

Matthew's Gospel – which relates that guards had been posted at the tomb to prevent Christ's disciples from stealing his corpse – speaks of the earth shaking and an angel with a shining face rolling back the stone to reveal the empty tomb, and then delivering the same message to the women. Luke says that the women found the stone already rolled aside and so they entered the tomb, where two men in shining garments appeared to them and asked why they sought the living among the dead, and told them that Christ was risen; the women then returned to the disciples, who did not believe the tale (though Peter went to confirm that the tomb was indeed empty).

Noli me tangere (1425–30) by the Renaissance painter Fra Angelico. According to John's Gospel, Christ spoke these words (meaning 'Don't touch me') to Mary Magdalene. Later in the same gospel, however, Christ invites the Apostle Thomas to touch his wounds, as proof of his real resurrection in the flesh.

John's story is simpler: Mary Magdalene found the tomb empty and ran to tell Peter and John, who then went to see for themselves; only when the men left again, and Mary was alone, did she see two angels seated within the tomb. Allowing for literary embellishment, and for the tendency of tales to grow in the telling, there is clearly a single tradition here: the women discovered the empty tomb first and then went to tell the men.

The Risen Lord

By itself, however, an empty tomb would not have warranted the claims the early Christians made about the risen Christ. For they did not merely believe that he had been restored to life in the manner of, say, Lazarus (who would one day die again); they believed, rather, that he had passed entirely beyond death, triumphed over it and entered into a new and eternal life.

When the risen Christ appears to his followers, he both is and is not as they knew him in his earthly ministry. His body has been not simply resuscitated, but transformed into a 'spiritual body' (to use the language of St Paul), at once concrete and yet transcendent of the normal limitations of time and space. He can appear and disappear at will; in Matthew, as the women are returning from the tomb, he 'suddenly' shows himself to them; in Luke, he is suddenly in the midst of his disciples; in John, he enters among them and departs again through locked doors. At the same time, he is not a ghost; as both Luke and John emphasize, he can be touched, he bears palpable wounds, he can even share food with his disciples. And, when at last he takes leave of his disciples, he is taken up bodily into heaven. In short, his body has somehow already entered into the transfigured reality of the Kingdom of God; and thus, by his resurrection, the Kingdom has already 'invaded' historical time.

VICTORY OVER DEATH

This was the earliest form of the Church's 'evangel' (its 'gospel' or 'good tidings'): namely, that Jesus is Lord. In his resurrection, God's Kingdom has triumphed, and Christ has been established as ruler over all of time. More importantly, he has decisively conquered all of those powers that formerly held humanity enslaved to sin, death and the devil. For the early Church, Easter was an event of total divine victory in every sphere of reality. According to Ephesians 4:8-10, Christ descended into the depths of the earth and ascended on high ('carrying captivity captive') 'in order that he might fill all things'. And this great act of conquest began even in Christ's death. The first Epistle of Peter twice speaks of Jesus in Hades evangelizing the dead, 'that they might, in spirit, live according to God' (4:6); it even says that he went to preach to those 'disobedient' spirits 'in prison' in Hades (3:19-20) – a reference to those souls who, like the rich man in one of Christ's parables, were excluded by their sins from the 'bosom of Abraham'.

Christ showing his wounds to his disciples; illumination from a late-15th-century codex by the Milanese Renaissance artist Cristoforo de Predis.

By his death, Christians believed, Christ had paid a ransom that redeemed all of humanity from bondage in the household of death. In later centuries, especially in some of the theology of the Western churches, this language of 'ransom' would sometimes be confused with the idea of a price paid to God as the due penalty for human guilt. But in the New Testament, and in the doctrines of the early Church, the metaphor was more properly understood as referring to the fee necessary to buy the freedom of slaves from a slaveholder (in this case, death and the devil).

Christ, however, having paid the price, did not then leave the kingdom of death intact; he also overthrew the ancient empire of injustice, cruelty, falsehood and sin. Henceforth, the power of everything that separated humanity from God lay shattered. This was the gospel with which the Church entered into history, and with which it would, in time, claim the Roman world for itself.

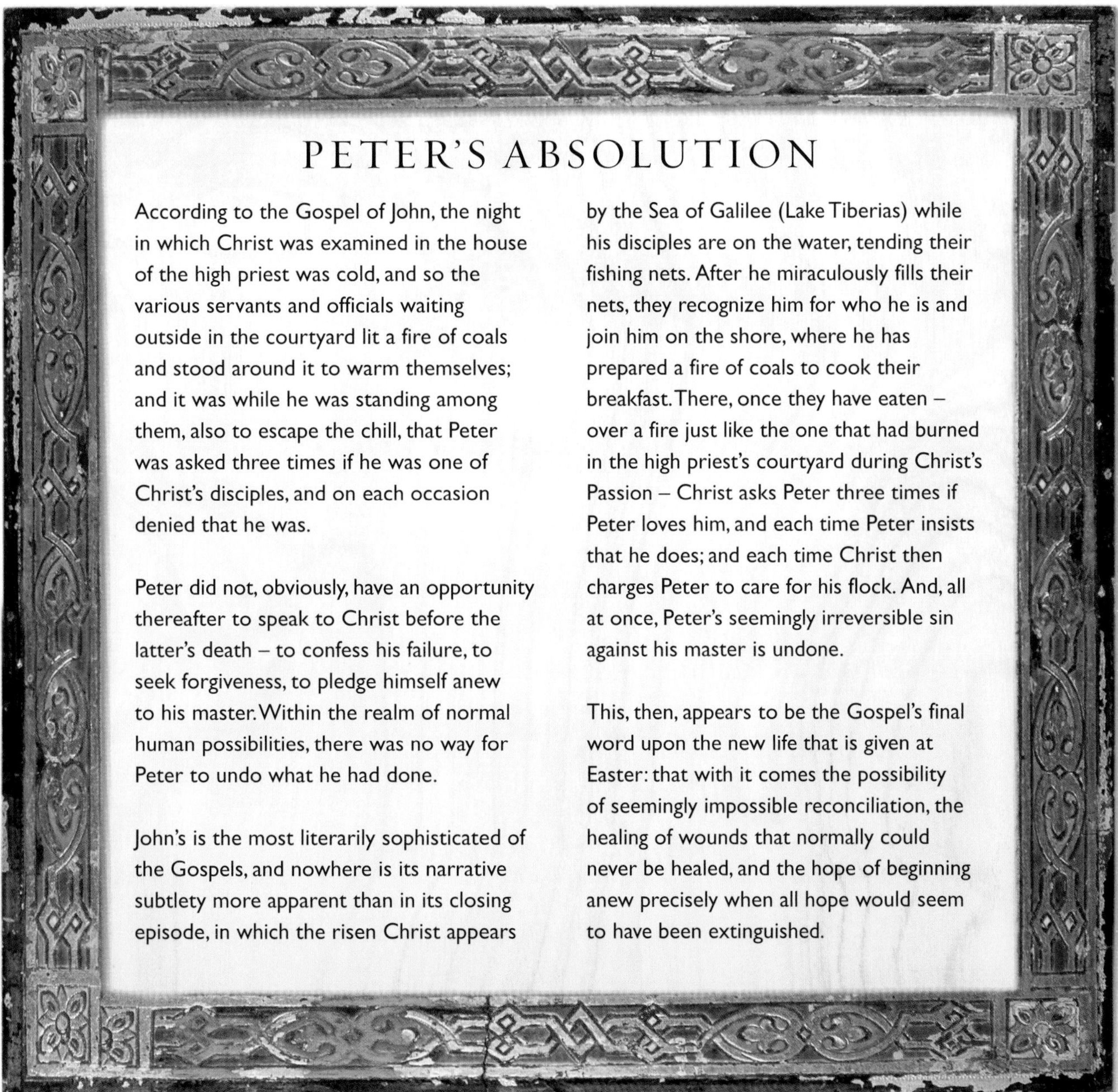

PETER'S ABSOLUTION

According to the Gospel of John, the night in which Christ was examined in the house of the high priest was cold, and so the various servants and officials waiting outside in the courtyard lit a fire of coals and stood around it to warm themselves; and it was while he was standing among them, also to escape the chill, that Peter was asked three times if he was one of Christ's disciples, and on each occasion denied that he was.

Peter did not, obviously, have an opportunity thereafter to speak to Christ before the latter's death – to confess his failure, to seek forgiveness, to pledge himself anew to his master. Within the realm of normal human possibilities, there was no way for Peter to undo what he had done.

John's is the most literarily sophisticated of the Gospels, and nowhere is its narrative subtlety more apparent than in its closing episode, in which the risen Christ appears by the Sea of Galilee (Lake Tiberias) while his disciples are on the water, tending their fishing nets. After he miraculously fills their nets, they recognize him for who he is and join him on the shore, where he has prepared a fire of coals to cook their breakfast. There, once they have eaten – over a fire just like the one that had burned in the high priest's courtyard during Christ's Passion – Christ asks Peter three times if Peter loves him, and each time Peter insists that he does; and each time Christ then charges Peter to care for his flock. And, all at once, Peter's seemingly irreversible sin against his master is undone.

This, then, appears to be the Gospel's final word upon the new life that is given at Easter: that with it comes the possibility of seemingly impossible reconciliation, the healing of wounds that normally could never be healed, and the hope of beginning anew precisely when all hope would seem to have been extinguished.

The Enigma of the Church

Considered purely as a historical phenomenon, the abrupt transition of Christ's followers from a posture of utter defeat and disillusionment to one of triumphant jubilation constitutes an altogether impenetrable enigma. After all, the Apostles were not just purveyors of a spiritual philosophy, who were merely continuing their master's ministry; the Easter proclamation was of an altogether different nature. And, given their persistence over many years in making that proclamation, and their willingness in many cases to give their lives rather than repudiate it, one may confidently say that it is an event that has no known parallel.

The most responsible historical judgment on this episode is that a profound shared experience transformed the disciples' understanding of the life and death of their master, and of his presence within time, and of the point and purpose of their own lives. Something quite extraordinary and unprecedented had clearly taken place.

THE CHURCH OF THE APOSTLES

According to the Gospel of John, Christ promised his disciples that, after he had departed from the world, he would send the Holy Spirit to lead them 'into all truth'; and, after the resurrection, he told the disciples that he was sending them forth, even as the Father had sent him, and then breathed the Holy Spirit out upon them, telling them that he was imparting to them his own power to forgive sins.

According to the Book of Acts (written, it is generally believed, by Luke), the final gift of the Holy Spirit to the disciples – and so, in a sense, the birth of the Church – came after Christ's ascension, on the day of the harvest festival of *Sukkot* or 'Pentecost' (that is, the fiftieth day after Passover). The Apostles were once again 12 in number, since Matthias, another disciple of Christ, had been elevated to the place formerly occupied by Judas, and were lodging in Jerusalem, where the risen Christ had instructed them to wait for the Spirit's advent. On the day of Pentecost, they were gathered together when the house in which they were staying seemed suddenly to be filled with a great rushing of wind, 'as from heaven', and tongues of fire appeared above their heads, and all at once they were given the power of speaking in foreign languages. They went out into the street to preach, where many Jews of the Diaspora were present who were amazed to hear Galileans speaking the tongues of their native lands (though others mistook their words for the meaningless babble of drunkards). The Apostles – Peter chief among them – proclaimed Christ's resurrection and the outpouring of the Spirit, and that day convinced approximately 3000 Jews to receive baptism into Christ.

The Church of the Apostles

The Church, at first, was located entirely in Jerusalem, under the leadership principally of Peter. As a community, it was distinguished in part by its disdain of riches. The Christians held all possessions in common, and the wealthy among them were obliged to sell their property to assist the poor members of the community. The Church was also, at first, exclusively Jewish. In fact, it was only gradually that the apostolic Church came to conclude that the gospel could be received by Gentiles without the additional requirement that they also become Jews, bound by the Law of Moses. Peter did, however, approve of the Apostle Philip's mission to the Samaritans, whom traditional Jews shunned, and even himself preached in Samaritan villages along with John.

As related in Acts, however, Peter's full acceptance of Gentile Christians *as* Gentiles came about only when a 'pious and God-fearing' Roman centurion named Cornelius – prompted by the vision of an angel – invited Peter to come and speak to him. Peter consented, despite the purity restrictions that would normally have

Pentecost, represented in a stained-glass window at St Vitus' Cathedral in Prague. The Christian feast of this name celebrates the descent of the Holy Spirit upon the Apostles on the fiftieth day after Easter Sunday.

c.10
St Paul is born as Saul in the city of Tarsus in the province of Cilicia, Asia Minor (southern Turkey)

c.34
The Protomartyr (first martyr) of Christianity, the Hellenistic Jew Stephen, is tried by the *Sanhedrin* for blasphemy and stoned to death

c.36
While on the road to Damascus to eradicate the Christian community there, Saul receives a blinding vision of the risen Christ and converts to Christianity

c.44–6
Paul undertakes his first mission, with Barnabas and John, to Cyprus

52
Paul completes his second missionary journey, to Corinth

c.58
Paul writes the Epistle to the Romans

58–60
Paul is arrested in Jerusalem and imprisoned by the Romans in Caesarea. As a Roman citizen, he invokes his right to trial in Rome

64
Peter is executed in Rome, during the widespread persecution of Christians as scapegoats for the Great Fire that destroyed Nero's Rome that year

c.67
Paul dies a martyr's death in Rome

prevented him from visiting a Gentile home. He did this because – just before the invitation arrived – he had a vision in which God commanded him to partake of foods of any kind, whether kosher or not. Then, as they were speaking, the Holy Spirit descended upon Cornelius and all the members of the centurion's household, and everyone present began speaking in tongues; whereupon Peter agreed to baptize them all.

Paul, the Apostle of the Risen Christ

Perhaps even more important for the Church's outreach to 'the uncircumcised' was the arrival among the Apostles of a man who had never known Jesus during his earthly mission, but who nonetheless understood himself to be an Apostle, directly commissioned by Christ to preach the gospel. He was a Jew of the Diaspora, from Tarsus in Asia Minor, named Saul: a zealous and observant Pharisee who, though from a 'Hellenized' background, and naturally fluent in Greek, was also a student of the famous Rabbi Gamaliel of Jerusalem and was a master of Hebrew scripture. He was also for a time probably the fiercest enemy of the Christians, entirely committed to eradicating the new movement. He was even an approving witness of the death of Stephen, the first Christian martyr, a Greek-speaking Jew who was stoned to death for alleged blasphemies against the Temple.

Saul, however, was transformed – more or less in an instant – from the Church's greatest persecutor to its most tireless missionary. According to Acts, it was as he was journeying towards the city of Damascus in Syria, in order to eliminate the Christian community there, that he encountered the risen Lord, in a blaze of light so brilliant that he was left blind for several days. His sight was finally restored by a Christian from Damascus named Ananias. Soon, he began to preach the resurrection of Jesus in the synagogues of the city, so persistently and blatantly that, according to Acts, he was forced to flee for his life. Thereafter, he never rested in his missionary efforts; he travelled from city to city within the empire, founding churches wherever he stayed. At some point, perhaps to signal his new life in Christ, he changed his name to Paul. Some time after his conversion – either immediately after leaving Damascus or after three years had elapsed – he went to Jerusalem to meet with Peter, James the brother of Jesus and the rest of the Church there, where he was recognized as an Apostle and given special responsibility for the mission to the uncircumcised.

One of the more remarkable features of Paul's ministry, considering his former zeal for defending the purity of Judaism, was his uncompromising insistence upon the absolute inclusiveness of the gospel. Naturally, as a Hellenized Jew, he was perfectly at ease in the greater intellectual and cultural environment of the empire, but his

THE MARTYRDOMS OF PETER AND PAUL

According to tradition, the Apostles Peter and Paul both ended their days in the city of Rome, and both were put to death for their faith. The truth of this tradition is attested often enough in the documents of the early Church to place it beyond any reasonable doubt.

A manuscript illumination by Fra Bartolommeo (c.1400) showing the two early Apostles and martyrs of the Church, SS Peter and Paul.

The Book of Acts tells how Paul visited Jerusalem during a famine (57) with relief sent principally by Gentile Christians. During his stay there, he was falsely accused of having brought some of his Greek companions into the Temple, denounced as a corrupter of the Law, attacked by a mob in the Temple precincts, and saved only by the arrival of Roman soldiers. The soldiers took him into custody, but first – unwisely as it turned out – allowed him to address the crowd, causing the unrest to continue. As Paul had been a Roman citizen since birth, the Roman commander could not have him flogged and interrogated, and so the next morning sent him to the *Sanhedrin* for questioning. There, however, Paul merely succeeded in dividing the council against itself, Pharisee against Saducee. At last, on learning of a plot to kill Paul, the Romans sent him to Caesarea, where he was imprisoned for two years.

Finally, Paul invoked his right as a citizen to trial before the emperor, and so was sent by ship to Rome. After an eventful journey, including a shipwreck near Malta, he reached the city and spent two years under house arrest, though all the while he continued to be an active member of the Church. The scriptural account ends there. Later tradition claims he was executed in the reign of Nero, during the latter's persecution of the Christians after the great fire that destroyed a large part of Rome in 64; as a citizen, however, Paul was spared the cross and died instead under the executioner's blade.

Peter too, according to tradition, was put to death during Nero's purge. Why he was in Rome we cannot say with certainty. Some late traditions claim that he lived there for 25 years. The only clear scriptural reference to his martyrdom appears in John's Gospel, where the risen Christ prophesies that, in his old age, Peter will stretch out his hands and be led where he will not wish to go. The apocryphal Acts of Peter report that he was crucified, but that he was – at his behest – nailed to the cross with his head pointing downward, as a sign that he was not worthy to die in the same manner as his Lord.

understanding of the radical hospitality of the gospel went far beyond mere cosmopolitan tolerance. Not only did he believe that the Church embraced both Jews and Gentiles; he was also convinced that Christ had entirely abolished the difference between them. Christianity was, in Paul's eyes, a new universalism that rendered the distinction between Jew and Greek – or between those who had been circumcised and those who had not – quite irrelevant. Indeed, Paul not only opposed the adoption of the Jewish Law by Gentile converts; he regarded it as a kind of faithlessness to the gospel.

The Calling of All Nations

In the letters he wrote to the various Christian communities he had founded or encountered, Paul unfolded a theology according to which all of God's promises to Israel had been fulfilled in Christ, but in a way that had miraculously allowed all the nations of the earth to be included within those promises. The expectation of the prophets that all nations would come to adore the God of Israel had been realized, but the Law had at the same time been made essentially obsolete: for what made Jews and Gentiles alike inheritors of God's covenant with Abraham was their common participation in Abraham's faith, not their obedience to the Mosaic code. After all, as Paul argued, it was a covenant that antedated the Law by centuries; the Law was dependent on the covenant, not the covenant on the Law.

> *'Now I beseech you, brethren, by the name of our Lord Jesus Christ, that ye all speak the same thing and that there be no divisions among you … For as the body is one, and hath many members, and all are members of that one body, being many are one body so also is Christ.'*
>
> St Paul, Epistle to the Corinthians, 1:10 and 12:12

It was a difficult message for pious Jews who happened to be Christians. It was also easily misunderstood. There is evidence in Paul's own writing, as well as in other of the epistles in the New Testament, that there were some who imagined that their faith not only liberated them from 'works of the Law', but relieved them of moral obligations. The Epistle of James, for instance, was written in large part to remind Christians that good works were required of them, and that the Church

was called always to provide for the poor, the widow and the orphan, to condemn injustices, and to provide an irreproachable moral example to the world.

If the early Church had not disengaged its evangel from the prescriptions of the Mosaic code, however, Christianity would have remained a marginal sect within Judaism. As such, it would almost certainly have disappeared within a relatively few generations. It was only through discovering that the gospel of the risen Christ had made as nothing the differences between peoples – even that most crucial of differences, the barrier between the children of Abraham and those who stood outside the Law of Moses – that the Church became a force that could transform its world.

So eloquent was St Paul in preaching to the citizens of the city of Ephesus in Asia Minor that some people who had previously 'used curious arts' burned their books in public. This depiction of the event is by the Flemish artist Maarten de Vos (1568).

THE GROWTH OF THE EARLY CHURCH

In its earliest days, Christianity disseminated its message principally through the synagogues. It was among communities of Hellenized Jews – at least, in the greater world of the Diaspora – that evangelization first spread beyond the Church's native confines. Moreover, it was quite common for Diaspora synagogues to include, at the margins of the community, a number of Gentiles who had adopted Jewish customs and beliefs and who, in many cases, were on their way to full conversion.

However, having no houses of worship of their own, Christians met in private dwellings. Their gatherings, therefore, naturally included not only a celebration of the Lord's Supper, but an actual shared meal. They met on the first day of the week, Sunday, the day of Jesus' resurrection. The worship of the community generally consisted in the singing of Psalms and hymns, mutual exhortation and teaching, prophecy, glossolalia (praying in tongues) and healings. This was the form in which the new faith expanded throughout the eastern half and into the western half of the Roman empire, establishing itself in cities like Antioch and Alexandria, as well as in Rome itself.

Orders of Authority

As the Church grew, the issue of authority became increasingly important. As the first generation of Christians died out, and with it the Apostles themselves, Christian communities relied upon the institution of the *episkopos* (bishop or 'overseer') or *presbyteros* (priest or elder) to preserve their historical continuity with the first Church in Jerusalem, as well as to maintain theological and moral rectitude. The institution had been established, as it happens, in apostolic times; and, wherever the Church took root, the bishop or priest, with the aid of deacons, was responsible for the baptism of converts, the administration of the Eucharist, the distribution of goods for the relief of the poor and the general governance of the community.

For the most part, though, the earliest Christians believed that Christ's return to earth was imminent, and so they probably rarely bothered to consider what fuller significance the bishop's office might have. But, as the first generation of believers passed on, the bishop's role came to be recognized as an indispensable instrument of Church unity and order. At the beginning of the second century, Bishop Ignatius of Antioch – in a series of letters he wrote as he was being transported to Rome to be executed for his faith – insisted that the Church existed only where a duly appointed bishop was to be found. Without the bishop, understood as a living link to the Apostles, specially commissioned by the Holy Spirit, no Eucharist could be celebrated, and no Christian community established. Ignatius'

The martyrdom of Ignatius of Antioch, by Giovanni Battista Crespi (1575–1633). Ignatius, the third bishop of Antioch and a disciple of John the Apostle, met a gruesome death in the Colosseum at Rome.

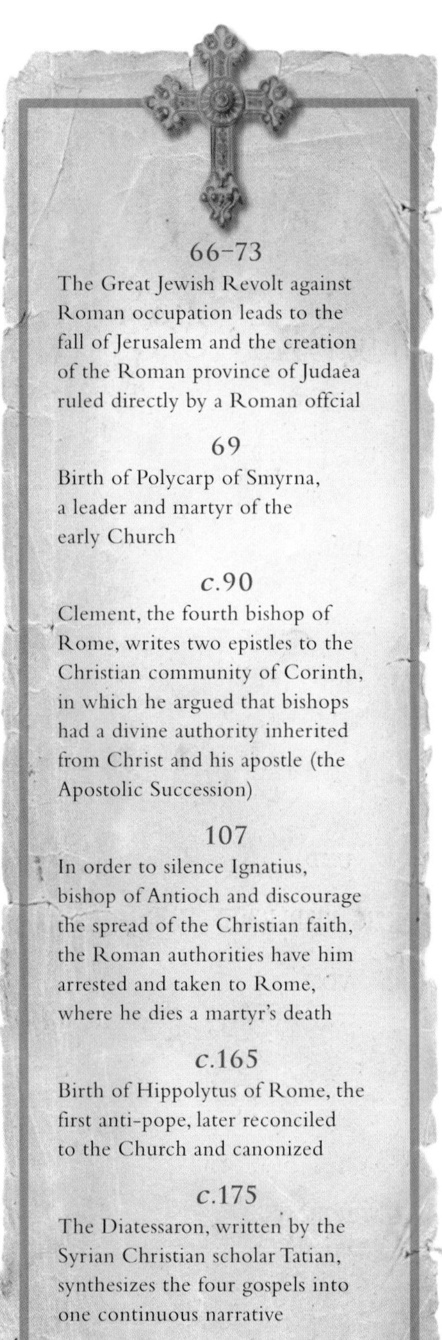

66–73
The Great Jewish Revolt against Roman occupation leads to the fall of Jerusalem and the creation of the Roman province of Judaea ruled directly by a Roman offcial

69
Birth of Polycarp of Smyrna, a leader and martyr of the early Church

*c.*90
Clement, the fourth bishop of Rome, writes two epistles to the Christian community of Corinth, in which he argued that bishops had a divine authority inherited from Christ and his apostle (the Apostolic Succession)

107
In order to silence Ignatius, bishop of Antioch and discourage the spread of the Christian faith, the Roman authorities have him arrested and taken to Rome, where he dies a martyr's death

*c.*165
Birth of Hippolytus of Rome, the first anti-pope, later reconciled to the Church and canonized

*c.*175
The Diatessaron, written by the Syrian Christian scholar Tatian, synthesizes the four gospels into one continuous narrative

stress upon the unique authority of the bishop was prompted in part by the prevalence in the Christian world of 'false teachers', such as the 'docetists' (from the Greek *dokein*, meaning 'to appear') who claimed that Christ had not really possessed a human body, but had only seemed a man of flesh and blood, and so had suffered only in appearance. Yet the institution of bishops was only an imperfect safeguard against dissent and division. Schisms were therefore part of the Church's life from a very early period.

From an early stage, churches in the more important cities began to enjoy a greater eminence than others. From at least the late second century onwards, the church in Rome began to regard itself as having a special prominence and dignity. As early as the middle of the third century, Bishop Stephen of Rome claimed that the authority Christ had granted Peter was the spiritual patrimony of the bishops of Rome.

The Word of God

Of course, the other principal source of authority and unity within the Church was scripture; and yet it was a considerable time before the Christian Bible came to exist in its final form. At first, the Christian

Bible was simply the Hebrew Bible, in Greek translation, generally the Alexandrian Jewish translation known as the Septuagint (from Latin *septuaginta* – 'seventy', referring to the number of scholars who are thought to have worked on translating the text). This translation, however, contained a number of later books originally written in Greek that did not appear in the Hebrew canon of scripture. The exact status of these additional books was never entirely settled. Certain of the early theologians of the Church regarded them simply as inspired scripture, some preferred to accord them only a secondary, 'deutero-canonical' value, and a few apparently paid little attention to them at all (though no one rejected them in the way that later Protestant tradition did, or classified them as 'apocrypha').

Situated at the foot of Mount Sinai in Egypt, St Catherine's Monastery, built in the sixth century, houses the second largest collection of early Christian codices and manuscripts in the world, including some of the oldest extant copies of the Gospels.

The development of the New Testament canon was a somewhat more involved process. There were various Christian texts, more or less universally recognized as 'scriptural', before the end of the first century. The four Gospels were regarded as authoritative from a very early date, though they were often read not as discrete documents, but in a combined, 'harmonized' form. The most virtuosic of these harmonies was called the Diatessaron (literally, 'taken from the four'), which was the work of the Christian philosopher Tatian (d. *c.*185), a second-century Hellenized Syrian. Several of Paul's letters had also been collected and were circulating among the churches by the end of the first century. The precise determination of what constituted legitimate Christian scripture, however, was probably prompted by the propagation of rival 'scriptures' and the rise of aberrant teachers in the second and third centuries. It became increasingly necessary to discern which texts could be said to be genuinely connected to the traditions of the Apostles and which could not. It took some time for a consensus to emerge. For instance, the visionary book *The Shepherd of Hermas* was considered part of the New Testament by many churches, a view that persisted in some places at late as the fourth century. Moreover, other books that became established parts of the Christian canon were not universally accepted for some considerable time: the Book of Hebrews, for example, or the epistles of James and Jude, as well as the third epistle of John.

A People Apart

In form, the early Church could be described as a form of 'mystery religion' – in other words, a faith into which a person was ritually initiated, that offered salvation through participation in a special set of 'mysteries' (that is, the sacraments), and that did not divulge its doctrines and practices to those outside its own circle. Moreover, since its adherents were forced to meet in private homes and usually in secret, early Christianity naturally gave rise to rumours. In so far

THE ANTI-POPE

Although the early Church placed great stress on unity among believers, and regarded the bishop as a privileged and necessary focus of that unity, it is not the case that Christians in any given city always agreed on who precisely their bishop was. Even in Rome, during the early centuries of the Church's history, there were often a number of men simultaneously claiming the episcopacy for themselves.

Perhaps the most famous such 'anti-pope' (that is, an alternative bishop or pope of Rome) was Hippolytus (*c.*165–*c.* 235), a Christian scholar and theologian of great erudition and short temper. He had been a severe critic of the theology of Bishop Zephyrinus, who presided over the church in Rome from about 199 to 217 (indeed, according to the doctrinal determinations of the later Church, Hippolytus was in the right). When on Zephyrinus's death the Roman church elected Calixtus, another 'heretic', as his successor, Hippolytus decided that the authority of the episcopacy had been entirely compromised. As a result, he broke communion with the new bishop and persuaded a number of the Christians in Rome to join him. They elected him as their bishop, and he continued in that office until 235, a period during which three different men presided as the 'other' bishop in Rome: Calixtus, Urban I and Pontian. In 235, however – as chance or providence would have it – the persecution inaugurated under Emperor Maximinus led to the arrest of both 'popes'.

Hippolytus and Pontian were both condemned to years of hard labour in the mines of Sardinia, and there – before dying together for the faith – they were reconciled with one another. Both resigned their common see, and one man, Bishop Anterus, was elected to succeed both of them; in this way, the two communities were reunited under a single pope. Although Anterus' tenure lasted only until 236, his successor Bishop Fabian (pope until 250) subsequently arranged to have the bodies of both Hippolytus and Pontian transported to Rome for interment as holy martyrs of the one Church.

as they were noticed at all, Christians appeared to constitute an eccentric, and perhaps somewhat sinister, sect and so scurrilous stories proliferated, claiming for example that Christians indulged in orgies, or practised infanticide and even cannibalism. But as Christians increased in number, and began to form a distinct and substantial community within the empire, a more accurate public perception of them crystallized.

Ultimately, even pagan critics of the new faith – however much they may have deplored the unpatriotic and irrational refusal of Christians to venerate the gods, and however they may have detested the 'rabble' that thronged to the Church – had to acknowledge that Christians were characterized in great part by their sobriety, their gentleness, their fidelity to their spouses, their care for the poor, their willingness to nurse the gravely ill even in times of plague and for their ability to exhibit virtues (like courage and self-restraint) that were generally thought impossible for persons of low estate, without the benefit of philosophical training. And it was this special character of the Christians that, in a very profound way, constituted the chief appeal of the gospel they preached.

THE AGE OF THE MARTYRS

In Greek, the word 'martyr' means simply 'witness', but in Christian usage, the term soon came to denote specifically someone who – like Christ – had borne witness to his or her faith by suffering or dying for it. Just as Christ had 'drawn all men' to himself by being crucified, so the martyrs of the early Church proclaimed the reality of God in their lives, and summoned others into fellowship with Christ, by enduring faithfully to the end whatever violence their beliefs provoked from others.

The earliest Christian martyrs, such as Stephen and the Apostle James, died at the hands of their fellow Jews, who condemned them as corrupters of the faith of Abraham. Both were stoned to death, in 34 and 62 respectively. The great majority of martyrs, however, were victims of pagan persecution. At first, of course, the Roman authorities could scarcely be expected to distinguish Christians from other Jews, and Judaism was tolerated by Rome (for the most part) on the grounds that its beliefs and practices could boast so great an antiquity. Many Romans may not have cared for the God of the Jews or for the exclusive devotion he demanded of his worshippers, but they recognized at the same time that his ordinances and the traditions attached to them were ancient and venerable.

Accordingly, Jews were exempted from the requirement – which was incumbent upon all other subject peoples – of honouring the gods of the empire, venerating the *genius* (the divine spirit) of the emperor or offferinng up prayers to the gods for the empire's welfare.

The First Pagan Persecutions

However, as the Christians developed into a separate community, deracinated from the synagogue and made up of Jews and Gentiles alike, they gradually lost the protection of Judaism's legal immunity. Moreover, pagan culture became conscious of Christianity as a distinct religion, one whose creed was new and therefore, in all likelihood, invalid. In Roman eyes, given the secretiveness of this new faith and the eccentricities of the religious language that its adherents sometimes employed, there was every reason to suspect Christians of depraved practices.

A 19th-century engraving showing the stoning to death of the first Christian martyr, St Stephen, in Jerusalem in 34. Stoning, or lapidation, was a form of execution prescribed by the Law of Moses for blasphemers.

The first systematic persecution of Christians occurred in Rome in 64, after a great fire had consumed a large part of the city. The emperor Nero found it convenient to lay the blame for the blaze on this small, peculiar cult, which had already aroused popular suspicion; according to the historical records, a large number of Christians (though it is hard to say how large) was arrested and put to death, often in quite spectacular and sadistic fashion. Nero's purge, however, was little more than an impromptu massacre; as far as we can tell, it did not herald a new imperial policy of systematic persecution. Nonetheless, it did establish in principle that the Christians could claim no legal protection for their practices, and thus that the refusal of Christians to make proper offerings in honour of the emperor or of the empire's gods could be treated as a criminal and seditious dereliction of civic duty. It was not long, therefore, before professing Christianity officially became a capital offence.

'My dear Pliny, you have done as you ought in examining the cases of those people who were charged with being Christians. It is impossible to lay down a general rule which will dictate a specific course of action. They must not be hunted down; if they are brought before you and the case is proven they must be punished; if, however some one should deny that he is a Christian, and make it clear that he is not by making sacrifice to our gods, although that person may have been suspect in the past, he should be pardoned for repentance. Pamphlets posted without the name of an author must play no part in any accusation. They create the worst sort of precedent and are out of keeping with the spirit of our age.'

TRAJAN, WRITING TO PLINY THE YOUNGER

Persecutions, however, were only sporadic. Local magistrates usually had to be stirred to action, by some discontent among the non-Christian population, or by some misfortune or sign of divine disfavour that could plausibly be attributed to the impiety of the Christians. A particularly revealing picture of the Christians' position in the early second century – usually uneventful, occasionally terrible but always precarious – emerges from a letter written to the emperor Trajan by the Roman writer and administrator Pliny the Younger during his tenure as governor of Bithynia (111–13). Pliny reports that recently, in response to complaints against Christians in his jurisdiction (at Amastris on the Black Sea coast), he has conducted trials of those denounced and exacted punishments; but he still craves advice on how to proceed. He confesses his uncertainty regarding which offences ought to be investigated or punished, whether any distinctions should be made among the accused on account of their age, whether one who has repented of his Christianity should be spared, and whether it is enough that one bear the name of Christian – without any other offence – for him to merit the full penalty of death under the law.

This is not to say, however, that Pliny felt any need to wait upon the emperor's instructions. He goes on to report that he has interrogated many of those who have been denounced to him as Christians. Those who have confessed he has had interrogated twice more, attempting to dissuade them from their convictions with threats. Those who have proved intransigent, however, he has had put to death, on the grounds that their sheer obstinacy was sufficient warrant for the sentence. Christians who are also Roman citizens, whom he is prevented by law from trying and sentencing himself, he has sent on to Rome.

Unfortunately, he says, as word of these proceedings spread, accusations multiplied, in many cases anonymously. Those who denied the accusations, or denied still being Christians, proved their sincerity by offering prayers, incense and wine to the emperor's image and, in some cases, by cursing Christ. In the course of his investigations, Pliny reports, he has discovered that Christian 'depravity' consists in no more than gathering for a weekly dawn meeting, singing hymns to Christ 'as

An artist's impression of the martyrdom of a group of Christians in the Roman Colosseum. This vast arena, built by the emperor Vespasian in 79, was the scene not only of gladiatorial combats but also the execution for public entertainment of criminals and other 'undesirables'. A favourite method of killing was 'exposure to the beasts'.

34
The death of St Stephen, the first martyr of the Church, by stoning

62
James the Just, an Apostle of Christ, is stoned to death in Jerusalem for violating Mosaic Law

64
The systematic persecution of Christians in the Roman empire begins, instigated by Nero following the Great Fire of Rome

***c*.100**
Justin of Caesarea, an important Christian apologist, is born in Nablus in Judaea; his writings include open letters to the emperors of Rome arguing the injustice of the persecution of Christians

111–13
Roman writer and administrator Pliny the Younger, during his tenure as governor of Bithynia and Pontus, conducts trials and executions of Christians

155
Martyrdom of Bishop Polycarp of Smyrna

250
Emperor Decius issues an edict aimed at suppressing the spread of Christianity

258
In a new round of persecution ordered by the emperor Valerian, Bishop Cyprian of Carthage is arrested and put to the sword for refusing to recant his beliefs

to a god'. vowing never to commit fraud, adultery, or breach of trust, and sharing an ordinary meal. To verify this, Pliny has had two female slaves – deaconesses – tortured, and has indeed found nothing more deplorable than an excess of superstition.

In his reply to Pliny, Trajan applauds his governor's methods. He only enjoins that Christians should not be sought out, that those who are accused and found guilty should be punished as prescribed – unless they repent and prove their contrition with offerings to the gods – and that anonymous accusations should be ignored. The patent harmlessness of Christian practices apparently did not impress him.

Imperial Purges

Not all persecutions, however, were local in nature. During the third century AD, a number of imperial campaigns to exterminate the Church arose and subsided, sometimes doing considerable damage to the faith, but ultimately leaving it stronger than it had been before. In 235, for instance, the emperor Maximinus Thrax made an abortive attempt to uproot the Church; in 250, the emperor Decius issued an edict requiring every citizen to make a token sacrifice at a pagan altar before an official witness, which led to the execution of certain prominent Christians who defied the law; in 257, the emperor Valerian renewed the persecution, more ferociously, and among its victims were the great bishop of Carthage, Cyprian (200–58), and bishop Sixtus II of Rome (d.258). The actual number of martyrs was not enormous, but their example impressed itself deeply upon the consciousness of the Church.

More importantly, while many Christians may have been terrified into recanting their beliefs, the faith of other Christians was actually strengthened by their tribulations. At almost the same time that Pliny was trying the Christians of Bithynia, Ignatius of Antioch was on his way to Rome, where he would face torture and execution. In the letters he wrote in transit to various church communities, Ignatius treats his impending sufferings and death as a participation in Christ's Passion, and as a way to deeper union with his Lord; he even implores his friends not to make any effort to save him from his fate, but rather to pray that he will be able to face his death with serene resolve. In the end, the willingness of Christians to die for Christ won them a reputation not only for stubbornness, but also for their courage and purity of spirit.

As the influential North African Christian theologian and apologist Tertullian of Carthage (*c*.155–*c*.230) succinctly expressed it:

> *'The more you mow us down, the more we grow. The blood of the martyrs is the seed of the Church.'*

THE DEATH OF POLYCARP

Polycarp, the revered bishop of Smyrna in Asia Minor (modern Turkey), was a contemporary and friend of Ignatius of Antioch. Born in 69, he became a vehement critic of aberrant strains of Christianity that denied the reality of Christ's physical body (the Docetists). Polycarp was also an influential champion of the theology and writings of St Paul. And he was a man of irreproachable character.

SS Polycarp and Sebastian are shown in a Medieval manuscript illumination destroying idols, to which the Roman authorities had required Christians to make sacrifice.

When he was well advanced in years (86, according to tradition), he was arrested along with a great many other Christians in Smyrna. The imperial proconsul demanded that Polycarp renounce his faith and make his sacrifice to the *genius* of Caesar. When he refused to do so, he was burned to death.

A somewhat embellished account of his death survives under the title *The Martyrdom of Polycarp*. The version we possess is not the earliest, but even so it is an excellent example of a genre that flourished in the early Church: edifying narratives of the deaths of heroes and heroines of the faith.

According to *The Martyrdom*, Polycarp was brought into the city's stadium, where many other Christians had already perished. The proconsul threatened the old man both with wild beasts and fire, but was unable to persuade Polycarp to renounce Christ, to swear by the emperor's genius, or to exhort others to turn from the faith. Polycarp was sentenced to the stake. When the old man mounted the pyre he prayed to God, thanking him for his many mercies and blessings, and especially for the honour of being allowed to die for Christ.

The Martyrdom also claims that the flames seemed to rise about Polycarp like a billowing sail, and that he stood in the midst of them like gold or silver being refined in a crucible, and that a fragrance like that of frankincense wafted from the pyre. When it became apparent that the fire would not kill him, the executioner was obliged to thrust a dagger into him, whereupon so great a quantity of blood flowed from his body that the flames were extinguished.

Colourful tales aside, it is profoundly ironic that repeated attempts to eradicate the Church – even by the cruellest of methods – only succeeded in generating a Christian literature completely suffused by a spirit of triumph.

THE GNOSTICS

In its first three centuries, the Church was threatened not only by division within and by persecution from without, but also by rival systems of salvation, some of which claimed to be truer and more enlightened forms of Christianity. During the second and third centuries AD, there arose a number of sects that are traditionally called the 'Gnostic' cults – a term deriving from their claim to offer a *gnosis* or privileged knowledge that would bring salvation to the enlightened. Many forms of Gnosticism claimed to have access to Apostolic traditions that had been kept secret from most Christians.

This manuscript illustration depicts the emperor Nero seated on his throne, talking to Saints Peter and Paul, while Simon Magus stands in the background. Nero and the proto-Gnostic Simon Magus were figures widely detested by the early Church, and both were identified with the Antichrist.

Some contemporary scholars would prefer to dispense with the category of 'Gnosticism' altogether, and to speak instead of 'alternative Christianities' – in other words, variants of the faith which, through sheer historical misfortune, ultimately lost out to mainstream 'orthodoxy', but which in their time were equally viable forms of early Christianity. This, though, is a difficult position to defend. Gnosticism (even Christian Gnosticism) was clearly not an organic outgrowth of the Apostolic Church, but rather a kind of syncretistic, trans-religious theosophy that drew from Christian, Jewish, Greek, Syrian, Mesopotamian, Egyptian and Persian sources, often simultaneously. As such, it may be likened to modern 'New Age' spirituality. The Naassene sect, for instance, worshipped 'Christ', but conflated his worship with that of Dionysus and Attis. And the scriptures used by those sects that claimed to be Christian – alternate Gospels, various acts of the Apostles, mystical discourses – were, like the traditions attached to them, late inventions with no credible claim to any historical links to the Apostolic Church. Even pagan observers were apparently able to tell the difference. The great Neoplatonist philosopher Plotinus (205–70) attacked Gnosticism vigorously, but never treated it as a species of Christianity.

A Fall Within the Divine World

The earliest Gnostic or proto-Gnostic teacher of whom we know was Simon Magus (or Simon the Magician) who makes a brief appearance in the Book of Acts, where he attempts to purchase supernatural powers from the Apostles Peter and John. According to the system that Simon taught, God the Father, in the beginning, conceived *Ennoia* (Thought), a sort of feminine manifestation of the divine intellect; she then created the orders of angels, and they in their turn created the cosmos. The angels rebelled, however, and took *Ennoia* prisoner, incarcerating her in the material world, where she was doomed to pass through successive incarnations (among them, Helen of Troy), forgetful of her divine home. At last, God himself descended to earth in the form of Simon to save her, eventually finding her – so the story goes – working in a brothel in Tyre. Once Simon had reminded her of her true estate, the two of them set off together to bring salvation to whomever they could persuade to accompany them on their return to the godhead.

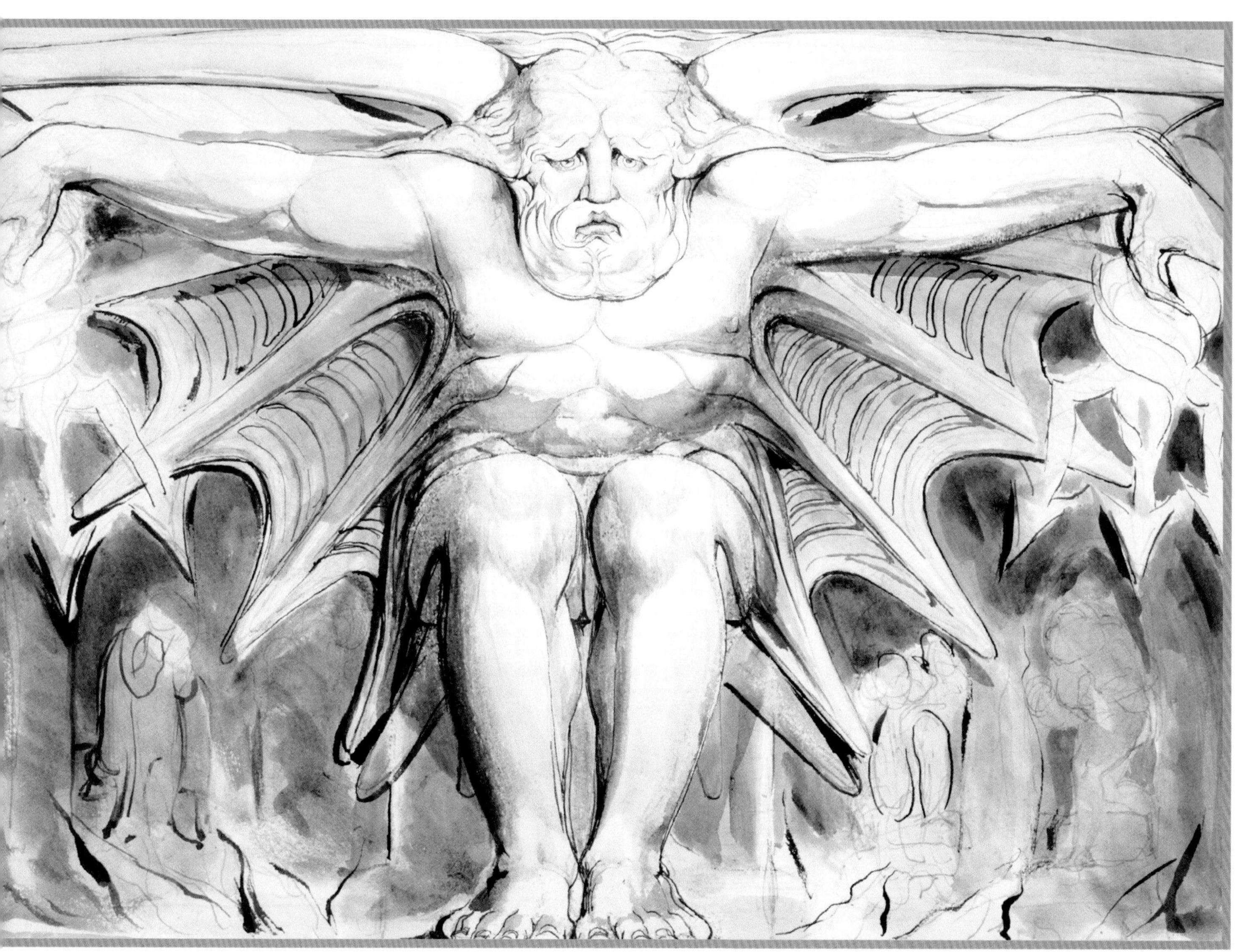

A Destroying Deity, *a sketch by the English Romantic artist and poet William Blake (1757–1827). Gnosticism taught that the world was created by a cruel deity who dispenses pitiless rough justice, and is identified with the God of the Old Testament. True salvation lay beyond this realm, for a select few.*

Simon's story contains a number of elements common to later, more developed schools of Gnostic speculation: the idea of a primordial fall within the divine realm itself; the claim that this world is the creation not of God but of inferior beings; an understanding of salvation as spiritual recollection followed by escape from the powers who rule this world. The great second-century systems devised by Valentinus, Basilides and other Gnostic sages all taught that the true God has no connection to this world, and that the material cosmos is the evil or defective creation of the '*archons*' or 'rulers' who reign in the planetary spheres above, or of a chief *archon*, the 'demiurge' or 'world-maker' (often identified with the God of the Old Testament). Many spoke of a divine *Pleroma* or 'Plenitude' of light, a sort of pre-cosmic community of divine beings called the 'aeons,' generated in eternity by the divine Father, who himself remained eternally inaccessible, even to his own offspring. According to some Gnostic systems, the lowest of the aeons *Sophia* or Wisdom, conceived an unlawful longing to know the hidden Father, and in this way fell from the fullness of the godhead; then she, in one way or another, generated the demiurge and the lower powers; and then, either by accident or through divine cunning, sparks of divine spirit became enmeshed within the machinery of the demiurge's cosmos.

LATE 4TH CENTURY BC
Beginning of the Hellenistic period and the fusion of Greek and Oriental wisdoms

2ND CENTURY BC
The birth of Jewish Apocalyptic literature

*c.*100 BC
Rise of Jewish Sethian Gnosticism

*c.*AD 40
Acts 8: Simon Magus attempts to purchase spiritual powers from SS Peter and John

EARLY 2ND CENTURY AD
Career of the Christian Gnostic Cerinthus

*c.*130
Carpocrates of Alexandria establishes an 'antinomian' Gnostic sect

2ND CENTURY AD
The rise of Ophite sects ('Venerators of the Serpent')

*c.*136
The Gnostic teacher Valentinus comes to Rome

144
Excommunication of Marcion of Sinope in Rome

*c.*150
The Gospel of Thomas is written

*c.*180
St Irenaeus of Lyon writes *Against the Heresies*

*c.*274
Death of the Persian Gnostic prophet Mani

The Deliverance of the Chosen

The Gnostic systems were not egalitarian creeds. The salvation they proclaimed was reserved for a very select few, since Gnostic doctrine regarded very few people as human in the fullest sense. The Gnostic Gospel of Thomas even states that women are inherently unworthy of the Kingdom. According to most systems, human nature may comprise as many as three distinct elements: body (*soma*), soul (*psyche*) and spirit (*pneuma*). The first and second of these are part of the demiurge's creation and so fall under the sway of the *archons*; the third, however, is a pure emanation of the divine world beyond, and has no natural relation to this world. Most human beings are composed from only one or two of these elements: there are the *somatikoi*, soulless brutes who simply dissolve back into the material world at death; or the *psychikoi*, who possess certain higher faculties of will and intellect, but who are nonetheless subjects of the demiurge. Salvation is possible only for the *pneumatikoi*, those who are 'spiritual' by nature, in whom dwells a spark of the eternal (though, according to some schools, a few of the *psychikoi* might also be rescued).

> *'These are the secret sayings which the living Jesus spoke and which Didymus Judas Thomas wrote down. And he said "Blessed are the solitary and elect, for you will find the Kingdom".'*
>
> Gospel of Thomas

Both the self and the cosmos are labyrinths in which the *pneuma*, the spirit, is imprisoned until it is awakened from its oblivion. Salvation consists principally in an inner awakening of the fallen pneuma; until then, it sleeps in the deepest depths of the self, trapped not only in flesh, but in the soul – or souls – created for it by the *archons*. According to some systems, the spirit is wrapped in a separate 'soul-garment' for each of the cosmic heavens through which it fell in the beginning; and, to be saved from rebirth here below, it must reascend through the spheres, not only abandoning its body to the earth, but shedding a 'soul' at each of the heavens it passes through. In some systems, this means seven souls must be stripped away, one for each of the seven planetary spheres; others, however, were less sanguine: according to Basilides, the number of heavens and of the souls corresponding to them is 365.

This ascent, moreover, will be fraught with perils, as the *archons* are jealous of their treasures and so will strive to prevent the *pneumatikos* from returning to the *Pleroma*. Accordingly, the mission of the saviour is, in large measure, to instruct his charges in the secret knowledge that will guide them safely home – a knowledge that includes a mastery of the magical incantations or special forms of address that the spirit will need to know after death, at each planetary sphere, in order to be able to elude the *archon* who resides there.

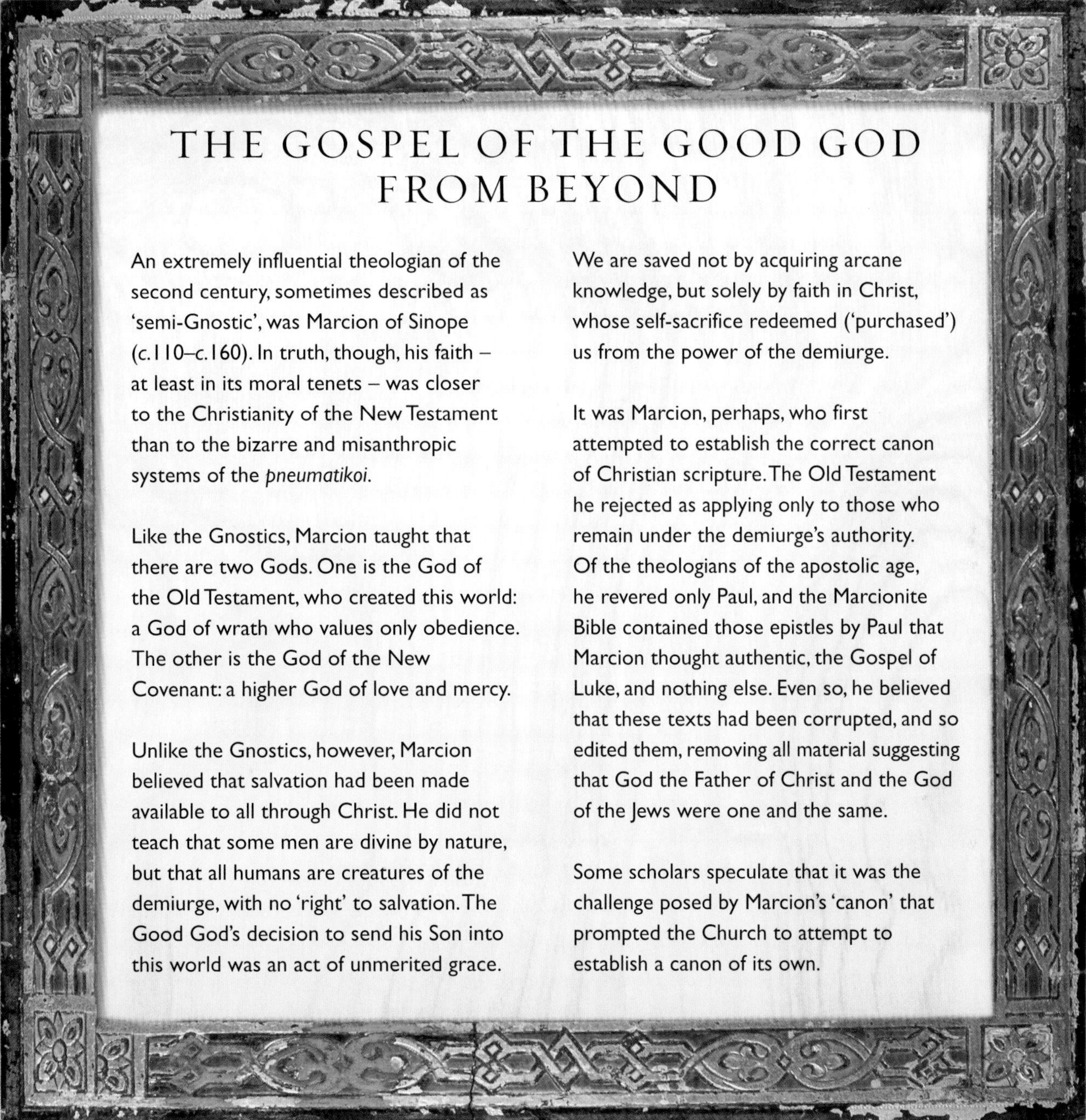

THE GOSPEL OF THE GOOD GOD FROM BEYOND

An extremely influential theologian of the second century, sometimes described as 'semi-Gnostic', was Marcion of Sinope (*c.*110–*c.*160). In truth, though, his faith – at least in its moral tenets – was closer to the Christianity of the New Testament than to the bizarre and misanthropic systems of the *pneumatikoi*.

Like the Gnostics, Marcion taught that there are two Gods. One is the God of the Old Testament, who created this world: a God of wrath who values only obedience. The other is the God of the New Covenant: a higher God of love and mercy.

Unlike the Gnostics, however, Marcion believed that salvation had been made available to all through Christ. He did not teach that some men are divine by nature, but that all humans are creatures of the demiurge, with no 'right' to salvation. The Good God's decision to send his Son into this world was an act of unmerited grace. We are saved not by acquiring arcane knowledge, but solely by faith in Christ, whose self-sacrifice redeemed ('purchased') us from the power of the demiurge.

It was Marcion, perhaps, who first attempted to establish the correct canon of Christian scripture. The Old Testament he rejected as applying only to those who remain under the demiurge's authority. Of the theologians of the apostolic age, he revered only Paul, and the Marcionite Bible contained those epistles by Paul that Marcion thought authentic, the Gospel of Luke, and nothing else. Even so, he believed that these texts had been corrupted, and so edited them, removing all material suggesting that God the Father of Christ and the God of the Jews were one and the same.

Some scholars speculate that it was the challenge posed by Marcion's 'canon' that prompted the Church to attempt to establish a canon of its own.

A Bitter Creed

The fabulous elements within Gnosticism did not produce a distinguished literature. Most Gnostic texts are characterized by their drearily elaborate mythologies, which abound in invention, but not in imagination. And much of that literature is marred by a streak of adolescent cruelty. In the Second Treatise of the Great Seth, for instance, Christ tells how he deceived the powers of this world by causing Simon of Cyrene to take on his appearance, and thus to be crucified in his place, while he watched from above, laughing at the stupidity of the *archons*.

Gnosticism spoke to a particular sort of spiritual discontent among persons of a certain type of temperament. It was not, however, a message of hope for a suffering humanity.

ALEXANDRIA IN THE EARLY CHRISTIAN CENTURIES

Without question, the greatest city of the ancient Mediterranean world was the Egyptian city of Alexandria, founded in 332 BC by Alexander the Great and ruled by the Greek dynasty of the Ptolemies from the time of Alexander's death in 323 BC to the death of the last Ptolemy, Cleopatra VII, in 30 BC, when Egypt was absorbed into the Roman empire. For many centuries, it was the principal home of Hellenistic science and scholarship, a city where Pagan, Jewish and Christian intellectual culture flourished, and where ideas from India, Persia, Africa and Europe ceaselessly intermingled. It was also the most violent city of its age.

It would be difficult to overstate how great a division existed between the educated and uneducated classes of Alexandria, or how profound a gulf separated the Pagans, Jews and Christians in one class from their co-religionists in the other. At the lowest level of society, religion was often little more than a tribal allegiance. Riots were frequent and murderous, and no community was safe from another. A perfect example of Alexandrian 'interfaith relations' is the anti-Jewish campaign of 38, when pagan gangs erected idols of the 'divine' emperor Caligula in the city's synagogues, Jewish homes were destroyed, and Jews were stripped of municipal citizenship, forced to retreat into ghettos and murdered or beaten if they ventured out. And, by Alexandrian standards, this was little more than a minor commotion; the street battles that occasionally erupted between pagans and Christians in the fourth century AD were so violent that they verged on civil war.

A City of Scholars

However, almost from its inception, Alexandria was also an unrivalled seat of learning and high culture. In the royal quarter of the city – the Brucheium – the first two Ptolemaic kings had established the grand 'Museum' (dedicated to the study of all the arts, humane and scientific) and the Great Library, a vast repository of texts from every land and culture known to Hellenistic civilization. The Library disappeared before the Christian period, despite a modern legend to the contrary, but the tradition of scholarship it inaugurated survived into the early seventh century AD. For many centuries, the greatest scholars in every tradition were often to be found in Alexandria; and at the higher levels of Alexandrian society, pagans, Jews and Christians associated freely. They pursued their studies in philosophy, literature, the sciences and rhetoric, frequently at one another's feet, while remaining aloof from the rabble of the lower city who spilled one another's blood with such enthusiasm and such frequency.

A Byzantine fresco painting of Clement of Alexandria. This influential teacher, who became head of the School of Alexandria, was notable for uniting Greek philosophy and exegesis with Christian doctrine.

A reconstruction of what the interior of the Ptolemaic Library of Alexandria might have looked like, with scholars poring over papyrus scrolls shelved in wall niches.

It was in Alexandria, also, that the first Christian institution of higher learning in the empire was established, midway through the second century, by the philosopher Pantaenus (d. before 200), a convert to Christianity from Stoicism. After Pantaenus, this 'Catechetical School of Alexandria' was led first by Clement of Alexandria (*c.*150–*c.*213) and then by the great Origen Adamantius (*c.*185–*c.*254), two men of immense erudition, who made free use in their teaching of Greek philosophy and Greek methods of textual interpretation. Origen, in fact, required his students to regard no path of wisdom as forbidden to them, and to apply themselves to the study not only of subjects such as geometry and astronomy, but of all the religious and philosophical texts of pagan culture.

Origen, the Father of the Fathers

Origen's importance in the history of theology can scarcely be exaggerated. He pioneered the practice of allegorical exegesis that would allow ancient and Medieval Christians to read the Old Testament as Christian scripture. At the same time, he was the first to undertake a scientific study of Hebrew scripture: in his *Hexapla*, he juxtaposed the Hebrew text with several Greek translations, in order to help scholars understand the precise meaning of the original. He was a tireless apologist, expositor of scripture, speculative theologian, philosopher and catechist, and furnished later theology with much of its conceptual grammar and terminology.

THE MYTH OF THE GREAT LIBRARY'S DESTRUCTION

An oft-repeated tale recounts that a Christian mob destroyed the Great Library of Alexandria in 391 and burnt its books in the street. According to some versions, the repository in question was the original library in the Brucheium, while others state that it was a 'daughter' library located in the Serapeum. This tale has entered so deeply into the popular imagination that it even sometimes appears in otherwise respectable books of history. It is, however, a myth, originated in the late 18th century, when the great historian Edward Gibbon read an unwarranted meaning into a single sentence from the Christian chronicler Paul Orosius (*fl.* 414–17).

The subtext of the legend is that the Christians of the fourth century were intensely hostile to the science, literature, and scholarship of classical culture, and that such matters were the special preserve of the pagans of Alexandria. This too is an 18th-century myth. The city's scholarly and scientific class comprised Christians as well as pagans, and Christian scholars, rhetoricians, philosophers and scientists were active in Alexandria right up until the city fell to Arab Muslim invaders in 642.

Regarding the library in the Brucheium – whose size, again, is impossible to determine – many ancient historians believed that it (or a large part of its collection) had already gone up in flames following Julius Caesar's assault on the city in 48 or 47 BC, during his wars with Pompey. Some historians now also claim that, if any part of the original library remained, it vanished in 272, during the emperor Aurelian's campaigns to reunite the empire. Whether either story is true, the Great Library of the Ptolemies no longer existed by the late fourth century.

As for the 'daughter' library, it may have been situated within the enclosure of the Serapeum; there were, at any rate, library stacks in the temple. However, the Pagan historian Ammianus Marcellinus (*c.*330–95) indicates that whatever library had once been there was long gone before the Serapeum's demolition in 391. More importantly, none of the original accounts of the temple's destruction mentions a library, not even the account written by the devout pagan Eunapius of Sardis (*c.*345–*c.*420), who despised Christians and who, as an erudite man, would have been enraged by the burning of precious texts.

Later Medieval legend claimed that the actual final destruction of the 'Library' or libraries of Alexandria was the work of the Arab conquerors of the seventh century AD. Of this, however, no account exists that was written before the 12th century.

Whatever the case, the scurrilous story of the Great Library's destruction by Christians is untrue. It may tell us something about modern misconceptions regarding the past, but tells us nothing about Christian or pagan antiquity.

The Church, though, never granted Origen the title of 'Saint'. In large part this was because, long after his death, certain of his speculations were declared heretical. For instance, he believed that human souls existed before their lives in the body, and had turned away from God in eternity, and that God had created this world as a sort of moral academy by which to restore them to innocence. He also taught universal salvation, meaning the ultimate rescue not only of all human beings, but of the devil and his angels. He also, it is said, had himself emasculated by a surgeon, which was a thing not unheard of among men of 'philosophical' or 'spiritual' temper in Alexandria in the third century, but which most Christians even in his time regarded as a violation of a body created by God. That said, Origen was also a martyr of the Church. During the Decian persecution of 250, when he was living in Asia Minor, he was severely tortured, despite his advanced years; he never fully recovered, and died only a few years later.

The Razing of the Temple of Serapis

Perhaps the most infamous episode of inter-religious violence in Alexandria occurred in 391, around the time when Christianity became the official religion of the Roman empire. The emperor Theodosius I (347–95) had recently imposed a ban on all pagan sacrifices, and many temples had already fallen into disuse. The patriarch of Alexandria, Bishop Theophilus, decided to renovate one of them as a church. When, however, workmen discovered hidden caverns beneath the temple and exhumed a number of human skulls, local pagans saw this as a desecration of a holy site and began attacking Christians throughout the city. Christian crowds retaliated and open warfare soon broke out in the streets. As the tide of battle turned against them, a number of pagans took refuge in the fortified enclosure of the Serapeum, the enormous temple compound dedicated to Serapis (a god invented by the early Ptolemies, as a fusion of Greek and Egyptian deities); as the pagans retreated into the compound, they seized a number of Christians as hostages, whom they susbsequently tortured and murdered.

> *'At Alexandria were invaluable libraries, and the unanimous testimony of ancient records declares that 700,000 books, brought together by the unremitting energy of the Ptolemies were burned in the Alexandrine wars, when the city was sacked under the dictator Caesar.'*
>
> Ammianus Marcellinus, *The Later Roman Empire*, 390–91

When word of this reached Theodosius, he pardoned the pagan rioters; he considered the Christians who had died in the Serapeum martyrs and did not wish the glory of their deaths to be overshadowed by acts of vengeance. At the same time he ordered that the Serapeum itself be demolished. A military detachment, supported by Christian civilians, accomplished the task in a single day. One particularly fearless soldier volunteered to be the first to strike a blow against the massive idol of Serapis (which supposedly had the power to bring an end to the world if touched by impious hands) by taking an axe to its face. Not only did the world remain intact, but – as other blows were struck – it is said that thousands of rats poured out of the idol's rotten interior, prompting several pagan witnesses to change sides and become Christians.

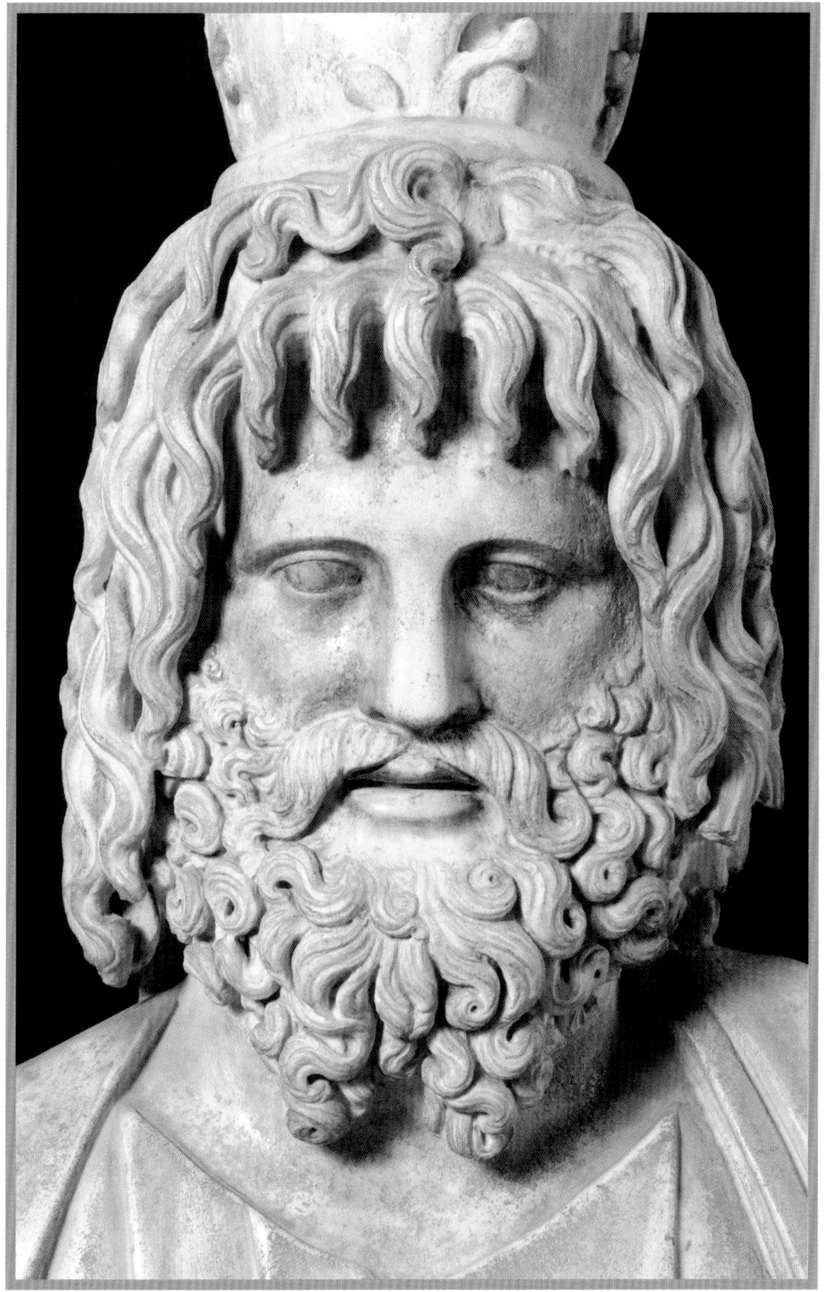

A bust of the head of the god Serapis. A fusion of Greek and Egyptian deities, the worship of Serapis was banned by Emperor Theodosius I.

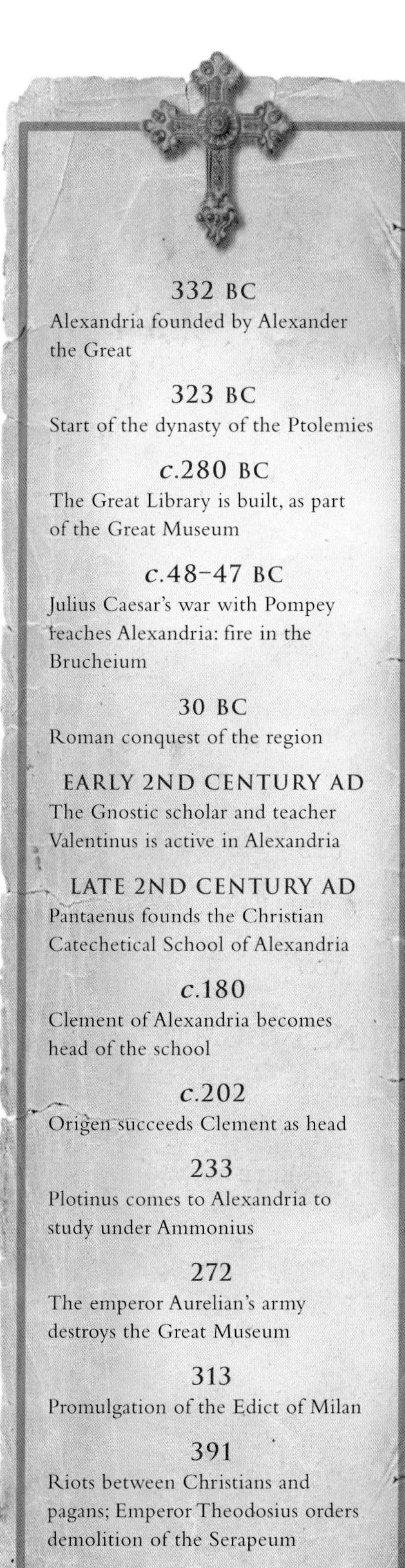

332 BC
Alexandria founded by Alexander the Great

323 BC
Start of the dynasty of the Ptolemies

***c.*280 BC**
The Great Library is built, as part of the Great Museum

***c.*48–47 BC**
Julius Caesar's war with Pompey reaches Alexandria: fire in the Brucheium

30 BC
Roman conquest of the region

EARLY 2ND CENTURY AD
The Gnostic scholar and teacher Valentinus is active in Alexandria

LATE 2ND CENTURY AD
Pantaenus founds the Christian Catechetical School of Alexandria

***c.*180**
Clement of Alexandria becomes head of the school

***c.*202**
Origen succeeds Clement as head

233
Plotinus comes to Alexandria to study under Ammonius

272
The emperor Aurelian's army destroys the Great Museum

313
Promulgation of the Edict of Milan

391
Riots between Christians and pagans; Emperor Theodosius orders demolition of the Serapeum

The riots of 391 did not abate all at once; many persons died, while many others – especially among the pagan community – fled the city. After peace was restored, a number of other heathen temples were razed and, at the emperor's command, their idols were melted down and made into vessels to be distributed to the poor. Alexandria remained a great centre of scholarship and science for more than two centuries, though now it was primarily a Christian city. It was rarely, however, a city ruled by charity.

CONSTANTINE THE GREAT AND THE BIRTH OF CHRISTENDOM

At the dawn of the fourth century AD, the Christians of the Roman world still practised a faith that was officially proscribed, but they were sufficiently numerous and well established to consider themselves safe from legal molestation. There were still sporadic outbreaks of violence, but no systematic imperial effort had been made to eradicate the faith since the Decian persecution of 250 and its sequel, the persecution instituted by the emperor Valerian (d.260) in 257, both of which had claimed the lives of some prominent bishops; and both of these purges had proved futile and had ended fairly quickly. By the year 303, Christians had every reason to feel secure in their position.

In that year, however, the last and most terrible imperial persecution of the Church began, when the emperor Diocletian (245–316), the Augustus (or chief emperor) of the eastern half of the empire, issued an edict requiring all Christians to make sacrifices to the old gods. Supposedly, Diocletian was inspired to renew the anti-Christian measures of an earlier generation because, on a visit to the prophet of Apollo in Didyma to obtain a divine oracle, he was told that the presence of Christians in the empire had rendered the god silent. He therefore resolved to wipe out this foreign impiety once and for all and win back the favour of heaven. The campaign against the Christians was prosecuted with a special enthusiasm by Diocletian's ferocious lieutenant, Galerius (d.311), whose loathing of the Christians was boundless (his mother allegedly was a priestess in one of the old cults).

Constantine's foundation of a new capital of the empire in the East on the Bosphorus saw the settlement of Nova Roma (Constantinople) develop rapidly into a magnificent city of grand architecture and opulent art. This mosaic of Christ Pantokrator is from the church of Hagia Sophia (Holy Wisdom) in Istanbul.

This 'Great Persecution' was truly a time of terror. Believers were imprisoned, tortured and killed; martyrs' tombs were desecrated, churches destroyed and Christian texts burned. When Diocletian abdicated for reasons of health in 305, Galerius became Augustus of the East and appointed his equally brutal nephew Maximinus (d.313) as Caesar (deputy emperor). Together they waged war on the Church for another six years. In 311, however, Galerius contracted an agonizing disease (possibly bowel cancer), which he suspected was retribution sent by the Christian God. And so, before his death, he issued an edict absolving Christians of the obligation to worship Roman gods. In the winter of 312, the persecution largely ceased.

Nevertheless, the Christians of the empire had been savagely reminded that they were a minority with no legal rights. They could scarcely have imagined that, just two years after Galerius' death, a Christian would be emperor.

The Emblem of Christ Appearing to Constantine *by Peter Paul Rubens (1622). The Christian historian Eusebius (c.275–339) wrote of this incident: 'The Christ of God appeared to Constantine with the sign which had appeared to him in the sky, and urged him to make himself a copy of the sign … and to use this as protection against the attacks of the enemy.'*

A Sign in the Heavens

Constantine the Great (*c.*280–337) was the son of Constantius Chlorus, who became Caesar of the West in 293 and Augustus in 305. When Constantius died in 306, while on campaign in Britain with his son, the latter was acclaimed emperor by his troops. Six years of civil war ensued, culminating in Constantine's defeat of his brother-in-law Maxentius at the Battle of the Milvian Bridge near Rome in 312.

Before this decisive engagement, however, Constantine experienced a religious conversion that prompted him to go into battle with a Christian symbol – probably a combination of the Greek letters X (*chi*) and P (*rho*), the first two letters in 'Christos' – painted on the shields of his soldiers. According to one version of the story, he had been instructed in a dream to adopt the symbol; according to another (and, apparently, to Constantine himself) he and his troops had seen a great cross in the heavens at some point before the battle.

In any event, as the new Augustus of the West, Constantine – along with Licinius (d.325), the Eastern Augustus – promulgated the Edict of Milan, which granted

Christians complete toleration for their faith and full legal rights. After 324, with his defeat of Licinius, Constantine was emperor of both East and West, and during his long reign he demonstrated his loyalty to his new faith by shifting state patronage and property away from the old cults to the Church, by making somewhat sporadic attempts to discourage pagan idolatry, and by building a great many churches. In 325, he convened the first 'ecumenical' (or 'universal') council of the Church to resolve differences of doctrine within the Church. In 330, he moved the seat of government to Asia Minor, to the ancient city of Byzantium. Now renamed Constantinople, this 'New Rome' was dedicated – unlike the old Rome – exclusively to Christ.

The 'labarum' or 'chi-rho' symbol: it was either this or a simple cross that Constantine claimed he had seen in the sky and had been instructed in a dream to paint upon his soldiers' shields before the Battle of the Milvian Bridge.

Even during his lifetime, Constantine was celebrated as a kind of Apostle, and his struggles to consolidate the empire as a kind of global evangelism. He was, if nothing else, an observant practitioner of his faith. That said, he was hardly a model of Christian charity and clemency. There was a touch of officious military brutality in the way in which he enforced several of his decrees. What is more, he may have been responsible for the murders of his wife Fausta and son Crispus in 326. On the other hand, he did attempt in significant ways to bring imperial policy into closer conformity with Christian teachings. He endowed the Church with the power and resources to provide for the poor and the sick, and to care for widows and orphans, on a massive scale. He abolished certain of the more barbaric criminal penalties, including crucifixion. And he made it easier for householders to free their slaves, in part by giving the Church legal authority to certify emancipation.

Constantine delayed his own baptism until the end of his life, since the responsibilities of his office obliged him to do things incompatible with full membership in the body of Christ. When, therefore, he fell fatally ill in 337, and was forced to retire to his deathbed, he exchanged his robes of imperial purple for the white baptismal garments of a catechumen and was baptized. Shortly thereafter he died.

> *'The bishop of Constantinople shall have the primacy of honour after the bishop of Rome, because Constantinople is the new Rome.'*
>
> COUNCIL OF CONSTANTINOPLE (CANON 3), 381

THE LAST PAGAN EMPEROR

The new course upon which Constantine had set the empire during his long reign was irreversible. His son, Constantius II (317–61), retained his father's creed, not so much out of conviction as out of political prudence.

There was, however, one last great attempt to revive the fading pagan order. Constantine's nephew Julian (332–63), whose father and brother had been murdered under Constantius II as possible rivals for the imperial throne, secretly converted to paganism in 351 (hence he was known to posterity as 'Julian the Apostate'). Quite by chance, Constantius II found it expedient to make Julian his Caesar in 355, and then to send him into Gaul to make war on the barbarian Franks and Alamanni. Julian proved to be an unexpectedly brilliant, courageous

MAGIC AND RELIGION

Though Julian the Apostate decried the 'irrationality' of Christianity, the 'higher' paganism to which he himself subscribed abounded in what the Church regarded as the grossest kinds of superstition. These included secret rites of initiation, blood sacrifice, astrology, divination, 'theurgy' (that is, magical invocations of the gods, sometimes into children, or into statuary), and a childlike faith in the 'divine revelations' contained in mystical texts such as the *Chaldean Oracles* (a fascinating farrago of Hellenistic and Asiatic hermeticism).

Much third- and fourth-century paganism was marked by a special fascination with everything exotic and outlandish: Eastern devotions and philosophies, alchemy, Egyptian and Chaldean magic, occultism, necromancy and demonology. Nor was this true only of vulgar popular religion. At every level of society, among the educated and uneducated alike, there was a longing for salvation from the conditions of earthly life, and for any spiritual techniques or recondite wisdoms that might aid the soul in its flight. A great many mystery religions promised to free their adherents from the material world's endless cycles of birth and death, but so did many schools of philosophy. The later Platonists, for example, especially from the time of Iamblichus (*c.*250–*c.*330) to that of Proclus (*c.*410–85), used magical rituals to communicate with gods and benign daemons, to secure divine assistance, and to thwart the malevolent daemons on high who might seek to impede the soul in its ascent to God.

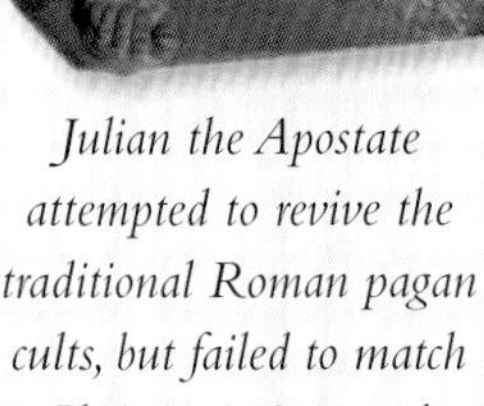

Julian the Apostate attempted to revive the traditional Roman pagan cults, but failed to match Christianity's appeal.

Naturally, this was an opportune time for conjurers, charlatans and confidence tricksters. Many temples were specially designed to 'assist' the faithful in seeing or hearing the god in whom they had placed their trust. Mechanical devices, optical tricks and combustible chemicals were used to simulate miracles and divine visitations. To give the impression that an idol had been inhabited by a divine spirit and brought to life, a clockwork automaton would be used; a hidden speaking trumpet would produce the voice of an unseen god; light reflected from a hidden pan of water onto a temple ceiling suggested a numinous presence; a skull cunningly fashioned from wax would deliver an oracle and then 'miraculously' melt away; a darkened temple vault could suddenly be transformed into the starry firmament by light reflected from fish scales embedded in the masonry; and so on. Needless to say, the effect of such devices was considerably enhanced by the votary's ardent desire to be convinced in the first place.

and successful general, and in 360, in reaction to an imperial attempt to remove him from command, his troops proclaimed him Augustus. Civil war would inevitably have followed, but Constantius conveniently died before it became necessary. On ascending to the purple, Julian publicly declared his reversion to the ancient faith, and then spent much of his extremely brief reign (November, 361 to June, 363) attempting to wrest control of Roman society away from the 'Galilaeans'.

Julian was an intelligent and formidable man, energetic, often remarkably generous, and blessed with a considerable literary gift and an enthusiasm (though not much capacity) for philosophy; he was also mildly vindictive and deeply superstitious, and suffered from an insatiable appetite for magic, esoterica and animal sacrifice. He was, simply stated, a religious fanatic. Unofficially, he countenanced any degree of violence against the Christians; officially, he enacted various discriminatory policies against them, such as a law forbidding them to teach classical texts. He did not, however, attempt to suppress the Church; rather, he granted equal toleration to *all* Christian sects, in order to foment greater discord among them.

'Julian knew that toleration of the Christians would intensify their divisions…experience had taught him that no wild beasts are such dangerous enemies to man as Christians are to one another.'
AMMIANUS MARCELLINUS, *THE ROMAN HISTORY*, 390–91

In the end, Julian's great cause was a failure, in part because he died after only 20 months in power, but ultimately because there was no real popular passion for his pagan revivalism; even many pagans regarded him as a credulous extremist. He had hoped to make the old faith attractive to those who had forsaken it, not only by giving it a doctrinal and institutional coherence like that of the Church, but by imbuing it with a moral dimension comparable to Christianity's. This was an impossible project. As he was forced to lament in a letter that he wrote to a pagan priest, 'It is a disgrace that these impious Galilaeans care not only for their own poor, but for ours as well.'

Julian died from a spear wound sustained as he retreated up the River Tigris, during a catastrophic campaign against the Persians. Legend says that, in his final moments, he cried out, 'You have conquered, O Galilaean!' He never actually uttered those words, in all likelihood; but they were true nonetheless.

303
Beginning of the last great persecution of Christians in the Roman empire

306
Constantine installed as emperor of the West; issues edict of toleration for Christians in his part of the empire

311
Persecution of Christians ends in the Roman empire

313
The Edict of Milan, granting Christians freedom of worship, is promulgated in both the eastern and the western empires

321
Constantine declares Sunday as the day of rest in the Christian calendar

325
The first Council of Nicaea defines the nature of orthodox Christian belief

330
Founding of Constantinople ('Nova Roma') as the new imperial capital

337
Constantine dies after being baptized on his deathbed

359
At the Synod of Rimini, Constantius II makes a final attempt to impose a variant of the Nicene Creed as the common statement of faith for the eastern and western churches

361
Death of Constantius II; Julian the Apostate, the last pagan emperor, comes to power

CITIES OF THE DESERT: THE RISE OF MONASTICISM

It was in the Egyptian deserts, late in the third century, that Christian asceticism was born. At first, the retreat of individual Christians to the wastelands was a flight not only from temptation, but from a hostile world; but, after the Edict of Milan, the number of hermits – if anything – increased, almost as if in reaction to the Church's new social respectability. In the fourth and fifth centuries, the enthusiasm for the monastic life became so great that, as a famous quip put it, the desert had become a city.

The ascetic life was held in high regard among both Christians and pagans; hence the Christian 'desert fathers' (and, for that matter, desert mothers) were drawn from every class and station. They saw their embrace of poverty and their devotion to prayer and fasting not just as obedience to Christ's commandments, but also as an imitation of his example, and of the example of John the Baptist.

The Way of the Pure Heart

The ascetics' chief concerns were the purification of the heart and the perfection of charity in their wills. The former required detachment from worldly affairs and possessions, the purging of lust, envy, ambition and anger from the soul, discipline of the mind and appetites, resistance to diabolic temptations and the cultivation of true humility. The latter required selfless service to others, a refusal to pass judgment and the practice of radical forgiveness. Indeed, many of the desert fathers' stories and sayings have been preserved, and they provide a remarkable picture of the desert as a school where one learnt the art of forgiving others without reserve.

Built in the sixth century AD, St Simeon Monastery stands on a hilltop near the city of Aswan in Upper Egypt. Early Arabic and Coptic sources call this institution Anba Hatre, after an anchorite who retired to the desert to imitate the life of St Anthony.

The problem with any such movement when it becomes popular is that it can become as much a fashion as a vocation, and attract persons not really suited to the life. By the late fourth century and well into the fifth, there were some monks who – far from living according to the exacting precepts of charity established by the great desert ascetics – were typical, volatile products of the brutal lower class milieu of the Egyptian cities. Such men, no doubt in all good conscience, did not hesitate during times of strife between pagans and Christians, or during times of doctrinal dispute within the Church, to indulge in vandalism or even in violence in defence of what they saw as the true faith. Yet, for all their infamous antics, they were not able to prevent the original ideals of the desert fathers from continuing to bear fruit in later generations.

Anthony the Great

The earliest desert fathers were hermits or 'anchorites', who pursued their spiritual disciplines mostly in isolation. The most famous of these was St Anthony of Egypt (251–356), a child of wealthy parents who from an early age led a sober life of self abnegation, and who in 285 sold all his worldly goods, gave the money to the poor, and withdrew to the desert west of Alexandria, and then to an old abandoned Roman fort on a mountain near the Nile. There he remained for 20 years, sustained by local Christian villagers, who passed food – and received spiritual counsel – through a small aperture in the wall.

In 305, Anthony emerged from his cell, quite sane and healthy. Other hermits had gathered near his retreat over the years, and so he set about forging them into a more orderly monastic community. He preached, gave spiritual advice to visitors, participated in theological arguments, debated with non-Christians, and even apparently visited Alexandria twice. After the Edict of Milan, he retired further into the desert, receiving visitors, sometimes venturing out to visit the monastery he had organized, and devoting himself to prayer and contemplation. He died at the age of 105. His *Life*, by the great Alexandrian bishop St Athanasius (*c.*293–373), became one of the most popular, widely disseminated and influential books of Christian antiquity.

Pachomius and Macarius

Perhaps almost as important as Anthony for the later development of Christian monasticism was St Pachomius (*c.*290–346), a former soldier who withdrew to the desert in around 314, and who was the originator of 'coenobitic' – or regulated

c.250
Paul the Hermit, the first recognized Christian recluse, takes refuge in the Egyptian desert to escape the Decian persecution, living for 20 years on Mt Pispir

285
St Anthony of Egypt renounces his worldly wealth and departs to live in the inhospitable Wadi el Natrun outside Alexandria in Egypt's Western Desert

c.300
Birth of Macarius the Great, hermit and author of important works on the spiritual life

c.317
Abba Pachomius, originator of coenobitic (community) monasticism, founds a contemplative community at Tabennisi, an island in the Nile

356
Death of St Anthony at the age of 105

c.365
Bishop Athanasius of Alexandria writes the *Vita Antonii* (Life of Anthony)

c.368
Basil of Caesarea codifies the ethical precepts of monastic life in his *Asketika*

c.390
Evagrius Ponticus records and systematizes the oral teachings of the desert fathers

During his years of islolation in the desert, St Anthony is said to have endured every possible assault by the devil, including enticing mirages of women or terrifying visions of wild beasts, and even physical attacks by demons. His temptation by the devil provided rich subject matter for numerous painters; this depiction (1647) is by the Flemish artist David Teniers the Younger.

communal – monasticism. He was the first to construct a monastic settlement in which all the monks' cells were situated within the same walls, and in which uniform hours were prescribed for prayer, meals, work and sleep. During his life, he established nine monasteries and two convents, which together housed more than 7000 persons. His monastic rule also set the pattern for all later rules, such as that of St. Basil the Great (329–79) in the East and that of St Benedict of Nursia (*c*.480–*c*.547) in the West.

As beloved as Anthony, and perhaps more important for the evolution of the contemplative dimension of Christian monasticism, was St Macarius the Great (300–91), who took up the hermit's life at about the age of 30, and soon won unsought renown as a spiritual guide, a master of spiritual discourses, a healer, and a prophet. He was a 'mystical theologian' primarily, who wrote about the light of God shining within the sanctified soul, and about the presence of God within the heart transfigured by love.

Of works written by Macarius himself, however, many scholars are willing to recognize only one, his *Epistle to the Friends of God*; but there are 50 Macarian Homilies, composed either by him or by disciples of his teachings, which occupy an honoured place within the tradition of Christian contemplative writings. And there are a number of other texts ascribed to him that might better be described as belonging to a greater 'Macarian tradition'. All of these writings are to this day especially cherished in the Eastern Christian world.

AN ENTERPRISING DEVIL

Beginning in the late fourth century, various collections of short anecdotes about the desert fathers – mostly brief souvenirs of their spiritual instructions and personal examples – were compiled, and came collectively to be known as the *Apophthegmata Patrum* ('Sayings of the Fathers'). They provide a fascinating portrait of the life of the Christian Thebaid (the upper Egyptian desert), as well as of many of the individual monks: Abba Anthony, Abba Macarius, Abba Evagrius, Abba Sisois, Abba John the Dwarf and so on. The Sayings also contain a number of legends that vividly express the high esteem in which the desert fathers were held.

One story tells of Satan holding court, receiving the adoration of his demonic lieutenants and inquiring into their recent exploits. The first of the demons to approach the throne reports that he has caused riots, wars and much bloodshed; but when he reveals that it took him a month to do so, Satan has him chastized. A second demon tells how he has raised storms at sea and sunk ships, sending many men to their deaths; but, on learning that it took him 20 days, Satan also punishes him severely. A third demon relates how he sowed discord at a wedding, resulting in the death of the bridegroom; but, as this took him ten days, he too is scourged for his idleness. A fourth demon then reports that for 40 years he tormented a single monk of the desert, before finally succeeding in making the hermit have a lustful thought in the night. On hearing this, Satan rises from his throne to kiss his servant; then he places his own crown on the demon's head, and commands the latter to sit beside him on his throne, proclaiming: 'You have performed a brave and mighty deed!'

The Great Evagrius

The most brilliant man ever to join the ranks of the desert fathers was Evagrius Ponticus (346–99), who not only possessed the sort of formal philosophical and theological training that most of his fellow monks lacked, but who in fact had abandoned a theological career in Constantinople to take up the ascetic life. His writings were remarkable not only for their philosophical sophistication, but for the precision with which they described the methods, psychological states, and special experiential qualities of the contemplative life. For instance, his exposition of the eight spiritually destructive *logismoi* – that is, self-sustaining sequences of desire, imagination, will and intellectual intention – exhibits a degree of psychological subtlety and moral insight unprecedented in the contemplative literature of Christians or pagans.

Evagrius' contributions to later Christian thought were immense and crucial, but – like Origen – he was never canonized as a saint, and for many of the same reasons as Origen. Theologically, Evagrius was an heir to the Origenist tradition, and so many of his teachings were condemned at the same time as Origen's, at the Second Council of Constantinople in 553. But his writings constituted a kind of subterranean current within the theology of later centuries; and they re-emerged into plain view in the great 18th-century Eastern Orthodox mystical anthology, the *Philokalia*.

'It is said that Pachomius at first practised asceticism alone in a cave, but that a holy angel appeared to him and commanded him to call together some young monks, and live with them … A tablet was then given to him, which is still carefully preserved. On this tablet were inscribed injunctions by which he was bound to permit everyone to eat, to drink, to work and to fast.'

SOZOMEN, *THE ECCLESIASTICAL HISTORY*, BOOK 3:14, *c.*440

CHRISTIANITY IN ARMENIA AND INDIA

Many modern Christians have little conception of quite how far the gospel spread in the early centuries of the Church, nor what a large variety of cultures have composed – and still compose – the greater Christian world. Western Christians are perhaps especially apt to forget that, in the early years of the faith, the gospel fared somewhat better in the East, and travelled far along the thriving trade routes opened up by Hellenistic culture.

Of all Christian nations – that is, nations in which Christianity is or has been the faith not only of the people but of the state – the oldest is Armenia. It was around the year 300 that the Armenian royal household received baptism and adopted Christianity as the royal religion some 13 years before the Christians of the Roman empire were granted the right to practise their faith by the Edict of Milan.

The First Christian Kingdom

In many ways, the history of ancient Armenia resembled that of Judea. It had been a subject nation for centuries by the beginning of the Christian era. It was conquered by the Persians under Darius I (550–486 BC), by Alexander the Great, by the Seleucids and – after a brief period of independence – by the Romans in 66 BC. For many centuries thereafter, situated as it was between the Roman and Persian empires, it was dominated now by one, now by the other, and even on some occasions by both; and it absorbed their religious influences.

According to tradition, however, the influence of Christianity began as early as the apostolic age. The Apostle Thaddeus is said to have arrived in Armenia in 43 and was joined by the Apostle Bartholomew in 60. Both died there as martyrs, along with a large number of other Christians. And, in the early second and early third centuries, many more Armenian Christians died at the hands of the Persians.

Yet the actual founder of Armenian Christianity – as a national religion with an indigenous institutional structure – was St Gregory the Illuminator (240–332), a Parthian prince who fled his homeland as a youth along with other refugees from a Persian invasion, and was educated as a Christian in Caesarea. In 287, he returned to his homeland to preach the gospel following the restoration of the Armenian monarchy under Tiridates III. Tiridates, however, was an ardent devotee of the old gods and had Gregory arrested and thrown into a dungeon, where he remained for around 13 years while his coreligionists suffered terrible persecution. According to tradition, the king – suffering a painful illness – finally released Gregory, was healed by him, and (along with his entire household) converted to Christianity. Gregory then returned to Caesarea, was confirmed as the 'Catholicos' (or supreme Primate) of Armenia, and was greeted on his return by the king, in full royal procession. Mass conversions and baptisms supposedly followed.

A Byzantine icon of St Gregory the Illuminator, who brought Christianity to Armenia.

Evangelism and Tradition

National legend may exaggerate the ease with which Christianity triumphed. Local forms of paganisms persisted for many years in Armenia. But, with Gregory, a national Armenian Orthodox Church was established, with an organized hierarchy. Churches were built, pagan shrines were reconsecrated as churches, monasteries were founded, and a cathedral was built for the Catholicos in the city of Echmiadzin. All the evidence suggests that the new faith was extremely successful.

In 365, a more robust campaign of Christianization in Armenia was inaugurated at the general synod summoned by the Catholicos Nerses (a descendant of Gregory): legal reforms were instituted, and hospitals, orphanages, and homes for the blind, for lepers, and for widows and orphans were built. Under the Catholicos Sahak I (r.387–439), a scholarly priest named Mesrop was commissioned to create an alphabet for the Armenian language, and a great age of translation of Christian texts from Syriac and Greek began, including – from 404 to 433 – the Bible. Church schools were also established.

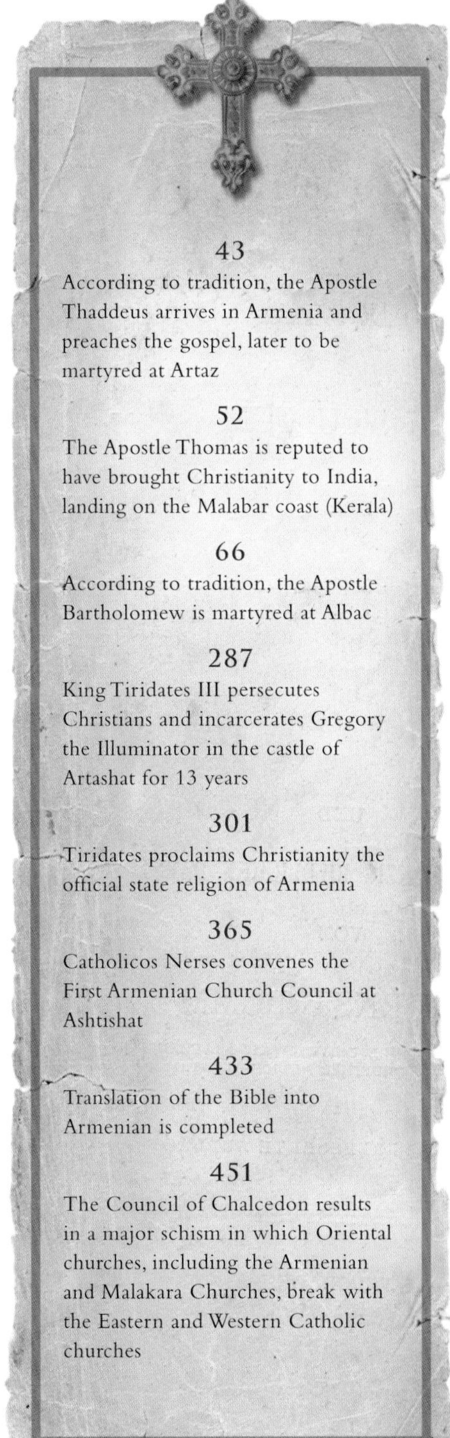

43
According to tradition, the Apostle Thaddeus arrives in Armenia and preaches the gospel, later to be martyred at Artaz

52
The Apostle Thomas is reputed to have brought Christianity to India, landing on the Malabar coast (Kerala)

66
According to tradition, the Apostle Bartholomew is martyred at Albac

287
King Tiridates III persecutes Christians and incarcerates Gregory the Illuminator in the castle of Artashat for 13 years

301
Tiridates proclaims Christianity the official state religion of Armenia

365
Catholicos Nerses convenes the First Armenian Church Council at Ashtishat

433
Translation of the Bible into Armenian is completed

451
The Council of Chalcedon results in a major schism in which Oriental churches, including the Armenian and Malakara Churches, break with the Eastern and Western Catholic churches

In common with certain other 'Oriental churches', the Armenian Church broke with the imperial Church of Constantinople and Rome after the Council of Chalcedon in 451, which the Armenian Church rejected officially in 506. This schism left Armenian Christianity somewhat isolated – a condition that was exacerbated by the Islamic conquest of the country in the seventh century.

The St Thomas Christians of India

No less ancient than Armenian Christianity, perhaps, is the native Christianity of India. From very ancient times, there has been an established community of Christians among the Malayalam-speaking peoples of the southwestern Malabar coastal region of Kerala. They are mostly the descendants of East Syrian merchants who travelled along the trade routes that passed through the Red Sea and settled there. These 'Nasranis' or 'Malankara Orthodox Christians' (as they are known) call themselves the 'Thomas Christians' because they believe that Christianity was originally brought to Kerala in 52 by the Apostle Thomas, who remained in the country until his martyrdom in Mylapur, in Madras, around 72.

'We the Apostles … apportioned the regions of the earth among us … and India fell to the lot of Judas Thomas, also named Didymus. He did not wish to go, protesting weakness of the flesh, and saying "How can I, a Hebrew, proclaim the truth to the Indians?" … In the night, though, the Saviour appeared to him, saying, "Fear not, Thomas. Depart for India, and preach the word, and my grace shall be with you".'

The Apocryphal Acts of Thomas

There is no reason to reject this story as legend. The trade routes to India were already quite ancient by the first century AD, and were frequented by merchants from the Near East and the greater Mediterranean world; and there was a small Jewish community in Kerala from before the Christian period. A late second or early third-century Gnostic text, *The Acts of Thomas*, tells of the Apostle's journey to India; this highly romanticized account nevertheless draws upon an established tradition. The fourth-century Christian historian Eusebius records that Pantaenus, founder of the Christian School of Alexandria, travelled to India as a missionary in the second century, only to find Christianity already established there.

We can say with certainty, however, that East Syrian Christian refugees, fleeing persecution under the Persian emperor Shapur II (309–79), came in great numbers to Kerala, and that by the late fifth century the Indian Church was ecclesiastically united with the Syrian 'Church of the East' – another 'Oriental' church that broke with Constantinople and Rome some time after the Council of Chalcedon (but for reasons radically different from those of the Armenians). Later waves of East Syrian immigration took place in the eighth and ninth centuries.

All, it seems, were quite hospitably received by the native Indian rulers, perhaps because theirs was a prosperous merchant population. They were granted legal charters for their community, accorded an extremely high caste in Indian society (only a step below Brahmins), and given extensive jurisdiction over their own people. From early on, Christian processions were allowed to display the full sumptuous ornament usually reserved for the ruling caste. In turn, certain Indian practices – usually associated with Hindu beliefs – were adopted by the Thomas Christians. It even became common for Christian men to withdraw from the world in their sixty-fourth year to devote the rest of their lives to contemplation and prayer, in keeping with ancient Hindu practice.

THE LEGEND OF KING ABGAR

According to a very old and popular legend known throughout the ancient and Medieval Christian world, Christianity penetrated into the eastern reaches of Syria not only in the days of the Apostles, but during the time of Christ's earthly ministry. The tale is recounted in two ancient Christian sources, Eusebius' *Ecclesiastical History* and *The Teaching of Addai*, supposedly written in the first century. Both works contain letters – in slightly different versions – allegedly exchanged between King Abgar V the Black of Edessa in Syria, and Jesus himself.

Legend recounts that, in place of a visit from Christ, Abgar received an image of Christ painted from life.

According to the legend, certain ambassadors from Edessa and their scribe Hannan, while passing through Jerusalem on their way home to Syria, heard of Christ's miraculous powers. They brought word of this new wonder-worker back to Abgar, who had long been afflicted by leprosy, and the king immediately sent Hannan back to Palestine with a letter for Jesus, entreating him to come to Edessa. In the letter, Abgar speaks of the marvellous things he has been told: how Christ has restored sight to the blind, caused the lame to walk, cast out devils, and raised the dead; 'from this I have concluded you are either a god descended from heaven,' he says, 'or the son of God'; he then begs Christ to come and heal him of his disease and offers Christ the protection and hospitality of his 'small yet very beautiful city'.

According to the tale, Jesus sent a response back with Hannan. In this letter he praises Abgar for 'having believed without having seen', and then explains that he cannot leave his homeland until he has accomplished the mission for which his Father has sent him into the world. He promises, however, that when he has ascended, he will send one of his disciples to heal the king. According to *The Teaching of Addai,* Hannan even painted a portrait of Christ to take with him back to the king's palace.

After Christ's ascension, the story continues, one of the 72 disciples who also followed Christ was sent by the Apostles into Syria. This disciple – one Addai by name – fulfilled Christ's promise to Abgar and healed him of his leprosy. The king then received baptism and ordained it for his subjects, and Addai became the bishop in Edessa. Addai was succeeded by Aggai, a local convert; but the next king, Manu, restored pagan worship to his city, and Aggai died a martyr.

ANCIENT SPLENDOUR: CHRISTIANITY IN ETHIOPIA

A modern Westerner encountering the Ethiopian Orthodox Church for the first time often experiences a sort of delighted disorientation. One cannot help but be overwhelmed by the sheer sensory splendour of the *Tewahedo* (as the Church is called in Ethiopia): the stern grandeur of the worship, the opulent vestments, the sumptuous processional 'parasols', the grand elaborate liturgies, the ornate gold crosses, the vivid icons, the drums and sistrums and ritual dance and mesmerizing pentatonic chant.

An image of Christ in an Ethiopian church. As Islam spread from the eighth century onwards, mountainous Ethiopia remained a bastion of Christianity in an otherwise Muslim-dominated North and East Africa.

The Ethiopian Church is also pervaded by an almost irresistible air of mystery: its claim that it possesses the Ark of the Covenant, for instance, or the national belief that the emperors of Ethiopia descended from Menelik I, the son of King Solomon and the queen of Sheba. But, even for those not drawn to grand spectacle or the enigmas of ancient history, the *Tewahedo* can exert a rare fascination, since it constitutes the sole living link to a magnificent civilization that vanished long ago. At its zenith, this civilization formed not only the southernmost frontier of ancient Christendom, but also one of its most remarkable manifestations.

Two Shipwrecked Sailors

That frontier might never have been reached but for a fortunate mischance. Sometime in the early decades of the fourth century AD, two Christian merchants from Tyre named Frumentius and Aedesius – brothers who had been raised in Alexandria – took passage aboard a trading vessel bound for India, but never reached their destination. Their ship foundered in the Red Sea, off the East African coast, and though both safely reached the Ethiopian shore, the men who found them did not put them on another ship, but took them instead to the imperial city of Aksum, high up on the Tigray Plateau of the mountainous north. Here the two brothers were sold into the service of the royal court: Aedesius as a cupbearer of the emperor and Frumentius as tutor to the crown prince Ezanas. And this, it seems, is how Ethiopia became a Christian empire; for, after ascending the throne, Ezanas and his court converted to the faith the two Alexandrians had introduced to the royal household. Later, Ezanas permitted Aedesius to return to Tyre and sent Frumentius to Alexandria to ask the patriarch to appoint a bishop for Ethiopia, to which the patriarch responded by assigning Frumentius to the post and sending him back to oversee the evangelization of the Aksumite empire.

This, at least, is one version of the story of how the gospel came to Ethiopia. In other versions, certain narrative details are different. But there is little doubt that, in its broad outlines, the tale is true. Not that the arrival of the two brothers

Ethiopian Christian clergy in their exquisite vestments assemble for the Timkat *festival (19 January) that celebrates Epiphany. During this feast, a replica of the Ark of the Covenant is taken in procession to its church and rituals commemorating Christ's baptism in the Jordan are celebrated.*

marked the first contact between Ethiopia with Christianity or, for that matter, with monotheism. For centuries, Aksum had controlled most of the significant trade routes from the African interior, as well as the thriving Red Sea port of Adulis, where traders brought goods from the Roman empire, Asia and the Near East to sell for African horn, ivory, precious metals, frankincense, and slaves, and where merchants from the Mediterranean world had long been settled, Christians among them. Moreover, Judaism was already well established in the empire; the exact origins of the *Falasha* – the native Jews of northern Ethiopia – are impossible to determine, but their conversion to Judaism certainly came long before the Christian era. All that said, however, the kingdom that Ezanas inherited was a pagan state, devoted to a host of Near Eastern and African gods, and it might have remained one indefinitely had it not been for that shipwreck in the Red Sea.

Imperial Zenith

For two centuries after Frumentius' return from Alexandria, Christianity continued to spread throughout Ethiopia, expanding constantly southward from Aksum. Monks and priests proselytized, churches proliferated, pagan shrines were reconsecrated, and a vast body of Greek, Syriac and Coptic Christian literature was translated into the native Aksumite language of Ge'ez (a Semitic tongue that survives today only in the scripture and liturgies of the *Tewahedo*). Of particular importance was the introduction of organized monasticism into the country in around 480. Especially revered in Ethiopian tradition are a number of foreign monks collectively known as the 'Nine Saints', who not only founded numerous

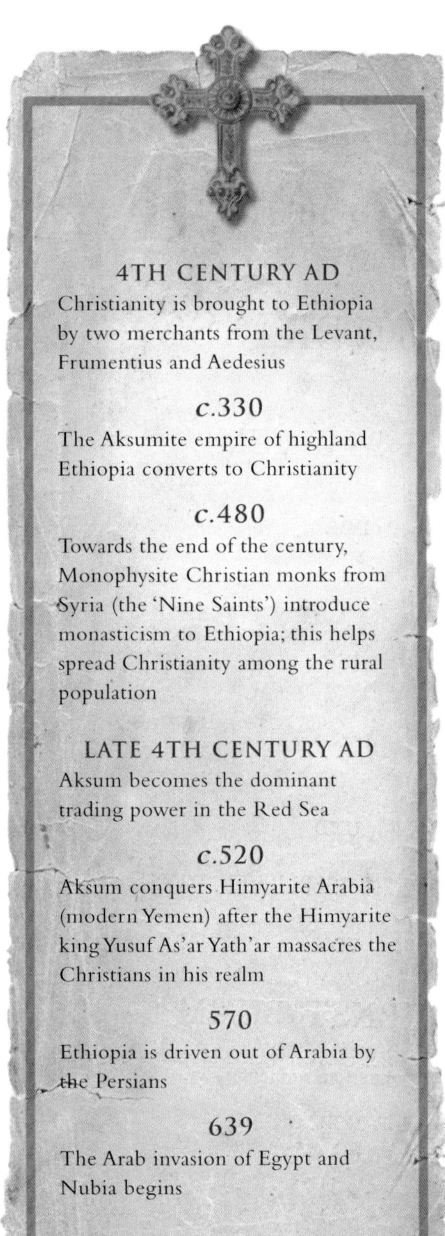

monasteries (often on almost inaccessible mountain peaks), but made a particularly rigorous form of asceticism one of the key traits of East African Christianity. They and the other monks of the late fifth century inspired an era of robust Christianization that soon swept away most of the lingering traces of the old paganism in Ethiopia, and put in its place a unified – and remarkably fervent – Christian culture.

4TH CENTURY AD
Christianity is brought to Ethiopia by two merchants from the Levant, Frumentius and Aedesius
c.330
The Aksumite empire of highland Ethiopia converts to Christianity
c.480
Towards the end of the century, Monophysite Christian monks from Syria (the 'Nine Saints') introduce monasticism to Ethiopia; this helps spread Christianity among the rural population
LATE 4TH CENTURY AD
Aksum becomes the dominant trading power in the Red Sea
c.520
Aksum conquers Himyarite Arabia (modern Yemen) after the Himyarite king Yusuf As'ar Yath'ar massacres the Christians in his realm
570
Ethiopia is driven out of Arabia by the Persians
639
The Arab invasion of Egypt and Nubia begins

In many ways, this was the golden age of Aksumite civilization. It was a period during which literature, music and all the arts flourished, almost exclusively in the service of the new faith, and during which Aksum's mercantile and military power continued to grow, extending even over parts of the Arabian peninsula. Commercial and cultural ties to Constantinople and Alexandria were strong, and no other power in the Red Sea or Indian Ocean rivalled Ethiopia for dominance of regional trade. It was also during these centuries that many of the most distinctive traditions of Ethiopian Christianity probably began to appear: for example, the adoption of Jewish practices such as observance of the Saturday Sabbath, abstinence from 'unclean' foods, and circumcision of male infants; also the extremely demanding fasting laws, which oblige Ethiopian Orthodox Christians to refrain from all animal products for some 250 days a year. These were also the years when the Ge'ez Bible was beginning to take shape, at a time when the exact canon of scripture was still indeterminate throughout the Christian world, with the result that the Ethiopian Bible comprises some 81 books, including many works in both the Old and New Testaments that no other tradition accepts.

Imperial Decline

During the latter half of the fifth century, when Alexandria separated from the Churches of Rome and Constantinople on account of the Council of Chalcedon, Aksum remained loyal to its original patriarchate (thus today Ethiopian Orthodoxy is still considered a branch of the Coptic Orthodox Church of Egypt). This perhaps somewhat weakened ties with the Roman empire, but not disastrously so. The real decline of the Aksumite empire began in the mid-6th century, when it was driven from Arabia, and became precipitous in the seventh century, with the Muslim conquest of Egypt and Nubia, the rise of Arab shipping in the Red Sea, and the virtual isolation of Ethiopia from the rest of Christendom. The economic consequences were quite devastating, the administration and army of the empire collapsed, and in subsequent years Ethiopian civilization was forced to retire into itself. The vitality of the Church, though, seems never to have suffered; its profound spirituality, liturgical beauty and special history (both real and legendary) provided the principal foundation upon which Ethiopian culture continued to rest, and the chief inspiration for the most splendid achievements of that culture for many centuries to come.

THE LOST ARK

A monk watches over the chest containing his monastery's replica of the Ark.

No aspect of Ethiopian religion is more distinctive than the belief – held by Christians and Jews alike – that the Ark of the Covenant, which was once housed in Solomon's Temple, now resides in a small sanctuary on the grounds of the cathedral of St Mary of Zion in Aksum. Only one guardian, a monk of extraordinary personal sanctity, ever enters its presence; and he, as death approaches, is obliged to name his own successor.

The Aksumite Ark (or *Tabot*) is more than a feature of pious folklore. It lies at the heart of Ethiopian Orthodoxy: the *Tewahedo*'s holiest symbol of God's abiding glory in the Earth, and of the incarnate presence of that glory in Christ. Every church or monastery, in order to be consecrated, must possess a replica of the Ark, locked in its tabernacle. Once each year, these replicas are brought out – in sealed chests and heavily veiled – for the Epiphany (or *Timkat*) procession. The Ark in Aksum, though, is never moved.

The great 13th-century Ethiopian epic, the *Kebra Negast* ('Glory of the Kings') tells of the Ark's secret removal from Jerusalem to Ethiopia by Menilek I; but this is a late reconstruction of a much older tradition. Before being brought to Aksum, the Ark supposedly resided at Tana Cherkos, an island in Ethiopia's Lake Tana where, to this day, monks still keep other alleged relics of Solomon's Temple. Some scholars think that the Ark may indeed have been taken south in the seventh century BC, perhaps after the corruption of Temple worship by King Manasseh. This is, after all, the period when the Ark disappears from the Biblical record; and, not long after, the prophet Zephaniah speaks of the 'dispersed' Israelites 'beyond the rivers of Ethiopia' (Zeph. 3:10). Whatever the case, the story is extremely ancient, and its spiritual significance for Ethiopian Christianity is inexhaustible.

ONE GOD IN THREE PERSONS: THE EARLIEST CHURCH COUNCILS

From the very beginnings of the Church, Christians had called Christ the 'Son of God' or 'God the Son', and had spoken of – and prayed and baptized in the name of – 'the Father, Son and Holy Spirit'. Before the Edict of Milan in 313, however, Christians rarely had any opportunity to discuss in what sense they understood Jesus to be divine, or what precisely they understood the relation of the Father to the Son or of either to the Spirit to be.

With the conversion of the Roman emperor Constantine, however, it became possible for matters of doctrine to be debated openly and thoroughly, and Christians soon discovered that they had many significant disagreements among themselves regarding many of the most basic elements of their faith. Scripture and the traditional liturgical practices of the Apostolic Churches had established certain general theological terms that all Christians accepted, but provided very little in the way of a conceptual clarification of those terms.

The Son of the One God

The old Greek way of speaking of the most high God was to refer to him by the definite article – 'the God', '*ho Theos*' – while a god was simply spoken of as a '*theos*'. In Christian usage, the name '*ho Theos*' was generally applied only to the Father, while Christ (or occasionally the Spirit) was more cautiously called '*theos*'. This rule, however, was anything but absolute: in the Gospel of John – where the pre-incarnate Son is identified as the divine '*Logos*' who 'was with God' and who 'was God (*theos*)' – the Apostle Thomas addresses the risen Christ as 'my Lord and my God (*ho Theos*)'. And, also in the Gospel of John, Christ declares 'I and the Father are one'.

What did this mean? In what way was Christ God? Was he equal with the Father, or a lesser emanation of the Father, or a kind of 'secondary God?' And, if the latter, what was the nature of his divine status in relation to the 'proper' divinity of the Father? Various answers to these questions had been ventured during the first three centuries of the Church. Some theologians (particularly in Rome) had proposed one or another species of 'modalism': that is, they speculated that the one God assumed different modes of existence for various purposes, now existing as Father, now as Son. Others advanced one or another version of 'adoptionism': they believed that Christ had been a man who had been adopted into divine Sonship by the Father. Still others were 'subordinationist': they claimed that the Father alone was God in the fullest sense, that the Son was a lesser expression of God, and the Spirit a still more diminished expression of the Son.

The painting in the dome of St Isaacs Cathedral, Saint Petersburg, Russia, illustrates Christ, the saints and the holy family. Divergent views on the nature of Christ soon emerged as the early Church debated the tenets of the Christian faith.

321
Arius is expelled from Alexandria

c.323
Arius publishes his *Thalia*

324
Constantine's defeat of Licinius

325
The First Council of Nicaea

326
Athanasius becomes patriarch of Alexandria

336
Athanasius is exiled from Alexandria after refusing Arius communion; death of Arius

356
Athanasius is exiled again, flees arrest and goes into hiding in the desert

362–5
Athanasius endures two further spells of exile from Alexandria

c.375
St Basil of Caesarea publishes *On the Holy Spirit*

379
Theodosius becomes emperor; St Gregory of Nazianzus becomes bishop of Constantinople and delivers his five 'Theological Orations' on the divinity of the Holy Spirit

381
First Council of Constantinople

382–3
St Gregory of Nyssa publishes his treatises *Against Eunomius*

The subordinationist tendency was especially pronounced in Alexandria. In fact, it was typical not only of Christians, but of Jews and Pagans also. The great Jewish scholar Philo, a contemporary of Jesus, had already argued that, intermediate between God and this world, was the divine Logos, the 'Son of God,' through whom the world was created and governed; for God himself, in his transcendent majesty, could not come into contact with lower reality. The Pagan Platonists believed that the ultimate divine principle – the One – was utterly transcendent of the world, and was 'related' to it only through an order of lesser, derivative divine principles. Within this environment, it was natural for many Christians to think of the divine Logos as a sort of heavenly high priest who acted as an intermediary between creatures and the inaccessible Father. Even the greatest of pre-Constantinian Alexandrian theologians, Origen, was a subordinationist.

Controversy and Creed

Theological opinions so vastly different from one another could not coexist indefinitely after the conversion of Constantine, now that the Church enjoyed the luxury – and bore the burden – of defining its beliefs with genuine precision. And, as chance or providence would have it, no sooner had the Church been granted legal rights and imperial favor than it suffered an enormous doctrinal crisis.

An Alexandrian priest named Arius (*c.*250–336) began to preach what can only be called a form of radical subordinationism: unlike, say, Origen, he not only denied the perfect coequality of Father and Son, but denied even that the Son was co-eternal with the Father, or even really 'divine' except in a purely honorific sense.

According to Arius, the *Logos* (the Son) was in fact a creature; he was the highest of creatures, admittedly, brought into being before all other things, and so exalted as to be called 'God' in relation to all other creatures, but nonetheless – to quote Arius' most notorious maxim – 'There was a time when he was not.' Only the Father, he taught, is 'unoriginate'.

'Alexander [bishop of Alexandria] attempted one day too ambitious a discourse about the unity of the Holy Trinity. Arius, one of the presbyters under his jurisdiction, a man possessed of no inconsiderable logical acumen, said: "If the Father begat the Son, the one that was begotten has a beginning of existence and from this it is evident that there was a time when the Son was not. It therefore necessarily follows that he had his essence from nothing". Alexander convened a council of many prelates and excommunicated Arius and the supporters of his heresy.'

Socrates Scholasticus, *The Ecclesiastical History*, *c.*440

A depiction of an early Ecumenical Council. The first and second Councils of Nicaea (in 325 and 787, respectively) were the first and last of seven such meetings convoked, three of them in Constantinople.

Arius' views were condemned and he was expelled from Alexandria in 321, but he spent his time in exile composing a long defence of his views – in prose and verse – entitled the *Thalia* ('Banquet') and in composing popular songs by which to spread his ideas among common Christians. When Constantine defeated Licinius in 324 and assumed control of the Eastern Christian world, he discovered that his newly adopted faith was convulsed by internal dissensions. He was not amused. He required unity of his Church no less than of his empire, and so at his command the first 'Ecumenical Council' (that is, a Council of the universal Church) was convoked in 325 to resolve the dispute. Three hundred and eighteen (almost exclusively Eastern) bishops gathered at Nicaea, near Constantinople, with Arius in attendance.

Once again, Arius' teachings were condemned, and a common statement of faith – the first version of the 'Nicene Creed' – was produced. It not only affirmed that the divine Son was 'begotten, not made', and was 'true God from true God', but

'GOD BECAME MAN THAT MAN MIGHT BECOME GOD'

That the Church spent the better part of a century agonizing over the difference between words like '*homoousios*' and '*homoiousios*' – a difference on paper, after all, of only a single letter – has frequently been an object of scorn and incredulity to those who see it as a contest between indistinguishable abstractions. But, for the Christians of the fourth century, the entire intelligibility of their faith was at stake. Many issues informed the debate – scripture, liturgy, the common understanding of the faithful – but chief among them was the nature of salvation.

If one thinks of salvation in the rather trivial sense of being allowed to go to heaven, then one will not be able to understand the prevailing mindset of the fourth-century Church. For the theologians of that time, salvation meant an intimate and immediate union with God, by which the human being would literally be 'divinized': that is, made to become (in the language of II Peter 1:4) a partaker of the divine nature – not, of course, to become God (*ho Theos*), but to become divine (*theios* or *theos*). They believed that Christ had assumed human form so as to free humanity from bondage to death and make it capable of a direct indwelling of the divine presence. This has always remained the explicit teaching of the Eastern Churches, and has never ceased to be the theological position of the Roman Catholic tradition (though it has often been forgotten).

For Athanasius or the Cappadocians, the paramount question was how such union with the transcendent God was possible for finite creatures. If – to use a formula that they and many others accepted – 'God became man that man might become God', could it possibly be the case that the Son or the Spirit was a lesser God or, even worse, merely a creature? Only God is capable of joining creatures to God; any inferior intermediary will always be infinitely remote from God himself. The Cappadocian arguments against the Eunomians were many, complex and subtle; but perhaps the most effective was the simplest: if it is the Son who joins us to the Father, and only God can join us to God, then the Son is God; and if, in the sacraments of the Church and the life of faith, it is the Spirit who joins us to the Son, and only God can join us to God, then the Spirit too must be God.

described the Son as 'consubstantial (*homoousios*)' with the Father. This was an audacious formula in the eyes of many – the word occurs nowhere in scripture – but ultimately all but seven of the bishops present subscribed to the new creed, and Arius was sent away to Illyricum (the Roman province covering much of the Balkans).

The controversy, however, did not end there. In the wake of the Council of Nicaea, any number of theologians proposed alternative solutions to the controversy. Among those who rejected the Nicene formula, there were the 'homoeans' who preferred to describe the Son as being 'of similar substance (*homoiousios*)' with the Father; and there were the 'anomoeans' who regarded the Son as being altogether 'unlike' the Father. More importantly, the emperor was persuaded by certain women within his household to turn a kindlier eye on Arius; in 336, he even commanded the bishop of Constantinople to give Arius communion. Arius entered the city in triumph, and would indeed have received communion, had he not suddenly died of natural (though rather grisly) causes the night before. Still, at the time of Constantine's death in 337, it was the Arian position that enjoyed the favour of the imperial court.

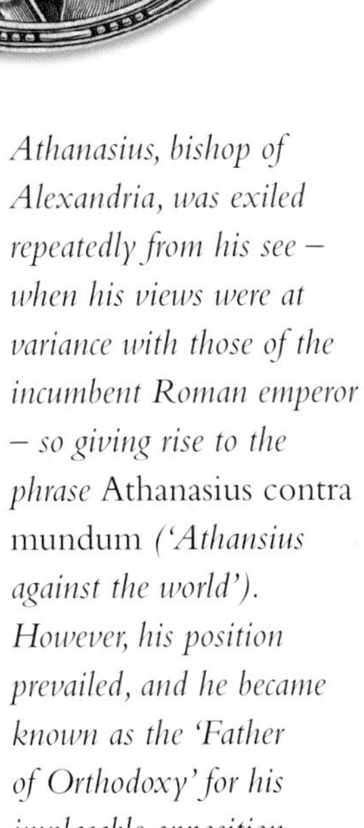

Athanasius, bishop of Alexandria, was exiled repeatedly from his see – when his views were at variance with those of the incumbent Roman emperor – so giving rise to the phrase Athanasius contra mundum *('Athansius against the world'). However, his position prevailed, and he became known as the 'Father of Orthodoxy' for his implacable opposition to Arianism.*

The Final Settlement

For many decades, the most redoubtable champion of Nicene orthodoxy was St Athanasius (*c.*296–373), a brilliant theologian who, as a young deacon, had been present at the Council, and who had been installed as patriarch of Alexandria the following year. Athanasius's fortunes in many ways were a perfect reflection of the fortunes of the orthodox party. With an almost comic regularity – no fewer than five times – he was deposed as bishop or forced to flee his see and was then restored, according to the inclinations of whichever emperor was in power.

The 'Arian controversy' did not reach its conclusion until Theodosius I (347–95), a Nicene Christian, had assumed power in the East, in 379. An uncompromising 'anomoean' named Eunomius insisted that God is, by definition, the 'ungenerated'. Hence, neither the Son nor the Spirit can be God in any proper sense, and must be essentially unlike the Father. The great opponents of 'Eunomianism' were three remarkable theologians, known collectively as the 'Cappadocian fathers': St Basil of Caesarea (329–79), his friend St Gregory of Nazianzus (*c.*330–*c.*389), and (the most brilliant of the three) Basil's younger brother St Gregory of Nyssa (*c.*335–*c.*394). It was their theology – marked as it was by an extraordinary clarity and profundity – that shaped the outcome of the second Ecumenical Council in 381, the First Council of Constantinople, which produced the final version of the Nicene Creed, and which affirmed once again that, in Christ, no less than the eternal God had entered into human history.

'We believe in One God, the Father, Almighty, Maker of all that is, seen and unseen. And in One Lord Jesus Christ, the Son of God, begotten of the Father, Only-begotten, that is from the substance of the Father; God from God, Light from Light, True God from True God, begotten not made, consubstantial with the Father, by whom all things were made, both things in heaven and in earth; who for us and for our salvation came down and was incarnate, was made man, suffered, and rose again on the third day, ascended into heaven, and is coming to judge living and dead. And in the Holy Ghost.'

Creed of the Council of Nicaea, 325

THE AGE OF THE FATHERS

The first few centuries of the Church's history are usually referred to as the 'patristic period' – in other words, the period of the 'Church Fathers'. These were the theologians who first enunciated the principles of Christian biblical exegesis, first attempted to establish and refine a Christian dogmatic vocabulary, and first employed the methods and the riches of Greek philosophy to deepen and clarify the Church's understanding of what had been revealed in Christ.

In many ways, this was the golden age of Christian thought; the accomplishments of that time were arguably never surpassed – or even equalled – in later centuries. If nothing else, the writings of the Fathers were frequently marked by a kind of speculative audacity that the theologians of later years, under the restrictions of more precisely defined dogmas, found all but impossible. The thought of the greatest of the Fathers flourished in an atmosphere of spacious liberty; it possessed an originality and power of inspiration that could not endure indefinitely, but that still often feels more lively and immediate than the theology of later centuries.

Defenders of the Faith

The first theologians of the patristic age are known as the 'Apostolic Fathers', because they were the earliest successors of the Apostles as leaders of the Church. The Apostolic Fathers include such figures as Clement, the late first-century bishop of Rome, and the second-century martyrs Ignatius of Antioch and Polycarp of Smyrna.

Aristides, one of the apologists of the early Church. In common with the writings of other defenders of the faith, it is almost certain that Aristides' document never reached its intended recipient, Emperor Antoninus Pius.

From the middle to the late second century, moreover, there arose a number of men known to posterity as the 'Apologists', who dedicated themselves to defending Christian beliefs to the pagan world by employing the language and methods of Greek philosophy. Among these were Quadratus, who addressed a defence of Christianity to the emperor Hadrian (76–138) in around 125, Aristides, who produced a similar defence for the emperor Antoninus Pius (86–161) in around 145, and Melito of Sardis, who addressed his apology to the emperor Marcus Aurelius (121–80). The greatest of the apologists was Justin Martyr (*c.*100–*c.*165), who employed the Stoic conception of a divine 'Reason' (*Logos*) pervading all things – partially present in all rational intellects – to explain who the eternal Son of God, incarnate in Jesus, was.

Perhaps the finest theological mind of that period, however, belonged to St Irenaeus of Lyons (*c.*130–*c.*200), whose work *Against the Heresies*, written in around 180, not only mounted a vigorous attack on the teachings of the Gnostics, but unfolded a subtle theology of humanity's 'recapitulation' in Christ. A perhaps equally original thinker was the North African lawyer Tertullian (*c*.155–*c*.230), a theologian who railed against pagan wisdom while making use of Stoic metaphysics to explain the Trinity.

The Great Age of the Fathers

The 'high patristic age' began with the great Alexandrians Clement and Origen – especially the latter – who not only made use of Greek philosophical concepts and methods to explicate their faith, but who began the work of developing a distinctively Christian philosophy. They were also the first great systematic exegetes of scripture. Moreover, they placed a particular emphasis upon the cultivation of the spiritual life, and so laid the foundations for the later Christian mystical tradition. Simply put, Origen's influence on later Christian thought – even after many of his ideas had been condemned as unorthodox – defies summary.

The first theologians of the patristic age whose teachings came to define Christian orthodoxy, however, arose in the fourth century: arguably the single most crucial century in the development of Christian thought. Athanasius, the scourge of Arianism, was a dogmatic theologian of considerable virtuosity; his short treatise *On the Incarnation of the Logos of God* is one of the masterpieces of the early Church's reflections on salvation and deification in Christ, profoundly impressive in its comprehensiveness and range.

> *'If the Tiber reaches the walls, if the Nile does not rise to the fields, if the sky does not move or if the earth does, if there is famine, if there is plague, the cry immediately goes up: "Throw the Christians to the lion!" What, all of them to the one lion?'*
>
> Tertullian of Carthage, *Apology*, Chapter 40.2, *c*.197

Moreover, the three Cappadocian Fathers – Basil, Gregory of Nazianzus and Gregory of Nyssa – were not only the most intellectually redoubtable defenders of Nicene orthodoxy in the later years of the Arian controversy, but could boast all the classical attainments of the educated class. Of the three, Gregory of Nazianzus was the most eloquent and theoretically rigorous, but the most original and philosophically daring was Gregory of Nyssa: his reflections on the Trinity possessed a conceptual scope and sophistication altogether unprecedented in Christian thought; he was the first philosopher in the Greek tradition (pagan or Christian) to develop a coherent metaphysics of the infinite; his understanding of the dynamics of the relation between the finite soul and the infinite God was revolutionary in its

c.125
The apologist Quadratus addresses his defence of Christianity to the emperor Hadrian

c.150–5
St Justin Martyr writes his *First Apology* to Antoninus Pius and the Roman senate

c.180
St Irenaeus of Lyon writes *Against the Heresies*

4TH CENTURY AD
The writings of the Cappadocian Fathers contribute substantially to the definition of the Trinity

354
St Augustine of Hippo born in Thagaste in North Africa

413–26
St Augustine writes his major work, *The City of God*

c.420
Augustine opposes the British monk Pelagius for the lattter's understanding of divine grace and human merit

431
Disputes over the relation of Christ's divinity to his humanity leads St Cyril of Alexandria to seek the deposition of Nestorius as archbishop of Constantinople at the Council of Ephesus

c.630
St Isidore of Seville compiles his *Etymologiae*, a summation of all the learning of antiquity

c.740
St John of Damascus produces *On the Orthodox Faith*

The writings of St Augustine are seminal works of theological enquiry. His Confessions *explored the interior life of the soul in a way for which there existed no previous model. His enormous treatise* The City of God *interpreted the whole of human history in the light of Christian belief, while his work* On the Trinity *brought the sort of intense Trinitarian reflections begun by the Cappadocian fathers to a new depth and complexity.*

revision of the traditional philosophical categories of Greek thought; and his spiritual writings are classics of contemplative theology.

No single theologian writing in Greek or Syriac in the patristic period exercised an influence in the Christian East comparable to that exercised in the West by the great North African St Augustine of Hippo (354–430), a man whose restless originality, philosophical sophistication, literary genius and sheer intellectual power set him apart not only from his contemporaries, but from all but a very few other theologians. The greatest works in his immense corpus of writings rank high among the enduring monuments of the Christian intellectual tradition.

It is not an exaggeration to say also that Augustine bequeathed to later Western theology almost the entirety of its conceptual grammar, its principal terms and distinctions and its governing themes. In his later years, he established a pattern of theological reflection on sin and on the relation between divine grace and human freedom that definitively shaped all subsequent Western theology. In a very real sense, Western Christianity is Augustinian Christianity.

The Later Masters

Over the next few centuries, the chief focus of doctrinal disputation in the Church was Christology: that is, the theology of the relation of Christ's divinity to his humanity. No theologian in this area was more distinguished than St Cyril of Alexandria (*c.*375–444). The only greater 'Christologian' of the patristic period was St Maximus the Confessor (*c.*580–662), who may well have possessed the single most impressive philosophical intellect in the history of Christian theology. His metaphysics of creation, his Trinitarian theology, his spiritual teachings, his anthropology – no less than his Christology – are difficult and complex, but always marked by genius.

Maximus' metaphysical vision was, in part, inspired by the writings of the 'Pseudo-Dionysius', a Syrian writer who flourished around the year 500, who assumed the New Testament pseudonym of Dionysius the Areopagite, and who produced certain treatises in which he used the resources of late Platonic philosophy to unfold the Christian understanding of divine transcendence. He was, in fact, one of the most influential figures in the history of Christian philosophy, East and West, though his true identity remains unknown.

The patristic period is usually said to have ended – in the West – with St Isidore of Seville (*c.*560–636) and – in the East – with St John of Damascus (*c.*675–749). Isidore produced compendia of etymology, the humane disciplines, the arts and sciences, moral theology, scriptural biography and ecclesiastical regulations. John, though a far more innovative and rigorous philosopher, is celebrated chiefly for his systematization of all previous patristic thought in *On the Orthodox Faith*, the first great work of Christian 'scholasticism'. The works of both men signal a change in Christian intellectual culture; one senses that in their time the first great creative surge of Christian thought had at last begun to subside.

PROBLEMS OF TRANSLATION

Such was the force of St Augustine's intellect that some of his ideas entered permanently into Western theology. The most obvious, perhaps, is that of 'predestination', the idea that God from eternity elects some to save, while 'reprobating' the rest to damnation, which Augustine believed to be the teaching of St Paul.

Such an idea never really arose in the Eastern Christian world. In large part, this difference is attributable to the vagaries of translation. The Latin word 'praedestinare' is a far stronger verb than the original Greek 'proorizein', which really means little more than to 'mark out in advance'. More importantly, Augustine's interpretations of certain passages in Paul were quite novel. For instance, he read Romans chapters 9–11 as a discourse on the predestination and reprobation of souls, even though those chapters appear really to concern the estrangement and ultimate reconciliation of Israel and the Church; Paul does not discuss salvation there at all, except to opine that all of Israel will be saved.

Similar problems of translation probably account for the significant differences between Eastern and Western understandings of original sin. All Christians believe that we are born in sin – that is, enslaved to death, suffering corruption in our bodies, minds and desires, alienated from God – but only in the West did the idea arise that a newborn infant is somehow already guilty of transgression in God's eyes. In part, this is because the Latin text of Romans 5:12 with which Augustine was familiar contained a mistranslation of the final clause of the verse, one that seemed to suggest that 'in' Adam 'all sinned'. The actual Greek text, however, says nothing of the sort; it says either that as a result of death all sinned, or that because sin is general all things die; but it does not impute guilt to those who have not yet committed any evil.

THE FALL OF ROME AND THE RISE OF A NEW WESTERN CHRISTENDOM

Well before Constantine's decision to relocate the imperial capital to Byzantium, the Western Roman empire had suffered a long and steady decline. In every sphere – social, political, economic, cultural and demographic – the Eastern empire had long enjoyed an enormous advantage over the West. Rome, in fact, had already long ceased to be the emperor's natural home. Diocletian (245–316) had kept court in Nicomedia, and several emperors before him had chosen to reside in Milan or in the southern Danube valley. In the last years of the Western empire, the imperial seat was often Ravenna.

The empire as a whole had endured incursions by 'barbarian' tribes (Germanic, Balkan and others) from the mid-third century on; but, with the general decline of the Latinate population of the West, the 'barbarians' slowly began to displace the older peoples of the Roman West, often simply through migration, settlement and partial assimilation. 'Barbarians' began to occupy agricultural regions left fallow by rural demographic attrition, and swelled the ranks of the imperial military, assuming positions even of command and, ultimately, of aristocratic privilege.

Barbarian Invasions

This is not to say that the rise of the new Germanic powers of the West did not entail great bloodshed and destruction. The Goths, Vandals, Alemanni, Burgundians, Gepidae, Franks and so forth were all warrior peoples, with strongly defined codes of honour, and no great aversion to the perils of battle. Moreover, from the middle of the fourth century onwards, the economic weakness of many Western cities and the decay of Western agriculture went hand in hand with a general decline of military defences, which left the old Western empire ripe for spoliation.

At the beginning of the fifth century, it was the semi-Vandal imperial regent Flavius Stilicho (365–408) who was responsible for protecting the Western empire and the city of Rome itself from the depredations of Visigoths and Ostrogoths. In 395, leadership of the Visigoths had been assumed by the dynamic Alaric (*c.*370–410), formerly an officer in the Roman army in the East. On becoming chief of the Visigoths, he set out to redress the failure of the imperial treasury to pay his people certain subventions they had been promised; he marched towards Constantinople before being diverted to Greece, where his men plundered many cities. In 397, the Eastern Emperor

The Forum in Rome. Following the sack of the city by the Visigoth Alaric in 410, it took just 70 years for the moribund Western Roman empire to collapse. The Eastern empire, by contrast, endured until the fall of Constantinople to the Ottomans in 1453.

A painting of the meeting between Attila and Pope Leo I near Mantua in 452. The pope persuaded Attila not to attack Rome, and pestilence forced him to abandon Italy (and the Hunnish leader died the next year on his way to make war against the Eastern empire). However, the Western Roman empire from which the Huns retreated was already as much 'barbarian' as Roman.

Arcadius placated Alaric by making him a Roman 'master of soldiers'. However, still unsatisfied, Alaric led his army into Italy in 401.

In 402 and again the next year, Stilicho defeated the Goths, and Alaric briefly withdrew. There was an inexhaustible supply of barbarians, however. Stilicho repelled the Ostrogoths in 406 and the Gauls in 407; also in 407, he was even obliged to call upon Alaric's aid. Yet in 408, under suspicion of plotting to seize the imperial throne for his sons, Stilicho was executed, and Roman 'purists' in the government and military massacred the families of Gothic soldiers in the Roman army. Naturally, these Goths defected to Alaric, and when the emperor Flavius Honorius refused to grant Alaric's people land and compensation, Alaric led his forces against Rome itself. He besieged the city in 408, but relented when the senate offered him tribute. Honorius, however, remained intransigent and the siege was resumed the next year. Again, Alaric was paid off and withdrew. In 410, however, weary of the emperor's continued failure to honour his promises, Alaric again besieged Rome. Allies in the city opened the gates to him, and – for the first time in 800 years – Rome was occupied by a foreign invader.

The Visigoths kept control of the city for three days, plundering it of many of its riches, but causing little damage and leaving its citizens unmolested. Above all, they took care not to touch the city's churches. For these barbarians were Christians.

The Evangelization of the Germanic Tribes

The first significant Christian mission to the Goths was undertaken in the mid-fourth century by Ulfilas (*c*.311–*c*.382), a Gothic scholar supposedly of Christian Cappadocian extraction. He was not only the first man to spread the Gospel among the German tribesman; it was he who first devised the Gothic alphabet

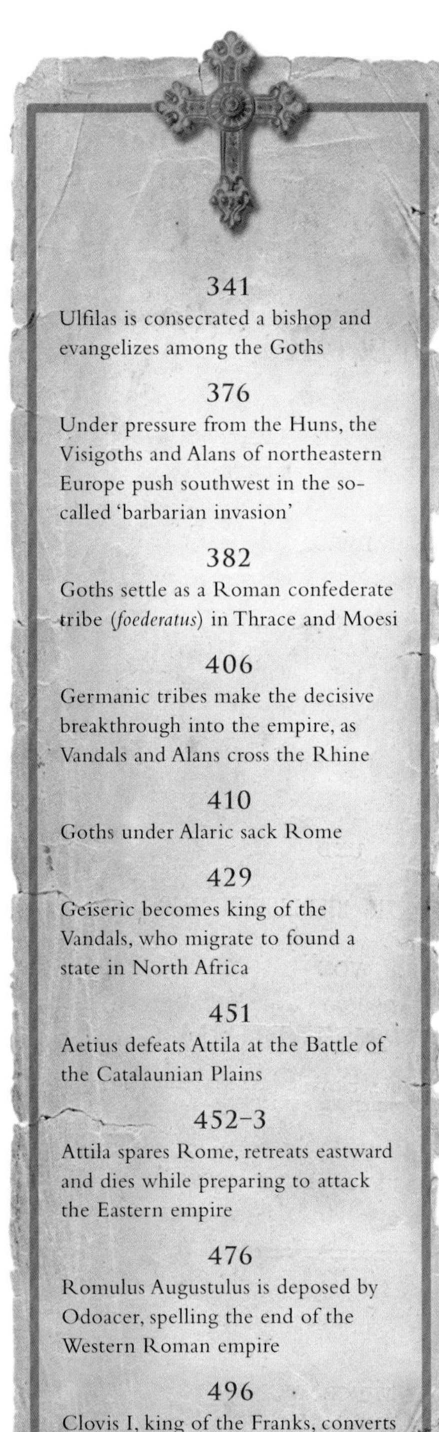

(based on both Greek and Latin scripts), and first translated the Bible (if not completely) into a Germanic tongue.

In 341, Ulfilas led an embassy to Constantinople, where he was consecrated by the city's bishop – Eusebius of Nicomedia – as bishop to the Gothic peoples. A persuasive evangelist, over the next 30 years he gathered a large community of Christian Goths around himself. In 375, however, he was forced to lead his flock into Roman territory, claiming imperial protection against persecutions by other Goths. But the process of conversion that he had set in motion proved inexorable, and the 'baptism of the barbarians' continued over the next few centuries.

341
Ulfilas is consecrated a bishop and evangelizes among the Goths
376
Under pressure from the Huns, the Visigoths and Alans of northeastern Europe push southwest in the so-called 'barbarian invasion'
382
Goths settle as a Roman confederate tribe (*foederatus*) in Thrace and Moesi
406
Germanic tribes make the decisive breakthrough into the empire, as Vandals and Alans cross the Rhine
410
Goths under Alaric sack Rome
429
Geiseric becomes king of the Vandals, who migrate to found a state in North Africa
451
Aetius defeats Attila at the Battle of the Catalaunian Plains
452–3
Attila spares Rome, retreats eastward and dies while preparing to attack the Eastern empire
476
Romulus Augustulus is deposed by Odoacer, spelling the end of the Western Roman empire
496
Clovis I, king of the Franks, converts to Catholicism

Essential to Ulfilas' Christianity, though, was its Arian theology, inherited from Eusebius of Nicomedia and others. As a result, Arianism became the characteristic theology not only of the Visigoths and Ostrogoths, but of other Germanic tribes, such as the Burgundians and Vandals, and became very much a part of their own sense of cultural identity, and of what distinguished them from the Catholic Romans.

The Barbarian Epoch

During the fifth century, new barbarian kingdoms arose throughout the former territories of the Western empire – in Spain, Gaul, Italy and elsewhere. In 428, the Vandals even invaded Roman North Africa, thus definitively eclipsing the old imperial order in the Western Mediterranean world. When St Augustine of Hippo died in 430, his city was on the verge of defeat; and, in 435, the city of Carthage fell to the invaders.

The Western empire persisted for a time formally. There were emperors, at any rate, all of whom were more or less creatures of barbarian kings, or at least dependent upon them. When, in 451, Attila led his Huns – the terror of Eastern and Western empires alike – into Gaul and then, in 452, into Italy, Visigoths, Alemanni and Franks fought alongside the Western Romans. In 476, the German warlord Odoacer deposed the last occupant of the Western imperial throne – the exquisitely well-named Romulus Augustulus ('little Augustus') – and ruled as king of Italy.

Though Arians, the Germanic kings rarely interfered with the Catholic hierarchy of the Roman Christians. And, ultimately, the Arian creed would be replaced among the barbarian peoples by Nicene orthodoxy. Perhaps most significant in this regard was the conversion to Catholicism of Clovis (466–511), who became king of the Salic Franks in 481. Clovis' Merovingian Dynasty was powerful and influential in its own right, and the Carolingian Dynasty that succeeded it more than 200 years later became the mightiest and largest European empire of the post-Roman and pre-modern age.

THE CITY OF GOD

Before Alaric's sack of Rome in 410, the great city had not fallen to a foreign invader since 390 BC, when Celts under Brennus had passed through the gates and besieged the city's population on the Capitoline. For centuries, Rome had been the 'eternal city'. invincible, the centre of the world. Thus its seizure by a hostile army had a symbolic impact that went far beyond the relatively minor physical damage inflicted on it by its temporary occupiers. Some adherents of paganism even believed that the empire had declined to so weak a state because it had forsaken worship of the old gods.

Such speculations prompted St Augustine to compose his most ambitious work, *On the City of God, Against the Pagans*. In this enormous book, Augustine reflected upon the entirety of human history, by way of a contrast drawn between two cities: the *civitas terrena* ('earthly city') and the *civitas Dei* ('city of God'). These two cities, he argued, are ultimately irreconcilable with one another; they comprise two distinct polities, each of whose values and virtues could not be more antagonistic to those of the other. Every soul is properly a citizen of one city or the other; but in historical time the two peoples are inextricably involved with one another.

The virtues of the pagans, Augustine argued, were in fact 'splendid vices'. Pagan culture valued chiefly martial virtues, glorified violence, and served principally the human desire for praise and renown.

The city of God, however, is a society that presumes that peace is the proper and normal condition of creation; it practises virtues such as charity, and seeks to praise not 'great men' but God. Thus the fall of Rome is of no ultimate consequence; the earthly city is by its nature transient; only the heavenly Jerusalem – the city of endless peace – is truly eternal.

Alaric, chief of the Visigoths, leading his troops into Rome in 410.

WESTERN MONASTICISM AND THE PRESERVATION OF WESTERN LEARNING

According to myth propagated by the 18th-century historian Edward Gibbon, the decline of Rome and the advent of the so-called 'Dark Ages' were precipitated by the rise of Christianity. This is simply false. The ravages that caused the Western empire's slow collapse had nothing whatever to do with the new religion; moreover, had it not been for the Christian monasteries of Western Europe, practically nothing of classical Latin antiquity would have survived the empire's disintegration.

Christian monasticism, as already noted, began in the deserts of the East, but soon migrated to the West; and no single figure was more important in bringing Egyptian asceticism to the Latin Christian world than John Cassian (360–435), or John the Eremite, the founder of the Abbey of St Victor in Marseilles. Cassian's origins are impossible to determine. It is believed by some that he was a Gaul of Roman origin who travelled eastward and spent time among the desert fathers before returning home. He may, however, have been born in the East; one ancient source claims that he was a Scythian. In any event, he was in Bethlehem when he took up the monastic life; and from there he journeyed to Egypt to receive spiritual instruction from the hermits of the Thebaid.

'What good is it if the Eucharistic table is overloaded with golden chalices when your brother is dying of hunger? Start by satisfying his hunger and then with what is left you may adorn the altar as well.'

ST JOHN CHRYSOSTOM, *HOMILY ON THE GOSPEL OF ST MATTHEW*

Cassian travelled to Constantinople in around 399, where the patriarch of the city, the great Christian master of rhetoric St John Chrysostom (literally 'Golden Mouth'), ordained him a deacon and made him treasurer of the cathedral. It may, in fact, have been his loyalty to Chrysostom that prompted Cassian to leave the East. The patriarch acquired formidable enemies in Constantinople – not least for his public reproaches of the rich and powerful for their wasteful extravagances and neglect of the poor – and in 403 he was deposed from his see on spurious charges and banished to Armenia. Cassian conducted an embassy to Rome in the hope of persuading Pope Innocent I (d.417) to try to intervene on Chrysostom's behalf; the pope, with the help of the Western emperor Honorius, used what influence he could, but he had no actual authority in the East and his efforts proved futile.

While still in Rome, in 405, Cassian was ordained to the priesthood. Thereafter, it seems, he applied himself to establishing an organized Christian monasticism in Gaul. In 415 he founded not only his famous monastery in Marseilles, but a convent as well, and spent the remainder of his life as an abbot. His work known

A reliquary bust of St John Cassian. His two major works codify the wisdom of the desert fathers. The Institutes *treat matters of organization, while the* Collationes *deal with 'the training of the inner man and the perfection of the heart'.*

as the *Collationes* (or *Conferences*) contained somewhat stylized reminiscences of the Egyptian desert fathers, as well as collections of their teachings in the form of discourses, and concerned principally the inner spiritual states of the Christian ascetic. His *Institutes of the Monastic Life*, by contrast, concerned the rules that governed the life of the ascetic and the eight chief temptations with which the Christian contemplative must struggle.

St Benedict and the Rule

The true father of the distinctively Western monastic tradition was the remarkable St Benedict of Nursia (*c.*480–*c.*547), an educated Italian of the privileged class who, as a young man, withdrew to live a hermit's life and soon won a reputation for extraordinary sanctity. After a few years, he was invited to become abbot of a monastery near his retreat; the rigours he demanded of his monks, however, were deemed intolerable by some and (allegedly) an attempt was made to poison him. He returned to his hermit's life, but disciples soon gathered around him, and he founded a dozen monasteries on a model he devised. Thereafter he removed himself farther south, to a region not yet fully converted to Christianity, and founded his great monastery of Monte Cassino, a point more or less midway between Naples and Rome. Of his monks, Benedict demanded a willingness to abide by the rules of the community, devotion to prayer, obedience to the abbot and service to the poor and the ill.

Perhaps Benedict's greatest contribution to Western monastic culture – apart from his personal example – was the *Rule* he composed for communities of monks. By comparison to Eastern rules of coenobitic

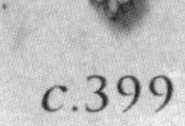

c.399
John Cassian (John the Eremite) arrives in Constantinople

403
The rulers of the Eastern empire depose and banish St John Chrysostom, archbishop of Constantinople

415
John Cassian founds the Abbey of St Victor in Marseilles, France; his writings on the coenobitic life strongly influence St Benedict

c.524
In prison awaiting execution, the Christian philosopher Boethius writes *Consolation of Philosophy*

c.535–40
St Benedict of Nursia, founder of the Benedictine order, writes his *Rule*, a book of precepts governing monastic life

c.545
Cassiodorus founds the Vivarium monastery at Squillace in southern Italy; its library preserves important sacred and secular texts

c.580
Pope St Gregory the Great writes his *Dialogues*, a collection of narratives that includes a life of St Benedict

monasticism (such as St Basil the Great's) it is marked by a certain mildness and prudence: monks are allowed a full night's sleep, warm clothes and adequate food; and the physically infirm or immature are to be spared exertions of which they are not capable. The *Rule*'s principal aim is to establish a code of communal harmony, love of God, prayer and service to others. But it is a rigorous rule for all that, precisely prescribing the pattern both of the novitiate and of the fully avowed life of poverty, chastity, and obedience.

What is more, the *Rule* is a model of clarity. It sets the daily *horae canonicae* (that is, the 'canonical hours') at which the community as a whole must gather for common prayer and worship, it describes with exactitude how the monastery is to be administered and how it is to receive guests, it precisely delineates the duties of the abbot and his monks, and it prescribes disciplines for the reconciliation of monks who have erred. It also apportions the day into roughly equal periods of manual or scriptorial labour, private study and communal observances.

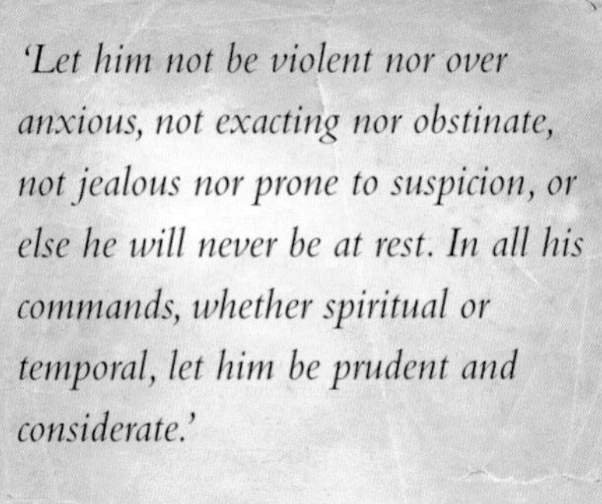

'Let him not be violent nor over anxious, not exacting nor obstinate, not jealous nor prone to suspicion, or else he will never be at rest. In all his commands, whether spiritual or temporal, let him be prudent and considerate.'

THE RULE OF ST BENEDICT, RULE 64 (ON THE IDEAL BEARING OF AN ABBOT)

As a whole, the special spirit that Benedict imparted to Western Christian monasticism was one of wise moderation: an emphasis more on simplicity than on austerity, more on the homely forms of self-abnegation than on the heroic and more on the discipline of the flesh than on its chastisement. Certain later forms of Western monasticism would more nearly approximate the somewhat severer example of the East; but the Benedictine approach to the ascetic life remained dominant in Western practice.

SHORING UP THE FRAGMENTS

Had it not been for the monastic institutions established by Benedict and others, with their libraries and scriptoria, the cultural devastation of Western Europe consequent upon the decline of the Western empire would have been complete. As the West was progressively sealed off from the high civilization of the Eastern Christian world, and knowledge of Greek became scarce in the West, the only institution that could boast any continuity with the culture of antiquity was the

Incidents in the Life of St Benedict *(1407–09), an altarpiece panel by the Florentine Renaissance painter Lorenzo Monaco. The central scene shows Benedict's follower St Maurus saving St Placidus from drowning by walking on water, a power bestowed upon him by Benedict.*

Church. In the sixth century, the Christian philosopher Boethius (*c.*475–524) undertook to shore up such fragments as he could against the darkness by producing translations of all of Plato and Aristotle, as well as commentaries upon them, and by preparing manuals of music, mathematics, geometry and astronomy. His grand project, however, was only partially complete when it was rather abruptly curtailed by his execution at the hands of the Ostrogoth king of Italy, Theodoric (d.526), on spurious charges. Thereafter, it was almost exclusively the labour of monks that preserved anything of classical Western literature and learning from the general ruin.

No figure was more important in this regard than Cassiodorus (490–*c.*585), a monk of patrician caste who spent the earlier part of his adult life as a civil official in the Ostrogoth administration in Italy, serving under Theodoric, Athalaric (516–34) and others. Some time after 540, however, he founded a

THE UNIVERSE IN A SINGLE RAY OF THE SUN

We have no biography of St Benedict of Nursia other than the *Second Book of Dialogues* by Pope St Gregory the Great (c.540–604), and this is in no sense a work of historical scholarship. In addition to the more mundane episodes of Benedict's life, Gregory's book recounts a number of miraculous deeds and mystical experiences, some of which at least seem to be of a legendary nature. For instance, Gregory reports that the conspiracy by the monks of Benedict's first monastery to poison their abbot came to light when the latter blessed the wine in which the poison had been mixed and the carafe promptly shattered.

One of the incidents of St Benedict's life related by St Gregory was his blessing of poisoned wine, which caused the vessel to break. The scene was depicted by the 15th-century painter Bartolomeo di Giovanni.

Gregory also tells of Benedict causing water to gush from a rock or oil to pour forth inexhaustibly from a single vessel. Benedict also confers the power to walk on water upon one of his followers, St Maurus, so he can save another from drowning. And he is also credited with the ability to discern the innermost thoughts and desires of others.

One story, however, that may well reflect an actual event is recounted in the thirty-fourth chapter of Gregory's text. Here Gregory tells how Benedict, when he was approaching his final days on earth, was granted an extraordinary vision of God's infinite glory embracing and transfusing all things.

Late one night, claims Gregory, Benedict found himself suddenly bathed in an unearthly light. It was at once perfectly visible and yet somehow more radiant than the light of the sun – pouring down on him from above, and dispelling all darkness by its pure brightness.

This extraordinary radiance was a vision of the supernatural sun of God's splendour. More mysteriously still, in the midst of all that brilliance, Benedict seemed somehow to glimpse the entirety of creation, gathered into one, and wholly contained within a single ray of that celestial light. And, so long as the vision lasted, Benedict saw, as it were, the infinity of God's transcendence, power and beauty, which no finite mind can comprehend.

monastery called the Vivarium, near modern Squillace in Calabria in southern Italy, where manuscripts were gathered and preserved, and monks were set to work copying and preserving works of Roman antiquity and Greek Christian thought. In later centuries, as a result of the Vivarium's example, various monasteries throughout Western Europe – from the Mediterranean to Britain – became repositories of the writings of Virgil, Ovid, Cicero, Pliny, Horace, Statius, Persius, Lucan, Suetonius, Seneca, Martial, Apuleius, Juvenal, Terence and so on, as well as of such portions of Plato, Aristotle and the Greek Church Fathers as were available in Latin.

Cassiodorus was also one of the earliest Christian encyclopaedists – that is, men who produced compendia of the sciences and arts, as well as manuals for study and instruction. His *Institutes of Divine and Secular Letters* contains – alongside his treatments of Christian scripture and theology – the programme of the seven liberal arts: the '*trivium*' of grammar, logic and rhetoric, and the '*quadrivium*' of geometry, arithmetic, music and astronomy, which became the course of elementary and higher education in the later Middle Ages. Cassiodorus also wrote a treatise on the soul, a history of humankind from the time of Adam and Eve called the *Chronicon*, an exposition of music theory and of the other 'liberal arts and disciplines', and an anthology of the work of classical grammarians.

A Carolingian ivory relief showing St Gregory with the Scribes. Monasteries were crucial in preserving the works of Classical antiquity.

These efforts may perhaps seem small in proportion to the magnitude of what had been lost in the fall of the Western Roman empire. Nevertheless, but for Christian scholarship and the tenuous links to the past that it strove to keep intact, the so-called 'Dark Ages' would have been very dark indeed.

CHRISTENDOM

As the Western imperial order disintegrated, a new reality took shape: Christian Europe. Barbarian kingdoms absorbed lands that had once enjoyed the protection of Rome, the settled Roman populations of the Western provinces became the subjects of Germanic overlords – usually 'heretics' or even, in some cases, heathens – and the ancient Latin civilization that had once stretched from the British Isles to North Africa and from Iberia to the Balkans dissolved into a collection of largely unread texts and ill-preserved monuments. Henceforth, the unity of the West – despite the episodic empires of European history – would be a cultural unity: which is to say, a religious unity.

The first Christian king of France, Clovis I – son of the pagan Childeric I (d.482) and grandson of Merovech (eponymous founder of the Merovingian dynasty) – was baptized at the instigation of his wife, St Clothilda. This illustration of the occasion is taken from the 14th-century Les grandes chroniques de France.

Throughout the fourth century and well into the fifth, the most thoroughly civilized province of the Western empire – most plentifully endowed with institutions of higher education, blessed with the richest literary culture, perennially prosperous and governed by a particularly refined patrician class – was Gaul. The settled aristocracy comprised both pagans and Christians, who existed in largely untroubled harmony with one another; and, among the very educated, friendships frequently transcended creed. It was not to last, however. The only cultural institutions that were still intact at the end of the fifth century were the Church and its monasteries.

A Pioneer of Gallic Christianity

Perhaps the greatest Gallic Christian figure of the first century of Roman Christianity was St Martin of Tours (316–97), the patron saint of France: a tireless evangelist and one of the earliest apostles of monasticism in the West. According to his biographers, Sulpicius Severus and the Christian poet and bishop of Poitiers Venantius Fortunatus (*c.*540–*c.*600), Martin chose as a boy of ten to abandon the paganism of his parents and seek baptism. As a young man, he was conscripted into the army but refused to fight and was briefly imprisoned. After a period of instruction at the feet of St Hilary of Poitiers (*c.*315–*c.*367) – the great defender of Nicene theology – Martin travelled to the Balkans as a missionary. Then, in 360, after a sojourn in Italy, he returned home and founded the first monastic community in Gaul, in Ligugé. In 371, he was appointed bishop of Tours; near his new see he founded the great monastery of Marmoutier, from which he conducted missions into the still pagan hinterlands of the Gallic countryside.

It was during Martin's episcopacy, in 385, that the usurper Magnus Maximus (d.388) – who ruled over Britain, Iberia, Gaul and parts of Germany – had a Spanish bishop, Priscillian of Ávila, tried in Trier (Augusta Treverorum, the imperial seat) and executed on charges of heresy and witchcraft. There was no precedent or warrant in Christian tradition for such an act. Under the old pagan dispensation, piety towards the gods had been regarded as inseparable from loyalty to the empire, and Roman magistrates had had the power to institute

extraordinary inquisitions and to execute atheists or devotees of proscribed cults. But the emperor was a Christian, and the killing of Priscillian was contrary to all Christian practice, and Martin distinguished himself by his willingness to reproach Maximus openly for his brutality.

The Dawn of Christian France

In the fifth century, the barbarians came. The Visigoths settled south of the River Loire, in Aquitaine, early in the century, and then over time took control of Provence and most of Spain. The Alemanni settled farther to the north, in Alsace and its vicinity. The Burgundians occupied the better part of the lands by the Rhône. And the Franks spread westward from the Rhineland into southern Gaul.

Gaul's native Roman culture was not, however, extinguished all at once. The old aristocracy proved durable and adaptable, and so remained largely enfranchised, in city and countryside alike; and much of the old civil administration of the provinces remained in place. There were losses and displacements among the ancient Gallic peoples as the new Germanic kingdoms replaced the old imperial regime; but Gallo-Roman civilization began to influence the invaders as well. The reigns of the Visigoth kings Euric (420–84) and Alaric II (d.507), for instance, were marked by an almost Roman sense of civil order and higher culture. And, whether Arians or pagans, the German kings left the Catholic Church in Gaul largely undisturbed. As a result, the transition from Roman to barbarian rule was relatively untroubled – at least for the patrician class.

St Martin of Tours appealed directly to the emperor Julian (the Apostate) to be released from military service on the grounds of faith; to avert accusations of cowardice, he volunteered to place himself at the front of the battle line protected by nothing more than the sign of the cross. His offer was refused and he was imprisoned. St Martin's renunciation is depicted in this fresco from 1312–17 by Simone Martini.

Catholic France, however, began to emerge from the welter of Germanic kingdoms among the Salic Franks. King Clovis I (*c*.466–511) not only unified the Franks, but conquered territories occupied by Burgundians, Alemanni and Visigoths, and ultimately established his rule over all of Gaul apart from Burgundy and Provence. Through his marriage to the Burgundian princess St Clothilda (d. *c*.545), Clovis was persuaded to abandon the gods of his ancestors and to embrace Christianity – and, since his queen was a Catholic, Nicene rather than Arian Christianity.

Farther west, moreover, beyond the Pyrenees, Roman Iberia had also been invaded by Germanic tribes throughout the fifth century – Visigoths, Vandals, Suevi and so forth – with the Visigoths ultimately emerging as the rulers of Spain.

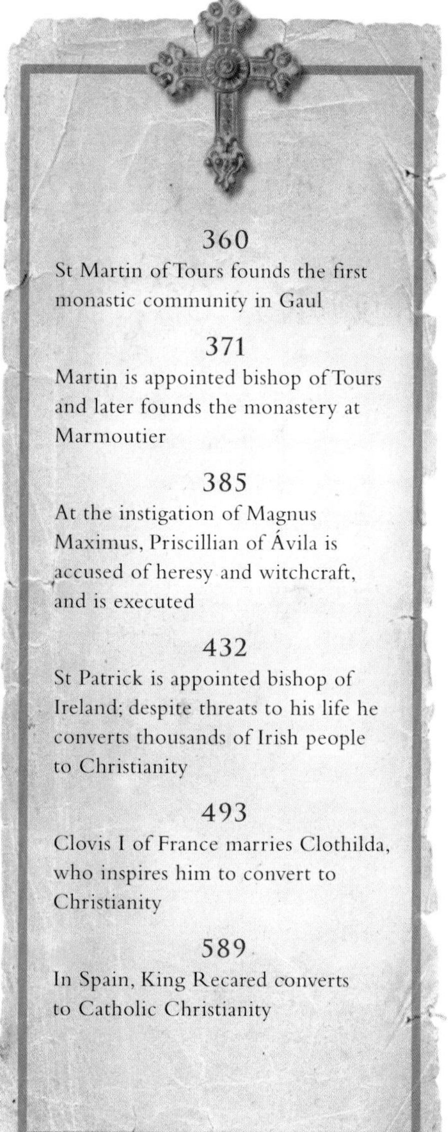

360
St Martin of Tours founds the first monastic community in Gaul

371
Martin is appointed bishop of Tours and later founds the monastery at Marmoutier

385
At the instigation of Magnus Maximus, Priscillian of Ávila is accused of heresy and witchcraft, and is executed

432
St Patrick is appointed bishop of Ireland; despite threats to his life he converts thousands of Irish people to Christianity

493
Clovis I of France marries Clothilda, who inspires him to convert to Christianity

589
In Spain, King Recared converts to Catholic Christianity

When, in 589, King Recared converted to Catholic Christianity, the triumph of Nicene Christianity in the old Roman West was assured.

The British Isles

Roman Britain, while perhaps not quite so idyllic as Roman Gaul, was a prosperous, refined society; but, as imperial protection waned in the last decades of the fourth century, and especially after the last Roman armies departed early in the fifth, the 'barbarians' of the north (Picts, Welshmen, Irishmen, Danes, Saxons, Angles and Jutes) began to raid, invade or simply settle in Britain. The British King Vortigern (fl.425–50) is said actually to have invited the Saxons into his realm to support him in his struggle against the Scots and Picts, and recompensed them with arable land. Yet by the late sixth century, pagan Germanic peoples had conquered England, and the old Roman civilization had been swept away.

Christianity, however – Catholic Christianity – persisted and gradually conquered the conquerors. Undoubtedly the most famous representative of the old Roman Christian order in the age of barbarian hegemony was St Patrick, the fifth-century apostle to Ireland. The son of a Roman Briton deacon, he was captured at the age of 16 by Irish raiders and endured six years of slavery before escaping and returning to Britain. He journeyed to Gaul and there was made a priest. Ultimately, though, inspired by a dream, he resolved to return to the country of his captivity to preach the gospel. In 432 he had the opportunity to do just this, when he was commissioned to replace the beleaguered bishop of Ireland, Palladius.

'Ireland is far more favoured than Britain by latitude, and by its mild and healthy climate … There are no reptiles, and no snake can exist there; for although often brought over from Britain, as soon as the ship nears land, they breathe the scent of its air and die.'

The Venerable Bede,
Ecclesiastical History, 731
(alluding to a legend that St Patrick banished all snakes from Ireland in the fifth century)

In Ireland, he travelled widely, made disciples and baptized. His was not the first mission to Ireland, certainly, but it was the most ambitious. Irish kings were sometimes indulgent, sometimes hostile; by Patrick's own estimate, he and his followers were taken captive a dozen times, and on at least one occasion he was bound in chains; and his life was frequently in danger – as were the lives of his disciples. He provoked the enmity of the Druids, naturally. But ultimately he counted kings and chieftains among his converts. He did not, of course, eradicate the old religions of Ireland; but if any man can be said to have converted an entire nation, Patrick would be that person.

THE DEFEAT OF THE DRUIDS

Far better known than the actual life of St Patrick are the innumerable legends that sprang up around his name in the centuries after his death (which is not, of course, to say that all of these legends are merely legendary). There is the story, for instance, of how the chieftain Dichu raised a sword to slay the Christian missionary only to find his arm frozen above his head until he professed obedience to Patrick. Or the tale of how Patrick came before the idol of the demon-god Crom-cruach – a gold–plated pillar to which infants were regularly offered – and reduced it to dust with a single touch of his crosier.

Perhaps the most colourful of these legends concerns Patrick's contest with the Druids in 433, early in his mission. Hearing that the kings of Ireland had gathered at Tara, the seat of the High King, for a great feast day, Patrick went there hoping to gain a hearing. As it happened, the royal assembly coincided with Easter. By royal decree, all fires were to be extinguished throughout the land until the sacred fire had been lit at Tara: a decree that Patrick and his disciples defied. On Easter eve they went to the top of the hill of Slane, across the valley from Tara, and lit a great Paschal bonfire at midnight. Supposedly the Druids of Tara exerted all their magical powers to put out the flames, but were unsuccessful. Then, in the morning, Patrick led an Easter procession across the valley.

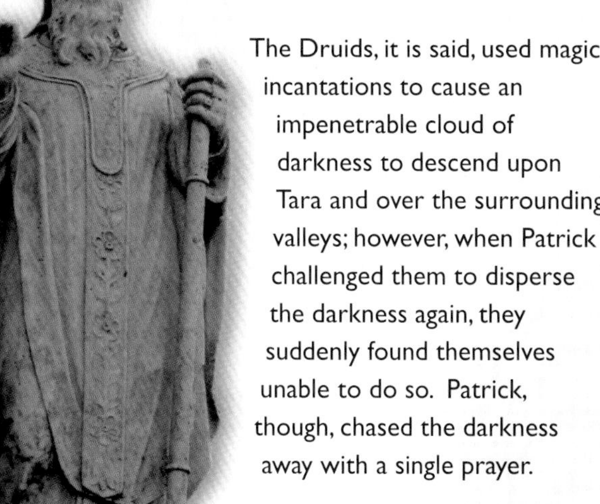

St Patrick (Patricius in Latin) converted thousands of Irish people to Christianity. This statue of the nation's patron saint stands at the Hill of Tara.

The Druids, it is said, used magic incantations to cause an impenetrable cloud of darkness to descend upon Tara and over the surrounding valleys; however, when Patrick challenged them to disperse the darkness again, they suddenly found themselves unable to do so. Patrick, though, chased the darkness away with a single prayer.

Nor does the tale end there. Lochru, the chief of the Druids, it continues, rose into the air and began flying around the brow of Tara. Patrick merely knelt in prayer, and the hapless heathen tumbled out of the sky to an abrupt demise at the foot of the hill. As one might expect, the Ard Righ – the High King – was persuaded by this to allow Patrick to preach the faith in all the lands of Eire.

It is a winsome tale – despite Lochru's grisly end – but, at the end of the day, it is hardly more remarkable than the unquestionably true story of a single man, with no great worldly resources at his disposal, succeeding by a life of sheer unwavering devotion in changing the faith of an entire people.

THE FORMATION OF ORTHODOX CHRISTOLOGY

The great dogmatic debate of the fourth century concerned the divinity of Christ; the great dogmatic debate of the fifth century (and after) concerned his humanity. Or, rather, it concerned the unity of his Person, and the relation of the divine to the human within that unity. And this, as it happened, would prove to be the most contentious doctrinal dispute in Christian history prior to the Reformation, and the most divisive. In addition to giving rise to a host of newer, more precise theological formulae, the ultimate effect of these 'Christological controversies' was a fragmented Church.

All the Christians of the time, of course, believed that Jesus was the incarnate Son of God; and all faithful members of the Nicene Church believed the divine Son to be co-eternal and co-equal with the Father. But in what sense then had he become a man? Had he merely assumed human flesh? Or had he assumed also a human soul, a human mind, a human will? If Christ was both God and man, did this mean that he was somehow a composite of the two, producing some sort of 'third genus'? Or did his divinity 'swallow up' his humanity? Or was he a kind of harmonious alliance within one body between two distinct personalities, one divine and one human?

Practical Doctrinal Issues

These were not abstract concerns. The Church taught that in Christ God had assumed our humanity in order to heal it of sin and death and to join it to himself in a divinizing union. And Gregory of Nazianzus, in the fourth century, had enunciated the principle by which Christological reflection had therefore to be governed: what had not been assumed had not been healed – which is to say, if any part of our humanity was absent from Christ, then that part of our humanity had never been saved.

Two figures from the Christology debate of the fourth and fifth centuries – left, St Gregory of Nazianzus (also known as St Gregory the Theologian) and, right, St Cyril of Alexandria – are depicted in this 14th-century icon painting.

The 'Mother of God'

The 'Christological crisis' began in Constantinople in 428, though its initial cause was a dispute not over Christ – at least, not directly – but over his mother. The trouble began when Nestorius (d.*c.*451), a theologian educated in Antioch, was made bishop of Constantinople on the recommendation of Emperor Theodosius II (401–50). Nestorius quickly distinguished himself by his eloquence and by his brashness, and both qualities were put on full display in a series of sermons he delivered – beginning on the first day of Christmas 428 – denouncing the established Constantinopolitan practice of referring to the Virgin Mary as the Theotokos: 'God-bearer' or 'Mother of God'. The title was not common in

Antioch and struck Nestorius as theologically dubious; as mother of Jesus the man, of course, Mary merited all praise, but no-one could be said to be mother of the eternal God.

Opinions differ on whether the 'heresy' called 'Nestorianism' was ever actually advanced by Nestorius himself; but one prominent Antiochian approach to Christology tended to emphasize the complete integrity of both the humanity and the divinity of Christ, almost to the point of dividing Christ into two distinct agencies – 'the son of Mary' and 'the Son of God' – who coexisted within the one prosopon (that is, the 'personality' or 'character') of Jesus of Nazareth. The so-called Nestorian heresy is the teaching that, in Christ, the divine *Logos* intimately associated himself with a naturally and completely human person. Whether this was indeed Nestorius' view, his refusal to call Mary the 'Mother of God' seemed to many Christians effectively to deny that God had really become human. A moral association between the *Logos* and a man would not be a real incarnation – and, again, what was not assumed by Christ was not healed by Christ.

> *'When the followers of Cyril saw the vehemence of the emperor ... they roused up a disturbance and discord among the people with an outcry ... And one passion was in them all, Jews and Pagans and all the sects, and they were busying themselves that they should accept without examination the things which were done without examination against me; and at the the same time all of them, even those that had participated with me at table and in prayer and in thought, suddenly found themselves at one in opposition to me.'*
>
> NESTORIUS (ON THE HUE AND CRY RAISED AGAINST HIM AFTER THE COUNCIL OF EPHESUS, 431)

Nestorius' great opponent was the brilliant, if sometimes intemperate, Bishop Cyril of Alexandria (*c.*375–444), who – in good Alexandrian fashion – believed that the doctrine of the incarnation was only true if, in Christ, the one divine Person of the eternal *Logos* had, while remaining God, become a man: that is, only if, in the most radical sense, there was one Person in Christ, the 'eternal *Logos* as a man'. Mary is indeed the Theotokos, because the man who was her son was also God the Son. Cyril sought and received the support of Pope Celestine I (d.432) against Nestorius, and in 431 a council was convened in Ephesus, whose ultimate result – after a few political complications – was that Nestorius was condemned and sent into perpetual exile.

ONE INCARNATE NATURE

The controversy, however, was just beginning; and now the source of the difficulty was Alexandria. For, if the Antiochian tendency was to stress the integrity of the divine and human natures to the neglect of the unity of Christ's Person, the Alexandrian tendency was the opposite. Cyril himself was wont to speak of Jesus as possessing a 'single incarnate nature', which to the ears of many Christians elsewhere seemed to suggest that, in Christ, the divine nature had wholly displaced the human nature: which, again, would mean that God had not really become a man.

As it happens, the word 'nature' (*physis*), as used in Alexandria, often had the connotation of 'substance' or 'concrete reality', but in other parts of the Church the word had a somewhat more abstract meaning. Cyril was intelligent enough to recognize that terminology was not consistent throughout the Christian world, and so subscribed in 433 to a declaration – intended as a compromise between the Alexandrian and Antiochian positions – that Christ was one Person (that is, the eternal Son of God) possessing two complete natures (divine and human). Not all of his theological kith, though, were willing to follow his lead.

After Cyril's death, the cause of 'monophysitism' (that is, the doctrine that Christ possessed only one *physis* or nature) was taken up with a special vigour – though without much philosophical finesse – by a fervent disciple of Alexandrian theology named Eutyches (*c*.375–454). According to him, there were 'two natures before the Incarnation, and one after'. In other words, in the Incarnation, Christ's humanity was wholly assumed into his divinity. In 448, Eutyches' position was condemned at a synod in Constantinople. In 449, Pope Leo I 'the Great' (d.461) lent his support to the Constantinopolitan synod by issuing the document known as 'Leo's Tome', in which he upheld the doctrine of Christ's two natures – inseparable but unconfused – within the unity of the one divine Person of the incarnate *Logos*. Eutyches, however, turned for succour to the patriarch of Alexandria, Dioscurus (d.454), who used his influence with the emperor to convene a new council at

In ancient times Ephesus in present-day Turkey was an important sea port and centre of commerce. At its heart stood the Roman library, originally built in 115–25 and dedicated to the proconsul Celsus. A mile to the north of the library stands the Church of St Mary, where the Council of Ephesus was convened in 431.

412
Cyril becomes patriarch of Alexandria

428
Nestorius becomes patriarch of Constantinople

431
The Council of Ephesus; Nestorius deposed

433
Cyril agrees to accept the language of Christ's 'two natures'

448
Synod of Constantinople condemns Eutyches' teaching of a single nature (divine) in Christ

449
'Leo's Tome'; the 'Robber Council of Ephesus' adopts Eutychianism

451
The Council of Chalcedon

634
The Synod of Cyprus adopts monothelitism

638
Emperor Heraclius issues the 'Ecthesis', which proclaims monothelitism imperial doctrine

655
Pope Martin I is exiled to the Crimea without trial and dies

662
Maximus tried, condemned, tortured, mutilated, exiled and dies

680–1
Third Council of Constantinople condemns monothelitism and monoenergism

Ephesus – known in later Church history as the 'Robber Synod' – which restored Eutyches to communion and condemned the 'dyophysite' (or 'two natures') position. In 451, however, under the emperor Marcian (396–457), the great Council of Chalcedon (the Fourth Ecumenical Council) was convened, which reaffirmed the 'dyophysite' position, condemned monophysitism and adopted Leo's Tome as an authoritative statement of orthodox doctrine.

The Aftermath

Chalcedon marked the end of an undivided Catholic order. Monophysite communions – the Coptic Church of Egypt, the Ethiopian Church, the Syrian Jacobite Church, the Armenian Church – broke with Constantinople and Rome. So did the Nestorian communion, in East Syria and Persia. Collectively, these are now often referred to as the 'Oriental Churches'.

The great tragedy of the Christological controversies was that, for the most part, the Churches were divided more by language than by belief. The so-called Monophysites, for instance, never meant to deny the full and inviolable humanity of Christ. The so-called Nestorians never meant to deny the real unity of God and man in Christ. There were, however, powerful political forces at play as well: the division of the 'Oriental' Churches from Rome and Constantinople was partly the result of indigenous resentment of imperial power.

Over the next two centuries, various attempts were made by Byzantine emperors to placate the Monophysites, with one or another theological compromise. The patriarch of Constantinople, Sergius I (d.638) proposed two different conciliatory formulae. The first was 'monoenergism': the theory that Christ – though he possessed two natures – possessed only one 'operation' or 'activity', and that divine; this was favoured by the emperor Heraclius (*c*.575–641), but was ultimately rejected by both the Greek and Latin Churches as implicitly denying Christ's full humanity. Sergius then proposed instead the theory of 'monothelitism', according to which Christ – though he possessed two natures – nevertheless possessed only a single will, and that divine. This was the position favoured by Emperor Constans II (630–68).

The most devastatingly subtle critique of the monothelite position was that of the great Maximus the Confessor (*c*.580–662), who was repaid for his opposition to imperial policy by having his tongue torn out and his right hand hacked off, before being banished to die in exile. Pope St Martin I (d.655), Maximus' ally, was also sent into exile in the Crimea, and he too soon succumbed to the ordeal.

THE DEATH OF HYPATIA

One of the more monstrous tales of violence to emerge from the perpetually violent streets of ancient Alexandria is that of the death of the female pagan philosopher and mathematician Hypatia (*c*.355–415), who was savagely assassinated and dismembered by the Parabolani of Alexandria, originally a Christian charitable fraternity devoted to the impoverished ill. Cyril of Alexandria has often been accused of direct complicity in her murder, but of this he was innocent. Nevertheless, she was definitely killed because she was suspected of having prevented a *rapprochement* between Cyril and the imperial prefect Orestes.

This 20th-century engraving is often used to represent Hypatia. A brilliant lecturer in mathematics and Platonic philosophy, later tradition credited her with several commentaries on arithmetical and geometric texts.

Hypatia's death has often been mythologized as a kind of martyrdom; it is fashionable to claim that she was murdered by Christian zealots on account of her paganism, her scientific researches and her sex. For (so the legend goes) the Christians of the time, in addition to hating all non-Christians, were hostile to learning and science, and especially despised women who presumed to dabble in such things.

Actually, there was no pronounced prejudice against woman scholars in the fifth century, especially not in the Eastern empire, among either Christians or pagans; such women were to be found in both communities. And learning and science were pursuits of the educated class, which comprised Christians and pagans alike.

Hypatia, moreover, was apparently on extremely good terms with the Christian intellectuals of Alexandria, not being a habitué of the local pagan cults, and she numbered many Christians among her students and associates. The warmest portrait of her that we possess, as well as the frankest account of her murder, was written by the Christian Church historian Socrates.

Hypatia died because she inadvertently became involved in one of the conflicts that were constantly erupting in Alexandria between the warring tribes in the streets. But, in the social and intellectual world to which she belonged, all the attainments of classical culture were the common property of all philosophies, including the Christian 'philosophy'.

'After tearing her body in pieces, they took her mangled limbs to a place called Cinaron, and there burnt them. This affair brought down great opprobrium, not only upon Cyril, but also upon the whole Alexandrian Church. And surely nothing can be farther from the spirit of Christianity than the allowance of massacres, fights and transactions of that sort.'

SOCRATES SCHOLASTICUS, *ECCLESIASTICAL HISTORY* (ON THE MURDER OF HYPATIA), 440S

THE LAST EPOCH OF THE UNITED CHRISTIAN EMPIRE

By the beginning of the sixth century, the Roman West was no more. Of Latin imperial civilization there now remained only a few moribund institutions, a few noble houses, an indigenous peasantry and an occasionally beleaguered Church. Over the course of the sixth century, however, much of the ancient Christian Roman world was briefly reunited – and even to a certain extent revitalized – through the efforts of the Byzantine emperor Justinian I (483–565) and his formidable wife Theodora (*c.*497–548).

It is something of a testament to the fluidity of Byzantine society that a man of Justinian's provenance should have become emperor at all. He was an Illyrian and a descendant of peasants. But his uncle Justin I (d.527) had become Augustus of the East in 518, having achieved his lofty eminence by rising first through the ranks of the military; and Justin saw to it that his nephew received an excellent education in Constantinople – though the latter, his native tongue being Latin, spoke a heavily accented Greek to his dying day. Justinian was made Caesar of the East in 525 by his uncle, and then elevated to the station of Augustus – and so co-emperor – in 527; and on his uncle's death, later that same year, he became sole Augustus.

An 18th-century print of a coin bearing the profile of Justinian I. His reign spanned almost four decades, during which he reconquered much of the empire lost during the fifth century, including North Africa, Italy and parts of Spain.

An Inauspicious Background

Theodora's pedigree was, if anything, less respectable than her husband's. She was the child of a bear-trainer at the hippodrome and had been an actress (and, like most actresses of her time, a woman of negotiable morals). When Justinian met her, though, she was a penitent convert to Monophysitism who had forsaken the stage for wool-spinning. He was captivated by her great beauty and by her extraordinary intelligence, but was legally prevented from marrying her sacramentally on account of her original profession. In 525, however, he changed the law and made her his wife; and in 527, on becoming Augustus, he conferred upon her the title of Augusta. This was more than merely honorific: theirs was, to a very real extent, a dual regency, even if Justinian alone possessed executive power.

Theodora's advice was invaluable to Justinian, her vision of restored imperial magnificence as ambitious as her husband's and her resolve perhaps superior to his. She was entrusted with diplomatic responsibilities of a sort enjoyed by no previous emperor's wife, and Justinian did not hesitate to accord her recognition in his official decrees and court documents. She succeeded in bringing an end to

the imperial persecution of the Monophysites. Through her influence, laws were passed to improve the condition of women – high-born and low – in the empire. Indeed, the truly creative and brilliant period of Justinian's rule, it could be argued, ended with Theodora's death.

The court of Theodora is depicted in this sixth-century mosaic panel in the church of San Vitale, Ravenna. Theodora, a tall figure robed in purple, is flanked by ladies-in-waiting and male servants.

The Reconquest

The Byzantine empire's great enemy when Justinian came to power was Persia's Sassanid empire, and both early and late in his reign his armies were engaged in campaigns to the East. He was also forced at various times to commit forces to the north to defend imperial provinces in the Balkans against Slavs, Bulgars, Avars and Huns. But his chief military aspiration was to regain for the empire

Like the Roman army from which it evolved, the Byzantine army valued intelligence and discipline in its soldiers but was considerably more sophisticated in its organization and tactics. This allegorical painting by the Italian Mannerist artist Giuseppe Cesari (1568–1640) shows Romans and barbarians joining battle.

the Western lands now under barbarian rule, especially those where Catholic Christians had been forced to submit to governance by Arian 'heretics'. In North Africa, the settled Nicene Christian communities had suffered persecution at the hands of their Vandal masters; and even in Italy, the formerly tolerant Ostrogoths had begun to take prejudicial measures against the native Catholics.

Justinian's campaign to 'liberate' the West was conducted in large part by the brilliant General Belisarius (*c.*505–65), who had already distinguished himself as a master tactician against the Persians. In August of 533, a Byzantine invasion force reached North Africa, and by March the following year Belisarius had broken the power of the Vandals in Africa, Corsica, Sardinia and elsewhere. In 535, the recapture of Italy began with Belisarius' invasion and swift conquest of Sicily, followed by his invasion of Italy itself and the occupation first of Naples and then of Rome. In Rome, for several months in 537 and 538, the Byzantines found themselves besieged by an Ostrogothic counterinsurgency; but Belisarius' men survived and, on breaking siege, drove inexorably north, capturing Ravenna – the seat of government – in 540. There a new imperial prefect was installed and the Byzantine government of Italy properly inaugurated.

Ultimately, however, Belisarius' military genius, as well as the admiration he inspired not only among his own men but even among many of the Ostrogoths – who offered to proclaim him their emperor – roused disquiet in Justinian. Belisarius had politely refused the honour offered him by the Ostrogoths, but Justinian seems to have feared for his throne nevertheless, and soon the Byzantine forces in Italy found themselves without sufficient reinforcements at crucial moments. This proved disastrous after the new administration in Ravenna – through its excessive taxation – had provoked a new Ostrogoth insurgency in 542. Belisarius' strategies were flawless, but his forces were too small; he lost control of all the cities of Italy other than Ancona, Otranto and Ravenna itself, and in 549 he was removed from command and recalled.

Justinian, however, had no intention of abandoning Italy to the barbarians. In 552, he sent a massive invasion force under the command of General Narses (*c.*480–574), a eunuch who had risen to power in the imperial guard, and an old rival of Belisarius (in fact, he had served in Italy in 538–9, but had been recalled then for his inability to work effectively with Belisarius). Narses was also an excellent tactician and, enjoying the troop strengths that Belisarius had been denied, he quickly defeated the Ostrogoths. At about the same time, Byzantine forces reclaimed the southern reaches of the Iberian peninsula for the empire.

Though the Byzantine empire never succeeded in restoring the West to its ancient imperial splendour, the Byzantine 'exarchates' of Ravenna and North Africa remained in place for more than two centuries; ultimately, though, the economic duress of constant warfare with barbarians in the East, and the impotence of Christian forces in the face of the Islamic invasions of North Africa in the seventh century, brought Byzantine power in the West to an end. The 'Italian gateway' to Byzantine culture, however, would remain open for centuries to come, with profound benefits for both sides.

Reforms and Rebellions

Justinian and Theodora were quite avid in their desire for a reform of Byzantine law and administration, and it is arguable that their greatest contribution to imperial glory lay not in the acquisition of territories, but in the re-organization of military, mercantile, civil and ecclesial

525
Justinian is made Caesar of the East and marries Theodora

527
He becomes co-emperor and, after his uncle's death, sole Augustus; Theodora is given the title of Augusta

529
Justinian Codex (*Corpus juris civilis*) marks the start of legal reforms

532
Uprising in Constantinople leads to destruction of civil offices and of Hagia Sophia

533–4
Byzantine forces led by Belisarius invade North Africa, defeating the Vandals in Africa, Corsica and Sardinia

537
The new church in Constantinople, Holy Wisdom, is completed

537–8
Ostrogothic counterinsurgents mount an unsuccessful siege on Byzantine forces occupying Rome

540
With the capture of Ravenna, Italy falls; an imperial prefect is installed

549
Justinian recalls Belisarius

552
A new invasion force, led by Narses, defeats the Ostrogoths in Italy; Byzantine forces reclaim southern parts of the Iberian peninsula

government. They were clearly sincere in their desire to improve the conditions of their subjects. Theirs was a great age of public works: the building of hospitals, orphan asylums, almshouses and hostels; churches, monasteries and convents; aqueducts, bridges and roads.

Beginning in 529, the 'Justinian Codex' (also called the *Corpus juris civilis*) – a thorough revision and codification of Roman law – as well as other legal enactments, began to appear, along with curricular material for the education of lawyers. The process of legal reform continued to the end of Justinian's reign in 565. In many respects, the law under Justinian was 'Christianized', even if one could not describe it as ideally Christian. It made the manumission of slaves easier, extended greater rights to women, made divorce (which was usually disastrous for women) extremely difficult, promulgated laws protecting children and greatly reduced the number of capital offences. At the same time, Justinian's laws regarding non-Christians and Christian 'heretics' were, to say the least, prejudicial. He ultimately required universal baptism of his subjects, made it illegal for heretics or pagans to teach, removed pagan professors from the ancient Academy in Athens and persecuted those who were 'aberrant' in religion.

> *'Governing under the authority of God our empire, which was delivered to us by the Heavenly Majesty, we both conduct wars successfully and render peace honourable, and we uphold the condition of the state. We so lift up our minds towards the help of the omnipotent God that we do not place our trust in weapons or our soldiers or military leaders or our own talents, but we invest all our hopes in the providence of the Supreme Trinity alone.'*
>
> JUSTINIAN I, *CORPUS JURIS CIVILIS*, *c.*530

Justinian was reasonably successful in rooting out corruption in the civil administration of the empire, which naturally provoked enmity from a broad variety of 'interested' parties. There was even a violent popular revolt in Constantinople in 532, which led to the destruction of many civil offices and part of the imperial palace, and from which Justinian would have fled had not his dauntless wife urged him to remain firm and to send the generals Belisarius and Mundus (assisted by Narses) to quell the revolt with whatever forces they could marshal within the city; this they did, ultimately driving the rebels into the hippodrome and slaughtering them there.

Justinian made quite vigorous attempts to reconcile the Catholic and Monophysite Churches – as much from political motives as out of deference to his wife's spiritual predilections – but they ultimately came to nothing. Their principal consequence was the Second Council of Constantinople in 553, which merely reaffirmed the doctrines of Chalcedon and, if anything, confirmed the schism.

All told, whether Justinian's reconquest of the West was ultimately worth the expense it exacted, the years of his reign (especially those before Theodora's death) were a period of remarkable cultural and political creativity. They laid the foundation for the resplendent Christian Byzantine civilization – in all its strengths and weaknesses – of later centuries.

THE HOLY WISDOM

For centuries Holy Wisdom was the most astonishing church in Christendom. Its vast dome measures more than 30 metres (100 ft) across and over 55 metres (180 ft) high.

Of all the grand public works and monuments that adorned Justinian's reign, none was more magnificent than the 'Great Church' of Hagia Sophia ('Holy Wisdom') in Constantinople, designed by Anthemius of Tralles and Isidore of Miletus, and completed in just five years. It was and is among the world's greatest architectural achievements, and was for centuries the chief glory of the eastern Christian world. However, it would never have been built had the original Hagia Sophia (a much smaller edifice) not been destroyed in the riots of 532.

In its full splendour, before centuries of spoliation stripped it of its treasures, the interior of Holy Wisdom was a magnificent tumult of gold, silver, porphyry, lapis-lazuli and polychromatic marbles. It was adorned with immense mosaic icons (added in many cases long after Justinian's time), and with inlays of semi-precious stone. One of its most remarkable features, however, was the quality of the light that filled the enormous central space of the building – a light not infrequently described as 'ethereal' or 'celestial' or 'mystical'. The peculiar quality of this light resulted from the single most impressive architectural feature of the edifice: the gigantic dome that seemed to 'hover' above the nave.

The appearance of weightlessness was achieved by constructing a continuous arcade of 40 windows at the base of the dome, above the main oblong structure of the building, making it appear that the dome floated above the church on a ring of light. In fact, the great weight of the dome was supported by four large and elegantly tapered pendentives resting on four large piers and creating four enormous arches. To the east and west of the central dome, lesser semi-domes descend in a kind of cascade.

It is said that, on first entering the Great Church after its completion in 537, Justinian cried out, 'Solomon, I have surpassed you!'

THE 'CHURCH OF THE EAST': THE NESTORIAN MISSIONS

We often tend to think of ancient and medieval Christendom principally as Roman and Byzantine (or Catholic and Orthodox) with only a few scattered 'Oriental' communions at the margins. But, in the early Middle Ages, the largest (or, to be more precise, most widespread) Christian communion in the world was the Syrian Nestorian Church, also called the East Syrian or Assyrian Church, or (more simply) the 'Church of the East'.

From the late fifth century, as they were progressively cut off from, and ultimately driven out of, West Syria and the greater Byzantine world, the Nestorians had no choice but to make a home for themselves beyond the eastern frontiers of the empire, in those parts of Syria controlled by Persia and in the Persian Empire itself.

East Syrian Christianity was a scholarly and ascetical tradition from a very early period, and always distinct in sensibility from the more Hellenized intellectual culture of Antioch, farther to the west. The city of Nisibis had been the chief East Syrian centre of learning until it was conquered by Persia in 363 and the scholars of the city had removed themselves in great numbers to Edessa. Among these was one of the most revered of Syrian saints, Ephraim Syrus (*c.*306–73): a theologian, scholar, poet, hymnode and servant of the ill, who founded a hospital in Edessa. But about a century later, on account of their refusal to subscribe to the formula of Chalcedon, the Byzantine emperor Zeno (d.491) expelled the Nestorians from Edessa, and they were forced to retreat to Nisibis again, and to the shelter of the Persian empire.

The Nestorian East had quickly become a theological world unto itself. In 498, the bishop of Nisibis assumed the title 'Patriarch of the East'. In 553, the Second Council of Constantinople formally condemned the teachings of Theodore of Mopsuestia (*c.*350–429), the Antiochian theologian and biblical exegete whose writings were foundational for East Syrian theology. By the late sixth century, the Assyrian Church had made its own

The Syrian capital of Seleucia-Ctesiphon was thought to be the largest city in the world from 570 to 637. Seen here are the remains of the façade and open audience hall of the Sassanian palace at Ctesiphon in present-day Iraq.

pronouncements regarding the proper terminology of Christology. And, while the Persian empire came to tolerate the Nestorians, it persecuted those other forms of Syrian Christianity (principally Monophysite) that attempted to establish themselves within its boundaries.

The Church of the East, however, was quite equal to the task of self-governance. The School of Nisibis was a disciplined and monastic community that fostered the study of philosophy and theology. Nisibis and Jundishapur – as far as we can tell – became centres of the medical training for which Nestorian Christian monks and missionaries were so justly renowned in subsequent centuries. And the zeal of the East Syrian Church for winning converts did not falter before the prospect of vast geographical distances or dangerously alien cultures. Not only did it establish itself over time in the Mesopotamian region of the Persian empire, but in eastern Anatolia, Kurdistan, Turkestan and well beyond. All of Asia east of the Euphrates was open to its monks, and to no other Christians. In 635, Patriarch Yashuyab II (d.643) inaugurated a mission to China that flourished right through the age of the khans.

Monasteries, Schools and Hospitals

East Syrian Christian missions naturally followed the trade routes to the Far East. Merchant caravans from the Arabian peninsula, India, Central Asia and China passed through the Syrian city of Seleucia-Ctesiphon, and the monks of the Assyrian Church – trained in technical, scribal and medical skills – followed where those routes led, to find places where their training would make them and the gospel they had to preach welcome. By providing trained physicians and scholars and by building schools, libraries and hospitals, the East Syrian Church often proved itself an immense benefit to the areas where it settled.

Semitic Christianity had been well established in the Arabian peninsula in the fourth century, and in the late fifth century Syrian missions built a number of schools and monasteries there. There were both Jacobite (that is, Monophysite) and Nestorian Christians in the peninsula in the fifth and sixth centuries, but the latter predominated. Even after the rise of Islam drove Christianity and Judaism out of Arabia, Christianity persisted among some of the nomadic desert people and in isolated pockets for at least a century.

The late fifth century also saw the beginning of the Assyrian missions to Turkestan and, in time, to the Mongols.

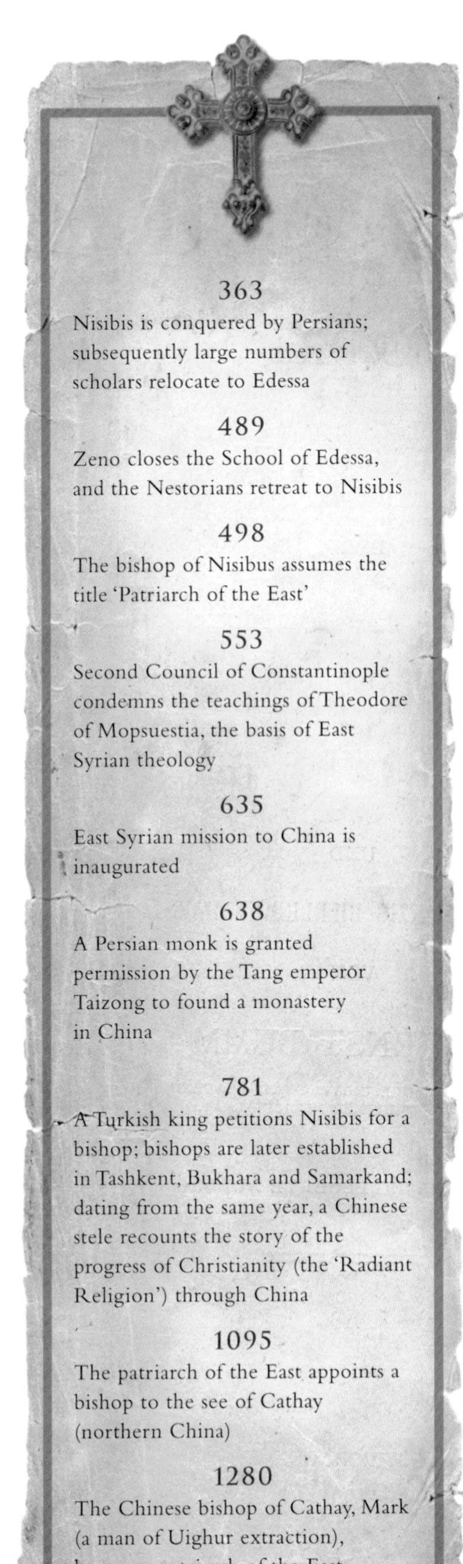

363
Nisibis is conquered by Persians; subsequently large numbers of scholars relocate to Edessa

489
Zeno closes the School of Edessa, and the Nestorians retreat to Nisibis

498
The bishop of Nisibus assumes the title 'Patriarch of the East'

553
Second Council of Constantinople condemns the teachings of Theodore of Mopsuestia, the basis of East Syrian theology

635
East Syrian mission to China is inaugurated

638
A Persian monk is granted permission by the Tang emperor Taizong to found a monastery in China

781
A Turkish king petitions Nisibis for a bishop; bishops are later established in Tashkent, Bukhara and Samarkand; dating from the same year, a Chinese stele recounts the story of the progress of Christianity (the 'Radiant Religion') through China

1095
The patriarch of the East appoints a bishop to the see of Cathay (northern China)

1280
The Chinese bishop of Cathay, Mark (a man of Uighur extraction), becomes patriarch of the East

We know that in 781 a Turkish king petitioned Nisibis for a bishop. And bishops were also established in Tashkent, Bukhara and Samarkand. These missions were soon extended to the Keraits, Uighurs and other Central Asian tribes.

The Radiant Religion

In 1625, Jesuit missionaries in Sian-fu in China's Shaanxi province discovered a stone stele bearing a long inscription, dating from 781, recounting the progress of the 'Radiant (or Illustrious) Religion' – that is, Christianity – in China. By the time of the Jesuit missions, the Chinese outposts of the East Syrian Church were no more; and, needless to say, the Roman Catholic world until then had had no idea that any form of Christianity had penetrated so far into the east. But for several centuries the Church of the East had extended from Syria to 'far Cathay'. According to the Sian–fu stele, it was the Tang emperor Taizong (d.649) who first received a Nestorian missionary, a Persian monk, whom he then gave permission to preach and, in 638, to found a monastery. Over the next two centuries, churches and monasteries were established in at least ten provinces.

'When the pure, bright Illustrious Religion
Was introduced to our Tang Dynasty,
The Scriptures were translated, and churches built,
And the vessel set in motion for the living and the dead;
Every kind of blessing was then obtained,
And all the kingdoms enjoyed a state of peace.'

Part of the inscription on the Nestorian Stele found in Shaanxi province, China

The East Syrian Church in China suffered a reversal of fortunes in the ninth century, when the emperor Wuzong (d.846) laicized all the native priests and monks in the Middle Kingdom; the setback, however, was only temporary. There were still monasteries in China in the 11th century, and around 1095 the patriarch of the East, Sebaryeshu III, appointed a bishop to the see of Cathay (northern China). Even as late as the 13th century, when the Radiant Religion enjoyed the favour of the Mongol court of Kublai Khan (1215–95), Chinese monasteries were still being built. And in 1280 the Chinese bishop of Cathay became the Syrian patriarch of the East, under the name Yahbalaha III (d.1317).

We can never know with certainty how far the East Syrian missions of late antiquity and the Middle Ages reached. The Thomas Christians of India were East Syrian in theology, loyalty and population from an early period, and the new immigrants who swelled the numbers of the Malankara Christians in the eighth and the ninth centuries were definitely East Syrian. As early as the sixth century, the traveller and writer Cosmas Indicopleustes (probably a Nestorian Persian) encountered East Syrian Christians on the remote island of Socotra in the Indian Ocean; and there are passing references in texts from later centuries to one or another bishop of Socotra. And East Syrian missions penetrated into Tibet before the late eighth century.

There is even some textual and physical evidence of East Syrian Christians in Sri Lanka, Java, Sumatra, Japan, Korea, Myanmar, Malaya, Vietnam and Thailand. Whether indeed the Church of the East spread quite so far remains a matter of scholarly debate; but – given the extent of the missions of which we know – it would be unwise to assume that there was any part of Asia (apart perhaps from the far north) untouched by them.

MARY THE MOTHER OF CHRIST AND THE GODDESS GUAN YIN

Many scholars believe that the eastward missions of the Assyrian Church, even in parts of Asia from which they were later driven out, left something of themselves behind in the form of subtle influences on the practices, devotions and art of other faiths. For instance, it has been suggested (not altogether implausibly) that one of the reasons that Tibetan monastic ritual differs from that of other forms of Buddhist monasticism – the elaborate robes, incense, holy water and so on – is that the liturgies of the Christians monks of the Church of the East left their mark upon it.

Guan Yin, the goddess of compassion, is one of the deities most commonly seen on altars in Chinese temples. Worshippers often ask her to provide sons, wealth and protection.

One of the more interesting speculations in this regard concerns the Chinese Buddhist goddess of compassion Guan Yin, a figure that was originally male. Guan Yin is a manifestation of the Indian bodhisattva, Avalokitesvara. The portrayal of Guan Yin as female may have begun as early as the fifth century in China, but it was not a universal practice until perhaps the 11th century.

Any veneration of a feminine saviour is something of an anomaly in Buddhist devotion; the earliest forms of Buddhism denied that any woman could achieve saving enlightenment, and the bodhisattvas of later Buddhism were always depicted as men. On the other hand, a bodhisattva supposedly can assume any form he chooses; and a devotion to the female manifestation of Avalokitesvara, in the form of the goddess Tara, can also be found in Tibetan Tantric Buddhism.

Even so, many scholars believe that the special characteristics of the veneration of Guan Yin in China – and especially her later iconography – might reflect something of the Christian veneration of the Virgin Mary.

This may or may not be true. Something, however, that is incontestably true is that in Japan during the period of the Tokugawa shogunate – beginning in 1603 – Christians were persecuted and had to conceal their faith, and consequently many chose to venerate Mary in the guise of Guan Yin (or Kannon, as she is known in Japan).

Small statues of the so-called Mary-Kannon have been preserved to this day. They are usually adorned by a single discreet cross, which one must search carefully to find.

A NEW POWER IN THE WORLD: THE RISE OF ISLAM

By the beginning of the seventh century, Christianity had enjoyed centuries of largely unimpeded expansion; in one form or another, it had established itself in Asia and Asia Minor, the Near East and North Africa, eastern and western Europe. It had suffered local persecutions, but – at least, since the days of Constantine – had encountered no cultural power comparable to itself. By the end of the century, however, it would find itself challenged – and even, in vast stretches of the formerly Christian world, overwhelmed – by one of the most potent religious, political and cultural forces known to history: Islam.

Muhammad (*c.*570–632) – according to Muslim belief the last and greatest of God's prophets on earth – spent his early adulthood as a merchant. Born in the city of Mecca, near the west coast of the Arabian peninsula, and brought up for a time among desert nomads, he became the ward of his uncle – a Meccan merchant – when still young, and on occasion apparently travelled with his uncle's caravans into Syria. According to Islamic tradition, however, he experienced a profound and terrifying vision of the Angel Jibril (Gabriel) when he was 40 years old, in around 610, in which he was called to become God's messenger (*rasul*) to the world.

The message he proclaimed was sublimely simple in its principles, and was, according to Muslim belief, the same message that had been proclaimed by all God's prophets since Adam, including Moses and Jesus – though it had been distorted by the Jews and the Christians. It was the message of submission (which is what 'Islam' means) to the will of God: obedience to divine law, prayer, reverence, good works and faithfulness. Islam was, above all, the strictest of monotheisms, reserving all devotion for God alone, hostile to any hint of polytheism or idolatry and censorious of the Christian doctrine of the Trinity.

The Dome of the Rock in Jerusalem is thought to be the oldest surviving Islamic monument. Its spiritual significance to adherents of Islam stems from the belief that Muhammad himself once ascended to heaven from this sacred place.

Muhammad and his followers at first struggled to convert the Meccans from the indigenous Arabian polytheism, and were even obliged to leave the city for a time to take up residence in Medina, some 275 miles (440 km) to the north. But by 629 he and his movement had become sufficiently powerful that he was able to return to Mecca without encountering any resistance, and to purge the city of its idols and to establish Islam as its law and its faith. By the time Muhammad died, only three years later, almost all of the Arabian peninsula was committed to Islam.

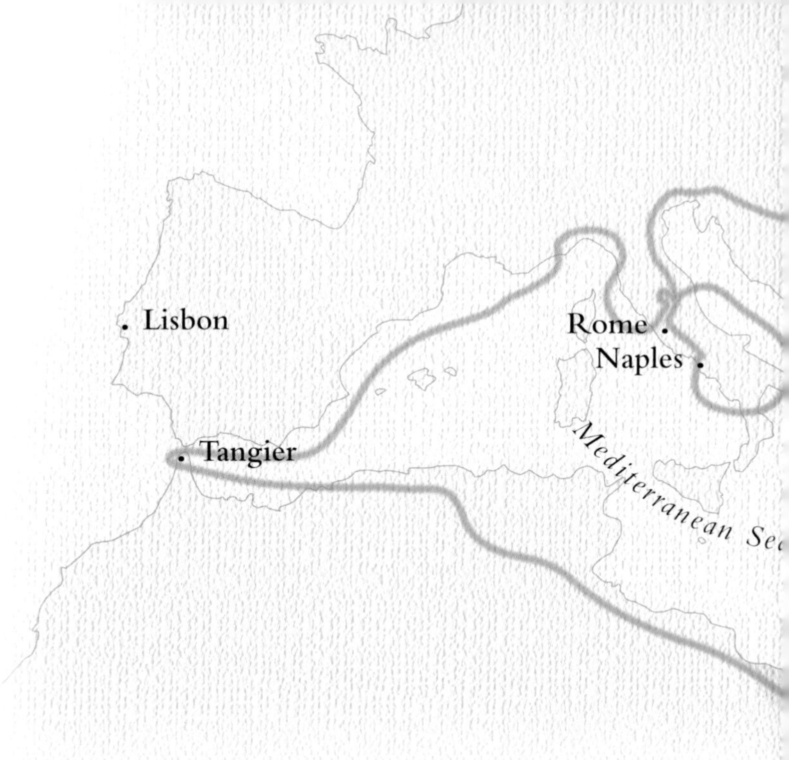

Area of Islam
- 632, at the death of Muhammad
- 634, at the death of Abu Bakr, the first caliph
- 656, at the death of Uthman, the third caliph
- 750, at the fall of the Ummayad dynasty
- extent of Byzantine empire, 632

The Islamic Empire

Islam is not merely a spiritual philosophy or ethical teaching, but a political order as well. There is no division between religion and state in Islamic thought, and Muhammad was not only a prophet, but a ruler. Thus, upon his death, it was necessary to find a successor (in Arabic, a *caliph*): not, of course, to his prophetic office, which was unique, but to his role as sovereign of the *umma* (the Islamic community).

> *'This is the site on which I shall build. Goods can come here via the Tigris and the Euphrates, and various canals. Only a place like this can support the army and the populace ... Build, then, with God's blessing.'*
>
> Words of Caliph Al-Mansur on founding Baghdad in 762, as reported by the chronicler Al-Tabari (*c.*839–923)

The early years of the caliphate were a period of remarkable military expansion. After subduing a number of still recalcitrant Arab tribes, the soldiers of the caliphate were able – with astonishing rapidity – to exploit the weaknesses of the Persian and Byzantine empires (weaknesses induced in large measure by the constant warfare between them) and to occupy immense territories from both – indeed, in the case of Persia, to conquer the empire itself. Within ten years of the death of Muhammad, Arab forces had captured Syria, Palestine, Egypt, Armenia, Iraq and Iran. At the end of the first period of the caliphate (the 'patriarchal period') 20 years later, the empire of Islam reached from beyond Tripoli in the west almost to Kabul in the east, and from Aden in the south to the lands between the Caspian and Black Seas and to Turkestan in the north.

From 661–750, moreover, under the Ummayad dynasty, the Islamic Empire conquered even more of the Christian world. By the end of the first decade of the eighth century, the caliphate comprised most of North Africa, stretching far to the west of Roman Tingis (Tangier), as well as all of Portugal and Spain (with the exception of the small kingdom of Asturias in northern Spain) and much of transalpine Gaul. The Abbasid dynasty that succeeded the Ummayad went on to conquer many of the Mediterranean islands, such as Sicily and the Balearics.

During the years of the Abbasids, there were occasional divisions within the empire – in 756, for instance, an independent caliphate was established in Spain –

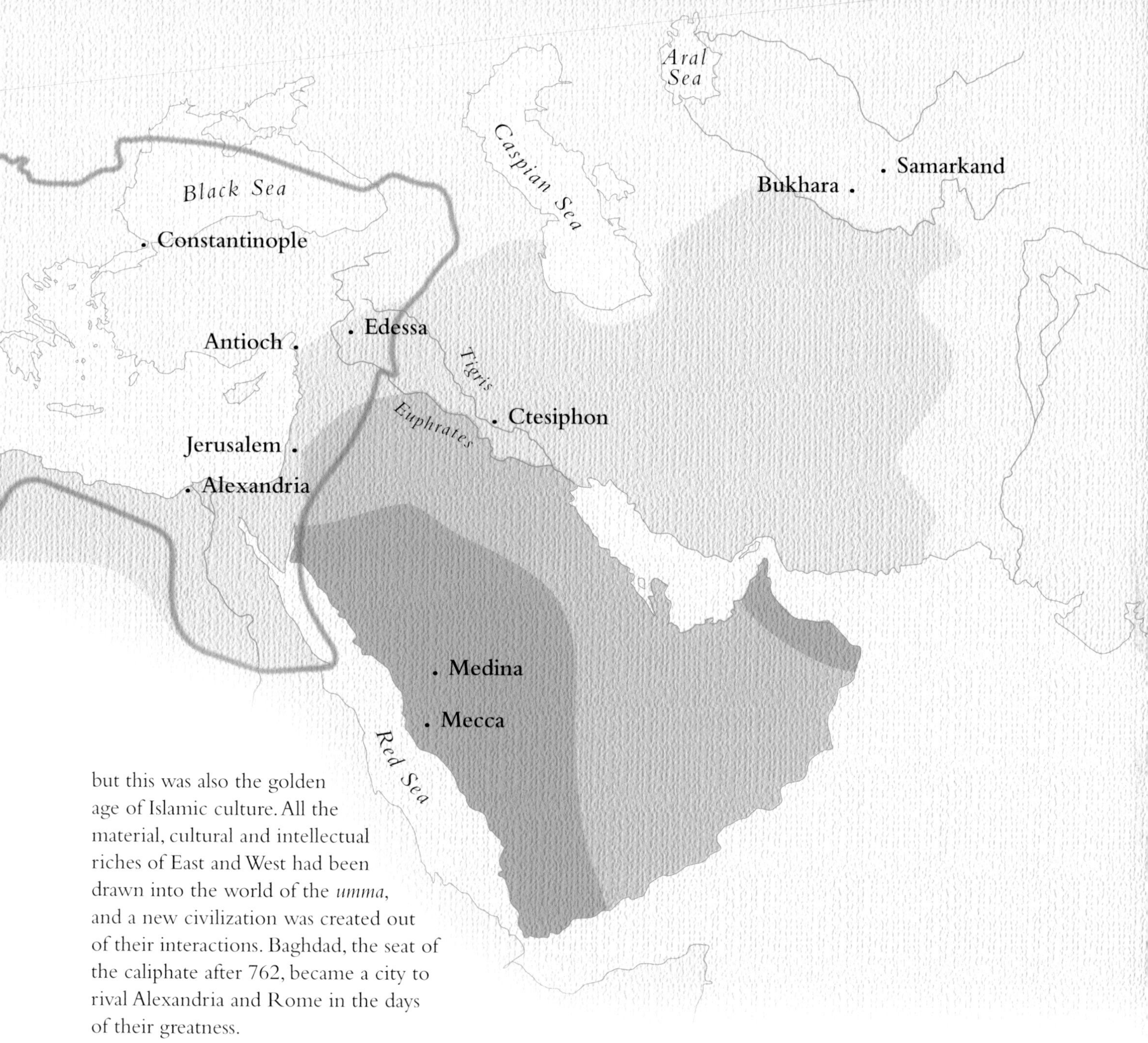

but this was also the golden age of Islamic culture. All the material, cultural and intellectual riches of East and West had been drawn into the world of the *umma*, and a new civilization was created out of their interactions. Baghdad, the seat of the caliphate after 762, became a city to rival Alexandria and Rome in the days of their greatness.

The Christian world, however, in little more than a century, had been reduced to a fragment of its former dimensions. Rather than continuing to expand in all directions, it found itself for the first time confronted by a geopolitical power as great as – or greater than – itself.

Map showing the extent of the Islamic empire immediately after the death of Muhammad and during the ensuing caliphates. In less than a century Islamic armies conquered a vast empire from Spain to Central Asia.

The House of Wisdom

One often hears it asserted today that, during the so-called Dark Ages, Christendom was reduced to barbarism, while classical culture – including philosophy, science and medicine – became the exclusive preserve of the Islamic world. This is, to say the least, an exaggeration. In part, it is a claim that reflects the tendency of many to think of medieval Christendom as comprising nothing but western Europe, and so to forget the brilliant Byzantine civilization of the east or the great achievements of the Syrian scholars of Persia and beyond. It is also a claim, however, that so oversimplifies the history of the period as to reduce it to caricature.

HOSPITALS IN THE EAST

The superiority of the medical training available in the Islamic world over that found in the western Christian world, at least from the early centuries of the caliphate to the 11th century, was enormous. Much of that superiority was the result of Syrian Christian tradition, and of the subsequent development of ever better medical techniques by Muslim and Syrian Christian physicians. But medical science was more advanced in the East as a whole than in the West, and the Byzantine empire should be given credit too for its contributions to the art of healing the ill, and of easing the suffering of the incurable.

Until quite recently, historians of medicine believed that medieval hospitals, in either the East or the West, were little more than hospices and shelters, providing nothing resembling systematic medical treatment and making no particular effort to restore their patients to health. In fact, though, in the eastern Christian Roman world, at least as early as the sixth century (and probably earlier) there were free hospitals served by physicians and surgeons, with fixed regimes of treatment and convalescent care, and with regular and trained staffs.

In their developed form, the hospitals of Byzantium offered a variety of specializations: some were sanatoria for the ill and injured, some were homes for the aged and infirm, some were foundling homes or orphanages and some were shelters for the poor. They were also generally almshouses, and provided food for the hungry.

In later centuries, Muslim society and – after the first crusade – Latin Christian society established hospitals of their own on the Byzantine model, the most famous of which was the massive Hospital of St John erected in Jerusalem by the Hospitallers in 1099, in imitation of which hospitals were built all over western Europe throughout the later Middle Ages.

Public hospitals had been an established feature of imperial Christian culture from the time of Constantine onwards, and providing medical care for the poor and afflicted had been a duty of monks from the earliest days of coenobitic monasticism. But the idea of a hospital as an institution devoted to the systematic and methodical care and cure of the ill seems to have originated specifically in Constantinople.

That said, it is most definitely the case that the Islamic empire was able – like all great empires – to produce a synthesis of the cultures it absorbed: Greek, Syrian, Persian, Chaldean, North African, Indian and so on. And, in assuming the Persian empire into itself, it inherited the entirety of Near Eastern Christian, Jewish and Persian scholarship and medicine. Thus, most definitely, from the end of the ninth century to the middle of the 13th, the Islamic world enjoyed a genuine measure of scientific superiority over Western Christendom, and even rivalled Byzantium in its achievements (though, in the area of technological innovation, western Europe in many respects surpassed both the Islamic and the Byzantine worlds). True there was, from the 12th century through to the 15th, a late introduction into the Christian West from the Islamic world of Greek classics not hitherto translated into Latin. But – to give all sides their due – Eastern Christian scholarship (particularly Syrian) had a considerable part to play in that story.

The traditional Arabic interest in astrology – held from the earliest times, when stars were used for navigation in the desert – was developed into a rigorous science by Islamic scholars after they were introduced to astrological texts from Greece, India and Persia. This early-16th-century print shows Arabian astrologers examining the sky.

Before the rise of Islam, Syrian Christians had carried Greek medical, scientific and philosophical wisdom far eastward, and had already translated a great many Greek texts – classical and technical – into their own, Semitic tongue. The Christian academies of Edessa, Nisibis and Jundishapur were the principal vehicles of Greek thought's eastern migrations after the fifth century, and the latter two were the chief repositories of the medical learning for which Nestorian monks were so renowned. Under the caliphate, it was Syriac-speaking Christians who at first provided the caste of scholars and physicians who brought the achievements of Greek and Roman antiquity into Islamic culture.

After the caliphate was moved to Baghdad, a grand library and academy – the House of Wisdom – was established and administered principally by Syrian Christians. There the translation of Greek texts into Arabic, either directly from the Greek or from Syriac versions, was a constant occupation. Perhaps the greatest translator of all was the caliph's chief physician, the Nestorian Christian Hunayn ibn Ishaq (808–73) who, in addition to his own treatises, produced an enormous number of accurate Syriac and Arabic renderings of Greek philosophical and medical texts.

From Baghdad and the House of Wisdom, a vast body of translations went forth into the greater Islamic world, including Muslim Spain. And from Spain a great deal of the intellectual patrimony of ancient Greece at last entered into Latin translations, produced by Mozarabic Christians (that is, the Arabic-speaking Christians of Spain), western European scholars and Spanish Jews.

c.610
According to tradition, the Prophet Muhammad – in a vision of the Angel Jibril (Gabriel) – is called to be God's messenger; his early attempts to convert the citizens of Mecca are largely unsuccessful and he is forced to flee to Medina

629
As the movement gains momentum, Muhammad returns to Mecca and establishes Islam as its law and its faith

632
Muhammad dies; by this time most of the Arabian peninsula has converted to Islam; a caliphate is established to ensure a successor to Muhammad

632–42
Within ten years of Muhammad's death, caliphate forces occupy large areas of the Persian and Byzantine empires

661–750
Islamic expansion continues under the Ummayad dynasty, encompassing most of North Africa, all of Portugal and Spain and much of transalpine Gaul

756
An independent caliphate is established in Spain

c.762
The Abbasid dynasty moves its capital to the newly founded city of Baghdad, ushering in a golden age of Islamic civilization; the House of Wisdom is established as a major centre of learning

CHARLEMAGNE

Even as the Abbasid dynasty was presiding over the first great flourishing of Islamic civilization, a new empire was arising in the Christian West – one that would not endure nearly so long as the caliphate, perhaps, but that would lay the foundation for the political culture, laws, customs and achievements of western medieval Christendom. This was the empire of the Franks, the Carolingian empire, so named because its founder was the Frankish king Karl der Grosse (*c.*742–814): in English, Charles the Great; in Latin, Carolus Magnus; in the French of his time, Charlemagne.

Long after his death Charlemagne continued to be remembered as one of the great leaders of Christian Europe, whose exploits in the company of his paladins are described in heroic terms in the French poems known as the chansons de geste. *This 19th-century statue of the emperor and two knights stands near the cathedral of Notre Dame in Paris.*

At its height, the Carolingian empire embraced almost all of continental western European Christendom, from west of the Pyrenees to east of Bavaria (as far as Moravia, if one includes tributary nations), and from Rome to the north of Saxony.

High King of the Franks

Charlemagne's grandfather was Charles Martel (*c.*688–741), the brilliant *major domus* (mayor of the palace) of the Eastern Frankish empire who – in the days when the Merovingian dynasty had been reduced to a purely nominal monarchy – united all the Franks under one rule, waged constant war to fend off the pagan Germanic tribes of the north, subdued Burgundy and, at Poitiers in 732, defeated the Muslim forces of Abd ar-Rahman, emir of Córdoba, thus bringing to a halt the expansion of Islamic rule in western Europe. Charlemagne's father, moreover, was Pepin III (*c.*714–68), who had further consolidated and expanded Frankish power, and who had – with the blessing of Pope Zacharias (d.752) – removed the last of the Merovingians from power and assumed the royal title for himself in 751.

Charlemagne had begun to accompany his father on campaigns as a boy, and from an early age, it seems, he was endowed with extraordinary energy, resolve, physical courage and concern for the protection of his dominions and of the Church. As king of the Franks – especially after the death of his brother Carloman in 771 – he permitted no rival to his rule. When the Lombard court in Italy attempted to force Pope Adrian I (d.795) to anoint Carloman's sons as kings, Charlemagne simply entered Italy and in 774 made himself king of the Lombards as well.

Many of Charlemagne's fiercest and most violent campaigns, however, were fought against the pagan Saxons of the north, whom he wished not only to subdue but to convert. Between 775 and 777, he succeeded in securing the fealty of the Saxon lords, and throughout Saxony there were baptisms en masse. Only a few years later, however, the Saxons rebelled, and Charlemagne's response was draconian. He did not hesitate to execute the rebels in great numbers, or to wage merciless war against those who resisted his

Charlemagne's unrelenting war against the Saxons from 775 to 804 resulted in the total subjugation and Christianization of these northern pagans. The subject of this 19th-century engraving is the submission to Charlemagne (mounted, at right) of the Saxon leader Wittekind (centre) in 785.

rule; finally, in 804, he succeeded in pacifying them. He insisted, moreover, upon a programme of thorough Christianization, and some of his anti-pagan decrees would be difficult to disapprove of; his Capitulary for Saxony, for example, made it a crime for anyone – prompted by some heathen belief in magic – to burn accused sorcerers or (grimly enough) to devour their flesh. Nevertheless, the means he used to convert the Saxons were often so coercive that even members of his own court were disturbed by their violence.

King and Emperor

The one major military defeat suffered by Charlemagne occurred in 778, when he entered into an alliance with certain Muslims of northern Spain against the emir of Córdoba. His forces besieged Zaragoza without success and, on their retreat through the Pyrenees, were attacked by Basques and suffered many losses. It was here, at the pass at Roncesvalles, that Hruolandus (Roland), the Warden of the Breton March, was killed, thus inspiring the legends and epics of Roland (or Orlando) that were written in later centuries.

To the east, though, Charlemagne's conquests continued. Ten years after the retreat from Spain, he took control of Bavaria by deposing the duke, his own cousin Tassilo. He conquered the northern Frisians, and his northern expansion was halted only when the Danes erected a massive fortification across the southern neck of the Danish peninsula. He made the Avars of Austria and Hungary and the Slavs of the Danube into tributary peoples. And slowly it became obvious that the king of the Franks was in fact the lord of a great empire.

732
Charles Martel defeats Muslim forces at Poitiers and halts the Ummayid invasion of Western Europe

751
Pepin III ousts the last Merovingian ruler and assumes the title of king of the Franks

768
Following his death, Pepin's two sons inherit the kingdom of the Franks

771
The younger brother, Carloman, dies; Charlemagne becomes sole ruler

774
Thwarting a move by the Lombard court to anoint Carloman's sons as kings, Charlemagne conquers the kingdom of the Lombards

778
Charlemagne's forces suffer heavy losses at the pass at Roncesvalles in the Pyrenees

780
Alcuin founds an academy at Aix-la-Chapelle

788
Charlemagne takes control of Bavaria and conquers the northern Frisians; he demands tribute from Austrian, Hungarian and Slavic peoples

800
Pope Leo III crowns Charlemagne 'Imperator Augustus' on Christmas Day

812
Byzantine emperor Michael I Rhangabe recognizes Charlemagne as emperor of the West

The title of emperor, however, was no trivial matter. It belonged by right – if not by actual power – to the Augustus in Constantinople, the sacred sovereign of all Catholic peoples. Furthermore, it was a symbol of continuity with the ancient Roman empire, and even if that continuity was little more than a myth, it lent an aura of eternal validity to the Catholic order. Even the pope was technically a subject of the Byzantine throne. But, by the end of the eighth century, the papacy had ambitions of its own, and wanted to exercise sovereignty over Roman Italy. More importantly, when the pope was in need of support or protection, Charlemagne was able to provide it, whereas the Byzantine emperor could not.

Thus, in Rome on Christmas Day 800, in response to the 'spontaneous' acclamation of the Roman people, Pope Leo III (d.816) crowned Charlemagne emperor. In legal terms, the pope's gesture was merely symbolic – he had no power to confer imperial dignity upon anyone – but even so it was a gesture that entered into the lore of the later Holy Roman Empire of western Europe.

> *'Charlemagne cultivated the liberal arts most assiduously ... In the study of grammar, he sat under Peter of Pisa, while in other studies his master was Alcuin, a Saxon of Britain by birth and the most learned man of his day ... At Aix he built a church of extraordinary beauty, where he could attend services morning and evening.'*
>
> EINHARD, *LIFE OF CHARLEMAGNE*, *c.*815

The Carolingian Renaissance

Charlemagne installed his imperial court at Aix-la-Chapelle (Aachen) in western Germany. Constantinople may not have relished the prospect of a Frankish emperor, with Rome and the papacy under his sway, but in 812 the emperor Michael I Rhangabe (d. *c.*843) bowed to the inevitable and officially recognized Charlemagne as emperor of the West.

Charlemagne took his new imperial dignity very much to heart. He even exchanged ambassadors with the caliphate in Baghdad, and set about creating a court worthy of an emperor of the Roman peoples. To this end he gathered scholars and men of letters from all over his realm and beyond. From England he summoned the poet, teacher and sometime philosopher Alcuin of York (*c.*732–804) to preside over the Palatine academy for the education of young nobles in Aix-la-Chapelle. He summoned the greatest scholars of Italy and Ireland (where knowledge of Greek and the classical tradition had not entirely faded away). He assembled a library of classical and patristic texts, and acted as a patron

CHRIST OUR GOOD LIEGE LORD – THE *HELIAND*

It was no easy matter for the Franks to instruct the newly (and forcibly) converted Saxons in the elements of the Christian faith. Saxon culture was martial and tribal; it was largely immune to the appeal of abstract speculation, and the stories of the Gospels were alien to its sensibilities. It was necessary, therefore, to produce a 'translation' of Christian scripture not only into the Saxon tongue but into, so to speak, the Saxon cultural grammar.

The oddest and most splendid attempt to do this was a long poem in Old Saxon now known as the *Heliand*, which means 'Saviour', written by an anonymous poet and commissioned by Louis I 'the Pious' (778–840), the son of Charlemagne. It is a retelling, in traditional Saxon alliterative verse, of the life of Christ, from conception to Ascension, in about 6000 lines.

While we possess no perfectly intact version of the *Heliand*, the four extant manuscripts provide us with a nearly complete text. It is definitely the work of a writer of some considerable skill. The most astonishing feature of the poem, however, is the portrayal of Christ and his Apostles. It is, first and foremost, a heroic portrayal. Christ's role as teacher is given only limited space – though a somewhat summary account of his teachings, distilled principally from the Sermon on the Mount, is provided – and the emphasis is placed instead upon his role as a leader of men.

In the *Heliand*, Christ is the liege lord of the Kingdom, the great Prince of Peace, and the Apostles are his 'eorls' (earls) and vassals. He is a generous and courageous master; his disciples are impetuous warriors, bold for truth; and the entire drama of his earthly mission is saturated in an atmosphere of fealty and honour. And no more striking evidence is given in the poem of Christ's regal magnanimity than the miracle he performed at the wedding at Cana, where the guests – gathered in a great mead hall, seated at long tables upon benches, quaffing from tankards and feasting on good meats – are provided by Christ with that noblest gift of a bountiful lord: good wine.

of the arts. He instituted a curriculum of Latin studies – literature and rhetoric – in all the cathedral schools and monasteries of his dominions. Charlemagne even undertook to learn to speak Latin himself, plus a smattering of Greek, and made some effort to acquaint himself with the writings of Augustine and other luminaries of the Church.

A scene from Les Grandes Chroniques de France *(late 14th century) shows Charlemagne entering a church after his coronation.*

Charlemagne's empire did not long survive him. His heirs partitioned his territories, more or less in keeping with ancient Frankish practices, and within two generations the Carolingian empire had dissolved into a collection of discrete kingdoms. But he had created a new social and political order, and had brought to its first fruition the emerging civilization of western Christendom – neither West nor East Roman, but rather a new Christian order, with its own character, its own genius and its own destiny.

Thereafter, though, relations between the Frankish West and the 'Roman' East were rarely cordial; and it was only a matter of time before the Eastern and Western Churches went their separate ways.

THE FACE OF GOD: THE ICONOCLAST CONTROVERSY

Anyone who enters an Eastern Orthodox church today will immediately be struck by the centrality and ubiquity of sacred icons: brilliantly coloured, highly stylized images of Christ, the saints and significant events from scripture and Christian history, rendered in gesso, tempera and gold leaf. The altar stands behind a great screen of icons called an 'iconostasis', the dome or ceiling is adorned by an image of Christ Pantokrator ('Christ the Universal Ruler'), and the faithful reverently kiss icons as they enter the church.

Sacred iconography is so established and vital a part of Orthodox tradition that it is difficult to imagine Eastern Christian worship without it. And yet, in the eighth and ninth centuries, a great theological debate over the permissibility of such images in the life of the Church arose and quickly assumed the dimensions of a full-blown crisis: theological, ecclesiastical, social and political.

THE FIRST ERA OF ICONOCLASM

The popularity of sacred images, and their use in churches and homes, had expanded considerably in the eastern empire by the beginning of the eighth century. The practice, as yet, had no explicit theological rationale; it simply flowed from the indigenous piety and aesthetic predilections of Byzantine society. But, with the accession to the throne of a Syrian emperor, Leo III 'the Isaurian' (*c.*675–741), in 717, the use of icons became a matter of (hostile) state attention. Whether Leo was an ardent enemy of icons when he first took power we cannot say; but by 726, when he issued his first public pronouncement against them, he clearly was. In 730, he officially proscribed their use. He even ordered the removal of a large icon of Christ from above the great entrance of the imperial palace, the Chalke Gate, and its replacement with a simple cross.

After the iconoclast controversy of the eighth and ninth centuries, the veneration of icons in the Eastern Orthodox Church became firmly entrenched in its doctrine for hundreds of years to come. Here, frescoes painted in 1644 on the walls of the Church of Laying Our Lady's Holy Robe in Moscow illustrate the life history of the Virgin Mary.

Precisely what prompted Leo to embrace 'iconoclasm' (literally, the 'shattering of images') is uncertain. It has been suggested that, as a Syrian, he may have been swayed by either Nestorian (East Syrian) or Monophysite (West Syrian) ideas, or by a general native Syrian distrust of sacred images. Others have suggested that he may have been influenced by certain iconoclast bishops of Asia Minor. Still others have suggested the influence of Islamic ideas. And, of course, Leo may simply have believed that icons violated the Mosaic prohibition of idolatry.

Even more passionate in his iconoclasm was Leo's son Constantine V (718–75), whose persecution of the 'iconodules' (that is, 'venerators of images') was savage and relentless. He was especially merciless towards the monks, who tended to be

the most zealous and uncompromising among the champions of icons, and towards clergy that supported them. He did not hesitate to confiscate monastic properties, mutilate and blind transgressors, force monks and nuns to marry one another, or even to have monks murdered.

The Theology of Icons

The chief theological arguments advanced by the iconoclasts are known to us principally from the accounts of their opponents, but sufficient evidence remains to confirm the general accuracy of those accounts. We know that, in the eyes of the iconoclasts, the veneration of sacred images was contrary to the spirit of the second commandment and to the practices and teachings of the ancient Church. Moreover, they argued, the adoration of material objects was a corruption of Christian piety; and the attempt to represent the living God by means so thoroughly unworthy of his divine dignity was blasphemous. Still more importantly, perhaps, they objected to icons on the grounds that images could not properly represent Christ as the incarnate God, since they could not depict his ineffable, invisible and infinite divinity. To believe otherwise, they argued, was either to confuse his divinity with his humanity (after the fashion of the Monophysites) or to abstract his humanity from his divinity (after the fashion of the Nestorians).

'In ancient times, God the incorporeal and uncircumscribed was not depicted at all. But now that God has appeared in the flesh and lived among men, I make an image of the God who can be seen. I do not worship matter but the creator of matter, who for my sake became material and deigned to dwell in matter, who through matter brought about my salvation.'

JOHN OF DAMASCUS (675–749), EXPLAINING HIS REVERENCE FOR ICONS

By far the most effective and brilliant defender of the iconodule position was John of Damascus (*c.*675–749), who, as he lived under Muslim rule, was beyond the reach of imperial persecution. He argued, in part, that icons were – contrary to the claims of their enemies – an established aspect of Christian tradition from the earliest years of the faith. They had always, if nothing else, he claimed, served as means of instruction for the faithful. He also sternly dismissed the iconoclasts' disdain of matter. Matter, he reminded them in sound Christian fashion, is the good creation of God, and through it one can worship and adore its creator. Moreover, matter itself becomes worthy of veneration when it is transformed into a vehicle of divine enlightenment, sanctification or salvation. Supremely adorable, of course, is the material body of the incarnate *Logos*; but also venerable are the wood of Christ's cross, the ink and paper used to write the Gospels, and the wood, paint and glue used in the making of icons.

However, for John it is not the matter from which the images are fashioned that principally merits our veneration, but their power to show us the persons they depict. The prohibition on images in the Mosaic code, he argued, was appropriate in the days of Moses because God had not yet been fully revealed, and so all images of gods were false and misleading portraits of beings who did not exist. Now, however, God has revealed himself, and has in fact provided us with the perfect icon of himself. In the incarnation, we have seen the very face

THE SACRED ART

In the Eastern Orthodox Church and Catholic Churches of the Byzantine Rite, the art of the icon is a discipline not only of the eyes and hands, but of the soul. To be a true iconographer (literally, 'one who writes icons'), a person must have a special vocation or charism.

To create an icon is to pray, to contemplate the 'hypostasis' of the holy figure or figures one seeks to represent, and then – following certain established norms – to produce an image in which the living presence of the subject is truly glimpsed.

The elements traditionally used in making an icon are quite simple, but ideal for producing images that are vividly colourful and that do not fade over time. The 'canvas' is a mere piece of wood treated with glue. The pigments are egg-based temperas, many of which have a natural translucency that allows for a complex layering of hues.

Icons ranged in size from miniature to monumental, taking the form of pendants, panel paintings or more permanent representations, such as frescoes or murals.

The background in most icons (though not in all) is golden, representing the light of eternity. In the oldest icons, a pale bright yellow tempera was painted upon a shimmering gesso ground, made with crushed alabaster or marble; more common today is the use of bright gold leaf. The former method is aesthetically superior, arguably, inasmuch as it produces a more ethereal effect.

In Byzantine worship, the icons that surround the worshippers serve as windows upon eternity, as it were. In them, it is believed, one sees the communion of saints, the final Kingdom of God, the glory of creation redeemed. It is often said, moreover, that through the icon, not only does one see, but one is also seen. For the Kingdom really is present wherever and whenever the Eucharist is celebrated, eternity really invades time, and those whom the icons depict are indeed present. As with any window, an icon allows the gazes of those on the two sides to meet.

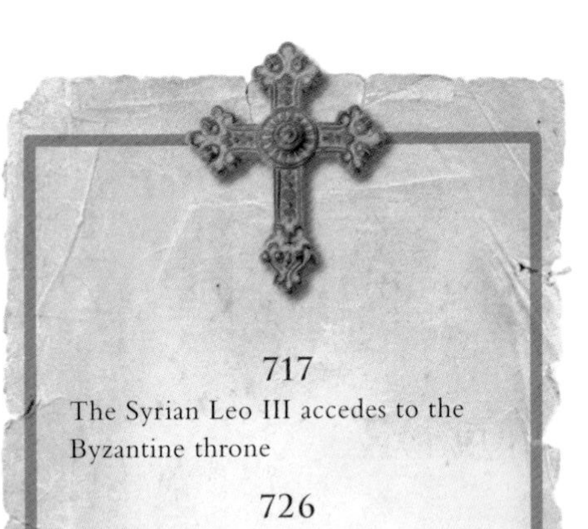

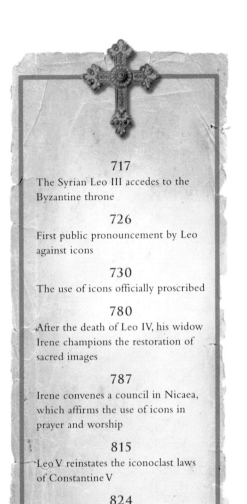

717
The Syrian Leo III accedes to the Byzantine throne

726
First public pronouncement by Leo against icons

730
The use of icons officially proscribed

780
After the death of Leo IV, his widow Irene champions the restoration of sacred images

787
Irene convenes a council in Nicaea, which affirms the use of icons in prayer and worship

815
Leo V reinstates the iconoclast laws of Constantine V

824
Icon defender Theodore the Studite is forced to flee Constantinople

843
Theodora, regent and mother of Michael III, revokes iconoclast laws and reinstates the use of icons in Church worship

of God, and so it is licit to imitate that divinely crafted icon in icons fashioned by human hands, as an affirmation that in Christ God has truly become a man.

Clearly John was unimpressed with the Christological justifications for iconoclasm. After all, it made no better sense to say that an icon was impotent to depict Christ's divinity than to say that his human body was impotent to reveal his divinity. Obviously, if one followed the logic of orthodox Christology, one had to believe that the human substance of Christ was also truly divine. Moreover, iconodule theology stressed that, in any icon, it is the 'hypostasis' – that is, the person – of the subject that is being revealed, and it is that person to whom the veneration is offered.

The Defeat of Iconoclasm

The first epoch of imperial iconoclasm came to an end as a result of the rise to power of the formidable Empress Irene (*c.*752–803). It was far from usual for a woman to rule the empire, but a combination of unforeseen circumstances – to say nothing of her remarkable intellect and will – brought Irene to the throne (or into its vicinity) nonetheless. As wife of Emperor Leo IV, she was appointed guardian of and co-emperor with her son Constantine VI on her husband's death in 780. At that point, the imperial prohibition of icons was half a century old, but she was of the iconodule party and took it upon herself to bring about the 'restoration of the sacred images'.

Her attempt to convoke a Church council in Constantinople in 786 was thwarted by soldiers of the city guard; but in 787 she succeeded in calling a council in Nicaea – the Seventh Ecumenical Council – at which the use of icons in prayer and worship was affirmed. The council clarified its position by drawing clear distinctions between *douleia* (that is, 'veneration'), which is perfectly appropriate in regard to sacred things such as icons, *hyperdouleia* ('superveneration'), which it is appropriate to offer to, say, the Mother of God, and *latreia* ('worship'), which can be offered to God alone.

The restoration of the icons was a triumphal affair, and Irene was canonized by the Church after her death; but iconoclasm was not yet entirely vanquished. In 813, Leo V 'the Armenian' (775–820) became emperor, and in 815 he reinstated the iconoclast laws of Constantine V and resumed the persecution of iconodules. The most important opponent of imperial policy and defender of the icons was Theodore the Studite (*c.*758–*c.*826), abbot of the Stoudion Monastery of Constantinople, who argued vigorously for both the antiquity and the spiritual benefits of the veneration of icons. For his impudence,

'The images which imposters once cast down, the pious emperors have restored.'

EARLY-NINTH-CENTURY INSCRIPTION AGAINST ICONOCLASM IN THE MOSAIC OF THE VIRGIN AND CHILD IN THE APSE OF HAGIA SOPHIA, CONSTANTINOPLE

Detail from a mosaic located at the eastern end of Hagia Sophia (Holy Wisdom), showing the Virgin and Child, dating from c.1118.

he was flogged and exiled. He was pardoned by Emperor Michael II 'the Armorian' (d.829) in 821, but – when the new emperor did not repudiate the iconoclast policies of his predecessor – he began again to agitate against the court and had to flee the city in 824.

The final restoration of the icons came about under the rule of yet another empress. When Emperor Theophilus died in 842, his son Michael III (838–67) became emperor at age four, with his mother Theodora as regent. She was a confirmed iconodule, and in 843, in her son's name, she revoked the iconoclast laws of the past three decades and reinstituted the use of icons in Church worship and private devotion once and for all.

FRANKS AND BYZANTINES: THE WIDENING GULF

The ninth century was in many ways propitious for both Western and Eastern Christendom. The 'Carolingian Renaissance' and political renewal of Charlemagne's reign was matched by a genuine revival of the arts and learning in the Byzantine world. But it was also a period in which it became clear that the now mostly nominal unity between the two halves of the ancient Catholic order could not persist indefinitely. In matters of faith and practice, East and West had always been strikingly distinct from one another. In matters of theology, they had been drifting apart for centuries. And, in matters of culture, they were now strangers one to the other.

Certain of the differences between Eastern and Western Church practices might seem rather trivial to us today: for instance, the Latin use of unleavened bread in the Eucharist as opposed to the Greek use of leavened; or the Latin preference for a celibate priesthood as opposed to the Greek preference for a married priesthood. But, when it proved convenient to make an issue of such differences, they could be an inexhaustible source of contention and recrimination.

There was, moreover, a more general atmosphere of theological incongruity between the two cultures on some issues. For instance, from at least the time of Augustine certain themes had emerged within Latin theology that were alien, or even repugnant, to Eastern tradition. Such themes included the notion of original sin as an inherited guilt, and the idea of predestination, and a rather distinctive understanding of the relation between created nature and divine grace.

For example, when Gregory of Nyssa in the fourth century wrote his treatise on infants who die prematurely, he assumed that unbaptized infants – having committed no sins – would enter into the presence of God. But when Augustine, some decades later, considered the fate of children who died before baptism, his understanding of sin and grace forced him to conclude that they must suffer eternal punishment. The opinions of individual theologians may not prove much; but so enormous a difference in perspectives, surely, reflected an immense difference also in the theological tempers of East and West.

The Procession of the Spirit

The single doctrinal dispute, however, that would ultimately become most emblematic of the division between East and West was the so-called Filioque Controversy. The Latin term *filioque* means simply 'and from the Son'; it was a phrase added to the Latin form of the Nicene Creed over a period of centuries,

though no equivalent phrase had been introduced into the Greek text. The form of the Creed produced by the Councils of Nicaea and Constantinople had merely repeated the assertion of John 15:26 that the Holy Spirit 'proceeds from the Father', and no subsequent council had ever modified it.

Pope John VIII's support of the council that reinstated Photius as successor to the patriarchate of Constantinople in 879 somewhat ameliorated relations between East and West. He is depicted here presiding over the Synod of Troyes, France, a year earlier, in 878.

It is true that there was a theological tradition in the East of speaking of the Holy Spirit as proceeding 'through the Son', and a similar formula had been advanced by Augustine in the West. But there was also a pronounced tendency among western theologians – Augustine most influentially – to condense this formula into the simple assertion that the Spirit proceeds 'from the Father and the Son'. Such language would not have been any cause for controversy had it remained confined to the realm of theology; but, in entering into the Creed – the universal declaration of the Orthodox Catholic faith – it became a poignantly obvious symbol of the growing division between the Greek and Latin Churches.

The 'filioque' clause was added to the Creed originally in Spain in 447, at the Synod of Toledo. Its purpose was to affirm the full divinity of the Son, over against the Arianism of the western barbarians, most particularly the Visigoths. And it was this modified version of the Creed that was adopted by the Catholic Franks of Gaul and that thus was favoured by Charlemagne. Rome, however, resolutely resisted the innovation. Pope Leo III (d.816) refused to acknowledge the revised Creed. He even had the original text of the Creed inscribed on twin tablets of silver (one in Greek, one in Latin) and displayed in St Peter's. It was not until 1014, scholars believe, that the version of the Creed including the filioque was first employed in Rome, at the behest of the Holy Roman Emperor Henry II (972–1024), on the occasion of his coronation mass.

FOURTH CENTURY
Gregory of Nyssa writes a treatise in which he postulates that unbaptized infants who die enter directly into the presence of God

FIFTH CENTURY
Augustine argues that children who die before baptism suffer eternal punishment

447
At the Synod of Toledo, the filioque clause is added to the Creed in Spain

731
Pope Gregory III convenes a council in Rome, which condemns iconoclasm as heresy

739
Following the attack on Ravenna by the Lombards, Gregory seeks protection from the Franks

791
Charlemagne condemns the iconodule council

862
Emperor Michael III replaces Ignatius as patriarch of Constantinople with Photius; a year later Pope Nicholas I convenes a council in Rome, which attempts to 'depose' Photius

879
Following a series of condemnations and reinstatements, a council in Constantinople vindicates Photius

1014
The filioque clause may have been used in Rome for the first time, during the coronation mass of Henry II

Pope and Patriarch

Even so, the filioque clause became an ancillary issue of dispute in the course of a larger struggle over jurisdictional prerogatives between the sees of Constantinople and Rome in the ninth century. Pope Nicholas I (*c*.820–67) attempted to insert himself into the internal affairs of the Constantinopolitan patriarchate in 862, after Emperor Michael III had removed Patriarch Ignatius I (d.877) from his position and replaced him with Patriarch Photius (*c*.820–after 900), a brilliant scholar and layman. The appointment seemed contrary to Western canons – though it was perfectly in keeping with Eastern practices – and in 863 the pope called a council in Rome that 'deposed' Photius. Photius responded simply by convoking a large ecumenical synod that 'excommunicated' and 'deposed' Nicholas. The sequel of this fracas is too complicated to recite in detail. As emperors and popes changed, so did the fortunes of Ignatius and Photius, and councils, condemnations, depositions and reinstatements multiplied. In 879, with the support of Pope John VIII (d.882), a council in Constantinople vindicated Photius.

In the course of the dispute, however, certain issues had been raised that until then had remained largely unaddressed. Many of them merely concerned the relative rights of the two sees – such as which should exercise episcopal jurisdiction over the Slavs – but others were of a more fundamental nature. Photius accused Rome of attempting to arrogate to itself authority it did not possess, and it was he who first made an explicit issue out of the filioque clause – even though Rome had not yet actually adopted it.

One Church in Two Empires

Disputes between the Constantinopolitan and Roman sees were matters not merely of ecclesiastical concern, but of imperial policy as well. The iconoclast controversy, for example, had a direct, and ultimately defining, effect upon the relations between the Byzantine and Carolingian courts. Early in the eighth century, before the Carolingian period, the policies of Leo the Isaurian had already alienated Pope Gregory II (669–731), who – though officially a subject of the eastern emperor and under the protection of the Byzantine exarchate in Ravenna – refused to obey Leo's iconoclast decrees. In 731, Pope Gregory III (d.741) convened a council in Rome that condemned iconoclasm as a heresy.

And so, when Ravenna was sacked by the Lombards in 739 and Rome lay largely unprotected against Lombard forces, Gregory turned to Pepin for aid, rather than to a heretical emperor. The new liaison between the papacy and the Franks was then fortified when Pope Stephen II (d.757) anointed Pepin king of the Franks and the latter obligingly inaugurated a military campaign against the Lombards in Italy. And, when

THE GREATEST OF THE PALADINS

The legendary hero wielding an axe to fight off attackers, in 'The Death of Roland'.

Throughout the Middle Ages, the legends of Charlemagne and his knights, or paladins, were among the most popular tales in western Europe, and inspired a rich and varied literature that persisted into (and reached some of its grandest heights during) the Renaissance. And, of all of Charlemagne's paladins, none enjoyed a more splendid mythic aggrandizement than Roland, that same Hruolandus (in Italian, Orlando), Lord of the Breton March, whose death in the Pyrenees in 778, during the Franks' retreat from Spain, was briefly recounted by Charlemagne's official biographer Einhard.

The massacre at Roncesvalles was the subject of the earliest of the Roland poems of which we know, the old French *Chanson de Roland.* The actual perpetrators of the ambuscade at Roncesvalles were Basques, but in the poem they are Moors, acting in league with Roland's wicked uncle Ganelon. In later *chansons de geste,* however, stories of Roland's early years began to multiply, with ever more fanciful elements mixed in. And his exploits – and those of his fellow paladins – soon began to appear in other tongues: German, Spanish, English and Italian.

This last language was especially hospitable to Roland's mythology. In *Paradiso,* Dante numbered Orlando among the great warrior martyrs whose souls shine like rubies in the sphere of Mars. And, in the 15th and 16th centuries, Orlando became the protagonist of the three greatest Italian Renaissance 'romances': Luigi Pulci's *Morgante,* Matteo Boiardo's *Orlando Innamorato* and Ludovico Ariosto's *Orlando Furioso.* In these delirious, violent, whimsical and fabulous epics, the Lord of the Breton March attained literary dimensions that no other figure in chivalric fiction – not even any of the knights of Arthur – ever equalled.

Coming as he did from a warrior culture, with a healthy appreciation for posthumous glory, the real Hruolandus – had he been able to foresee his literary posterity – might have thought his death at Roncesvalles an acceptable price to pay.

Charlemagne came to power, he did so as a Catholic monarch in an age of imperial heterodoxy, and so as a theological as well as political ally of Rome.

It is true that Charlemagne's 'unexpected' coronation occurred after the restoration of the icons in 787, but this did nothing to reconcile the Frankish court with the Byzantine. The Latin translation of the council's decrees failed to make the distinction – so vital to the Greek – between 'veneration' and 'worship', and so gave the impression that the labile Byzantines had abandoned iconoclasm only to embrace iconolatry. Thus, in 791, Charlemagne issued a condemnation of the iconodule council as well – proving that, even when East and West were actually in agreement, they were at odds.

THE CONVERSION OF THE SLAVS

The disputes of the early eighth century between the Byzantine emperor and the pope concerned more than iconoclasm; they were also arguments over ecclesial jurisdictions, and specifically over the question of whether Rome or Constantinople should wield authority over Calabrian Italy and over the peoples of the Balkans (for episcopal authority could not be severed from political authority). And in the ninth century, as the conversion of the Slavs progressed, these disputes over regional prerogatives only intensified, and served further to embitter relations between East and West, especially during the controversy surrounding the appointment of Patriarch Photius in Constantinople.

Considered in themselves, however, rather than in the light of their political ramifications, the ninth-century Christian missions to the Slavic world were not only enormously successful, but in many respects astonishing, not least in their civilizing effects.

Cyril and Methodius

The most famous of the missionaries to the Slavic world were two brothers from Thessalonica, St Cyril (*c*.827–69) and St Methodius (*c*.825–84), the great 'Apostles to the Slavs'. Both were theologians of considerable range, but their principal qualifications for evangelizing the pagans of the north were their special scholarly gifts, and most particularly their abilities as linguists. Few Greek or Latin theologians could speak Slavonic, and few Slavs could speak Greek or Latin; moreover, Slavonic was not a written language, and so the dissemination of Christian texts in the native tongue of the Slavs was impossible.

An Orthodox icon depicting Saints Cyril and Methodius. The brothers are venerated in eastern Orthodox Christianity and given the title 'Apostles to the Slavs'. They were canonized by the Roman Catholic Church in 1880.

Cyril had taught philosophy in Constantinople at the Patriarchal University, and had once, thanks to his mastery of Arabic and Hebrew, conducted a state embassy to the caliphate. Methodius was abbot of the great Polychron Monastery. In 860, the two brothers had been commissioned by the emperor to evangelize the Khazars north of the Black Sea (although the mission was a failure, as the Khazars ultimately adopted Judaism as their national faith). The two brothers began their mission to the Slavs, however, in 862, when Prince Ratislav (d. after 870) of Great Moravia sent to Constantinople, requesting missionaries capable of preaching to his people in their own language. Western priests had already penetrated into the region, but they insisted on preaching and celebrating the mass in Latin.

The emperor – in part, no doubt, out of a desire to establish Byzantine rather than Latin Christianity in Moravia, and Greek rather than Frankish rule – sent

ІС ХС
СТЫИ КИРИЛЛЪ
СТЫИ МЕѲОДИ
А Б В Г Д
Є Ж З И Ї
К Л М Н О
П Р С Т Ȣ
Ѵ Ф Х Ѿ Ц
Ч Ш Щ Ъ Ы
Ь Ѣ Є Ю Ж
Ѡ Ѧ Ѯ Ѱ Ѳ
Ѵ

860
Cyril and Methodius embark on a mission to evangelize the Khazars north of the Black Sea; they are unsuccessful

862
Prince Ratislav requests missionaries to preach to the people of Great Moravia in their own language

863
Sent to Great Moravia by the Byzantine emperor, Cyril and Methodius translate the Byzantine liturgy into Slavonic and conduct worship in the local vernacular; they are accused of impropriety by German clerics

867
Pope Nicholas I requests that they come to Rome

868
They arrive the following year and persuade the new pope, Adrian II, of the legitimacy of their mission; Cyril dies during the visit

870
Methodius is imprisoned by Germanic priests

873
Having been released on the orders of Pope John VIII, Methodius continues his work as archbishop of Sirmium

880
Methodius returns to Rome to renew papal support for the Slavonic liturgy

885
Methodius dies; Pope Stephen V later permits the expulsion of his followers from Moravia

Cyril and Methodius to Moravia in 863. The brothers translated the Byzantine liturgy into Slavonic, but in order to do this were obliged first to devise an alphabet for the language – the old Glagolitic alphabet, in all likelihood. (The later Cyrillic Slavic script, which is named after St Cyril, may also have been the invention of the two brothers, and in form it more nearly resembles the Greek alphabet than does the Glagolitic.) They began conducting worship in the vernacular, which was the Eastern Church practice in any event, and preaching in a language the local people could understand.

Soon, however, their vernacular liturgy aroused the hostility of the German archbishop in Salzburg and the German bishop in Passau. They saw these Byzantines as interlopers in a mission field they regarded as theirs by right, and they accused the two Greeks of theological impropriety on the grounds that Roman canons recognized no legitimate liturgical languages apart from Latin, Greek and Hebrew.

To settle the dispute, Pope Nicholas I (*c.*820–67) requested in 867 that Cyril and Methodius come to Rome. They complied and, on arriving in the city in 868, soon convinced the new pope, Adrian II (792–872), of the legitimacy of their mission. Cyril, however, died during the visit to Rome; and so it was Methodius alone who returned to Moravia, in possession now of a papal commission and an appointment as archbishop of Sirmium (the archdiocese that comprised all of Great Moravia, Pannonia and Serbia).

The Germanic priests of the region, however, did not relent in their intrigues. In 870, on purely spurious charges, they arrested, tried, beat and imprisoned Methodius; and no doubt he would have died in prison had not Pope John VIII (d.882) – whose pontificate began in 872 – demanded his release. From 873 to 879, he presided over his archdiocese, and in 880 returned to Rome to renew papal support for the Slavonic liturgy. But his Swabian suffragan bishop Wiching continued to conspire against him, and after Methodius' death in 885, Pope Stephen V (d.891), a timid and incompetent pontiff, authorized the suppression of the Slavonic rite and the expulsion of Methodius' followers from Moravia.

The Prince of the Rus

It was at the end of the tenth century – tradition says 988 – that Russia (or, at any rate, its people, the Rus) became Christian, under Prince Vladimir the Great (*c.*956–1015), monarch of Kiev and Novgorod, who secured unchallenged rule over his dominions in 980. During the early years of his rule, which were occupied with enlarging and consolidating his realm through conquest, he was a confirmed pagan, who erected temples to the various gods of the Rus, commissioned numerous idols,

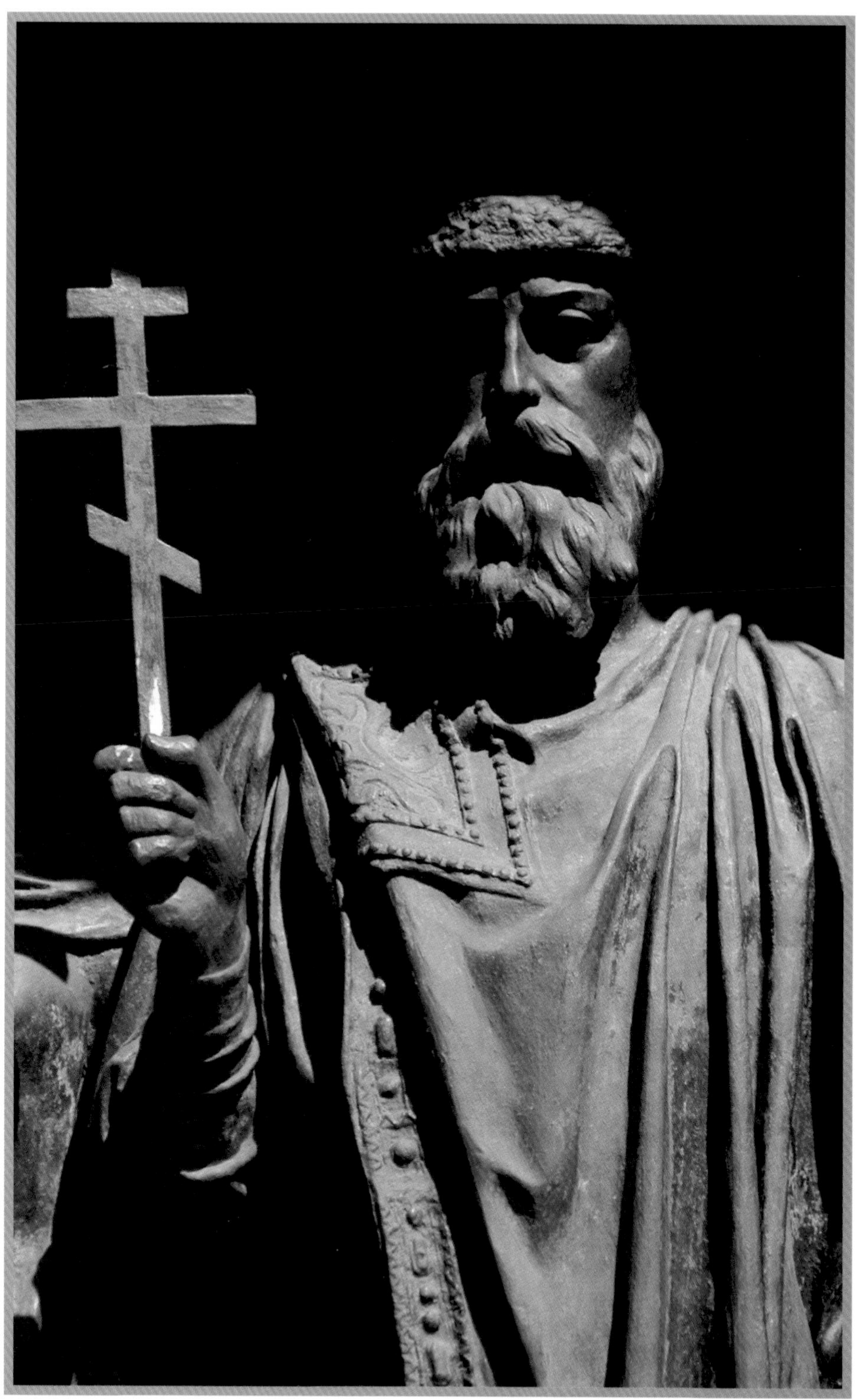

Detail of the Monument to the Millennium of Russia (1864), a representation of Prince Vladimir the Great, which stands in the ancient Slavonic city of Veliky Novgorod.

cultivated a special devotion to the thunder-god Perun (of whom he had a statue cast in gold, with a moustache in silver) and kept hundreds of concubines in addition to his seven wives.

According to a 12th-century chronicle, however, Vladimir sent out envoys in 987 to investigate the faiths of neighbouring races. Those who visited the Muslim Bulgars returned with reports complaining of the joylessness of a religion that prohibited alcohol; and those who visited German churches of the Latin rite reported that the worship was arid and graceless; but those who attended a glorious Divine Liturgy at Hagia Sophia reported that, during the worship, they no longer knew if they were in heaven or on earth, so ineffably beautiful was all that they saw and heard – whereupon Vladimir adopted Byzantine Christianity.

Whether or not this tale is entirely credible, what most definitely is true is that in 988 Vladimir – like many of the barbarians of the east, a rapt admirer of Byzantine civilization – petitioned Constantinople for the hand of Anna, sister of Emperor Basil II (957–1025). Such a marriage would probably have been unthinkable had Vladimir not been so powerful a prince and had Basil not so keenly desired a military alliance with him in order to suppress a Byzantine insurrection. The marriage of a Christian princess to a pagan was impossible, of course, but Vladimir accepted baptism, took the Christian name Basil in honour of the emperor, and married Anna. He then mandated the baptism of all his subjects and had all the idols of the Russian gods destroyed; the resplendent statue of Perun he had thrown into the River Dnieper.

'Then we went to the Greeks [Constantinople] and they led us to the place where they worship their God, and we knew not whether we were in heaven or earth, for on earth there is no such vision nor beauty, and we do not know how to describe it; we only know that God dwells among men. We cannot forget that beauty.'

ANON. PRIMARY CHRONICLE (*c.*986) OF THE DELEGATION SENT BY PRINCE VLADIMIR OF KIEV-RUS TO CONSTANTINOPLE

CHAMPION OF THE FAITH

Apparently Vladimir took his new faith rather seriously. Not only did he build monasteries and a great many churches, some of them quite magnificent; he devoted himself quite earnestly to creating a Christian Kievan culture on the Byzantine civic model, which required rather substantial social reforms: he built schools, hospitals, almshouses and orphanages; he established ecclesiastical courts and monastic shelters for the aged and infirm; he instituted laws designed to protect the weak against the powerful; and he came to be known as a friend of the poor, a just and gentle ruler and a fervent champion of the faith. And it is as St Vladimir that he is remembered in Orthodox tradition.

The first, Kievan age of Russian Christianity was something of a golden age – or so it is remembered in Russian lore. The capital city – Kiev – grew and prospered, it became a centre of trade and manufacture, its decorative arts flourished, its silversmiths were famed for their skill, and its churches (numbering in the hundreds) were renowned for their opulent loveliness.

The Kievan period came to an end in the early 13th century – after more than a century of declining fortunes and power – with the invasion of Russia by the Mongols under Batu Khan (*c.*1205–55), grandson of Genghis, in 1238. In 1240, the city was destroyed, and its people massacred. Thereafter, the centre of Russian Christianity shifted north, to the free – but considerably less civilized – city of Moscow.

THE PASSION-BEARERS

Among the most beloved of Russian saints are the two sons of Vladimir, Boris and Gleb. They are commemorated by the Orthodox Church as the holy 'passion-bearers', because of the Christ-like manner in which they met their deaths.

According to *The Lives of Boris and Gleb*, an 11th-century work, both were murdered by their ambitious and pitiless elder brother Svyatopolk 'the Accursed'. Prince Vladimir had divided his kingdom among his sons before his death, and Svyatopolk, as the eldest, was made prince of Kiev; but Svyatopolk coveted his brothers' principalities as well.

The willingness of Boris and Gleb to die rather than use violence, in imitation of Christ's passion, is among the most cherished stories of the Russian Church.

Supposedly, Boris was advised by his courtiers to march on Kiev before Svyatopolk could strike, but Boris was unwilling to use violence against his own brother solely for the sake of worldly power – an attitude shared by Gleb. Svyatopolk, burdened by no such scruples, sent assassins to kill Boris. When the killers arrived, they found Boris at his prayers in a tent; Boris supposedly implored God for the fortitude to face his faith without fear or anger, prayed that God would forgive Svyatopolk, and then lay down upon his sleeping couch, where the assassins promptly stabbed him several times. As his body was being carried to Kiev later, however, he was found still to be breathing, and so one of his brother's agents drove a spear into his heart.

Svyatopolk then sent for Gleb, claiming that their father was gravely ill. While Gleb was travelling to Kiev by boat, however, he discovered that his father was already dead and that Boris had been murdered by assassins. As he was weeping with grief, Svyatopolk's paid assassin – who turned out to be Gleb's personal cook – cut Gleb's throat with a kitchen knife and left his body in a thicket on the river bank.

That, at any rate, is the story preserved in sacred legend. Some historians question its veracity, not only in particular details, but as a whole; some even doubt Svyatopolk had any hand in his brothers' deaths. Whether accurate or not, though, the story of two princes who chose to die in Christ-like meekness rather than to wage war entered deeply into the spiritual imagination of Russian Orthodox tradition.

THE GREAT SCHISM

By the 11th century, the Byzantine and Latin halves of the Catholic world were to all intents and purposes separate entities, not only politically and culturally, but also ecclesiastically. For centuries the Eastern and Western Churches had been drifting ever farther apart, and behaving not simply as two rites within a single communion, but as rivals to each other – even though formally they still belonged to one Church.

The 'official' date of the Great Schism that divided the ancient Catholic Church into the Eastern Orthodox and Roman Catholic Churches is 1054: in that year, full communion between the sees of Constantinople and Rome was broken and – perhaps somewhat unexpectedly – never again restored. That said, communion between the Eastern and Western Churches was not entirely abrogated until much later, and then only by a very gradual process.

Papal Power and Papal Reform

As substantial as the theological and ritual differences between East and West had become by the 11th century, and as great as the cultural distance was that separated the elaborate and somewhat decadent civilization of the Byzantines from the plainer and still somewhat barbarous warrior culture of the Franks, the Church might have remained united indefinitely but for the imperial and ecclesial politics of the time. During the latter half of the 11th century, the Latin Church was governed by a succession of formidable popes, all of whom were committed to reform of the Western Church, regularization of its practices and a greater centralization of its authority.

The first of these reforming popes was Leo IX (1002–54), who was especially concerned to purge the Latin Church of clerical abuses, such as the buying of ecclesiastical offices ('simony'), or the appointment of clergy by secular rulers ('lay investiture'). He also wanted to eliminate 'Nicolaitism' – that is, married priests, or priests keeping mistresses. (The prevailing preference in the Latin West for a celibate priesthood was many centuries old, but it was not shared by all Western bishops; and since the Greek and Syrian East had a married priesthood, Rome could not claim the custom of priestly celibacy as some sort of universally binding 'doctrine'.) Leo knew he would accomplish nothing, though, without first strengthening the papacy. One of the advisors he appointed was his old and trusted friend Humbert of Silva Candida (*c.*1000–61), a scholar fluent in Greek, a Benedictine monk and preacher, and an implacable champion of universal papal jurisdiction.

A bull promulgated in 1052 by Leo IX. To further his programme of reform, Leo appointed allies as cardinals and convened a consistory of advisors (forerunner of the College of Cardinals formed in the 12th century).

The Emperor, the Pope, the Legate and the Patriarch

When Leo became pope in 1049, the throne in Constantinople was occupied by Constantine IX Monomachus (980–1055), a somewhat feckless man who had

A mosaic from Hagia Sophia, Istanbul, showing Christ flanked by the Empress Zoe and Emperor Constantine IX Monomachos. When she married Constantine, Zoe was already the influential widow of two former Byzantine rulers, Romanos III Argyros and Michael IV.

assumed power by marrying the Empress Zoe (*c.*978–1042). His principal accomplishments as emperor were to expand the University in Constantinople and to foster a renaissance of Byzantine arts and letters. Yet he also squandered immense portions of the imperial treasury on lavish building projects and various other extravagances, for the catastrophic economic effects of which he attempted to compensate by drastically reducing the military. As a result, he was unprepared to respond effectively to the insurrections that his profligacy provoked, or to the advance of the Seljuq Turks into Byzantine Armenia, or to the Patzinak invasions of Macedonia and Bulgaria, or to the Norman conquest of Byzantine Calabria.

The last of these – the Norman rampage through the south of Italy – was also a problem for Leo, not only because of the damage it inflicted on the Italian Church, but also because of the threat it posed to Rome. Leo petitioned the Holy Roman Emperor Henry III (1017–56) for military assistance; but Henry provided nothing. Leo, though, was resolved to launch a campaign against the Normans, and so sent an entirely inadequate papal army, which was defeated in June 1053. Leo was seized by the Normans and held hostage for nine months. On his release, he decided to send a delegation to Constantinople to investigate the possibility of an alliance with the Byzantines; and, as part of this embassy, he sent Humbert.

Constantine had already attempted to strike an alliance with the pope against the Normans, and had shown himself willing to make considerable concessions to Rome. He had been impeded in his designs, however, by the extremely influential patriarch of Constantinople Michael Cerularius (*c.*1000–59). As intent as Leo was upon asserting Rome's universal authority in the Catholic world, Cerularius was equally intent upon maintaining the autonomy of his see. In 1052, partly in response to the emperor's overtures to Rome, Cerularius had issued a number of

1049
Leo IX becomes pope (until 1054), and instigates a programme of Church reform

1054
(16 July) Papal legates from Rome instigate the Great Schism by issuing a bull against the patriarch of Constantinople

1067
The Seljuq Turks under Alp Arslan invade Asia Minor and capture the city of Caesarea Cappadocia

1071
(9 August) Byzantine forces are routed by the Seljuq Turks at the Battle of Manzikert near Lake Van in Armenia. Emperor Romanos IV is taken prisoner

1073
Hildebrand, a monk, ascends St Peter's throne as Pope Gregory VII

1074
Priests in the Latin Church are forbidden to marry

1075
Gregory VII proclaims his *Dictatus Papae*, 27 points of principle establishing the precedence of spiritual over secular authority

1076
At the Synod of Worms, Henry IV declares Gregory VII deposed

1077
Holy Roman Emperor Henry IV makes a penitential journey to beg absolution from Pope Gregory VII at Canossa, in the 'Investiture Controversy'

public attacks upon the doctrinal 'errors' and 'innovations' of the Roman Church. He may also have suppressed the Latin rite in his diocesan territories, though historians are not entirely certain of this.
To Cerularius' denunciations of the Latins, at any rate, Humbert had written a searingly rancorous response in 1053 entitled 'Against the Calumnies of the Greeks', in which he had argued vehemently for the authority of Rome over all Christian communions, as well as for papal sovereignty over all of the lands of the old Western empire (drawing, in the latter case, upon the 'Donation of Constantine', a forged document falsely ascribed to Constantine the Great). Leo's choice, then, of Humbert as his chief legate to Constantinople in 1054 was an act of either surpassing boldness or inconceivable folly (or perhaps both).

The Excommunications

When the papal legation arrived in Constantinople, Humbert and his two fellow legates delivered an insultingly imperious 'papal letter' to the patriarchal palace. The proud and irascible Cerularius took umbrage and refused thereafter to recognize or receive the legates. And Humbert – an intemperate and obstinate man at the best of times – made matters worse with his infantile antics during his public debates with the theologians of Constantinople: his method of debate consisted almost exclusively in strident demands for total submission by the Byzantines to the Roman pontiff and histrionic tirades against Greek doctrines and practices.

As it happened, Leo had died soon after dispatching the embassy to Constantinopole, and it is arguable that the legation's authority had expired with him; but he had also granted Humbert *carte blanche* in the form of a papal bull, to be used as the legates saw fit, and Humbert chose to exploit the papal interregnum to 'resolve' matters once and for all. Furious at the Byzantines for refusing to yield to his arguments either for papal supremacy or for any other of the Latin doctrines in dispute, and in a fit of pique over the patriarch's continued refusal to acknowledge the Latin embassy, he and his fellow legates strode into Hagia Sophia on Friday, 16 July 1054, during the Eucharistic celebration, and placed a bull on the altar 'excommunicating' Cerularius and his clergy.

Cerularius – already disposed to see the papal representatives as insolent barbarians – was predictably contemptuous of their behaviour, and simply 'excommunicated' the legates in turn. Such was his sway with the people, moreover, that Constantine IX had no choice but to assent to the patriarch's decision.

As for Humbert, he went on to serve as an advisor to several more popes, and in 1059 was partly responsible for forging a firm papal alliance with the Normans.

THE GREAT REFORMER

It was in the second half of the 11th century that the 'monarchical papacy' of the later Middle Ages emerged, as a result of the reforms inaugurated by Leo IX and continued by several of his successors. This would not in all likelihood have been possible had Rome not broken with the Eastern Church.

One of the popes who did much to advance the project of a reformed papacy – though his pontificate lasted little more than half a year – was Leo's cousin (and one of the Constantinople legates in 1054) Stephen IX (*c.*1000–58). He was a staunch advocate of priestly celibacy and the universal jurisdiction of the pope, and convened a synod to deal with the problem of simony.

The man who did the most to reform the Latin Church in the 11th century, however, was Pope Gregory VII (*c.*1020–85) – better remembered, perhaps, by his given name, Hildebrand. His measures to eradicate simony were relentless, he did not hesitate to depute papal legates to overrule restive bishops in their own dioceses, and he strove to suppress all liturgical usages in the West other than the Roman rite.

Gregory VII's resolve proved that so long as the pope was believed to hold the souls of all baptized persons in his power, no prince was wise to defy him.

His chief accomplishment, however, was to demonstrate the true extent of papal power. This he did in the course of the 'investiture controversy' that set Gregory at odds with the German King Henry (1050–1106), who later became the Holy Roman Emperor Henry IV. A papal synod of 1075 condemned the practice of lay investiture and excommunicated five of Henry's personal counsellors.

Backed by bishops from Germany and northern Italy, Henry defied the papal legates and convoked a synod of his own, which declared Gregory deposed. Gregory responded not only by excommunicating Henry (and his synod), but by declaring Henry deposed and his subjects absolved of all obedience to their monarch. Henry's support collapsed.

In January 1077, on his way to a meeting of nobles in Augsburg, Gregory heard that Henry had entered Italy, and so withdrew to the safety of the Tuscan castle of Canossa. Henry had come, however, as a penitent, and for three days stood barefoot in the snow outside Canossa, imploring the pope for forgiveness. Gregory at last relented. Henry's act of penance has gone down in history as the 'walk to Canossa'.

THE AFTERMATH

Communion between Eastern and Western Christians continued in some places, ceased in others, and gradually faded as the schism of 1054 became fixed in popular memory as some kind of defining event. Ultimately, of course, where Byzantine traditions prevailed – Greece, Syria and the Balkans – so did communion with Constantinople; where Latin traditions prevailed, so did communion with Rome. But the schism cannot really be located at any precise point in history; it is something that 'happened' but that never precisely 'occurred'. It came to pass in some ways much earlier, and in others much later, than 1054.

THE EARLY CRUSADES

The idea of a 'holy war' is alien to Christian theological tradition. It is self-evidently incompatible with the recorded teachings of Christ, and would have been abhorrent to the mind of the ancient Church. Of course, Christian rulers – such as Justinian and Charlemagne – had often enough shown themselves willing to coerce 'faith' from their more intractable subjects, for the sake of state unity. But none, as far as we know, ever presumed to represent his military adventures as divine missions.

At the very end of the 11th century, however, the notion that a war might be not merely 'just', but also a 'sacred cause', insinuated itself into Catholic thought. Ironically enough, this was in part the result of a concerted effort on the part of the Church to discourage and limit warfare. From the late tenth to the mid-11th century, Church synods in France had instituted the convention called the 'Peace of God', which threatened excommunication for private wars and attacks upon women, peasants, merchants, clergy or other non-combatants, and which required every house to pledge itself to preserve the peace. Other synods, over the course of the 11th century, introduced the 'Truce of God', which prohibited armed conflict on so many days of the year – penitential periods, holy days, harvests, and from Wednesday evening to Monday morning every week – that ultimately more than three-quarters of the calendar were off limits.

High Ideals and Low Motives

It may seem somewhat ironic, then, that it was at the Council of Clermont in 1095 – which reaffirmed and expanded the Truce of God – that Pope Urban II (*c.*1035–99) called for the First Crusade. But chief among the guiding ideals of the Truce was a commitment to protect the defenceless against the depredations of violent men, and Urban was responding to tales coming from the East of Christians (native Easterners and Western pilgrims to the Holy Land) who had been robbed, enslaved and murdered by the Seljuq Turks, as well as to the appeals of the Byzantine Emperor Alexius I Comnenus (1057–1118) for military aid in resisting Seljuq aggressions in the Eastern Christian world – Anatolia, Armenia, Byzantine Asia Minor and West Syria.

The capture of Antioch during the First Crusade on 3 June 1098, from a manuscript illumination. This crusade's journey across Asia Minor had been bloody and arduous; from an original force of 100,000, only 40,000 made it to the gates of Antioch.

The cause of Crusade, however, attracted an element that in all likelihood the pope had not expected. Rather than armies of the chivalrous and saintly eager to rescue the oppressed, many of the forces that assembled consisted in little more than armed gangs of brigands. Several of these, in fact, began their journey by robbing and murdering Rhineland Jews in their thousands in 1096, and even attacking local bishops who attempted to protect the Jews within their diocesan boundaries – and then, as a rule, disbanding before ever actually reaching the East.

The properly organized crusader armies, however, were under the command principally of French noblemen, and began a more orderly eastward advance in

August 1096. In all, some 4000 knights assembled in Constantinople in 1097, bringing with them between 20,000 and 30,000 foot soldiers. Alexius, fearing with good cause that his new allies might ultimately prove as dangerous as his enemies, insisted that the knights swear to restore to the Eastern empire all Byzantine territories they might liberate.

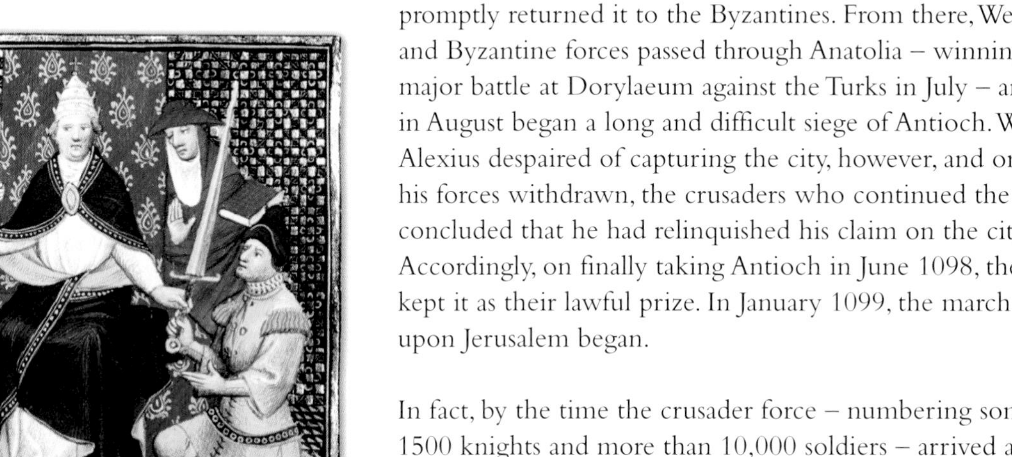

Pope Urban called for the conquest of 'Tierra Santa' at the Council of Clermont in 1095, thus instigating the First Crusade.

In June 1097, the crusaders recovered Nicaea from the invaders and indeed promptly returned it to the Byzantines. From there, Western and Byzantine forces passed through Anatolia – winning a major battle at Dorylaeum against the Turks in July – and in August began a long and difficult siege of Antioch. When Alexius despaired of capturing the city, however, and ordered his forces withdrawn, the crusaders who continued the siege concluded that he had relinquished his claim on the city. Accordingly, on finally taking Antioch in June 1098, they kept it as their lawful prize. In January 1099, the march upon Jerusalem began.

In fact, by the time the crusader force – numbering some 1500 knights and more than 10,000 soldiers – arrived at Jerusalem, the Seljuqs had already been driven out by the Egyptian Fatimids. This did not deter the crusaders, however. The siege lasted from early June to mid-July. When at last the walls were breached, the Norman commander Tancred of Hauteville (d.1112) promised protection for the city's inhabitants; but the crusader army disregarded his orders and – on entering the city – indiscriminately massacred Muslims, Jews and Arab Christians, not sparing women and children. The scale of the atrocity can scarcely be exaggerated.

Thereafter, a crusader protectorate was established in Jerusalem, which by late 1100 had evolved (or degenerated) into the Kingdom of Jerusalem under Baldwin I (*c.*1058–1118). Other crusader states were founded and castles erected as Beirut, Acre (modern Akko in northern Israel) and other cities fell and new crusaders arrived from the West. In this way, Western European feudalism was imported into the Near East and parts of North Africa, and feudal realms were established from the Euphrates to the Levant, and even in Tripoli. Nor did the crusaders hesitate to seize Byzantine territories, such as the port of Latakia, or to anger the Eastern Church by establishing Latin rather than Greek patriarchs in Antioch and Jerusalem.

Warfare and Cultural Interaction

Viewed as a whole, the Crusades were a sporadic undertaking, and largely pointless. Their chief function, it sometimes seemed, was to provide an outlet – in an age when the population of Western Europe had drastically increased – for the energies of the fading warrior caste of the last Western barbarians. They did,

THE ALBIGENSIAN CRUSADE

Not every Crusade was waged in the Holy Land. One was fought in France. During the 12th and 13th centuries, the church of the 'Albigensians' or 'Cathars' (from the Greek for 'pure ones') appeared in the south of France and in Italy. This was a sect of Gnostics who derived their teachings from the Bogomils of the East, a cult that began in Bulgaria in the 10th century and survived in the Christian East into the 15th. The Cathars regarded the material world as the creation of the devil, foreswore procreation, believed the universe a prison in which spirits were incarcerated through successive incarnations, held traditional Christian teachings in contempt and sought salvation through inner enlightenment and asceticism. They also led peaceable and sober lives.

When St Dominic (1170–1221) disputed with the Albigensians, legend recounts that both parties threw their books onto a fire; while those of the Cathars were consumed, Dominic's were miraculously spared.

Initially, Pope Innocent III (c.1160–1216) pursued a policy towards the Cathars of toleration and dialogue. But certain noble houses in the Languedoc region embraced the Cathar cause in the late 12th century and began in some cases to persecute the Catholic Church in their estates. The Comte de Foix, for example, evicted monks from their abbey in Pamiers, desecrated the chapel and seized the property for himself. The Vicomte de Béziers plundered and burned monasteries, imprisoned a bishop and an abbot, and – when the latter died – had his body propped up in a public pulpit. The Comte de Toulouse, Raymond VI, persecuted monks, sacked churches and conspired in assassinating a papal legate.

Innocent, unprepared for the crisis, began actively to promote the French crown's 'Crusade' against the south. For all its violence, however, this campaign proved largely ineffectual. It turned out to be little more than an excuse for the king of France to subdue Toulouse and the rest of the south, and for the nobles of the Norman north to steal southern fiefs from Catholic and Albigensian houses alike.

Finally, Pope Innocent IV (d.1254) – in part at the behest of King Louis IX of France (1214–70) – instituted a legal measure drawn from pre-Christian Roman law, contrary to Christian usage, but recently revived by the Holy Roman Empire: an inquisition. This succeeded where the 'Albigensian Crusade' had failed, and ultimately eradicated the Cathars.

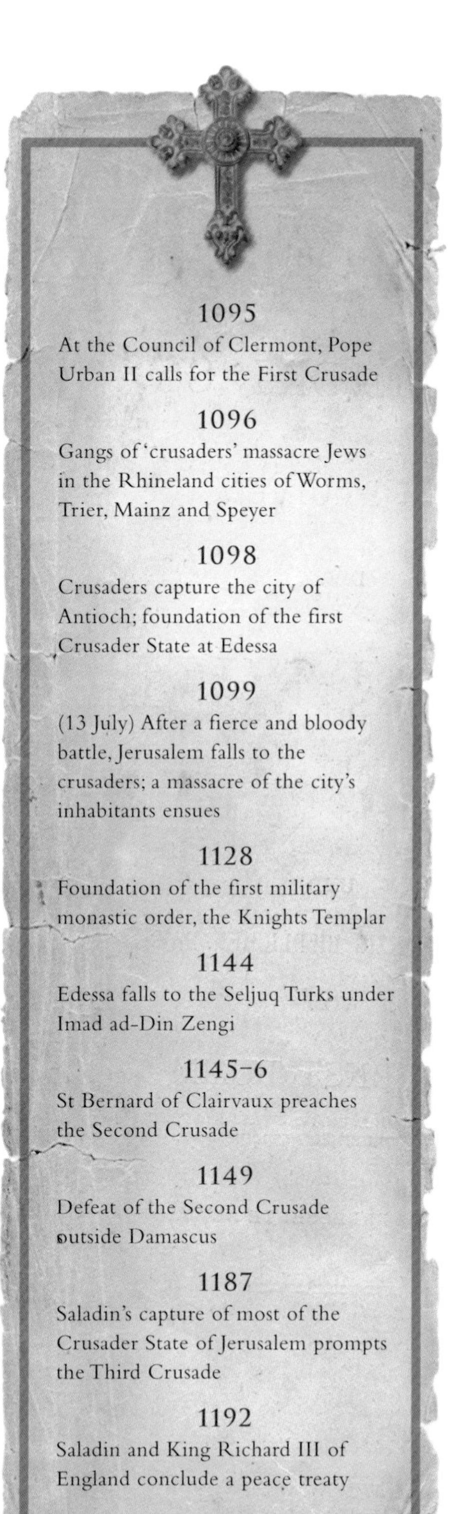

1095
At the Council of Clermont, Pope Urban II calls for the First Crusade

1096
Gangs of 'crusaders' massacre Jews in the Rhineland cities of Worms, Trier, Mainz and Speyer

1098
Crusaders capture the city of Antioch; foundation of the first Crusader State at Edessa

1099
(13 July) After a fierce and bloody battle, Jerusalem falls to the crusaders; a massacre of the city's inhabitants ensues

1128
Foundation of the first military monastic order, the Knights Templar

1144
Edessa falls to the Seljuq Turks under Imad ad-Din Zengi

1145–6
St Bernard of Clairvaux preaches the Second Crusade

1149
Defeat of the Second Crusade outside Damascus

1187
Saladin's capture of most of the Crusader State of Jerusalem prompts the Third Crusade

1192
Saladin and King Richard III of England conclude a peace treaty

however, rather contrary to the intentions of the crusaders, establish a generally stable – if intermittently bloody – cultural and mercantile contact between Western Christendom and the civilizations of the East, both Byzantine and Islamic. This allowed for a certain degree of fruitful cultural and intellectual interaction between East and West.

The Second Crusade was inaugurated in 1145 by Pope Eugenius III (d.1153) and was preached by, among others, St Bernard of Clairvaux (1090–1153) in France and Germany. Two main forces – one under the German King Conrad III (1093–1152) and the other under the French King Louis VII (1120–80) – departed for the East in 1147. Conrad's army was all but annihilated by the Turks in Anatolia in October, but was joined in November by Louis' army in Nicaea the following month. After a visit to Antioch in March of the following year, where Raymond of Poitiers (*c.*1115–49) reigned, both Conrad and Louis retreated to Constantinople and – with the assistance of other German and French nobles – undertook an assault upon Damascus with a force of some 50,000 men. It was a disaster. In July, after a siege of a few days, the crusaders had to retreat before a far superior force of Turkish reinforcements.

The crusader principalities of the 12th century did not expand beyond the territories captured in the days of the first Western campaigns; but they seemed stable enough to tempt a certain number of Western Christians to emigrate from Europe to the East. The Western Christian rulers of the second generation often learned to speak Arabic, married native women and adopted many regional customs. In addition to the armies of the crusader kings, there were two military monastic orders that added to the impression of a secure and settled feudal order: The Knights Templar, formed in 1128 to provide protection for Christian pilgrims to the Holy Land, and the Hospitallers, formed in the 11th century with the express purpose of building and maintaining hospitals for pilgrims (and for others in need), but also 'militarized' in the 12th century.

> *'It certainly seems amazing that on a single day in many different places, moved in unison by a violent inspiration, such massacres should have taken place, despite their widespread disapproval and their condemnation as contrary to religion. But we know that they could not have been avoided, since they occurred in the face of excommunication imposed by numerous clergymen, and of the threat of punishment on the part of many princes.'*
>
> HUGH OF FLAVIGNY (*c.*1065–1140) ON THE MASSACRE OF RHINELAND JEWS IN 1096

A 19th-century engraving depicting crusader forces abandoning their siege towers after a failed assault on Jerusalem during the Third Crusade.

This illusion of strength, however, was shattered by Salah al-Din – or, as he was known by Western Christians, Saladin (1137–93) – the daring, devout and often chivalrous Kurdish-born sultan and general whose *jihad* (or holy struggle) against the Latin occupiers recaptured almost all of the kingdom of Jerusalem in 1187, taking the city itself in October. He allowed those Christians who were able to do so to ransom themselves for a modest fee. Only the city of Tyre resisted his armies.

The fall of Jerusalem prompted Pope Gregory VIII (d.1187) to call for the Third Crusade. This war acquired a certain glamour in later legend, principally because of the relations between Saladin and the English King Richard III (1157–99), both of whom were masters of the craft of war, and each of whom often seemed to want to outdo the other in displays of courtly gallantry (though both could also be quite ruthless towards their enemies). Richard, for instance, after retaking the city of Acre from the Muslims in 1191, grew impatient with negotiations for the exchange of prisoners and executed all of his Muslim hostages (along with their families). Even so, communications between Richard and Saladin were never broken off, and – when they had fought each other to a standstill – they signed a peace treaty in September 1192. Richard left the Holy Land a month later, and five months after that Saladin died peacefully in Damascus.

BYZANTINE ZENITH AND NADIR

For more than a thousand years after the time of Constantine the Great, the city of Constantinople was one of the great wonders of the world; certainly no city of the West could match it for sheer grandeur. And compared to the Christian Byzantine civilization of the East – which could claim an unbroken continuity with ancient Hellenistic and Roman culture – the kingdoms and empires of the West always seemed painfully unrefined, at least in Byzantine eyes.

During the 11th and 12th centuries, moreover, the Byzantine world enjoyed something of a cultural and intellectual renewal. But this was also the period when its decline as a military power began in earnest, under the pressure of Islam, the barbarian tribes of the East, and even Western Christian armies.

Symeon the New Theologian

The 'Byzantine Renaissance' was marked in part by a spiritual awakening – specifically, a renewal of the theology and practice of contemplative prayer. And no figure was more significant in this regard than St Symeon the New Theologian (*c.*949–1022), a monk, mystic and poet whose writings profoundly shaped Eastern Orthodox spirituality in later centuries. The title 'Theologian' is a very high honorific in Eastern Christian tradition, indicating a special knowledge of the mysteries of the Holy Spirit, and Symeon is one of only three persons to whom the distinction has been accorded (along with St John the Divine and St Gregory of Nazianzus).

'Do not say that it is impossible to receive the Spirit of God. Do not say that it is possible to be made whole without Him. Do not say that one can possess Him without knowing it. Do not say that God does not manifest Himself to man. Do not say that men cannot perceive the divine light, or that it is impossible in this age! Never is it found to be impossible, my friends. On the contrary, it is entirely possible when one desires it'.

St Symeon the New Theologian (Hymn 27, verses 125–132)

Symeon (whose given name was George) was a child of the aristocracy, and his family expected him to enter the service of the imperial court; they sent him to Constantinople at age 11 for his formal education. When, though, at age 14, he made the acquaintance of a monk of the Stoudion monastery called Symeon the Pious, he placed himself under the older man's spiritual guidance. He did not immediately abandon his secular studies, but when he was 20 years old (or thereabout) he suffered the first of many intense mystical experiences, in which – in a state of inexpressible ecstasy – he had a vision of God as pure and eternal light.

He continued to pursue the career for which he had been educated, rising even to the rank of senator, but ultimately could not resist the call of the contemplative life. At 27, he entered the Stoudion monastery, taking his spiritual master's name as his own. His superiors, however, feared that his constant dependency on the elder Symeon's guidance might appear unseemly; and so they told him they would allow him to remain under his master's tutelage only if he would agree to live in another monastery.

The writings of St Symeon the New Theologian express his deep conviction that Christianity is rooted not in mere observances and outward form, but in a person's personal experience of the living Christ.

Symeon moved to the monastery of St Mamas, where in 980 he became abbot and led a revival of contemplative prayer among the monks. In 1009, though, well after his teacher's death, Symeon's disputes with the patriarch of Constantinople forced him to retire to a humble hermitage on the far shore of the Bosphorus. There disciples began to gather around him, drawn by his mystical discourses and by his personal example, and at his death he left behind him quite a sizeable community of monks dedicated to the life of mystical prayer.

Symeon's writings are daring in many respects. His descriptions of the mystical state – the rapture of union with God, the despondency of the return to normal consciousness – are effusive, opulent and often entrancing. He did not hesitate to use the frankest erotic imagery to portray the intimacy of the soul's union with God, or to employ metaphors of inebriation or romantic elation to describe the ecstasy of the soul seized by divine love. His greatest work is the *Hymns of Divine Love*, a collection of poems rich in the most extravagant metaphors, symbols and images and often extremely beautiful.

Scholars and Philosophers

The great rebirth of Byzantine learning encouraged by Emperor Constantine IX Monomachus (980–1055) had no greater champion than Michael Psellus (1017 – after 1078): a historian, rhetorician, philosopher, professor, legal scholar, scientific and medical encyclopaedist, occasional poet and statesman. As advisor to Constantine and succeeding emperors, it was chiefly Psellus who created the curriculum of the university in Constantinople, which was a marvel of comprehensiveness, variety and intellectual openness.

More than any other man, Psellus was responsible for the Medieval revival of serious philosophical studies in the Byzantine East. His special predilection for Platonism, moreover, led to the rise of the Christian – though not always entirely Christian – Platonism that became the

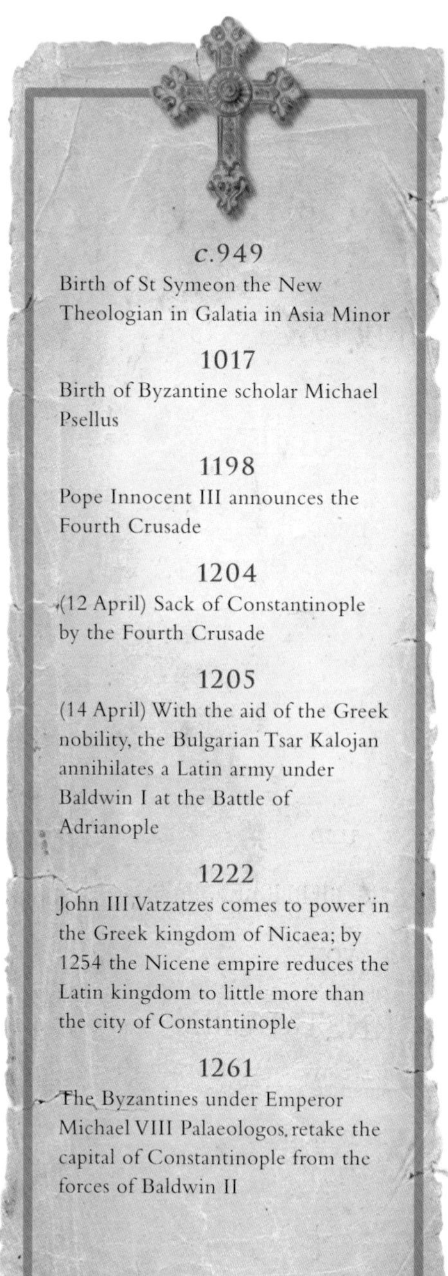

c.949
Birth of St Symeon the New Theologian in Galatia in Asia Minor

1017
Birth of Byzantine scholar Michael Psellus

1198
Pope Innocent III announces the Fourth Crusade

1204
(12 April) Sack of Constantinople by the Fourth Crusade

1205
(14 April) With the aid of the Greek nobility, the Bulgarian Tsar Kalojan annihilates a Latin army under Baldwin I at the Battle of Adrianople

1222
John III Vatzatzes comes to power in the Greek kingdom of Nicaea; by 1254 the Nicene empire reduces the Latin kingdom to little more than the city of Constantinople

1261
The Byzantines under Emperor Michael VIII Palaeologos, retake the capital of Constantinople from the forces of Baldwin II

THE 'CHILDREN'S CRUSADE'

One of the stranger stories to emerge from the age of the Crusades is that of the 'Children's Crusade' – a tale that owes more to legend than to historical fact. The story that was generally accepted for centuries was that a French or German child early in the 13th century claimed to have had a vision in which Jesus commissioned him to lead an army of children to the Holy Land to convert the Muslims not by force of arms, but by charity. Supposedly as many as 20,000 children joined the cause, expecting the Mediterranean to part before them so that they might cross over by foot. When the sea refused to oblige, however, wicked merchants in Marseilles offered many of the children free passage, and then sold those who accepted in the slave markets of Tunisia.

The true story appears to be more complex and less colourful. For one thing, the 'crusaders' were not in all likelihood children. What seems to be the case is that in 1212 two shepherd boys – a French boy name Stephen and a German named Nicholas – both claimed that Christ had appeared to them. The French youth claimed to have been given a letter by Jesus to be delivered to the French King Philip II (1165–1223) and, as he neared Paris, a large crowd gathered about him. The king, however, ordered the crowd dispersed. Some may indeed have set off for the Holy Land and ended up as slaves, but there is slight evidence for this.

The German shepherd boy, Nicholas, seems indeed to have intended to lead a Crusade to the Holy Land, and to have led thousands of pious souls into Italy. There, however, this crusader 'army' is thought to have fragmented into various contingents. Some may have gone to Genoa but failed to secure passage to the East. Others are said to have reached Rome – according to one version of the tale, Pope Innocent III gently absolved them of their crusader oath – and some may even have made their way to Marseilles and ultimate slavery. Again, though, there is no reliable evidence to that effect.

dominant intellectual tradition of Byzantine civilization in the later Middle Ages and that ultimately inspired the Platonist revival of the Western Renaissance. His devotion to pagan philosophy and his avid study of the religious and philosophical traditions of non-Christian peoples occasionally excited suspicions among certain citizens of Constantinople, and at one juncture he was obliged to issue a public profession of faith to reassure them of his orthodoxy.

The name 'Psellus' is a sobriquet meaning 'stammerer', perhaps given to him on account of some defect of his speech, even though he was an acknowledged master of the art of rhetoric. His eloquence is certainly evident in his extant writings, most particularly his *Chronographia*, a history of the Byzantine emperors from the late tenth through the late 11th centuries that is either (depending on how one reads it) a masterpiece of servile flattery and self-promotion or a wryly subversive satire on the hypocrisies of the court and society of Constantinople.

The Sack of Constantinople

During the 12th century, the rise of the crusader states and the growing presence of Latin Christians in the lands of the Christian East were, in the eyes of many

Byzantines, necessary evils at best, an intolerable menace at worst. And relations between the 'Greeks' and 'Latins' were rarely untroubled: the uneasy alliance between them was often punctuated by episodes of violent conflict. There had, moreover, been mercantile and strategic ties between the Byzantine throne and Venice from before the period of the Crusades that many Byzantines – out of financial self-interest, cultural prejudice, or religious intolerance – resented mightily.

By the last decades of the century, the situation was fairly grave. The emperor Manuel I Comnenus (1118–80), for instance, could hardly have been more favourably disposed towards the Latin West (even his first two wives were Latin Christians); but his attempts to forge and sustain ties with the West ultimately resulted in an increase in hostility between the two sides. In 1182, when Andronicus I Comnenus (*c.*1118–85) seized the Byzantine throne by force, a sizeable number of the native citizens of Constantinople celebrated by massacring the Western (mostly Italian) Christian men living in the city and selling their families to Muslim slave-traders.

The history of hatred between Greeks and Latins culminated in the tragedy – or travesty – of the Fourth Crusade. Called in 1198 by Pope Innocent III (*c.*1160–1216), this particular campaign never actually reached the Holy Land. Instead, the 'Crusade' degenerated into a mercenary expedition; involving themselves in a Byzantine dynastic struggle, the crusaders agreed to aid Alexius IV (d.1204) in capturing the imperial throne (which he thought his by right) in exchange for a large fee, additional troops for an invasion of Egypt and the submission of the Orthodox Church to the pope.

Pope Innocent III fiercely berated the crusaders who sacked Constantinople in 1204: 'How ... will the church of the Greeks return into ecclesiastical union and to a devotion for the Apostolic See, when she has seen in the Latins only an example of perdition ... so that she now, and with reason, detests the Latins more than dogs? As for those who were meant to be seeking the ends of Jesus Christ ... who made their swords, which they were supposed to use against the pagans, drip with Christian blood?'

In June of 1203, the crusader army attacked Constantinople and installed Alexius as emperor. He, however, lacked the funds necessary to pay for their services. The native Constantinopolitans, moreover, were enraged at the violence of the crusaders and at Alexius' agreement with them, and in January 1204 the new emperor was deposed by Alexius V Ducas Mourtzouphlus (d.1204) and executed by garrotte the following month.

On 12 April 1204, the crusader forces – weary of waiting for their pay – sacked the city of Constantinople, murdering unarmed civilians, raping women (including nuns), despoiling the churches and desecrating their altars. From this date until 1261 Constantinople was under the rule of a foreign army and its see occupied by a Latin 'patriarch'. The city would never recover from the crusaders' depredations; and the schism between East and West was now beyond all remedy.

THE HOLY ROMAN EMPIRE IN THE MIDDLE AGES

From the time of Constantine I onwards, the idea of a sacred Christian empire – and of a duly appointed emperor as the wellspring of all legitimate authority within Christendom – fixed itself in the lore of Eastern and Western Christian society alike. In the East, the Roman empire remained in some sense intact until the middle of the 15th century. In the West, though, with the rise of the barbarian kingdoms, the concept of a Christian emperor became somewhat more abstract.

Between 476 and 800, no one in the West could lay claim to the imperial title for himself. The only emperor there was resided in Constantinople, and his rule in the West – outside of the exarchates established under Justinian – was acknowledged only as a kind of legal formality (if it was recognized at all). For a thousand years, however, from 800 to 1806, the imperial dignity of Christian Rome was claimed by a single institution in the West: the Holy Roman Empire (which was never Roman, not always an empire and only rarely holy).

The Empire of the Franks

The term 'Holy Roman Empire' was coined in the 13th century, but the empire itself began on Christmas Day 800 with the coronation of Charlemagne in Rome. At that moment, the pope effectively transferred his fealty from the Byzantine emperor to the Frankish, and thus recognized the new empire as the true sacred polity of the Western Catholic world. This was chiefly a pragmatic act on the pope's part; he needed the military protection that the Franks could provide; but it also inaugurated a new imperial and ecclesiastical mythology that would shape the politics and religion of Western Europe for many centuries to come.

It also created the context for centuries of tension between the papacy and the empire. Under the old order, the emperor reigned because 'God' (for which one may read 'armies') had conferred the power upon him. No emperor had ever officially abandoned the ancient fiction that he ruled as the representative of the 'Senate and People of Rome' – a formula inherited from the old Roman Republic. But when the pope crowned Charlemagne, this quite unprecedented and as yet legally meaningless gesture seemed to suggest that the emperor derived his authority from the Church.

Internecine conflicts among the Franks after Charlemagne's death fortified the pope's position. Charlemagne's son Louis I 'the Pious' (778–840) took the imperial title he inherited from his father quite seriously, but his vassals were not always

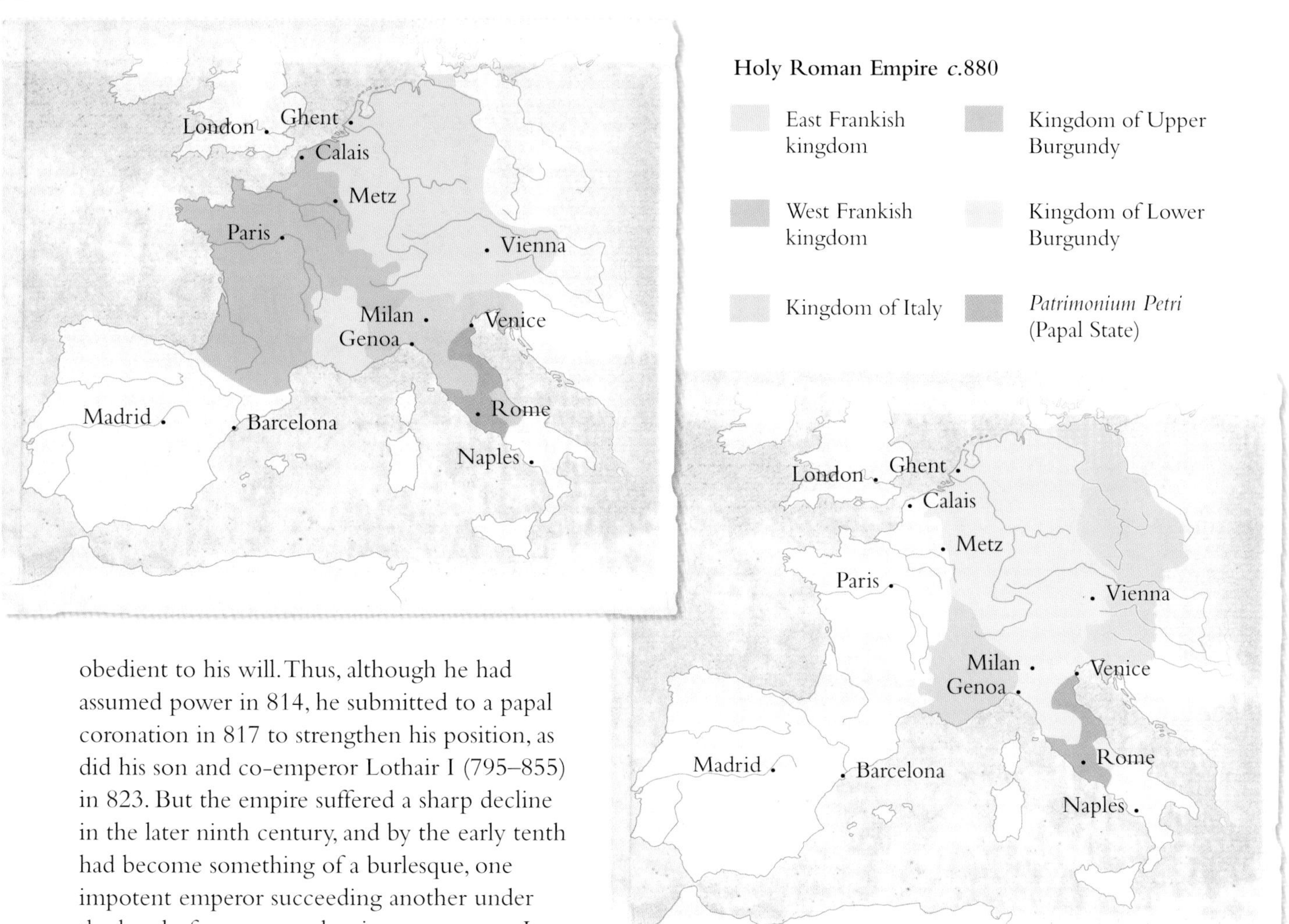

Holy Roman Empire *c.*1050

East Frankish (German) kingdom

Kingdom of Italy (in union with E. F. kingdom since 1004)

Kingdom of Burgundy (in union with E.F. kingdom since 1033)

Slavic principalities under E.F. sovereignty

Patrimonium Petri (Papal state)

obedient to his will. Thus, although he had assumed power in 814, he submitted to a papal coronation in 817 to strengthen his position, as did his son and co-emperor Lothair I (795–855) in 823. But the empire suffered a sharp decline in the later ninth century, and by the early tenth had become something of a burlesque, one impotent emperor succeeding another under the hand of one or another impotent pope. In 924, the title of emperor was entirely suppressed by the Crescentii, a noble Roman clan that did not care for rivals.

The German Empire

The empire, however, was only beginning. In 955, after his decisive victory over the invading Magyars, Otto I (912–73) – the Saxon king of Germany and liege of the kingdom of north Italy – was proclaimed emperor of the old Eastern Frankish empire. In 962, moreover, Pope John XII (*c.*937–64) – in desperate need of military protection from the king of Italy – confirmed Otto's title by crowning him in Rome.

The scope of Otto's empire – by comparison to Charlemagne's – was not vast. It comprised only Germany and northern Italy. The imperial title principally signified Otto's pledge to support and defend the papacy. The emperor did not even call himself 'Roman' as yet; that addition was made to the imperial title by Otto II (955–83) as a result of political tensions with the Byzantine emperor Basil II Bulgaroctonus (957–1025). And it was not until the reign of Conrad II (*c.*990–1039) that an emperor presumed to call his realm the 'Roman empire'.

The only emperor of this new 'Roman' order who seriously contemplated restoring the ancient Roman empire was the young and wildly self-deluding Otto III (980–1002), who had acceded to the throne when he was only three. He made

800
Coronation of Charlemagne in Rome by Pope Leo III

814
Charlemagne dies and is succeeded by his son Louis I the Pious

936
Otto I crowned emperor in Aachen; he bestows new power and wealth on the Church, making the *Reichskirchensystem* (State–Church system) the centre of his internal politics

955
Otto I wins a major victory over the Magyars at the Battle of Lechfeld

965
Harald Bluetooth of Denmark is baptized as the first Christian king of Scandinavia

1033
The unified kingdom of Burgundy and Provence is incorporated into the Holy Roman Empire

1075
Gregory VII's *Dictatus Papae* asserts the primacy of the Church, claiming that the imperial appanage and dignity were the pope's to confer

1152
Frederick Barbarossa becomes emperor (to 1190)

1220
Pope Honorius II crowns Frederick II Holy Roman emperor; his reign is marked by a protracted and bitter feud with the papacy

1254
Death of Conrad IV marks the end of the Hohenstaufen Dynasty

Rome his capital in 997, instituted extravagant court ceremonials on the Byzantine model, assumed a number of grand titles (among them 'Emperor of the World') and in 999 installed his ally Sylvester II (*c.*945–1003) as pope. His dream of world dominion was short-lived, however; an uprising in Rome in 1002 forced him to retreat to a monastery outside Ravenna, where he died while awaiting reinforcements.

Pope and Emperor

In the latter half of the 11th century, a succession of formidable popes helped to transform the papacy into a power capable of challenging an emperor. An alliance with the Norman kingdom of Sicily freed Rome from its former total subjection to imperial power. And there were many imperial subjects in Italy and Burgundy who disliked being ruled by a German and who naturally preferred to regard the pope as the true head of 'Roman' Christendom. The culmination of the struggle between pope and emperor was the 'Investiture Controversy' (see The Great Schism). Pope Gregory VII even went so far as to assert that the pope enjoyed complete supremacy over the emperor, and might depose an emperor if he saw fit.

Neither Henry nor any subsequent emperor ever granted the legitimacy of such claims. The Hohenstaufen Dynasty that ruled the empire – with only a brief interruption – from 1138 to 1254 generally supported its claim to imperial authority from the precepts of Roman Law, which the empire had recently revived in its own legal codes. According to the Hohenstaufens, imperial power was conferred by the diet of German princes, which elected the emperor as universal sovereign of the Christian people. The pope had no say in the matter, and papal coronation of the emperor was the seal – not the source – of that election.

In 1157, Frederick I Barbarossa (*c.*1123–90) adopted the title 'Holy Empire' for his realm, as if to suggest that it was sacred in and of itself. For much of the next century, the empire was engaged in a struggle to reassert its power in Germany and Italy, while the papacy was often intent on thwarting imperial designs. Frederick's son, Henry VI (1165–97), by his marriage to the Norman princess Constance, became king of Sicily and southern Italy and was able in some measure to reassert imperial claims in Italy. The last great Hohenstaufen emperor, Henry's son Frederick II (1194–1250), was for some years a successful and revered ruler; but, in the end, good relations with the German princes and with the papacy proved impossible to sustain, and after his death the empire in its Medieval form would survive only four more years.

When the imperial tradition began to re-emerge in 1273 – in a much altered form – it was under the rule of new dynasty: the Habsburgs.

THE GRAND EMPEROR

Of the many Holy Roman emperors, none was more remarkable – or had a more colourful reign – than Frederick II. Elected king of Germany at two, inheritor of the throne of Sicily at three, and crowned emperor at 22, Frederick's career was one of almost constant warfare – though not by preference. Born into the impossibly complicated politics of empire and papacy, and forced from an early age to fight to retain Sicily, his aim as emperor was to create a stable regime and good relations with Rome.

Frederick II (r. 1220–50) spent most of his reign fighting to retain or regain parts of his territories and attempting to establish a harmonious imperial order, agreeable both to the German diet and the pope.

He founded the University of Naples, formed a civil service, fostered trade, built a navy and attempted to reassert various imperial prerogatives in Italy (an aim frustrated by the powerful northern Italian Lombard League). At his coronation in 1220, he pledged himself to a Crusade, and in fact by his marriage to Yolande of Brienne in 1225 could claim the kingdom of Jerusalem as his own.

This Crusade was the occasion of his first contretemps with his erstwhile ally Pope Gregory IX (1170–1241), who for various reasons had turned against Frederick. When a contagion among his troops in 1227 delayed Frederick's departure for the Holy Land, Gregory accused him of procrastination and excommunicated him.

Frederick furiously denounced the pontiff but set off for the East in 1228, where he won Nazareth, Bethlehem and Jerusalem through negotiation with the sultan of Egypt. In 1229 he crowned himself king of Jerusalem – an act that, in the eyes of his admirers, marked him out as God's chosen ruler of Christendom.

Back home in 1230, however, he was obliged to drive a papal army out of Sicily; but by declining to reciprocate the pope's aggressions, he secured release from excommunication. His attempts further to fortify imperial power, however, were failures. Even his victory over the Lombard League in 1238 failed to secure the submission of all the northern Italian city-states. In 1239, the pope – fearing an invasion of Rome – once again excommunicated Frederick.

This led in 1240 to an imperial march upon the papal states, and probably only the pope's death averted the seizure of Rome. In 1245, however, Pope Innocent IV (d.1254) stripped Frederick of his imperial title at the Synod of Lyons. Thereafter the papal and imperial parties traded curses, but a series of unforeseen setbacks hampered Frederick's cause. His sudden death in 1250 ended the drama, though so large did he loom in the minds of his admirers that many refused to believe he had died – or, indeed, that he would not come again.

THE HIGH MIDDLE AGES

During the first millennium of Christian history, the eastern half of the Roman world enjoyed every advantage – demographic, economic and cultural – over the western. Moreover, in the long centuries of 'barbarian' government that succeeded the old Roman order, Western European society may have excelled in many practical technologies and in the arts of war, but by comparison to the Byzantine East it could scarcely be called a civilization.

In the second Christian millennium, however, Western Christendom came fully of age. The period extending roughly from the late 11th century through to the mid-14th is often – and justly – called the 'High Middle Ages'. It was a period of extraordinary cultural creativity (in part fertilized by increased contact with the Byzantine and Muslim East), demographic and economic expansion, and urban growth.

'When my whole soul is steeped in the enchantment of the beauty of the House of God, when the charm of many-coloured gems leads me to reflect, transmuting things that are material into the immaterial, on the diversity of the holy virtues, I have a feeling that I am really dwelling in some strange region of the universe which exists entirely neither in the slime of the earth nor entirely in the purity of Heaven.'

ABBOT SUGER OF ST-DENIS ON THE ARCHITECTURE OF THE ABBEY CHURCH OF ST-DENIS

CATHEDRALS

This period saw the rise of new architectural styles and new methods in the decorative arts; and the grandest achievements in both fields were the great cathedrals of the Middle Ages. The so-called Romanesque (or 'Norman style') cathedrals of the 11th and 12th centuries – with their barrel vaults and groin vaults, large supporting piers, rounded arches, massive carved façades and high roofs – were imposing structures. One need only visit some of the more impressive examples of the style – such as the cathedral of Pisa, whose construction began in 1064 – to appreciate how ingeniously and attractively Romanesque architecture could succeed in combining a variety of influences, and of blending the classical with the new.

The most glorious examples of Medieval architecture, however, were the great cathedrals built in the 12th century and after in the (misnamed) Gothic style. Massive as many of them were, they possessed a quality quite different from the heavy monumentality of Romanesque structures. They were so constructed as to allow as much light as possible to penetrate their interiors, and appeared almost delicate in form. Flying buttresses, apiculated 'ogival' arches, ribbed vaults and tall tenuous columns allowed for vast, high ceilings and numerous large window embrasures, allowing abundant sunlight to flow through their stained glass.

The apse of the Romanesque cathedral at Pisa in northern Italy, showing the mosaic of Christ Enthroned in Majesty *(1302) by the artist Cimabue.*

The earliest example of a large church in the Gothic style was the Abbey Basilica of St-Denis outside Paris, commissioned by Abbot Suger of St-Denis (*c.*1080–1151), almost as if to give tangible form to his own lyrical metaphysics of the divine light. The church was so splendid and so ethereal in its effect that it sparked an

EGO LUX
SUM MŪDI

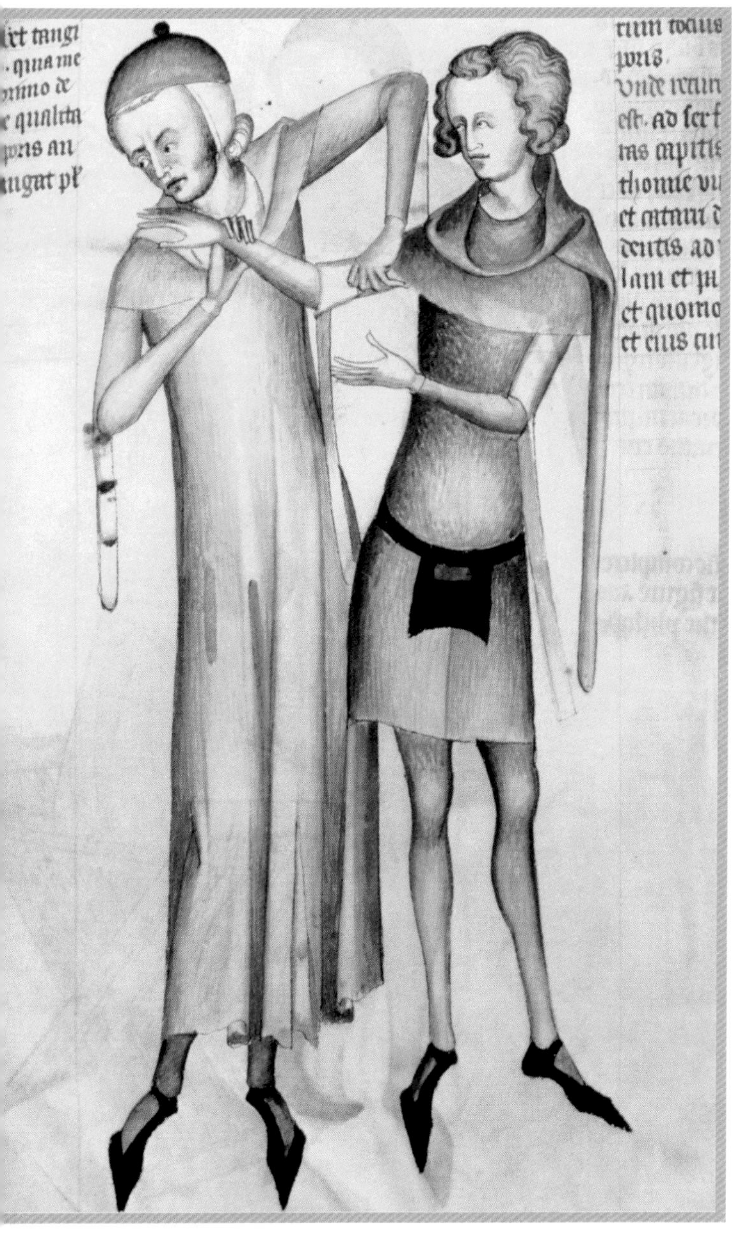

A doctor (left) taking the pulse of a student, in an illumination from a manuscript of 1345. The growth of universities from the late 12th century onwards promoted a flourishing of scholarship in the arts and sciences throughout Western Europe.

architectural revolution, first in France and then throughout Western Europe. It led to the magnificent French cathedrals of Notre Dame de Paris, Amiens, Rouens, Chartres, Bourges and others, and to many of the finest churches, chapels and cathedrals of Spain, Portugal, Germany, England and elsewhere.

Hospitals

One of the few benign consequences of the Crusades was the migration into Western Europe of the Byzantine model of the hospital, as well as of the more advanced medical techniques known to Byzantine, Syrian Christian and Muslim physicians. There was, of course, a long and honourable Christian tradition of building hospitals for the ill and destitute, in both East and West, generally as monastic establishments. The first public hospital in Western Europe was founded in the fourth century by the Roman noblewoman St Fabiola (d. *c.*399), who herself assisted in the care of its patients. But it was in the later Middle Ages that a great 'hospital movement' took shape. The Benedictines, for instance, obedient to the precepts of their founder, founded more than 2000 hospitals.

Perhaps most important for the rise of organized medical care in Medieval Europe was the Order of the Knights of St John of Jerusalem, also known as the Knights Hospitallers. Beginning in 1099, this order established a great number of hospitals in the Holy Land and in Europe – most famously, the immense Hospital of St John in Jerusalem. In addition to the traditional facilities of older Christian hospitals – shelters for the poor, hospices for the sick and dying, almshouses, food kitchens and orphanages – these establishments offered regimens of systematic diagnosis and remedy, and apparently even included areas of specialization, such as treatment of injuries and diseases of the eye.

> *'Tuitio fidei et obsequium pauperum' ['Defence of the faith and assistance to the poor'].*
>
> Motto of the Knights Hospitallers

One of the most important medical establishments of the 12th century was the Hospital of the Holy Spirit in Montpellier, founded in 1145, not only on account of its size, or of the quality of the care it provided, but on account of its role in training physicians. It was, in some ways, the first great teaching hospital of Western Europe and in 1221 it became the medical school of the University in Montpellier. By the end of the 13th century, a great many municipalities employed trained physicians for the care of the poor; and many of the best of these physicians were trained by the faculty in Montpellier.

Universities

Perhaps no accomplishment of the High Middle Ages was ultimately more significant for the later development of Western civilization than the cultivation of a new dedication to scholarship, not only in the abstract disciplines of philosophy and theology, but in the humane, natural, physical and theoretical sciences. From at least the time when the Cathedral School of Chartres reached its apogee, in the 11th and 12th centuries, the devotion of Western scholarship to 'natural philosophy' was pronounced. The bishop of Lincoln Robert Grosseteste (*c.*1175–1253), for instance, was the first known expositor of a systematic method for scientific experimentation. St Albert the Great (*c.*1200–80), the insatiably curious student of all disciplines, might justly be called the father of biological field research. He also undertook studies in mechanical physics, studying the velocity of falling bodies and the centres of gravity of objects; and he insisted that empirical experience – rather than metaphysical speculation – was the only sure source of true scientific knowledge.

Throughout the course of the 13th and 14th centuries, moreover, a number of Christian scholars began developing mathematical models by which to understand the laws of physical motion. Early in the 13th century, Gerard of Brussels ventured to measure the motion of physical bodies without reference to any received causal theories. After him, a succession of scholars in Oxford such as William of Ockham (*c.*1285 – *c.*1348), Walter Burleigh (1275 – after 1343), Thomas Bradwardine (*c.*1290–1349), William Heytesbury (*fl.* 1335), Richard Swineshead (*fl.* 1348), and John of Dumbleton (d. *c.*1349), while others in Paris such as Jean Buridan (1300–58), Nicholas Oresme (*c.*1320–82) and Albert of Saxony (*c.*1316–90) pursued the same course with ever greater sophistication.

Buridan, for instance, broke with several of the (erroneous) principles of Aristotelian science, developed a theory of 'impetus' and even ventured the speculation that the Earth might revolve on its axis. Oresme put forward the same hypothesis, fortified by even better arguments; his studies of physical movement allowed him to devise geometric models of such things as constant and accelerating motions, and also allowed him to answer objections from his critics to the theory of terrestrial rotation.

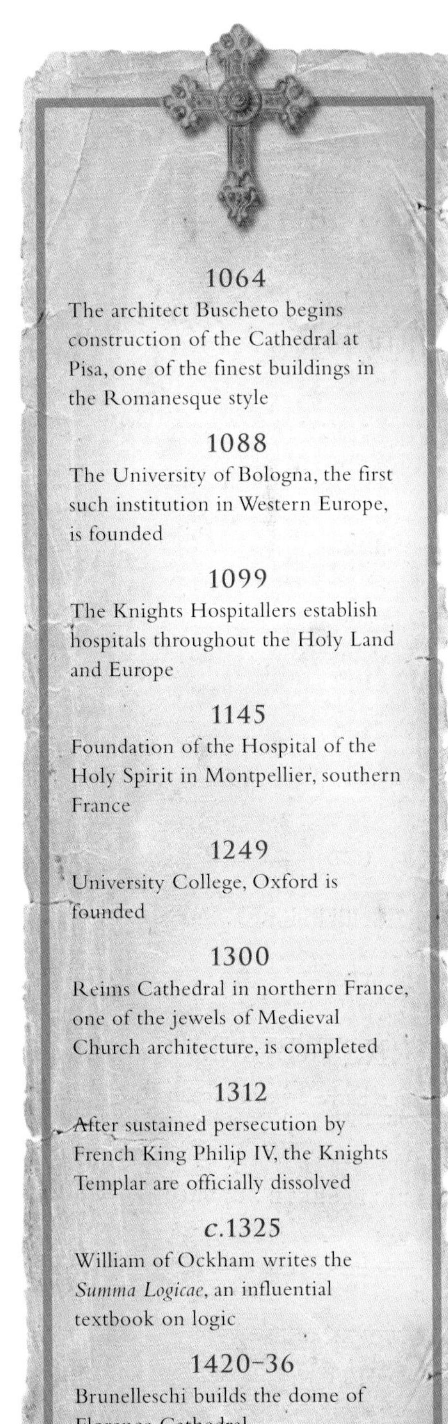

1064
The architect Buscheto begins construction of the Cathedral at Pisa, one of the finest buildings in the Romanesque style

1088
The University of Bologna, the first such institution in Western Europe, is founded

1099
The Knights Hospitallers establish hospitals throughout the Holy Land and Europe

1145
Foundation of the Hospital of the Holy Spirit in Montpellier, southern France

1249
University College, Oxford is founded

1300
Reims Cathedral in northern France, one of the jewels of Medieval Church architecture, is completed

1312
After sustained persecution by French King Philip IV, the Knights Templar are officially dissolved

c.1325
William of Ockham writes the *Summa Logicae*, an influential textbook on logic

1420-36
Brunelleschi builds the dome of Florence Cathedral

I COELVM CECINIT MEDIVMQVE IMVMQVE TRIBVNAL LVSTRAVITQVE ANIMO CVNCTA POETA SVO DOCTVS ADEST DANTES SVA QVEM FLORENTIA SAEPE
SIT CONSILIIS AC PIETATE PATREM NIL POTVIT TANTO MORS SAEVA NOCERE POETAE QVEM VIVVM VIRTVS CARMEN IMAGO FACIT

This fresco by Domenico di Michelino (1417–91), from the Church of Santa Maria del Fiore in Florence, shows Dante holding a copy of The Divine Comedy. *On the left of the painting is the entrance to Hell, while behind the poet rise the seven terraces of Mount Purgatory. The dome of the cathedral in Florence can be seen on the right.*

None of these studies would have advanced very far, of course, had it not been for the institution of the Medieval university. The first university established in Christendom – or perhaps in the world – was in Constantinople (849). The first true university in Western Europe, though, was probably that of Bologna in northern Italy, founded late in the 11th century. And the first major universities in the West were the late 12th-century universities of Paris and Oxford. Both taught theology and philosophy, law (ecclesiatical and secular) and the liberal arts. In the 13th century, the most notable foundations were those of Cambridge, Salamanca, Montpellier and Padua; and, in the 14th century, those of Rome, Florence, Prague, Vienna and Heidelberg.

Universities were principally ecclesiastical institutions, and dependent upon popes and princes for their charters. Even so, they not only tolerated but encouraged a remarkable freedom of inquiry and debate. They governed themselves, were legally and financially independent of their cities and were integrated with one another (i.e. they recognized each other's qualifications and certifications). And, since they all shared a common language – Latin – together they constituted a unified European intellectual community, transcending national boundaries.

THE DIVINE COMEDY

Among the literary monuments of the High Middle Ages, none is greater in scope and originality – or achieves a more comprehensive expression of all the spiritual, intellectual and social dimensions of its time – than the *Divine Comedy* of Dante Alighieri (1265–1321), the Florentine polymath, poet, classicist, political philosopher and (in his later years) champion of the imperial rather than the papal party.

Written in the 'vulgar tongue' – that is, Italian – rather than Latin, and composed when Dante was forced on account of his political sympathies to live in exile from his native city, the *Comedy* is an immense epic recounting the poet's journey through Hell, Purgatory and Heaven, beginning on Good Friday and ending just after Easter 1300.

In the first part of the *Comedy*, the *Inferno*, the poet finds himself in a dark wood from which ultimately he is able to pass over the border between this life and the next. The first part of his journey – for which his guide is the Roman poet Virgil – allows him to see the torments of the damned and even to converse with the spirits of those who have been imprisoned in Hell (including a certain number of persons he had known during their lives). It is in the *Inferno* that Dante's genius for dramatic characterization first becomes evident, especially in such episodes as the poet's meeting with Ulysses.

Many regard the second part of the poem, the *Purgatorio*, as the dramatically and spiritually richest, in large part because the souls Dante encounters upon the mount of purgation are not fixed forever in misery, as are the denizens of Hell, but rather are flawed persons engaged in a long and arduous process of spiritual regeneration.

Moreover, Dante himself participates in this process, slowly shedding many aspects of his past – including certain unworthy attachments – so that he might be prepared for the vision of Heaven. At the top of the mountain he finds the Earthly Paradise, where he meets and is gently chastened by the Lady Beatrice.

Beatrice was, in life, a young and lovely girl with whom Dante had little direct contact, and who died young, but with whom Dante was deeply fascinated; in the *Purgatorio*, she has been transformed into an allegorical figure of such radiant power that it is impossible to reduce her significance to any single symbol. And, since Virgil is a pagan who cannot enter Heaven, it is she who guides him on the final stage of his journey.

Dante's ascent through the planetary heavens to the divine empyrean beyond is the most dreamlike portion of the poem; the heavenly spheres are thronged with the spirits of saints and heroes, few of whom are as dramatically interesting as the souls Dante encountered below. But the poem ends when Dante – now under the guidance of St Bernard – is granted an ineffable vision of the divine Trinity, and the poem ends in an ecstatic failure of language.

REASON AND SUPERSTITION: MEDIEVAL CONTRADICTIONS

Western Medieval civilization reached its zenith in the 13th and early 14th centuries. Among the educated classes, it was an age that celebrated the authority of reason. But it was also a period of great violence, political and social, in which certain kinds of cruelty that Christian culture had traditionally forbidden (such as the ancient pagan practice of judicial torture) were revived, and certain kinds of gross superstition that Christian culture had traditionally suppressed (like a 'heathen' belief in and hysterical terror of black magic) re-emerged.

It was also a time of immense political and social transition. The great economic and demographic surge that had overflowed into the East at the beginning of the 12th century had, by the beginning of the 14th, clearly begun to abate.

The End of the Crusades

Over the course of the 13th century, the principal 'adventure' of the 12th-century West – the Crusades – died away in a prolonged diminuendo. The Fifth Crusade (1218–21), an ambitious invasion of Egypt intended to wrest Jerusalem from the sultan, failed through poor organization, and ultimately consisted principally in negotiations, culminating in a truce. The Sixth Crusade (1227–9) was a more impressive feat of negotiation – without military engagement – but succeeded only in gaining Frederick II the title of king of Jerusalem and in creating a decade of strife among the Christian barons of Cyprus and the Levant (and, anyway, in 1244 Jerusalem fell to Turkish forces).

> *'Then on Friday 18 May, 1291, before daybreak, there came the loud and terrible sound of the kettledrum ... the Saracens assaulted the city of Acre on every side... They came in countless numbers, all on foot; in front came men with great tall shields, after them men throwing Greek fire [a primitive form of napalm] and then men who shot bolts and feathered arrows so thickly that they seemed like rain falling from the sky.'*
>
> Anonymous Templar on the Fall of Acre to Mameluke forces in 1291

The Seventh Crusade (1248–50) was a large expedition into Egypt under the pious French king Louis IX (1214–70). Despite a few initial victories, such as the capture of the town of Damietta, the expedition was soon defeated, with Louis captured and ransomed for a huge sum. The Eighth Crusade (1270), also led by Louis, was putatively an attempt to save the Christians of the East (indigenous and Latin) from the monstrous ruthlessness of the Mameluke sultan of Egypt Baybars I (1223–77); but it was diverted to Tunis before ever heading east, and there was defeated not by arms, but by disease (from which the king and his son both died).

By the end of the century, the crusader states of the Holy Land had been destroyed. With the fall of Acre to the Mamelukes in 1291, the massacre

St Francis Receiving the Stigmata *(1440), by the Flemish painter Jan van Eyck. The monastic order that bears St Francis' name was founded in 1209, after he led his followers to Rome to seek an audience with Pope Innocent III.*

of most of its people and the enslavement of its survivors, the illusion that Western Christendom possessed either the power or a divine mandate to rule in the Holy Land was shattered.

Monks and Scholars

The 13th century was also marked by spiritual and intellectual movements – or, rather, movements at once spiritual and intellectual – that profoundly shaped Christian thought and piety in later centuries. Two important monastic orders, the Franciscans and the Dominicans, took shape and quickly developed distinctive traditions of theological and philosophical reflection that in many ways determined the main currents of later Catholic theology.

The Franciscan order, of course, sprang from the life and ministry of St Francis of Assisi (1181–1226), the fervent apostle of humility, poverty, service to the poor, love of all creation and Christ-like charity. Francis was a mystic, not a scholar; he

St Thomas Aquinas, from the Demidoff Altarpiece *(1476) by Carlo Crivelli. Thomas'* Summa Theologiae *was a magisterial investigation of all the principal elements of Catholic teaching.*

preferred the book of nature to books of philosophy, and was prone to visions and auditions; in his last years, his body was marked by the stigmata – the wounds of the crucified Christ – received during one such vision. But the Franciscan order's original spiritual impulse in no way prevented it from producing an intellectual tradition of great rigour, or scholars of considerable refinement.

St Bonaventure (*c.*1217–74), for instance, governor-general of the order from 1257 to 1274, was a university man and speculative theologian of enormous erudition who succeeded grandly in combining the mystical elations of Franciscan piety with the rational disciplines of academic philosophy. As a boy he had, he believed, been saved from death during a severe illness by St Francis, and on being certified a Master of Arts by the University of Paris in 1243 he repaid his heavenly benefactor by taking vows as a Franciscan and by continuing his studies in Paris at the Franciscan School. In his fully developed theology – expressed nowhere more exquisitely than in his brief, mystical and deeply metaphysical treatise *Itinerarium Mentis ad Deum* ('The Journey of the Mind to God') – he described a perfect integration of natural and supernatural wisdom, in a seamless ascent of thought from the empirical, through the theoretical, and finally into the contemplative knowledge of truth, culminating in the union of the soul with God in love.

The founder of the Dominican order, St Dominic (*c.*1170–1221), a son of the Castilian nobility, was first and foremost an evangelist, who began his mission preaching against the Albigensian church in southern France; it was his conviction that the gospel could be proclaimed convincingly only by those as willing to embrace a life of humility, poverty and sanctity as were the 'heretics'. His order in later years, though, put at least as great an emphasis on the need for a coherent and philosophically sophisticated defence of Christian doctrine.

The greatest figure in the Dominican intellectual tradition – and almost certainly the greatest Medieval Catholic philosopher – was St Thomas Aquinas (1224–74), the so-called 'Angelic Doctor', whose immense and extraordinarily varied oeuvre exhibits a philosophical range that sets it quite apart from any other of its time. There was also no more creative intellectual beneficiary of the late Medieval influx of translations of ancient philosophical texts and commentaries – particularly the works of Aristotle, which until then were almost entirely unknown in the West – from the Byzantine, Syrian Christian and Islamic East. Early in his studies, Thomas steeped himself in Greek patristic thought (in Latin translation), and he was able to create a brilliantly original synthesis of the Christian Neo-Platonism of the fathers (most importantly the Pseudo-Dionysius the Areopagite), Hellenistic and Arabic metaphysics and Aristotle. His special genius lay in his metaphysics of *esse* or being.

Thomas was a professor at the University of Paris and at the University of Naples and, obedient to the ethos of the Medieval university, his preferred style of reasoning was rigorously dialectical. His method in his major treatises was to pose a question, suggest an answer, present all conceivable objections to his answer as powerfully as he could, and then respond to those objections in order. His masterpieces – the *Summa Theologiae* and *Summa Contra Gentiles* – are models of lucid exposition and balance. Shortly before his death, though, a profound mystical

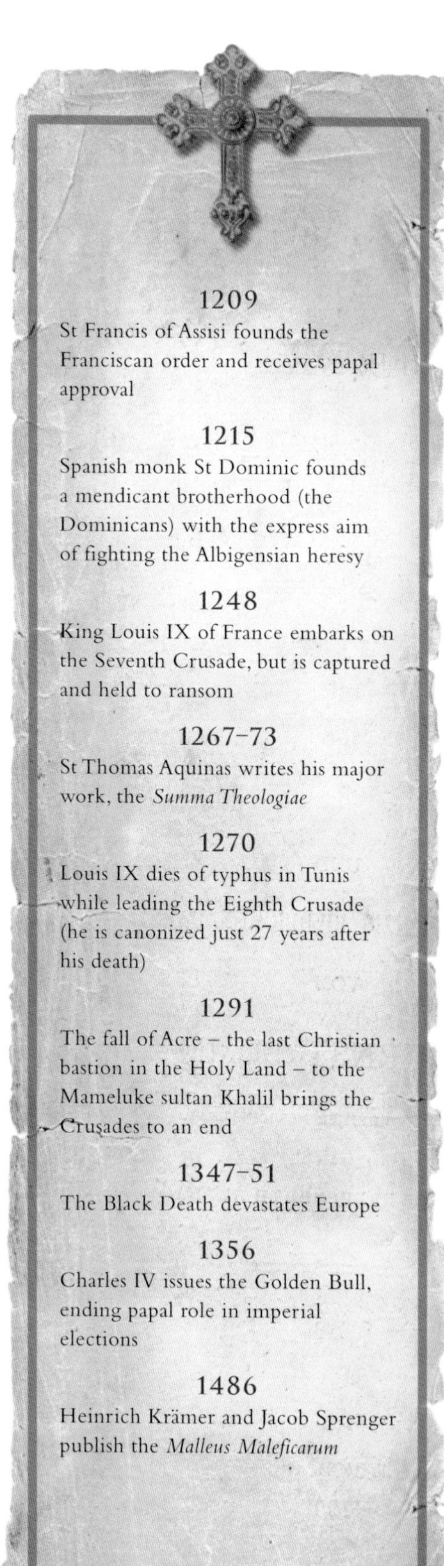

1209
St Francis of Assisi founds the Franciscan order and receives papal approval

1215
Spanish monk St Dominic founds a mendicant brotherhood (the Dominicans) with the express aim of fighting the Albigensian heresy

1248
King Louis IX of France embarks on the Seventh Crusade, but is captured and held to ransom

1267–73
St Thomas Aquinas writes his major work, the *Summa Theologiae*

1270
Louis IX dies of typhus in Tunis while leading the Eighth Crusade (he is canonized just 27 years after his death)

1291
The fall of Acre – the last Christian bastion in the Holy Land – to the Mameluke sultan Khalil brings the Crusades to an end

1347–51
The Black Death devastates Europe

1356
Charles IV issues the Golden Bull, ending papal role in imperial elections

1486
Heinrich Krämer and Jacob Sprenger publish the *Malleus Maleficarum*

experience left him (by his own account) with no desire to occupy himself further with 'names and forms'.

Witches and Diabolists

The late Middle Ages also saw the rise of a general belief in the reality of witchcraft. The old popular picture of the Middle Ages as a time of mad inquisitors burning thousands of 'witches' at the stake, though, is wildly inaccurate. For one thing, the true era of hysterical witch-hunting was the early modern period – the 16th and 17th centuries in particular – and, for another, secular courts were far more likely to prosecute and condemn suspected witches than were their ecclesiastical counterparts.

> *'They have slippery tongues, and are unable to conceal from their fellow-women those things which by evil arts they know; and, since they are weak, they find an easy and secret manner of vindicating themselves by witchcraft … All wickedness is but little to the wickedness of a woman. And to this may be added that, as they are very impressionable, they act accordingly.'*
>
> Heinrich Krämer and Jacob Sprenger, *Malleus Maleficarum*, 1486 ('Why Superstition is Chiefly Found in Women')

For most of the early and Medieval history of Christianity, the Church had ignored or dealt extremely leniently with 'magic' practices (which generally meant mere folk sorcery): usually a prescription of penance and reconciliation. Moreover, the Church had traditionally treated belief in the real efficacy of such magic as a pagan superstition; and those who reported extraordinary experiences of flying through the air or passing through locked doors were treated as, at worst, deluded. Lay magistrates, however, were not always of like mind. Pope Gregory VII (*c.*1022–85), for instance, was obliged formally to forbid the Danish courts to execute accused witches.

Nevertheless, in the late 13th century, a general belief in the existence of satanic covens began to spread and to insinuate itself into ecclesiastical culture. In 1374, Pope Gregory XI (1329–78) – reasoning that, since there is no real natural magic, any powers witches might actually possess must be the work of demons – allowed that witches might be tried by ecclesiastical courts as heretics. Pope Innocent VIII (1432–92) found rumours of a widespread conspiracy of child-devouring Satanists credible and in a bull of 1484 encouraged official investigations. In 1486, two Dominicans, Heinrich Krämer and Jacob Sprenger, printed the luridly ghastly *Malleus Maleficarum* ('The Hammer of Witches'), the infamous and influential manual of witch-hunting.

That said, not all clergymen were convinced. The bishop in Innsbruck, for instance, considered Krämer a deranged imbecile, thwarted his attempts to convict certain women in his diocese of witchcraft, and then had him expelled from the city. The same year that the *Malleus* appeared the Carmelite Jan van Beetz published an icily sceptical treatise on black magic. Ultimately, of all the institutions of its time, it was the Catholic Church that came most quickly to discount stories of witchcraft; and, during the witch-hunting hysteria of the 16th and later centuries, it was the Church (where it had the power to do so) that suppressed trials for witchcraft.

THE BLACK DEATH

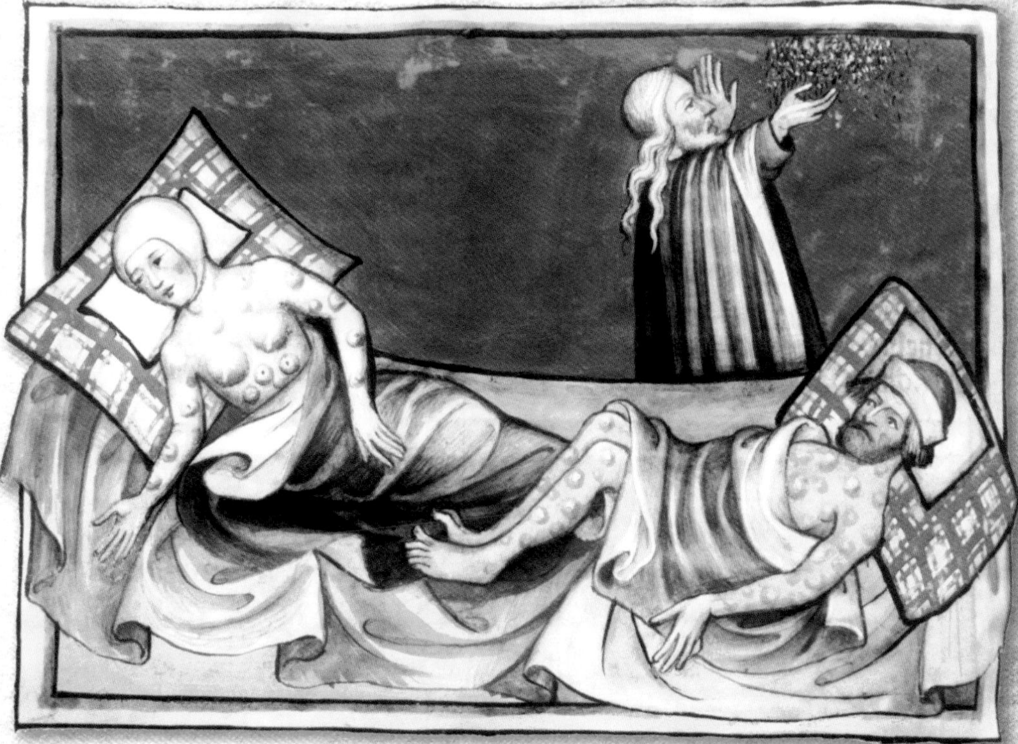

Victims of the Black Death. The devastation – social, economic and spiritual – wrought by the Plague was beyond all reckoning.

The long summer of the High Middle Ages – the period, that is, of Medieval Western civilization's most energetic creativity – gave way to autumnal decline for a great many reasons, but one stands out as the most decisive and most catastrophic: the arrival of the Black Death.

In 1347 a pestilence that had been ravaging Asia – bubonic plague combined (many historians believe) with pneumonic plague – entered Sicily on Genoese merchant ships returning from the Crimea; by the end of 1348 it had encircled the western Mediterranean, spreading to North Africa, Spain, Portugal and Italy, and had also reached France and England. In 1349 it spread to the Low Countries, German principalities and Hungary; in 1350 it reached the far north.

Infection brought certain and painful death, and since no one in the 14th century had any understanding of epidemiology, infection was impossible to prevent. The Black Death claimed millions of victims, from every social station: kings and queens, cardinals and archbishops, burghers and peasants all perished.

In some areas, Jews were made scapegoats and accused of inducing the disease by poisoning wells. In 1348, Pope Clement VI (*c.*1291–1352) had to issue a decree proclaiming their innocence and pointing out that they were dying alongside Christians.

During the last half of the century, there were five extended recurrences of the plague. By the beginning of the 15th century, it had claimed as many as 25 million lives: fully one-third of the population of Western Europe.

THE ORIENTAL CHURCHES IN THE LATER MIDDLE AGES

During the age of the Crusades, the ancient churches of the East that had severed ties with the imperial Church after the Council of Chalcedon (451), or that had simply over time become isolated from the rest of Christendom, were in many cases scarcely touched by the great events and movements of Christian Europe. Many, however, were profoundly affected by the coming of the Crusades, in some cases permanently.

The 'monothelite' Maronite Christians of Lebanon, for instance, not only allied themselves with the crusaders, as guides and soldiers, but in 1182 renounced their 'heresy' and accepted union with Rome.

Armenia

The Christians of Armenia, while unwilling to become Catholics, nevertheless had cause to be glad of the crusaders' arrival, at least at first. The eighth-century Muslim conquest of Armenia had in some sense liberated its people from Byzantine and Persian tyranny, and had allowed the Armenian Church to resist the attempts of the Byzantine Church to convert it to Chalcedonian orthodoxy with impunity. That said, Arab rule was on occasion quite harsh. And, in the late tenth century, as the caliphate declined in strength, the Seljuqs invaded and proved more cruel, voracious and destructive masters than their Arab predecessors.

An independent kingdom of Lesser Armenia was established in formerly Byzantine territory in 1080, a kingdom that over more than two centuries often found it convenient to make common cause with the Latins against the Turks. The crusaders, moreover, shared the Armenians' hostility to the Greeks. There were even marriages between the royal families of the crusader kingdoms and Armenia.

The alliance came at a price, however. Throughout the 12th century, the Latin Christians – who enjoyed the position of strength – pressed the Armenians to adopt the Chalcedonian formula and to submit to Rome. Negotiations regarding reunion were frequent, and in some cases seem to have been inspired by genuinely ecumenical motives: the Armenian Catholicos Nerses IV 'the Gracious' (1098–1173) advocated an ecumenical convocation of the Byzantine, Latin, Syrian, and Armenian Churches to seek a reunion of all.

In the 13th century, as a consequence of these talks, a schism erupted in the Armenian Church. A party of so-called 'uniates', led by the Catholicos Constantine I (d.1267), publicly adopted the Chalcedonian formula. Thereafter the Armenians were divided between the Westernizers and the traditionalists. Latin

Interior of the cathedral at Echmiadzin, the holiest city in Armenia and seat of the Catholicos, the head of the Armenian Apostolic Church.

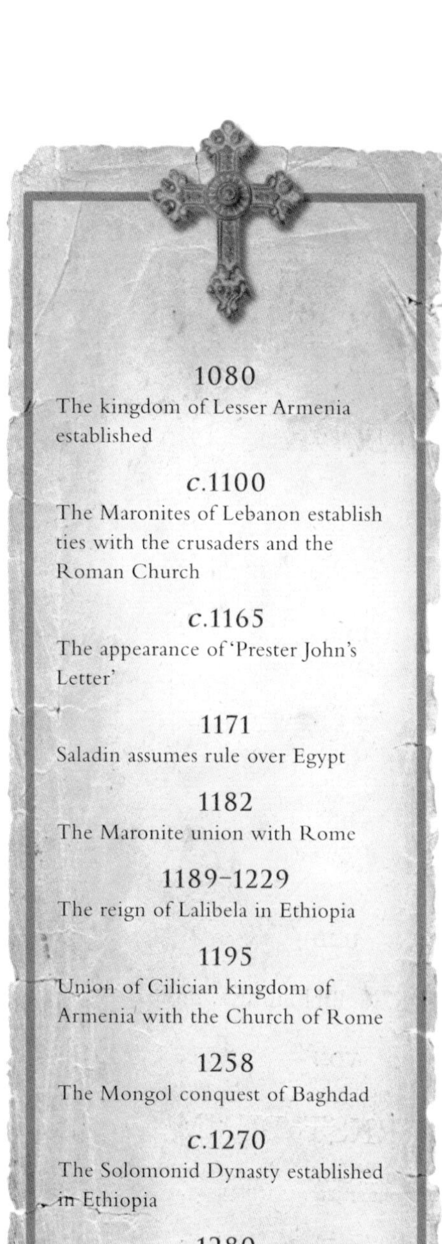

1080
The kingdom of Lesser Armenia established

c.1100
The Maronites of Lebanon establish ties with the crusaders and the Roman Church

c.1165
The appearance of 'Prester John's Letter'

1171
Saladin assumes rule over Egypt

1182
The Maronite union with Rome

1189–1229
The reign of Lalibela in Ethiopia

1195
Union of Cilician kingdom of Armenia with the Church of Rome

1258
The Mongol conquest of Baghdad

c.1270
The Solomonid Dynasty established in Ethiopia

1280
Yahbalaha III (Chinese Uighur) becomes patriarch of the Church of the East

1369
The Ming Dynasty comes to power in China

1439
Various official 'unions' between eastern churches and the Roman Church forged at the Council of Florence

missionaries were imported by the former, an alternative Catholicos was elected by the latter. Ultimately, however, the Armenians did not submit to Rome.

The Copts

The Copts of Egypt, like the Armenians, were relieved of Byzantine pressures to conform to the formula of Chalcedon by the Muslim conquests of the seventh century. The Arab invaders, unlike the Greeks, had no interest in suppressing the native religious culture of the Egyptian Church. The Coptic Christians were, nevertheless, reduced to a subject people, and on occasion were the victims of oppressions and violence. In general, though, they survived, and in many periods even thrived.

The age of the Crusades, however, was an unmitigated calamity for Egyptian Christians. Their Muslim rulers made no distinctions among different kinds of Christian, and it was not uncommon for them to suspect their Coptic subjects of secret sympathies for – or even conspiracies with – the crusaders. Of course, the Latin Christians harboured no love whatsoever for the Egyptian 'heretics'; the crusader kingdom of Jerusalem, for instance, barred them from entering the city as pilgrims to Christ's sepulchre. Nor were they well treated during the early reign of Saladin: they were forced to pay enormous and punitive taxes and to wear special garb to mark them out; they were forbidden even to mount horses; the cathedral of Alexandria was demolished, along with various churches and monasteries; signs of Coptic unrest were violently contained; and many of the Christians of Nubia (Coptic in faith) were killed or enslaved.

'Then Timur returned to Khorasan with the fixed purpose of taking revenge on the city of Seistan, whose inhabitants went out to him asking for peace and agreement, which he granted them on condition that they should hand over their arms to him ... And as soon as they had given this guarantee, he drew the sword against them and billeted upon them all the armies of death. Then he laid the city waste, leaving in it not a tree or a wall and destroyed it utterly, no mark or trace remaining.'

AHMED IBN ARABSHAH (1388–1450), *TAMERLANE OR TIMUR THE GREAT AMIR*

Conditions somewhat improved after Saladin's conquest of Jerusalem. But in the last years of the Crusades (the latter half of the 13th century) and long after, the situation of Egyptian Christians under the new sultanate, the Mamelukes, was often dire.

ETHIOPIA

The Christian empire of Ethiopia – though ecclesiastically united to the Coptic Church of Egypt – was largely isolated from the rest of the Christian world after the seventh century. However, protected as it was behind its vast mountain ranges, it remained impregnable to the Muslim armies that conquered Egypt and Nubia to the north. It had ceased to be a great mercantile power when it lost the Red Sea routes to Arab traders, and so had turned its diminished energies inward, away from the Eritrean Plain and southward from the Tigray Plateau, where it absorbed the lands and peoples of the East African highlands. One of these peoples, the Agew, were so well assimilated into Amharic culture that not only did they abandon their native tongue for Ge'ez and their native religion for Aksumite Christianity, they actually came to rule the Ethiopian empire, under the Zagwé Dynasty, from the late 12th to the late 13th centuries.

The greatest of the Zagwé emperors was Gebre Meskel Lalibela, who reigned probably from 1189 to 1229, and under whom, it is said, the 11 great granite churches in the Zagwé capital Roha (now called Lalibela) were built.

The Zagwés were overthrown in the late 13th century by the Amharic royal house from the Ethiopian kingdom of Shewa. Thus was born – or reborn – the 'Solomonid' Dynasty, so named because it based its claim to imperial power upon its supposed descent from King Solomon's son by the queen of Sheba, Menelik I. Much of the great literary, cultural, architectural and religious renaissance of Ethiopia's 13th and 14th centuries – though it had begun under the Zagwés – was an expression of the imperial mythology of Ethiopia as the new Holy Land, and of the Shewan emperors as the true successors of the Davidic line.

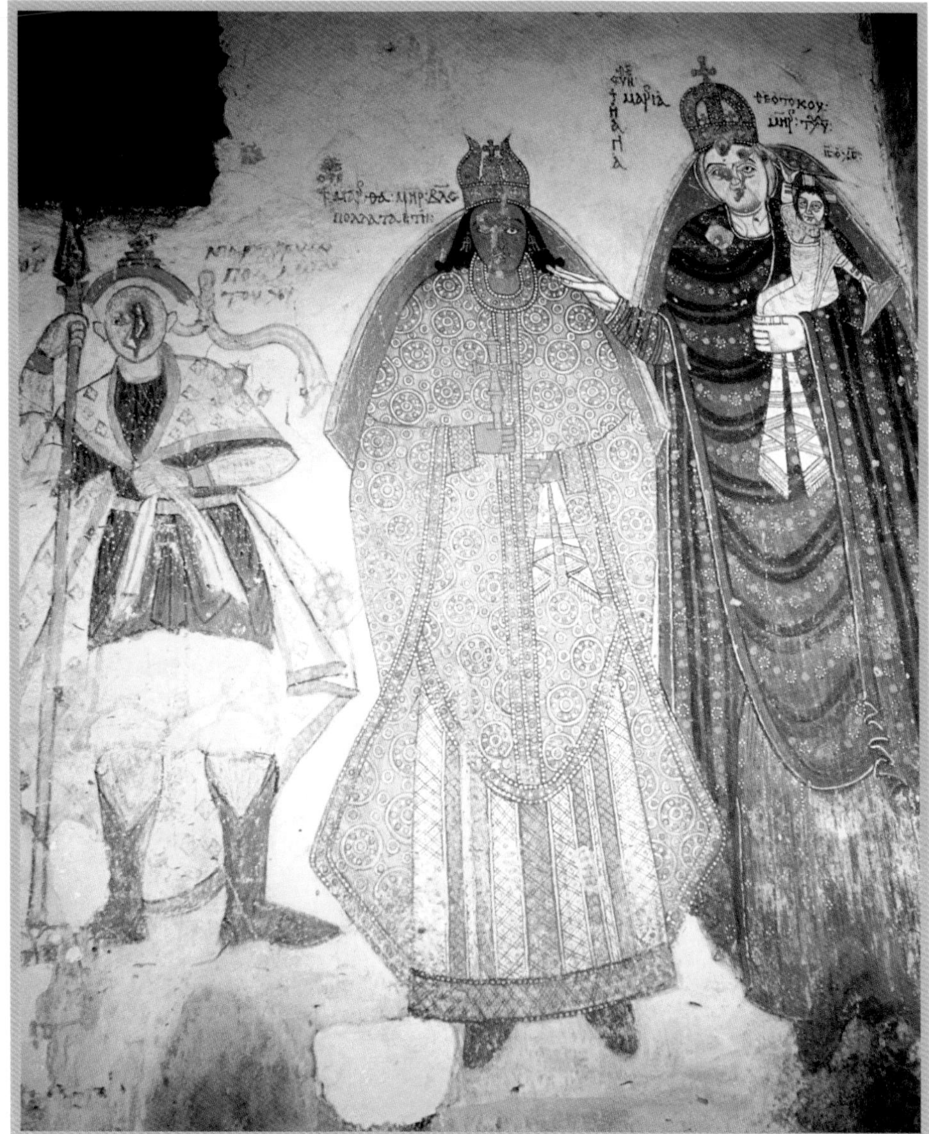

An early 12th-century fresco of Queen Martha of Nubia with the Virgin and Child, from the Basilica at Faras, the former capital of the northern Nubian kingdom of Nobatia (now in Sudan).

During much of the 14th century, Ethiopia was a considerable military power, engaged in an incessant struggle to prevent Islamic encroachments, and even to act as something of a protector of the Copts in Egypt. The emperor 'Amda Tseyon (r. 1314–44) established armed garrisons and conducted fierce campaigns in the more vulnerable south; and more than once he and his successors threatened to divert the waters of the Nile and so reduce Egypt to a desert if the Mamelukes did not desist from their persecutions of the Copts. And the emperor Zar'a Yakob (r. 1434–68) – among whose military achievements was the crushing defeat of the Adal sultanate's armies in 1445 – even threatened to invade Egypt.

The East Syrian Church

Of the Oriental communions, none suffered a more tragic history during the later Middle Ages than the East Syrian or 'Nestorian' Church. Though East Syrian scholars and physicians had for centuries occupied an honoured place in the caliphate, and though they had at times even been allowed to breach official restrictions on the building of new churches, still theirs was a subordinate community, and in the 12th century they were subjected to many of the same

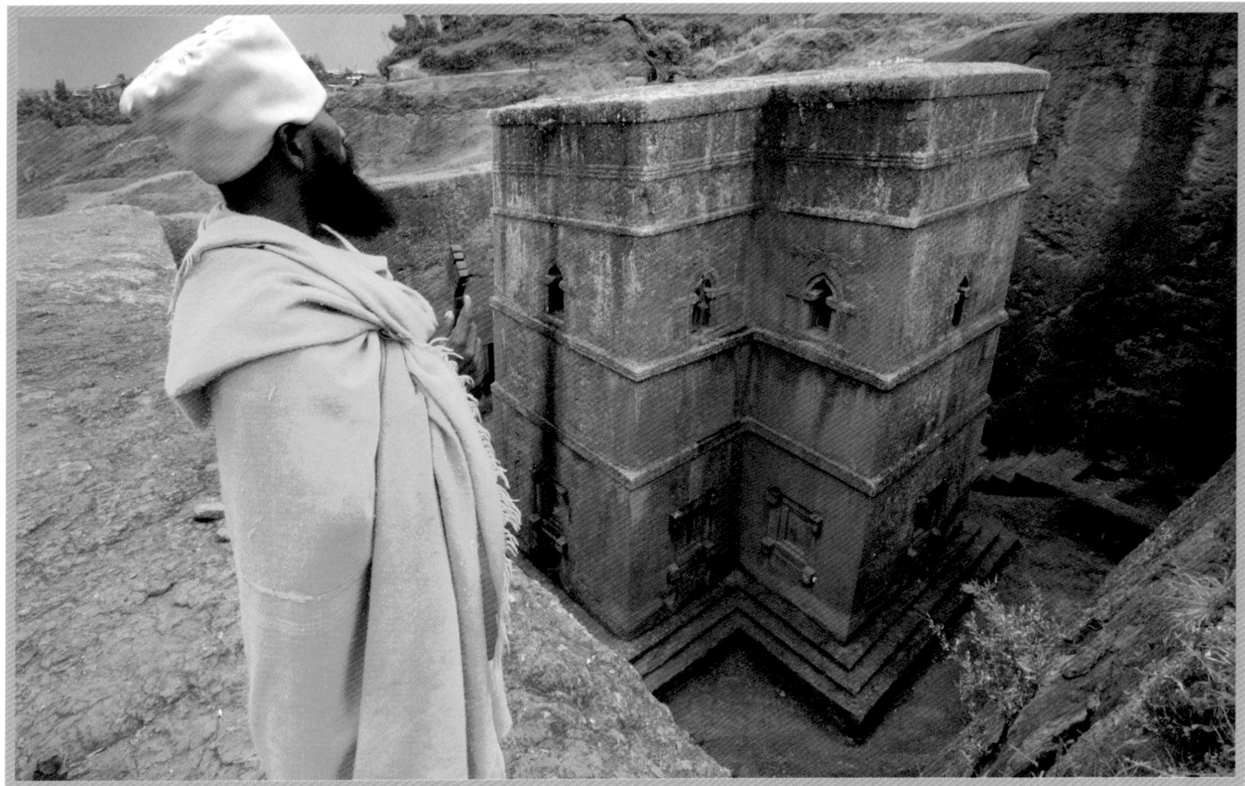

The 11 immense and imposing granite churches at Lalibela in highland Ethiopia, constructed in the early 13th century, were literally hewn from deep terraces of rock, from ground level down, and then connected to one another by deep trenches and tunnels. Pictured here is the Church of St George (Bete Giyorgis).

humiliating laws of behaviour and dress and many of the same ruinous taxes as were the Copts.

It was farther to the east, however, in Central and East Asia, that the Nestorian Church endured its greatest calamities: at the beginning of the 14th century, it was in geographic terms far and away the largest Church in Christendom; by the end of the century, it was among the smallest. Christians in Central Asia suffered terribly – as did everyone else around them – during the worst years of the Mongol conquests, when the 'Golden Horde' of Genghis Khan (*c.*1150–1227) was destroying every village and city (even such great cities as Samarkand and Bukhara) in its path. But, in fact, the later khans were rather indulgent of the Nestorians. Möngke Khan (1208–59), grandson of Genghis and elder brother of Kublai (1215–94) and Hülegu (1217–65), was reportedly drawn to Christianity. Hülegu took a Christian wife and, when his forces took Baghdad in 1258, those Christians who retreated into their churches during the slaughter were left unmolested. And Kublai tolerated and even perhaps somewhat favoured the East Syrian Church in China.

In the late 13th century, however, the great reversal began. In Baghdad, the Mongol ruler Ghazan Khan (r. 1295–1304) adopted Islam, and at once the East Syrian Christian community became the object of ferocious persecutions, including numerous massacres. In China, moreover, in 1369, the Ming Dynasty came to power and instituted a systematic extermination of foreign creeds, which quickly extinguished the Syrian Church in the Middle Kingdom. And in Central Asia the rampages of the Turkic Muslim warlord Timur (1336–1405) – among the most prolifically murderous psychotics of pre-modern history – left no living traces of East Syrian Christianity in their wake.

THE LEGEND OF PRESTER JOHN

In the age of the Crusades, the Latin West's rather nebulous knowledge of Oriental Christianity helped give rise to the popular romantic legend of Prester John (or John the Priest), a Christian king ruling over a rich and mighty Christian kingdom somewhere far to the East. In some accounts, he was credited with miraculous powers and said to rule over a domain verging on an earthly paradise. His kingdom was variously thought to lie in India, East Asia or Ethiopia.

Reports of the St Thomas Christians of India – or even perhaps an Indian episcopal embassy to Rome in the days of Pope Callixtus II (d.1124) – may have been the original inspiration for the legend. But the Cistercian monk Otto of Freising (*c.*1114–58) in his *Chronicon* of 1145, reports meeting a Bishop Hugh of Jabayl in Lebanon, who told him that King John – described as a Syrian and a descendant of one of the Magi who visited the Christ child – had recently defeated the Persians at Ecbatana.

This may be a confused account of the defeat of the Seljuqs by the Mongol khan Yelu Dashi (a Buddhist, as it happens) in Katwan, Persia in 1141. If so, it mirrors the story told in 1221 by the bishop of Acre Jacques de Vitry, on his return from the Fifth Crusade, of the victories won over the Muslims in the East by King David of India – either the son or grandson of Prester John. This King David, it seems reasonably certain, was actually none other than Genghis Khan.

The most fascinating episode in the development of this legend is 'Prester John's Letter' (see below), which – according to Alberic de Trois-Fontaines in the 13th century – first appeared in 1165. In this document (addressed supposedly to the Holy Roman emperor Frederick I, the Byzantine emperor Manuel I Comnenus and other Christian princes), Prester John, Christian king of the 'Three Indies' and guardian of St Thomas' tomb, boasts of the natural splendours and high civilization of his realm, and declares his intention to take Jerusalem. Copies of the letter – in many languages and variants – spread throughout Europe. Pope Alexander III (*c.*1100–81) allegedly even penned a reply in 1177.

In the 14th century and after, Europeans began to identify Prester John with the emperor of Ethiopia, and it was as a mysterious and powerful Ethiopian monarch that the Christian king of the East entered into later romances – most memorably, perhaps, in Ariosto's *Orlando Furioso*.

'Our land is the home of elephants, dromedaries, camels, crocodiles … hyenas, wild horses, wild oxen, and wild men – men with horns, one-eyed men, men with eyes before and behind, centaurs, fauns, satyrs, pygmies, forty-ell-high giants, cyclopses, and similar women … When we go to war, we have fourteen golden and bejewelled crosses borne before us instead of banners. Each of these crosses is followed by ten thousand horsemen and one hundred thousand foot soldiers … .'

'THE LETTER OF PRESTER JOHN' (1165)

BYZANTINE TWILIGHT

After the sack of Constantinople in 1204, the ancient Roman empire of the East was fragmented into autonomous principalities, some governed by French or Italian occupiers, others by the local Greek nobility. In 1208, Theodore I Lascaris (*c.* 1174–1221) established an imperial seat in Nicaea, but his dominion was not vast. Still, the Nicene empire soon became a prosperous and militarily secure realm, exercising control over most of West Anatolia, and fostering a culture of high Hellenism.

In 1259, the throne of Nicaea was seized by Michael Palaeologos (*c.*1224–82), who then in 1261 re-conquered Constantinople and installed himself as Emperor Michael VIII. In this way, the dynasty of the Palaeologoi was founded and the last age of the Byzantine empire inaugurated.

East and West

In order to restore the empire to something like its former greatness, the new emperor had to finance military campaigns to drive the Latin occupiers from the Greek islands and from the Morea in the Peloponnese, as well as to subdue the Greek provinces of Thessaly and Epirus, whose rulers viewed him as a usurper. He also had to restore Constantinople and strengthen its defences. None of this was possible without trade, and for this he was dependent upon Genoa, which was willing to provide him ships in exchange for the sort of preferential trading rights once enjoyed only by Venice. Most importantly, he had to take every measure possible to ensure that the French king of Naples and Sicily, Charles of Anjou (1226–85), did not succeed in his avowed intention of reclaiming Constantinople.

> *'But the crown jewels were made of glass and the banqueting plate was of pewter and clay'.*
>
> Nicephorus Gregoras (1295–1360) on the coronation of the Byzantine emperor John VI Cantacuzenas in 1347

To avert this last peril, Michael took the extraordinary step of petitioning the pope for protection, promising in return the submission of the Eastern Church to Rome. And indeed, at the Council of Lyons in 1274, representatives of the emperor accepted union with Rome on those terms. The Orthodox people, however, refused to comply with the emperor's decision, and by 1281 it was obvious that, despite Lyons and despite the draconian methods employed by Michael to quell dissent, no true union had occurred. So that year Charles launched his invasion of the Byzantine empire. His forces were defeated, however, before reaching Asia Minor, and his plans for another invasion were thwarted by a rebellion among his Sicilian subjects.

At the time of his death, Michael was despised by many of the Byzantines as an apostate, even though he had restored their empire, defeated the French pretender and made provisions for Constantinople's future defence. But no doubt a great many of his subjects were also aware that his military exertions against the Latins had weakened the defences of the eastern provinces, leaving them exposed to the Turks.

The investiture of Charles I of Anjou as king of Naples and Sicily by Pope Clement IV in 1262.

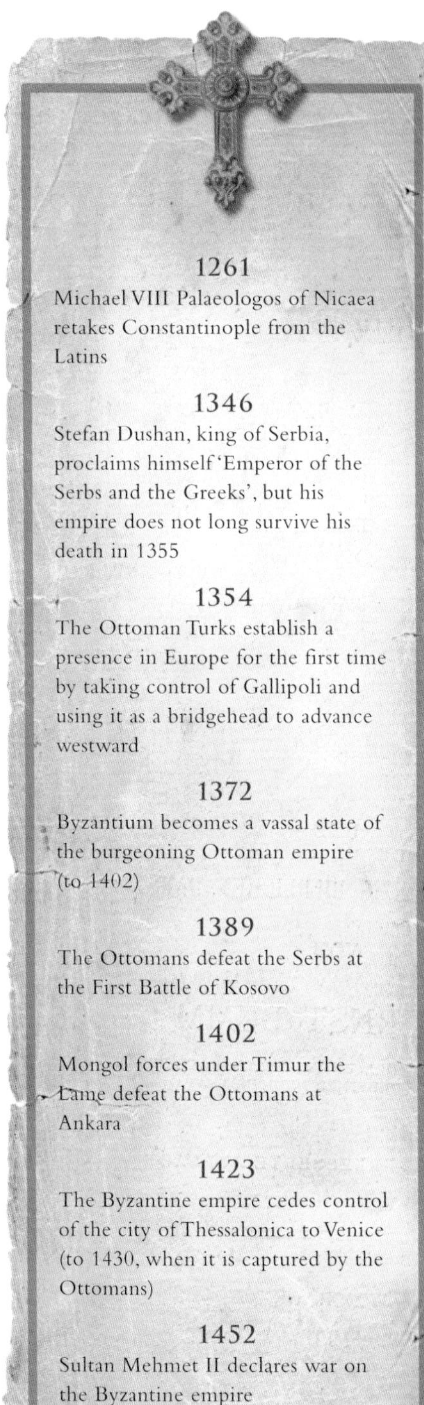

1261
Michael VIII Palaeologos of Nicaea retakes Constantinople from the Latins

1346
Stefan Dushan, king of Serbia, proclaims himself 'Emperor of the Serbs and the Greeks', but his empire does not long survive his death in 1355

1354
The Ottoman Turks establish a presence in Europe for the first time by taking control of Gallipoli and using it as a bridgehead to advance westward

1372
Byzantium becomes a vassal state of the burgeoning Ottoman empire (to 1402)

1389
The Ottomans defeat the Serbs at the First Battle of Kosovo

1402
Mongol forces under Timur the Lame defeat the Ottomans at Ankara

1423
The Byzantine empire cedes control of the city of Thessalonica to Venice (to 1430, when it is captured by the Ottomans)

1452
Sultan Mehmet II declares war on the Byzantine empire

The Long War

During the 14th century, the Palaeologan emperors were engaged in a ceaseless struggle to forestall the inevitable. Rebellions, insubordinate provinces, dependency on mercenary armies, Turkish raids on Byzantine territories, economic decline, the slow rise of the Ottomans in Asia Minor, civil conflicts – in short, every imaginable turmoil and tribulation – were the constant realities of Byzantine politics.

And then there were – as there had always been – the barbarians: specifically, the Serbs and the Bulgars. In 1346, the formidable Serbian king Stefan Dushan (1308–55) – an Orthodox monarch – declared himself 'Emperor of the Serbs and the Greeks', and by 1348 had conquered all of northern Greece. And, but for an alliance they had earlier forged with the Turks, the Byzantines might not have been able to prevent the loss of more of the empire. In 1347, the Black Death had come to Constantinople and other areas of the Byzantine east. The human and economic toll was devastating.

At mid-century, the gold in imperial coinage had been diluted with base metals (reducing its worth as an international currency), the crown jewels had been surrendered as surety on debts to Venice incurred during a civil war, the erosion of Byzantine power in the provinces was

Hesychasm's great defender was the Athonite monk and philosopher Gregory Palamas (1296–1359), who insisted that this practice in no way denied the infinite transcendence of God; he granted that God's essence is incomprehensible and invisible, but argued that by his energeiai *– his activities towards creation – God makes himself truly present in the hearts, minds and flesh of human beings. Palamas' arguments often oscillated between flashes of great insight and moments of incoherence, but his complex and profound mystical theology was affirmed by the Orthodox Church in his lifetime.*

inexorable, imperial trade principally enriched Italians rather than Greeks, wars with the Serbs and the Turks were incessant, and any possibility of Roman aid was contingent upon submission of the Eastern Church to the Western. In 1369, Emperor John V Palaeologos (1332–91), returning from a humiliating embassy to Rome to profess obedience to the Roman see, was even briefly arrested in Venice by his creditors for insolvency. In 1373, after Turkish forces had seized much of Macedonia, he was compelled to accept the suzerainty of the Turks and promise to pay tribute.

In 1390, Emperor Manuel II Palaeologos (1350–1425), in fact, was forced at one point to live as a hostage vassal at the Turkish court of the Ottoman sultan Bayezid I (*c.*1360–1402); and even when Manuel returned to Constantinople in 1391 Bayezid reminded him that his realm now extended no farther than the city walls. A journey Manuel made through Western Europe from 1399 to 1403 secured a wealth of promises for military aid, but promises proved rather feeble reinforcements. While he was abroad, however, the armies of Timur had descended upon the Ottoman forces at Ankara and crushed them, taking Bayezid prisoner. In the ensuing power struggles among Bayezid's sons, the military aid of Constantinople became a commodity with which the emperor could now barter. In 1413, it was with Byzantine help that Mehmet I (d.1421) defeated his last rival, his brother Musa, in Serbia. To show his gratitude, the new sultan absolved the Byzantine emperor of all further tribute and restored various territories – such as the city of Thessalonica – to the Byzantine throne. Manuel took advantage of Mehmet's clemency to rebuild the military defences of his empire and the fortifications of Constantinople, in preparation for Mehmet's death and for the disintegration of good relations with the Ottomans that would inevitably follow.

Cultural and Spiritual Renewal

During the long twilight of Byzantine civilization, even as the economy, military and government of the empire continued to decline, higher culture flourished. A rare devotion to Hellenism – antique, Alexandrian and Christian – pervaded the entire period from the days of Michael Psellus in the 11th century to the last years of the empire in the 15th. Emperor Andronicus II Palaeologos (*c.*1260–1332) was a generous patron to the scholars of Constantinople, among whom few were more distinguished than Theodore Metochites (1270–1332), the poet, philosopher, astronomer and commentator on Aristotle. Still more gifted was Theodore's student Nicephorus Gregoras (*c.*1295–1360), a philosopher, astronomer, historian and philologist.

During this period, as well, classical and patristic Latin literature entered the Byzantine world in Greek translations, many produced by Maximus Planudes (*c.*1260–1330), the grammarian, 'Greek Anthologist' and theologian. The brilliant

THE MYSTICS OF THE RHINELAND

In the 14th century, mystical theology enjoyed a revival not only in the Christian East, but in the West as well, most especially in the north. England, for example, produced a number of remarkable writers on contemplative prayer and the soul's union with God: Richard Rolle (*c.*1300–49), Walter Hilton (*c.*1340–96), Dame Juliana of Norwich (1342 – after 1416), and the anonymous author of the treatise *The Cloud of Unknowing*.

In the first half of the century, though, the richest mystical literature of Western Europe was produced by various German Dominicans: Meister Eckhart (*c.*1260–*c.*1327), Johannes Tauler (d.1361) and Heinrich Suso (*c.*1295–1366). Tauler was perhaps less purely mystical than the other two, but his descriptions of the soul's sanctification in its assimilation to Christ are as profound as any spiritual writings of the period. Suso was a student and, to the end of his life, a defender of Eckhart. This sometimes made things very uncomfortable for him, since Eckhart was among the most controversial figures in Christian history.

Meister Eckhart was both a brilliant speculative theologian and a majestically gifted writer. He was also given to expressing his more difficult ideas in almost willfully audacious language. He apparently regarded many of his teachings as entirely orthodox developments certain of the central tenets of the metaphysics of Thomas Aquinas, but he expressed himself in words and images that it is doubtful Thomas would have recognized.

Most famously, he asserted that the soul, in its ascent to union with God, must learn to detach itself not only from creatures, but even from God, at least as God is conceived by the finite mind. There is a 'God beyond God', he claimed, an infinite 'desert of divinity' where no concept of the divine applies. He spoke also of an uncreated 'spark' of God within the soul, and of a ground within the soul where God and soul are one.

Demetrius Cydones (*c.*1324 – *c.*1398), one of the Greek humanist scholars of the next generation, produced translations not only of Augustine but also of Thomas Aquinas, and was one of the first of a small circle of Byzantine Thomists (in fact, he ultimately joined the Latin Church).

The Palaeologan era, however, also saw a renewal of the Eastern Christian mystical tradition, particularly evident in the triumph of Hesychasm. Deriving from the Greek word *hesychia*, meaning 'quietude', this term denoted a special form of contemplative prayer that leads the devout person to an ecstatic experience of God as the Uncreated Light – a light reputed occasionally to become visible as a transfiguring radiance pouring from the body of the contemplative.

In the 14th century, Hesychasm was the special spiritual practice of the monks of Mount Athos (a promontory on the Chalcidice Peninsula in the Aegean that had been the home of numerous Orthodox monasteries since the tenth century). The Hesychasts had many detractors – as a result of both their theology and their techniques – but they also had one great defender: Gregory Palamas (1296–1359), perhaps the most important Orthodox theologian of the Middle Ages.

THE LAST CAESAR

The Roman empire of the West came to an end in the fifth century; but the Roman empire – as a continuous legal, cultural and political institution – persisted in the East for another millennium, and its capital, the 'New Rome' of Constantinople, was the seat of Roman emperors into the age of gunpowder and cannon; the last of them died only four decades before the discovery of the Americas.

Portrait of John VIII Palaeologos (1390–1448) by the School of Giovanni Bellini. John VIII's agreement to union with Rome in 1439 obliged the Eastern Church to consent to the addition of the 'filioque' clause to the Nicene Creed, accept the Western idea of Purgatory, and acknowledge the jurisdictional supremacy of Rome.

Constantinople had been the first Christian city of Europe, and had jealously preserved the high Hellenistic culture of the late empire for centuries. But geography alone made its ultimate survival as a Christian capital impossible. It was surrounded by too many enemies – Arabs, Slavs, Turks, Bulgars, Mongols, among others – and from the seventh century onwards was engaged in an almost continuous struggle with the immense power of Islam. With the rise of the Ottoman empire, the Byzantines were confronted with an enemy that could not be defeated, and that could not be resisted indefinitely.

A Forced Union

The favourable conditions that Manuel II Palaeologos had won for his subjects from Mehmet I ended soon after the latter's death in 1421. Sultan Murad II (1404–51) – mindful of the support that Manuel had given his rivals for the Ottoman throne – reversed Mehmet's indulgent policies towards the Greeks, briefly besieged Constantinople, and blockaded Thessalonica. Unable to mount an adequate defence of Thessalonica, the Byzantines were forced to sell the city to the stronger Venetians in 1423; in 1430, though, it fell to Murad's armies just the same.

By then, Manuel had been succeeded by his son, Emperor John VIII Palaeologos, who spent more or less the whole of his reign desperately attempting to secure Western military support against the Turks. Such support, though, was invariably contingent upon submission of the Greek Church to the Latin pontiff; and so, in 1439, at the Council of Florence, John – attended by the patriarch of Constantinople and around 700 Greek delegates – agreed to union with Rome and obedience to the pope.

Needless to say, many of the Greeks made concessions to Rome not out of conviction, but out of necessity; the reunion did, after all, amount to a more or less complete capitulation on all issues of disagreement with the Latin Church. Even so, all the Greek delegates subscribed, with the sole exception of the revered bishop of Ephesus, Mark Eugenicus (d.1444), who sincerely desired a return to unity between the Greek and Latin Churches, but who could not reconcile himself to reunion purchased at the price of betraying Orthodox tradition.

Nor, indeed, could most of the people of Constantinople or the greater Orthodox world. Even most of the delegates who had subscribed to the union, on returning

The siege of Constantinople, depicted on a 16th-century fresco. Mehmet II made meticulous preparations for taking the Byzantine capital, including having a gigantic siege-gun specially cast, which required 50 pairs of oxen to move it. In the face of the fierce Ottoman onslaught, it was only a matter of time before the city's 7000 Christian defenders were forced to capitulate.

to the East, repudiated the decree of Florence. A popular motto of the time proclaimed that, if the Byzantines were to be a subject people, it was 'better to be ruled by the sultan's turban than by the pope's triple crown'. A few notable Orthodox bishops remained loyal to the union, though: for instance, the great Byzantine humanist and philosopher, Basil Bessarion (1403–72), archbishop if Nicaea, who was made a cardinal by Pope Eugenius IV (*c*.1383–1447), and who lived his later years in Italy; and Isidore of Kiev (d.1463), metropolitan of Kiev and Moscow, who ultimately had to flee Russia for his commitment to the union, and who in 1458 was given by the pope the honorific – though meaningless – title of patriarch of Constantinople.

The Long War

In any event, Florence did in fact aid the emperor in procuring Western military assistance. In 1444, the king of Poland Władysław III (1424–44), who was also king of Hungary, with forces commanded by the governor of Transylvania Janos Hunyadi (*c*.1387–1456), succeeded in driving the Turks from Serbia, Albania and Bulgaria, and then – with a Venetian fleet sailing for the Bosphorus to prevent Ottoman forces from crossing into Europe – crossed the Danube to begin the march to Constantinople. The Venetians had failed to close the Bosphorus; however, the king of Serbia (to preserve a favourable peace signed with the Turks months earlier) conspired with the sultan to thwart the Christian expedition, and the Turks met and destroyed the armies of this new 'Crusade' at Varna.

Thereafter, the days of the Byzantine empire were numbered. In 1449, John VIII was succeeded by his brother, the emperor Constantine XI Palaeologos (1404–53). Constantine was a strong and gifted ruler, but his was a hopeless situation. He attempted, like his brother, to win military aid from the West by reaffirming the

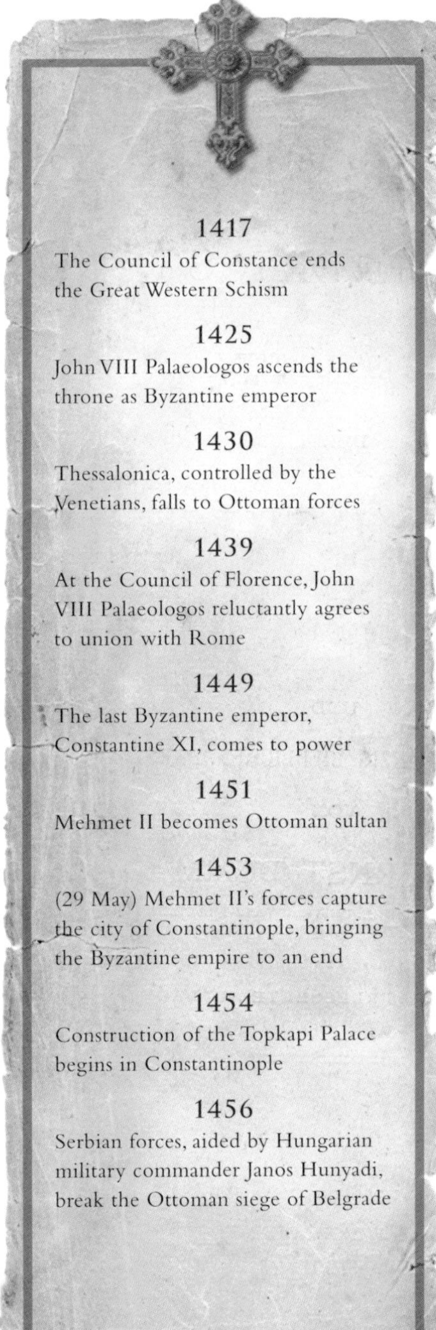

Greek Church's subjection to Rome, and even by publicly celebrating the union in Hagia Sophia in 1452. But, apart from inspiring vehement public protests, this accomplished nothing.

1417
The Council of Constance ends the Great Western Schism
1425
John VIII Palaeologos ascends the throne as Byzantine emperor
1430
Thessalonica, controlled by the Venetians, falls to Ottoman forces
1439
At the Council of Florence, John VIII Palaeologos reluctantly agrees to union with Rome
1449
The last Byzantine emperor, Constantine XI, comes to power
1451
Mehmet II becomes Ottoman sultan
1453
(29 May) Mehmet II's forces capture the city of Constantinople, bringing the Byzantine empire to an end
1454
Construction of the Topkapi Palace begins in Constantinople
1456
Serbian forces, aided by Hungarian military commander Janos Hunyadi, break the Ottoman siege of Belgrade

In 1449, a very young but very resolute Mehmet II (1432–81) had begun to gather his resources for a single grand assault upon Constantinople – which, along with its 'Great Church', Hagia Sophia – was a prize upon which he had set his heart with absolute fervour. And when, in 1451, Mehmet became sole sultan of the Ottoman empire, he began the final campaign in earnest, though not in haste. Not only did he sign a peace accord with the Hungarians to prevent them from entering the war on the Greek side, he also commissioned a Hungarian engineer to cast a cannon of unprecedented size and power. In addition, he signed a treaty with Venice to ensure that its fleets would not join battle on the Christian side.

The Final Siege

In 1452, Mehmet enlarged his fleet and built a near-impregnable fortress to allow his forces unobstructed passage across the Bosphorus. Then, in April 1453, the final siege of Constantinople began. The Byzantines had stretched a great chain across the mouth of the Golden Horn; but this delayed the Ottoman fleet only temporarily: the Turks simply carried their ships across land over greased logs to the city's harbour. And, once the bombardment of the city's walls began, it was only a matter of time before the Turkish forces broke through the city's defences.

After allowing his troops three days and nights of plunder, Sultan Mehmet II entered Constantinople and made directly for Hagia Sophia, which he ordered converted into a mosque.

Though Venice – true to its treaty with the sultan – sent the Byzantine emperor no reinforcements, it did allow the Byzantines to recruit soldiers and sailors from Crete (a Venetian possession), and the Venetians in Constantinople fought alongside the Greeks. Moreover, the extraordinarily able and courageous Genoese general Giovanni Giustiniani (d.1453), at his own expense, brought a force of 700 men to aid in the city's defence, and was given command of the ground defences by the emperor. Two hundred Neapolitan soldiers were also hired by Isidore of Kiev, with funds provided by the pope. In addition, a few Western Christians – such as the Spanish nobleman Don Francisco of Toledo – chose to join the fight on the Byzantine side, as did the Ottoman Prince Orhan.

POPE AND COUNCIL

The Council of Florence (reckoned by later Roman Catholic tradition as the seventeenth ecumenical council), at which the Orthodox and Roman Churches were formally – but not actually – reunited, concerned itself not merely with the reconciliation of Greeks and Latins. From 1439 to 1445, the council produced pacts of reunion with representatives from other eastern communions as well: the Armenians, the Syrian Monophysites (the 'Jacobites'), the East Syrian 'Nestorians' and the Maronites in Cyprus. Not all of these unions proved real or enduring.

The council was also important, however, in resolving certain internal Roman Catholic issues of authority. The period from 1378 to 1417 – known to history as the 'Great Western Schism' – had been a time of hierarchical turmoil for the Roman Church. In these years there existed two – and, ultimately, three – rival streams of papal succession. From 1309 to 1377, the papacy had, for a variety of reasons, kept its court at Avignon in southern France, and during those years the College of Cardinals had come to enjoy considerable powers. But the first pope elected after the court's return to Rome, Urban VI (c.1318–89), harboured so deep an antagonism towards his French cardinals that a number of them retreated to Avignon, where they repudiated the earlier papal election as having been made under duress, and elected Robert of Geneva (1342–94) as Pope Clement VII. Thereafter, there were two papal courts. The situation was further complicated in 1409 when cardinals from both colleges – in order to resolve the conflict – elected a third pope.

The confusion was settled at the Council of Constance in 1417, which variously dismissed all three claimants to the papacy – the Roman pope, Gregory XII (c.1325–1417), by personal resignation – and appointed Martin V (1368–1431) as sole pontiff. The Council of Constance also, however, plainly decreed that the authority of a general Church Council is superior to that of the pope, and that such councils should be frequent. This was the 'conciliar position' favoured by many at the time. The Council of Florence, however, clarified the Roman position by establishing precisely the opposite principle: that the pope wields supreme authority in the Church, in all matters.

The city held out far longer than might reasonably have been expected, but finally, in late May, the landward walls were breached. On the night of 28 May, when it was clear that the city would fall the next day, a great procession of the city's holy relics – attended by Eastern and Western Christians alike – took place, while in Hagia Sophia Orthodox and Catholics worshipped together and prepared for death. The emperor delivered a moving address to the leaders of the city on the transience of earthly life and the nobility of sacrifice for faith and country.

The next day the Turks broke into the city, after hours of battle at the breached walls. Giustiniani was grievously wounded and carried away from the battle (he died some days later aboard one of his ships). The emperor himself put off his imperial purple and joined the battle on foot. He was last seen when he, his cousin Theophilus Palaeologus, Don Francisco and another nobleman named John Dalmatus lifted their swords above their heads and together ran into the ranks of the Turks pouring through one of the city's gates.

RENAISSANCE CHRISTIAN THOUGHT

In the 15th century, even as the civilization of the Christian East was dying, the civilization of the Christian West was experiencing its great 'Renaissance'. In fact, the former reality helped to bring the latter about. There was a more or less continuous migration of texts and scholars from the East to the West during the last several decades of the empire, and the great 'Byzantine Renaissance' that had begun in the days of Michael Psellus, in the 11th century, and that had fitfully persisted for almost four centuries, was now obliged to surrender its riches to the West.

Of course, no single cause can be assigned for the extraordinary flowering of the arts, philosophy, speculative theology, scholarship and scientific inquiry that occurred at the end of the Western Middle Ages, or for the rise of the new 'humanism' of early modernity. The mundane explanations are plentiful – the rise of a new merchant class and a general improvement of the economy, the resulting shift of wealth away from landholders and the Church into a more diversified secular realm, the increasing availability of classical texts and so on. Whatever the case, in those years – beginning in Italy and then spreading outward – a new passion arose for the recovery of the 'lost wisdom' of the ancient world. Nor was this merely a 'secular' movement, as we now understand that word.

> *'The council is superior to the pope … since the representation of the church in the general council is surer and more infallible than the pope alone.'*
>
> NICHOLAS OF CUSA, *DE CONCORDIA CATHOLICA*, 1433

THE FIRST STIRRINGS

Had it not been for the devastation visited on Europe by the Black Death in the second half of the 14th century, the Renaissance might have begun to spread far sooner. In Italy, which for a variety of reasons had long enjoyed privileged access to the Byzantine and Islamic East, the first period of 'humanism' – that is, a concerted return to classical models, literary, philosophical and artistic, and an equally concerted effort to develop new artistic techniques, new literary forms and new sciences – began in the late 13th and early 14th centuries. Dante's *Divine Comedy* may have been the crowning literary achievement of Medieval civilization, but it was also profoundly innovative in style, and was inspired far more by classical than by Medieval literary forms. The true father of the later Italian revolution in painting – in terms both of method and of figuration – was Giotto (*c.*1270–1337).

Moreover, it was the late Medieval influx of Eastern texts that had nourished late scholasticism and the rise of the late Medieval university that created the intellectual conditions necessary for the remarkable developments of the 15th century. One of the greatest and most imaginative thinkers of the early Renaissance, for instance, was Cardinal Nicholas of Cusa (1401–64). It is true that Nicholas was sent by the pope to Constantinople on the eve of the Council of Florence, and there encountered Byzantine Platonism and Byzantine scholarship directly for the first time – indeed, it was while returning from the East that Nicholas experienced his reported great awakening regarding the nature of divine transcendence – but he had already been formed by texts and traditions available in the West, and so was able to absorb and transform Eastern Christian thought without difficulty in his own work. Thus his reflections upon the necessarily asymptotic approach of the finite mind towards knowledge of God, upon God as the 'coincidence of opposites', upon the nature of the infinite, upon God as the infinitely simple 'implication' of all that is 'explicated' in creation, upon the person of Christ, upon the nature of celestial movements, and so forth, were a perfect confluence of Western and Eastern streams of thought (passing through the medium, of course, of his own native genius).

A portrait of Nicholas of Cusa, by an unknown artist. Among his many accomplishments, Nicholas was a theologian, scientist, philosopher, mathematician, legal scholar and astronomer.

Byzantine Exodus

Without question, the Renaissance in Italy was nurtured by an infusion of Byzantine learning in the last days of the Eastern empire. And no figure was more influential in this regard than the great polymath George Gemistus Plethon (*c.*1352–1452), the brilliant Byzantine Platonist who – while acting as a delegate to the Council of Florence – delivered a famous oration 'Concerning the Differences between Aristotle and Plato' that inspired a new passion for Platonism in Florence: a passion that led ultimately to the founding of the *Academia Platonica* by Cosimo de' Medici (1389–1464).

This, as it happens, was a matter far closer to Plethon's heart than the reunion of the Churches. He was not really Christian in his beliefs, in any event; he was a secret adherent to a kind of late Neoplatonism, which drew upon many traditions (pagan, Zoroastrian, Chaldean, Jewish, Muslim and Christian), and which was formally polytheistic (though devoted, ultimately, to the one Great God). Plethon continued his sojourn in Florence after the Council of Florence to teach and proselytize for a new Hellenism, and through him an entire generation of Italian humanists was exposed to philosophical texts – and interpretations of those texts – to which they had hitherto had no access.

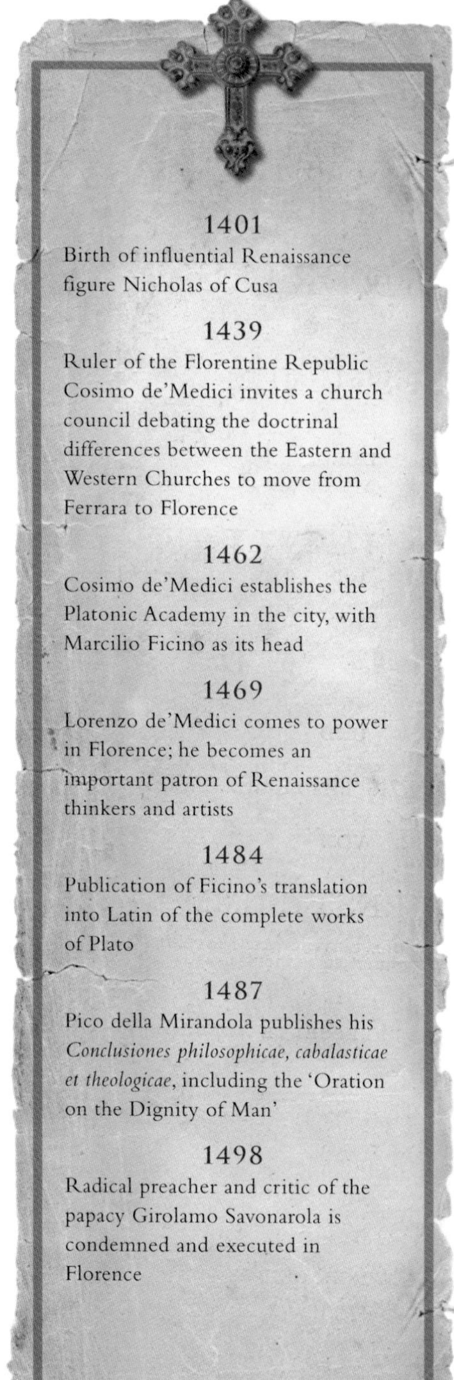

1401
Birth of influential Renaissance figure Nicholas of Cusa

1439
Ruler of the Florentine Republic Cosimo de'Medici invites a church council debating the doctrinal differences between the Eastern and Western Churches to move from Ferrara to Florence

1462
Cosimo de'Medici establishes the Platonic Academy in the city, with Marcilio Ficino as its head

1469
Lorenzo de'Medici comes to power in Florence; he becomes an important patron of Renaissance thinkers and artists

1484
Publication of Ficino's translation into Latin of the complete works of Plato

1487
Pico della Mirandola publishes his *Conclusiones philosophicae, cabalasticae et theologicae*, including the 'Oration on the Dignity of Man'

1498
Radical preacher and critic of the papacy Girolamo Savonarola is condemned and executed in Florence

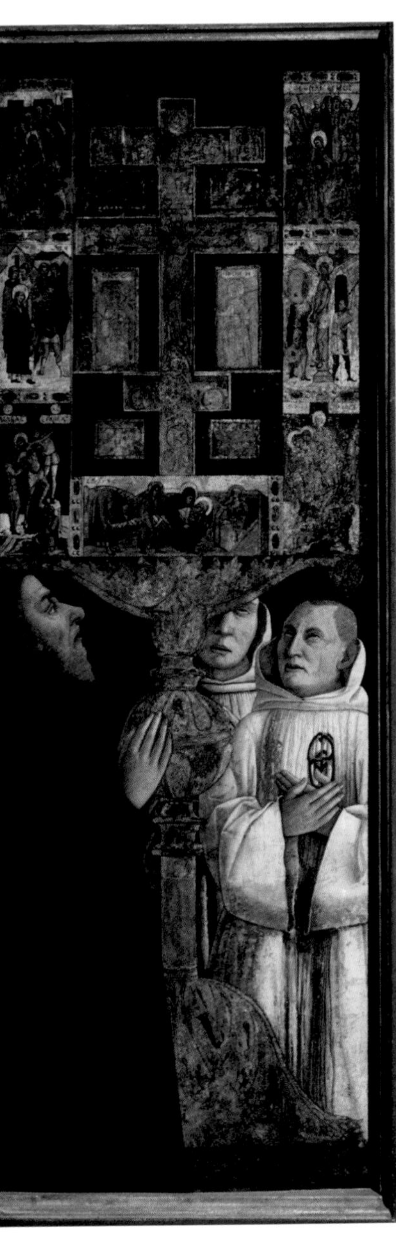

A painting (1472) by Gentile Bellini showing the influential Platonist Cardinal Bessarion. In Rome, Bessarion taught, sheltered Greek scholars fleeing the East, amassed precious Greek manuscripts and commissioned translations.

Almost as important in the transmission of Byzantine culture to Italy was Bishop – and later Cardinal – Basil Bessarion (1403–72), a former student of Plethon's, and as committed a Platonist (though a more committed Christian). He too was a delegate to the Council of Florence, and his loyalty to the pact of union obliged him to live in Italy as early as 1439.

The Academy

The intellectual centre of the early Italian Renaissance, though, was undoubtedly the Platonic Academy of Florence; and, of the many remarkable scholars directly or indirectly associated with it, two were particularly notable for their breadth of learning, intellectual daring and their influence Marsilio Ficino (1433–99) and the count of Concordia, Giovanni Pico della Mirandola (1463–94).

In addition to being a linguist, physician and philosopher, Ficino was a priest and a theologian. Though there was a period in his life, apparently, when he underwent a crisis of faith, he ultimately became one of the most learned, energetic and eloquent advocates not only of the new humanism, but of a new Christian Platonism, much like that of the Church Fathers, but open to other traditions of thought as well. Made the first head of the Platonic Academy in 1462, he devoted the new institution to the collection, study and translation of Eastern texts.

Ficino not only translated the works of Plato and Plotinus, but wrote commentaries on them that profoundly shaped Christian thought over the next two centuries. The theme most central to his thought was love, understood as the universal bond holding all things together, and as the transcendent power by which the human soul may be assimilated to God. All his writings are imbued by a quintessentially 'Greek' optimism regarding the dignity and divine destiny of the human being.

If anything, this optimism is even more pronounced in the work of Pico della Mirandola, a man of impetuous brilliance and eclectic intellectual sensibilities, who believed he could achieve an ideal synthesis of scholastic and humanist, Aristotelian and Platonic, and Eastern and Western wisdoms. Of noble birth, he studied at the universities of Ferrara and Padua, travelled through Italy, visited Paris (and its university) and in 1486 met Ficino in Florence.

Though he remained a convinced and devout Christian, Pico believed that all truth should be cherished, and drew ideas from Jewish, pagan, hermetic, Chaldean and Persian sources; and he was the first of the Renaissance Christian Kabbalists. His most famous work, the 'Oration on the Dignity of Man', was composed as the inaugural address of a great public debate he planned for 1487, to discuss 900 metaphysical theses he had published the year before. The debate never occurred, though, due to a papal condemnation of 13 of these theses. Pico withdrew to France in 1488, but was arrested and detained until the pope was persuaded to allow him to return to Florence. There Pico lived the rest of his life, devout to the last – though not absolved of all suspicion of heresy until 1492.

THE RADICAL FRIAR

A good friend of Pico's in Florence – though no friend of Italian humanism – was the Dominican preacher and, in many eyes, prophet, Girolamo Savonarola (1452–98): a man whose ecclesiastical and political career illustrates with special vividness many of the tensions of the early modern period in Europe.

Savonarola came from a devout and scholarly family, and was from an early age marked out by his moral austerity and intellectual seriousness. It was a sore trial to his pious soul to live in an age in which a new paganism (as he saw it) was spreading through the West, and in which the papacy was in the hands of worldly men. In 1475 he joined the Dominicans and devoted himself to teaching and to the study of his beloved Thomas Aquinas. He arrived in Florence in 1482 as a lecturer for a Dominican convent there, but – after a spiritual experience of some profundity – he began preaching sermons of a distinctly 'prophetic' nature; and in 1485 he began to predict that the Church, so desperately in need of reform, would suffer divine chastisement for its faithlessness before being renewed by the Holy Spirit.

In 1490, he began preaching against the tyranny and dishonesty of the city's rulers, the Medicis. When the Medicis were driven from power by the French king Charles VIII (1470–98) in 1494 (an event Savonarola had predicted two years before), the Dominican preacher became by default the city's ruler. He instituted a democratic republic, both just and transparent.

Savonarola's great nemesis in those years, however, was the almost theatrically corrupt Borgia pope Alexander VI (1431–1503), whose chief talent – apart from siring illegitimate offspring and squandering small fortunes on his pleasures – was political intrigue. Neither Alexander's attempt to lure Savonarola to Rome in 1495, nor a threat of excommunication, nor a brief suspension of his licence to preach, nor the offer of a cardinal's hat prevented Savonarola from denouncing the vices of the papal court.

Ultimately Savonarola's political enemies, within Florence and beyond, conspired to incite a riot among the more disaffected citizens of Florence. Savonarola was seized. Officers arrived from Rome to try him, charges were falsified, torture applied, and he was sentenced to death by hanging (his body to be burned afterwards). On the gallows, he bowed his head to receive plenary absolution from one of the pope's emissaries.

A statue of Savonarola in his native city of Ferrara in northern Italy.

SPAIN AND ITS INQUISITION

From the time of the eighth-century Muslim conquests in Iberia until the last decade of the 15th century, Spain was neither a unified country nor wholly governed by Christian monarchs. In 1492, however, with the fall of Granada – the last Muslim kingdom in the peninsula – the Catholic nation of Spain was born, under the rule of King Ferdinand II (1452–1516) and Queen Isabella I (1451–1504), who had already by their marriage forged a union between the independent kingdoms of Aragon and Castile.

Spain had been for centuries the most diverse country in Europe, with large populations of Christians, Jews and Muslims living – if not always in perfect harmony – at least in peaceful and remarkably tolerant concord. Ferdinand's ambition to convert Spain into a unified and powerful nation, however, prompted him to adopt a policy of enforced religious uniformity; and for this purpose he required the services of an Inquisition.

The Catholic Monarchs

Prince Ferdinand of Aragon married Princess Isabella of Castile in 1469. When Isabella's father died in 1474, her right of succession was disputed by some, but she proclaimed herself queen, and Ferdinand joined her in Castile, first as the king consort and then, in 1479, as king of Castile. That same year, Ferdinand succeeded his father as king of Aragon. In this way, the joint reign of the 'Catholic monarchs' of Spain began – though the two kingdoms were governed and administered separately. And in the spring of 1482, the campaign for Granada commenced.

'We further order in this edict that all Jews and Jewesses of whatever age that reside in our domain and territories leave with their sons and daughters, servants and relatives large or small, of all ages, by the end of July of this year, and that they dare not return to our lands and that they do not take a step across, such that if any Jew who does not accept this edict is found in our kingdom and domains or returns will be sentenced to death and confiscation of all their belongings.'

Ferdinand of Aragon and Isabella of Castile, Alhambra Decree, 31 March 1492

Ferdinand and Isabella made Spain into a powerful and wealthy nation. Having financed Columbus' voyage in 1492, they even had possessions in the Americas. In 1512, Ferdinand annexed the kingdom of Navarre. None of this, though, required the imposition of a single faith on all Spanish subjects. Nevertheless, it was political anxiety, and not personal animosity or prejudice, that led them to issue the notorious 'Alhambra Decree' of March 1492, which obliged all Jews living in their dominions to accept Christian baptism or to depart the country.

Aside from being cruel, pointless and economically harmful to Spain, this policy was contrary to the traditions of both kingdoms; the court of Aragon, in particular, had long admitted Jews into its service and protected the rights of their community. But the birth of Spain as a nation-state, and as an incipient empire, gave shape to a new ideology of religious and racial unity – an ideal ultimately known by the name of 'blood purity', (*limpieza de sangre*), despite the absurdity of such a concept after centuries of intermarriage

In this highly romanticized 19th-century painting by Antonio Rodriguez Villa, Moors are shown bringing tribute to Ferdinand and Isabella. In reality, the Reconquista *inaugurated an unprecedented persecution of Spain's non-Christian communities.*

among Christians, Jews and Muslims. Even those Jews and Muslims who converted to Christianity were not accorded the full dignities and rights of 'pure' Spaniards; and now, as baptized Christians, they fell under the authority of the Inquisition.

The Inquisition

Most of our impressions of the Spanish Inquisition are exaggerations, and can be traced back to a number of anti-Spanish legends of the 16th and 17th centuries. For most of its history, the Inquisition was a relatively weak institution, and in some times and places actually functioned as a benign and even lenient stay upon the more capricious and brutal practices of secular courts. Even so, it was an institution guilty of many gross injustices – especially in its first several decades – and one that used imprisonment, confiscation and even limited torture (usually chastisement with rods) to obtain the information it sought. It also, obviously, was willing to surrender those it condemned to the 'secular arm' to be killed in the name of doctrinal orthodoxy.

One should note, though, that the Inquisition was an office primarily of the Spanish crown. This does not entirely exculpate the papacy, of course. It was, after all, Pope Sixtus IV (1414–84) who authorized the early Inquisition. But he did so under pressure from Ferdinand, who threatened to withhold Spanish military protection against the Turks unless the pope agreed to give him licence to install an Inquisition in Castile and to appoint inquisitors. In 1478, the pope complied,

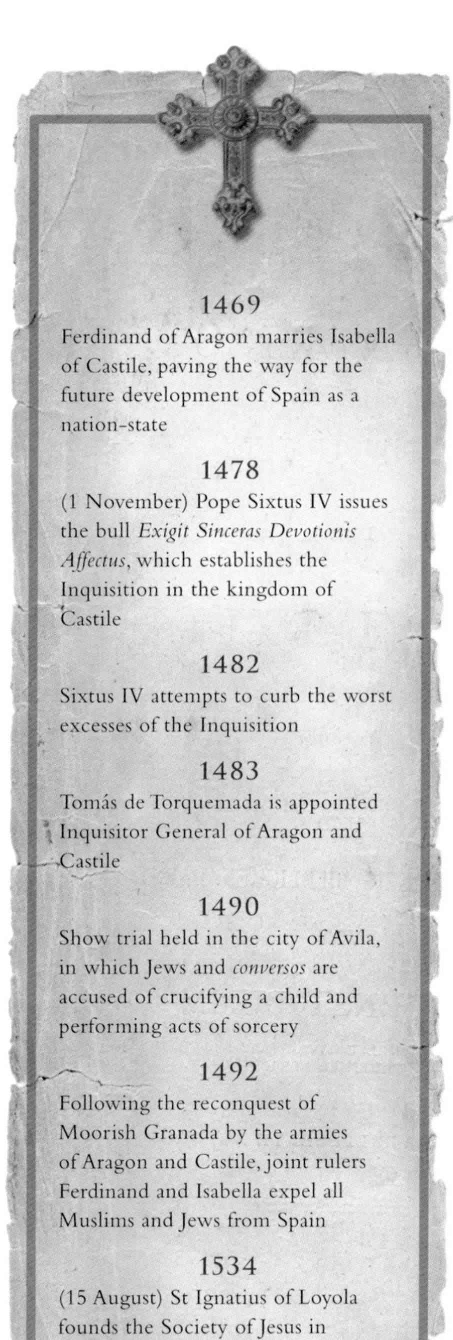

1469
Ferdinand of Aragon marries Isabella of Castile, paving the way for the future development of Spain as a nation-state

1478
(1 November) Pope Sixtus IV issues the bull *Exigit Sinceras Devotionis Affectus*, which establishes the Inquisition in the kingdom of Castile

1482
Sixtus IV attempts to curb the worst excesses of the Inquisition

1483
Tomás de Torquemada is appointed Inquisitor General of Aragon and Castile

1490
Show trial held in the city of Avila, in which Jews and *conversos* are accused of crucifying a child and performing acts of sorcery

1492
Following the reconquest of Moorish Granada by the armies of Aragon and Castile, joint rulers Ferdinand and Isabella expel all Muslims and Jews from Spain

1534
(15 August) St Ignatius of Loyola founds the Society of Jesus in Paris to undertake hospital and missionary work

and in February 1481 six 'heretics' of Seville became the first victims of the new office.

The Inquisition soon proved so harsh and corrupt, however, that Sixtus attempted to interfere in its operations. In a papal bull of April 1482, he uncompromisingly denounced its incarceration, torture, and condemnation of innocent persons and its theft of property (though he did not in principle object to the execution of real 'heretics'). Ferdinand, however, refused to recognize the bull, and in 1483 forced Sixtus to concede complete control of the Inquisition to the Spanish crown and to consent to the royal appointment of a 'Grand Inquisitor'. Sixtus did not, however, relent entirely. In 1484, for instance, he supported the Aragonese city of Teruel when it refused to allow the Inquisition entry – a refusal Ferdinand overcame the following year by force of arms.

The first Grand Inquisitor was the notorious Tomás de Torquemada (1420–98), a devout but brutish Dominican priest, who harboured a deep hostility towards Jewish and Muslim *conversos* whom he suspected of secret adherence to their original faiths. He was almost certainly the principal architect of the Alhambra Decree, and he presided over the Inquisition's most violent period. Before he was finally reined in by Pope Alexander VI (1431–1503), he was responsible for the expulsion of at least 40,000 Jews from their homes in Spain and for the execution of perhaps 2000 'heretics'.

St Ignatius and the Jesuits

Although Sixtus and his successor Innocent VIII (1432–92) continued to issue sporadic demands that the Inquisition exercise greater leniency, and attempted to intervene on behalf of *conversos* when the opportunity arose, their efforts were too feeble – and the national politics of *limpieza de sangre* too pervasive – to allow for any marked amelioration of the condition of convert families. Not even monks, priests or archbishops of Jewish descent could escape suspicion and harassment. There were, however, certain prominent Spaniards who rejected this new racialism – most conspicuously, perhaps, St Ignatius of Loyola (1491–1556), founder of the Jesuits, who went so far as to proclaim that he would have counted it a cause for pride had he been of Jewish extraction.

St Ignatius of Loyola was destined for a military career, but was inspired by the ideal of the 'chivalry' of holiness to become a priest.

THE INQUISITION AND THE WITCH-HUNTS

The disorienting truth about the Spanish Inquisition is that, for most of its history, it was more scrupulous in its attention to the rules of evidence, more likely to acquit and more lenient in its sentences than were the secular courts. For this reason, persons accused by their neighbours of witchcraft were generally fortunate if they lived in lands where the Inquisition was strong. From the time of Torquemada onwards, the Inquisition had the right to investigate 'superstitions,' and sorcery fell into this category. And there were rare instances in which the inquisitorial court did condemn persons for practising sorcery.

Nevertheless, Church courts almost invariably treated accusations of witchcraft and of Satanism with incredulity; where secular courts were inclined to consign the accused to the public executioner, ecclesial inquisitions were prone to demand hard evidence and, in its absence, to dismiss charges. In Spain, in the whole of the 14th and 15th centuries, we have evidence of only two prosecutions going to trial. In the mid-16th century, the Catalonian office of the Inquisition argued forcefully against all further prosecutions for witchcraft; and soon other Iberian tribunals added their voices to the recommendation.

In or around 1610, after a spasm of witch-hunting panic in Basque country – which had led to the execution of six people – the Spanish Inquisition actually went so far as to forbid even the discussion of witchcraft. The bishop of Pamplona wrote to the Inquisition to protest the injustices of these condemnations, and the inquisitor sent to investigate concluded that 'There were neither witches nor anyone bewitched before they were talked and written about'.

More than once, though, in following years, Iberian inquisitions were obliged to intervene when secular courts renewed prosecutions.

Ignatius was a son of the nobility who, in his youth, was intent upon achieving military glory; in 1521, however, while recovering in his family's castle from wounds sustained in battle, his readings in the lives of the saints led him to abandon the military life and his family's wealth. He devoted a year to penitential asceticism, and began writing his classic manual, the *Spiritual Exercises*. Then, after a pilgrimage to Jerusalem in 1523, he embarked on formal studies in Barcelona and Alcalá. He was briefly suspected of heresy, however, and imprisoned by the Inquisition, but was released on the condition he would not teach while still uncertified. So he went abroad to complete his studies, and it was in Paris in 1534 that the Society of Jesus was formed. He was ordained in 1537.

The Jesuits received papal approval of their rule in 1540, and Ignatius spent most of the last 15 years of his life in Rome. The new order soon attracted many of the most talented young men of western Europe; its emphasis upon scholarship in every field of learning, its missions to the farthest-flung regions of the world, its stated aim of making Christ known in every quarter of the globe – all these things imbued the Society of Jesus with a quality of what one can only call romance.

THE REFORMATION BEGINS

From the late 11th century onward, the power and wealth of the Catholic Church continued to grow. Not only was the Church in every nation a large landholder and an ally of princes, but the papacy itself was an armed state; and many men whose concerns and motives were anything but spiritual aspired to the papal crown. The 15th and 16th centuries were marred by several corrupt pontificates, and even the most pious Catholics could hardly be unaware that their Church was often in the hands of deplorable men. By the late 15th century there was a strong desire among many of the faithful for reform.

The call for reform was, in fact, first issued more than a century before the Protestant Reformation began. In England, John Wycliffe (*c.*1330–84) argued that the Church should surrender its riches, serve rather than profit from the poor and acknowledge scripture as its sole source of doctrinal authority. His theology, moreover, was cast in the mould of that of the late Augustine: he believed firmly in predestination and in the impotence of human works to earn any merit before God. The latter position especially seemed to derogate certain of the Church's penitential disciplines, as well as a practice increasingly common after the 11th century: the granting of indulgences. These were 'certificates' of remission of the 'temporal punishment' (the penance) due for sin, given in return for meritorious service or gifts made to the Church in a sincere spirit of contrition. The Bohemian theologian Jan Hus (*c.*1370–1415), a leader of the Czech reform movement, was sentenced to the stake by the Council of Constance for propounding similar ideas, and for attacking the sale of indulgences in Bohemia in 1412.

> *'We … condemn, reprobate and reject completely the books and all the writings and sermons of the said Martin Luther, whether in Latin or any other language … We forbid each and every one of the faithful of either sex, in virtue of holy obedience and under the above penalties to be incurred automatically, to read, assert, preach, praise, print, publish or defend them.'*
>
> POPE LEO X, EXSURGE DOMINE (PAPAL BULL ISSUED AGAINST LUTHER ON 15 JUNE 1520)

A century later, however, circumstances were more propitious for the cause of reform. The steady growth of the middle class had produced a greater number of educated, financially independent and politically enfranchised Catholics. More importantly, the early modern period was the age of the full emergence of the nation state in Europe; monarchs began to claim 'absolute' power for themselves, and an inviolable sovereignty for their nations. Older, 'feudal' notions of overlapping spheres of authority, with reciprocal responsibilities, and subject to a higher authority in spiritual matters, had become rather passé; and the princes of Europe had begun to resent the two trans-national authorities that still presumed to interfere in their affairs: the Holy Roman Empire and the Church.

The French crown – the most absolutist of all European monarchies – effectively subdued the Church in its territories by forcing Rome to consent in 1438 and

Luther's protest against the abuses and (as he saw it) theological deviations of the Roman Church precipitated the first large schism within Western European Christianity. This painting by the Belgian artist Eugène Siberdt (1851– 1931) shows Luther in 1521, translating the Bible.

14TH CENTURY
The English theologian John Wycliffe publishes a series of attacks on corrupt practices in the Church

1412
Jan Hus is sentenced to death for attacking the sale of indulgences in Bohemia

1476
Pope Sixtus IV declares that remission from punishment for souls in Purgatory can be secured by financial favours

1517
Martin Luther writes his 'Ninety-Five Theses'

1519
The German scholar Thomas Müntzer states that reformation of the Church should include a programme of social improvement

1520
A papal bull condemns Luther's teachings; he responds by producing three more treatises and publicly burning the bull

1521
In a second papal bull, Luther is threatened with excommunication; Frederick III intervenes and Luther is summoned to defend himself at the Imperial Diet in Worms

1523
Luther attacks the teachings of 'radical reformers' such as Müntzer

1525
Müntzer is a leader of a peasant revolt in Germany; the rebellion is suppressed and Müntzer is executed

1516 to concordats that, among other things, gave the king authority over ecclesial appointments in France and restricted papal jurisdiction over French bishops. In Spain, too, from 1486 on, the power of the crown over the Spanish Catholic Church was all but total. And much the same was true in Portugal. In lands, however, where the Catholic Church could not so easily be subdued – as in England or the German states – the idea of a Church establishment directly subordinate to the monarch exercised a very definite appeal; and in those lands, the cause of Reformation often thrived.

MARTIN LUTHER

The one man who can be called the father of the Protestant Reformation – at least, in its German variant – is the monk, priest and theologian Martin Luther (1483–1546). Luther came from a moderately comfortable bourgeois background, received sound schooling, took his Bachelor's and Master's degrees from the University of Erfurt, and in 1505 (supposedly to keep a vow he made when caught in a terrifying thunderstorm) joined the Order of Augustinian Hermits. In 1508, the

Order sent him to the University of Wittenberg, where he encountered a number of scholars who were openly hostile to much of the metaphysics (and in particular the Aristotelianism) of Medieval scholasticism. In 1510, moreover, he visited Rome on behalf of his Order, and was deeply disturbed by the licentiousness of the superior hierarchy, the irreverence of the Roman clergy and the sheer worldliness of Italian Renaissance culture.

In an age when only a minority of the population was literate, Luther understood the benefits of the sermon as an instrument of reform. In this illustration he is depicted preaching, with one hand pointing to popes, monks and cardinals being swallowed by the mouth of Hell, and with the other to the Crucifix.

In 1512, he took his doctorate and assumed the chair in biblical theology, but his professional eminence apparently brought him no great satisfaction. By his own account, he was haunted by an unendurable feeling of unworthiness and guilt, a sense of his own impurities of thought and will and a deep fear of God's displeasure. He was delivered from his anxieties only when his readings of Paul led him to the conclusion that divine justice – unlike human justice – is a power that gratuitously makes the sinner just, and that it is not by works, but by faith, that one is justified. Here, he believed, he had discovered the true joyous tidings of the gospel: that human beings are not saved by their efforts to make themselves good in the eyes of God (an impossibility in any event), but by God's free gift of forgiveness.

Theological Differences

Over the next few years, Luther's hostility to scholastic method increased, his preference for Augustine's theology became more pronounced and his theology of justification by grace alone became more emphatic. But none of this would necessarily have led to a rupture within the Church had it not been for the 'indulgences controversy'. In 1476, the pope had allowed the merit vouchsafed by an indulgence to be applied to the soul of a person enduring 'temporal punishment' in Purgatory. The idea of Purgatory – that the soul undergoes a period of purgation after death for undischarged venial sins – had deep roots in Western Catholic tradition, and had been given clear definition at the Councils of Lyon and Florence. But the proclamation that one might secure remission from such punishment in exchange for financial contributions was obviously little more than a cynical scheme for generating revenue. Reacting to the especially shameless methods of one seller of indulgences, Luther in 1517 wrote his 'Ninety-Five Theses', a series of academic propositions for debate that suggested, rather cautiously, that such indulgences reflected a defective theology of grace.

> *'Those who believe themselves assured of salvation by papal letters will be eternally damned, along with their teachers.'*
>
> MARTIN LUTHER
> *NINETY-FIVE THESES*,
> 31 OCTOBER 1517
> (FROM THESIS 31)

The dispute that followed was unexpectedly fierce, in part because some of Luther's colleagues and allies were somewhat less circumspect than he was. Luther enjoyed the favour and protection of the Elector of Saxony, Frederick III (1463–1525), but even so was obliged to go into hiding when it seemed he might be extradited from Augsburg – to which he had been summoned to defend his

CHRISTIAN FREEDOM AND HUMAN FREEDOM

Thomas Müntzer (1490–1525) – a contemporary and, briefly, an admirer of Luther – was a priest and scholar who had himself begun agitating for reform as early as 1519, but who believed that the reformation of which Luther spoke could be complete only if it included a programme of social amelioration. Luther, after all, wrote movingly of the freedom of the Christian from the burden of the law; but such freedom surely involved more than mere spiritual consolation.

Müntzer soon became convinced that his pastoral vocation obliged him to act as an advocate for the poor against the abuses of the rich; and increasingly he came to believe that the highest authority for the Christian was not the Church, or even simply scripture, but the voice of the Holy Spirit speaking to the individual conscience. And by 1522 he became convinced that it was the will of God that a holy war should be waged by the poor against the social and political order. Ultimately, when a large peasant revolt broke out in Thuringia in 1525 – one that briefly established a fairly large alliance of 'commoners' and even took control of certain towns – Müntzer was among its leaders.

Luther was deeply shaken by the teachings of Müntzer and other of the 'radical reformers'. In 1523, he wrote a short treatise entitled 'Of Worldly Governance', in which he firmly asserted that civil authority is instituted by God, and rebellion against that authority a grave sin. He was not by any means unsympathetic to the complaints of the rebels, even if his own social views were not particularly egalitarian; over many years, the peasants of Germany had been deprived of many of the common rights that had been theirs since the early Middle Ages, and had consequently been left at the mercy of usurers and landlords. But when the revolt began, Luther nevertheless exhorted the peasants to desist from rebellion; and when they did not, he wrote a scorching tract – 'Against the Murderous and Thieving Hordes of Peasants' – in which he encouraged the legal authorities to slaughter the rebels without pity.

On 15 May 1525, at the Battle of Frankenhausen, the revolt was decisively defeated. Müntzer was captured, tortured, tried and executed. He did not recant his teachings, however; and Luther did not mourn his passing.

theses – to Rome. But the debate he had sparked could not now be extinguished, in large part because the new technology of the printing press had made his views known well beyond the close confines of the world of academic theology. In 1520, Rome issued a papal bull condemning a number of Luther's teachings. Luther responded by writing three especially provocative treatises – one calling on the secular princes of Germany to convene a council of reform, one denouncing a variety of Catholic teachings regarding the number of sacraments, the power of the pope and the authority of scripture, and one proclaiming the freedom of the Christian conscience – and by burning the bull in public. In January 1521, Rome promulgated a second bull, excommunicating Luther. Frederick III, however, convinced the Holy Roman emperor to allow Luther to defend himself before the Imperial Diet in Worms before recognizing the bull; and Luther – despite the apprehension of many of his friends – obeyed the emperor's summons.

THE GROWTH OF THE REFORMATION

The Protestant Reformation was an immense – but not a unified – religious, social and political movement. The spectrum of Protestant theology admitted of countless variants and intensities, from the most moderate and cautious to the most extreme and reckless.

The Magisterial Reforms – that is, the Lutheran and the Calvinist – rejected certain practices and doctrines of the Catholic Church but still affirmed all the classic dogmas and practices of the early Church: the Trinity, the two natures of Christ, infant baptism and so on. Both, moreover, were profoundly Augustinian in their theologies. But other reform movements were not so bound to tradition.

Reformation in Germany

When Luther arrived in Worms in April 1521 to appear before the Imperial Diet, not only was he greeted by crowds of supporters, his entourage included a large number of German knights. If, though, Emperor Charles V (1500–58) was impressed by this display of popular support, he did not show it; instead he simply instructed Luther to recant. Luther, in the presence of the Diet, refused, saying that, unless it could be proved to him from scripture that he had erred, he was bound by conscience to hold firm. Debate could not move him, and the Diet (no doubt noting that many of Luther's companions were 'men of action') allowed him to depart; in his absence, however, the Diet declared him an outlaw – a decision that forced him to go into hiding for almost a year. He continued to write during this time, however, and began his German translation of the Bible. The Reformation – or 'Evangelical Movement' – in the German principalities was now an inexorable force. From 1526 onwards, with some predictable vacillations, the emperor was increasingly obliged to concede the princes of Germany the right to govern the churches in their domains as their consciences dictated. In 1531, moreover, the Protestant princes formed the Schmalkaldic League, a defensive alliance, and in 1532, anxious over a possible Turkish invasion, the emperor agreed to an official truce with the Reformers (which lasted until 1544).

'I cannot and will not recant anything, for to act against the dictates of conscience is neither right nor safe.'

Martin Luther, Speech at the Diet of Worms, 18 April 1521

Under the pen of Luther, the principles of the movement became ever clearer: the 'priesthood of all believers', the complete dependency of the soul on God's grace, unmerited election to salvation, the 'bondage of the will' of fallen humanity (either to the devil or to God), the 'freedom of the Christian', salvation by faith and not by works, and the uselessness of such Catholic forms of 'works righteousness' as penance, the 'sacrifice of the mass' and clerical celibacy. One distinctive feature of Luther's theology – and so of the Evangelical Church – was his insistence on the real presence of Christ in the bread and wine of the Eucharist, a position he defended on the Christological grounds that, in the incarnation, Christ's humanity came to share perfectly in all the attributes of his divinity (including omnipresence). He preferred to speak of this presence, though, as occurring 'with' the substances of the bread and wine (a position known as 'consubstantiation') rather than as displacing those substances with the substances of Christ's body and blood ('transubstantiation').

With the help of intellectual allies such as Philipp Melanchthon (1497–1560), the brilliant humanist scholar who reformed the German educational system, Luther was able to create a genuinely Evangelical culture for the Protestant German states and Scandinavia. He remained a controversialist to the end, attacking enemies with the same zeal with which he preached the free gift of divine grace. His denunciations of the papacy – an institution 'founded by the devil' – of radical reformers and of Jews became, if anything, more intemperate as he aged. But at his death he left behind him a distinct, independent and doctrinally cogent Protestant Church.

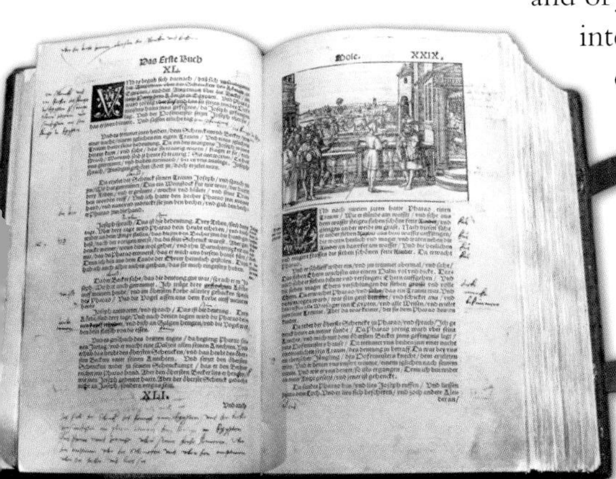

In hiding at the Elector of Saxony's castle at Wartburg in 1521, Luther worked on his translation of the Bible into German. Above is a copy of a Luther Bible with margin notes and corrections made in Luther's own hand.

Swiss Reformation

The other major stream of the 'Magisterial Reformation' is that which flowed from Switzerland, now principally associated with John Calvin (1509–64). A more important figure, though, for the *rise* of the Reformed tradition in Switzerland was Huldrych Zwingli (1484–1531), the priest and humanist scholar who, as early as 1516, began preaching against clerical abuses, and whose sermons 'from true, divine scripture', starting in 1520, inaugurated a popular movement in Switzerland against such practices as priestly celibacy and the keeping of fasts. In Zurich, from 1523, he succeeded in bringing about liturgical reforms, the stripping of the churches of images and of organs, the institution of Bible study and the taking of wives by many of the clergy (including Zwingli himself). He taught that doctrinal authority lies in the Bible alone, that the Church has no head but Christ, that prayers for the dead are of no avail, that the doctrine of Purgatory is unscriptural and that the Eucharist is in no sense a 'sacrifice'. His understanding of original sin was rather like that of the Greek fathers, in that he denied that it involved any inheritance of aboriginal guilt. Like Luther, he taught that justification is a free gift of God's grace alone. Unlike Luther, he denied the real presence of Christ's body and blood in the elements of the Eucharist, and argued that the

1520
In Switzerland Huldrych Zwingli openly questions certain dogmas of the Roman Catholic Church and founds a movement for reform

1521
At the Diet of Worms Martin Luther refuses to recant accusations against the Catholic Church; he is released, but the Diet declares him an outlaw

1523
Zwingli's reforms include removal of images and organs from churches

1526
Charles V grants German princes the right to govern churches in their own domains

1531
Protestant princes form the Schmalkaldic League. Michael Servetus proposes a form of Unitarianism

1532
Charles V agrees to a truce with the Reformers

1536
John Calvin's 'The Institutes of Christian Religion'; for the next two years Calvin works on Reformation in Geneva but is expelled in 1538

1541
After living in Strasbourg, Calvin returns to Geneva to implement his Protestant vision

1553
Servetus is tried and executed in Geneva for heresy

John Calvin, the French lawyer, humanist scholar and theologian whose work The Institutes of the Christian Religion – *the first edition of which appeared in 1536, when Calvin was not yet 27 – still constitutes the most systematic and lucid expression of the principles of 'Reformed' (as distinct from 'Lutheran' or 'Evangelical') Protestantism.*

human and divine natures in Christ remain eternally distinct in their attributes and operations. And Zwingli's teachings had spread to other cantons within Switzerland, and had helped to give form to a distinctively Swiss Reformed Church well before his death in battle, as a military chaplain, in 1564.

Calvin

The most important figure in the next generation of Reformers was, of course, John Calvin. As a young man in Paris, Calvin was active in the movement for reform within the Catholic Church, as a result of which he found it prudent to leave France in 1533. He went to Basel in Switzerland, where he came to adopt a more purely Protestant view of things. From 1536 to 1538 he lived in Geneva, where he worked on behalf of the city's nascent reformation until the (Protestant, but tepidly so) city council expelled him. He sojourned in Strasbourg, Germany until 1541, when Geneva invited him to return to help overcome the city's resistance – or indifference – to the Reformed cause.

In Geneva, Calvin was able – despite occasional conflict and failure – to create a Church organization and social order consonant with his theological vision. Churches were run by elders, duly constituted pastors preached and taught, and deacons looked after the needs of the community. Moreover, the Genevans' morals were now matters not only of social concern but of criminal law: licentiousness, dancing, gambling, profane speech, improprieties of dress or comportment, irreverence or blasphemy, absence from church and all other forms of moral laxity were to be reported by community invigilators and punished by magistrates, often in a vividly public way. And false doctrine was not to be tolerated. These measures point to certain profound differences between the Lutheran and Calvinist understandings of grace. Luther might well have regarded many of Calvin's vice laws as signs of an excessive anxiety regarding personal righteousness, and even as a form of justification by works. Calvin, though, believed that the gift of justification really makes men and women righteous, and that any society made up of the elect should reflect the sanctity instilled in human hearts by grace, as evidence of God's workings.

In most respects, the elements of Calvin's theology were typically Protestant: the unique authority of scripture, the absolute gratuity of justification, the impotence of the human will to merit salvation, the uselessness of fasts and penances, and predestination. In this last case, though, Calvin's emphasis differed from that of Luther. No other theologian ever put so great a stress upon the sheer sovereignty of God, as an explanation of the mystery of God's actions in creation and redemption. He went so far as to assert that God eternally foreordained even the original fall of humanity from grace, that he might by the working of his will display the glory of his sovereignty in the gratuitous salvation of the elect and in the fitting damnation of the derelict. This theology of absolute divine sovereignty became one of the most characteristic features of the high Reformed tradition.

THE DEATH OF SERVETUS

Whatever the Magisterial Reformation was, it certainly was not a movement for greater freedom of conscience – much less freedom of religion. The aim of reform was a stricter adherence to the rule of scripture (as interpreted by reforming theologians) and a renewal of piety and moral purpose among the faithful. But Protestant regimes were no more tolerant of aberrant theological opinions than were their Catholic counterparts.

Portrait of Michael Servetus, from a biography published in 1727. A renowned scholar in many fields of science, his life was cut short by his trial and eventual execution for heresy.

Prime evidence of this would be the case of Michael Servetus (*c.*1510–53), the Spanish physician, scholar of science, astrologer, discoverer of blood circulation and amateur theologian who – though a Catholic and attracted to the cause of reform – offended against Protestant and Catholic orthodoxy alike by publishing two books (the first in 1531, the second in 1532) attacking the doctrine of the Trinity, and proposing in its place a kind of complex Unitarianism.

In 1534, a proposed debate in Paris between Servetus and John Calvin failed to materialize, but Servetus clearly came in the years that followed to regard Calvin as his natural theological interlocutor. In 1546, he sent the manuscript of his treatise 'The Restitution of Christianity' (which attacked Nicene theology as extra-biblical) to Calvin in Geneva, and attempted to initiate a dialogue by post. After a few exchanges, however, Calvin terminated the correspondence and even refused to return the manuscript; he also vowed to his fellow Genevan reformer Guillaume Farel (1489–1565) that, if Servetus ever came to Geneva, he would not be allowed to leave alive.

Calvin was as good as his word. In 1553, Servetus – fleeing the inquisitor in Lyon – entered Geneva, where he was recognized, arrested and put on trial for heresy. Calvin argued forcefully in favour of execution, and – enraged by Servetus' defence of his positions before the court – peevishly remarked that he would have liked to see the Spaniard's eyes scratched out by chickens.

Servetus was convicted and sentenced to be burned at the stake. To his credit, perhaps, Calvin expressed a preference for quick and merciful decapitation. This did not prevent him later, however, from mocking Servetus' cries of torment amid the flames.

'For I do not disguise it that I considered it my duty to put a check, so far as I could, upon this most obstinate and ungovernable man, that his contagion might not spread further.'

JOHN CALVIN, LETTER REGARDING SERVETUS, SEPTEMBER 1553

THE ANABAPTISTS AND THE CATHOLIC REFORMATION

Though it is not uncommon to think of the Reformation as a movement more or less exhausted by the two main schools of the 'Magisterial Reformation' – the Lutheran and the Calvinist – it was in fact a larger and more diverse historical phenomenon. Not only was reform not limited to the institutions of the German and Swiss Protestant churches; it was not confined to Protestantism. If Lutheranism and Calvinism together constituted the 'broad middle' of the Reformation, to their 'left' lay a number of more radical Protestantisms, and to their 'right' the reform movement within the Catholic Church.

The name commonly applied to the majority of 'radical' or 'free' Protestant reformers was 'Anabaptists', which means 'Re-baptizers'. The name derives from the fact that these reformers taught that baptism – being the emblem of a sincere conversion of the heart to faith in Christ – could be undertaken only by adults; hence they performed baptisms on persons who had already been baptized as infants. (This was, incidentally, a capital crime for baptizer and baptized alike.) They rejected the term Anabaptist, however, on the not unreasonable grounds that, according to their beliefs, they had never truly been baptized before they themselves freely consented to the ritual.

The Protestant reforms of Huldrych Zwingli, pictured in this 1531 engraving by Hans Asper, were not sufficiently rapid or far-reaching for Konrad Grebel. Grebel broke with Zwingli in 1524 and founded the Swiss Brethren.

As a rule, this branch of the Reformation – at least in its earliest forms – was deeply influenced by Zwingli's theology. Its followers therefore felt no great anxiety in withholding baptism from their own children, since they believed that no guilt could attach to the soul before the age of reason. Unlike Zwingli, however, Anabaptist communities tended towards political and social separatism, and regarded civil allegiances, litigations, military service and civil oaths as contrary to genuine Christian adherence. Some of them were political radicals as well, inspired by a theocratic Messianism, but in general they were non-violent on principle. And, inasmuch as their views were repugnant to Catholic and Protestant authorities alike, they were persecuted by both. If any 16th-century Western communion could identify itself with the 'Church of the martyrs', it was theirs.

The Swiss Brethren

One of the earliest Anabaptist communities was the Swiss Brethren, founded in Zurich by the humanist scholar Konrad Grebel (*c.*1498–1526), an early admirer of Zwingli who became disenchanted with the graduality and moderate nature of the latter's reforms (and his acceptance of infant baptism). In January 1525, in defiance of the admonitions of the city council, Grebel began administering baptism to persons 'already' baptized. His movement spread, but he was twice

Menno Simonsz, an early leader of the Anabaptist movement in Holland. His moderate leadership and pacifist beliefs helped to unify the non-violent wing of the Dutch Anabaptists.

1521
Balthasar Hubmaier becomes one of the leaders of the Swiss 'Anabaptist' movement

1525
Konrad Grebel, founder of the Swiss Brethren, practises 're-baptism' in Zurich; Hubmaier is arrested

1528
Hubmaier is burned at the stake in Vienna

1533
In Strasbourg, Melchior Hoffman, a radical Anabaptist, is imprisoned; his followers retreat to Münster in Westphalia

1534
John of Leiden declares Münster the New Jerusalem and introduces adult baptism. Radical Anabaptist supporters seize control of the city hall but are besieged by royal forces; Jan Mathijsz is killed but John of Leiden proclaims himself 'king' of the new 'Zion of God'

1535
Catholic and Lutheran soldiers retake Münster. Insurrection among Dutch Anabaptists and the death of some of their number causes Menno Simonsz to denounce violence; his outspokenness condemns him to life as a fugitive

1536
John of Leiden and two other Anabaptist leaders are tortured and killed

1545–63
The Council of Trent institutes wide-scale reforms of the Catholic Church

prosecuted and jailed, was constantly harassed and died young. His example, though, inspired Balthasar Hubmaier (1485–1528), a German Anabaptist who in 1521 became one of the leaders of the Swiss movement – only to be arrested in Zurich in 1525 and forced to recant – and then became a leader of the Anabaptist movement in Moravia (where conditions were not so adverse). He was burned at the stake in Vienna in 1528.

A more radical and less peaceful strain of Anabaptism drew inspiration from the teachings of Melchior Hoffman (*c.*1495–1543), the German lay theologian – originally an ally of Luther and promoter of the German Reformation – whose conviction that he was living at the end of time led him to evolve a particularly eschatological interpretation of the reform movement, and finally to embrace Anabaptism. His beliefs, however, were eccentric even among the Anabaptists: he prophesied that Christ would return in 1533, and that he – Hoffman – would establish the New Jerusalem in Strasbourg.

That very city, evidently insensible of the honour it had been accorded, placed Hoffman in prison, where he died a decade later. Nevertheless,

Persecution of Anabaptists by Catholics and Protestants was even more severe than that of the early Christians by pagan Rome. The 'heretics' were subjected to imprisonment, torture and even execution, often by burning alive. This illustration depicts Anneken Henriks, a 16th-century Dutch Anabaptist martyr, being tied to a ladder and hoisted towards the fire.

his teachings won some particularly zealous adherents, with occasionally violent consequences – such as the brief, bloody history of the 'kingdom' founded by Anabaptist radicals in Münster in 1534 – which served only to provoke fiercer persecutions of the Anabaptists in both Catholic and Protestant lands.

Yet the Anabaptists were, by overwhelming majority, convinced pacifists. Typical of the movement was Menno Simonsz (1496–1561), the Dutch founder of the Mennonites. Menno was ordained a priest in 1524, but by 1528 had become convinced of the validity of many Reformation principles, and ultimately came to embrace the doctrine of adult baptism. There were radicals among the Dutch Anabaptists, however, some of whom were involved in insurrectionary activities leading, in 1535, to an engagement with Dutch soldiers that left several persons dead. Menno openly denounced the behaviour of the radicals, arguing that violence was forbidden to Christians, and that all baptized men and women were called to lives of charity, even under persecution.

Menno himself probably submitted to 're-baptism' in early 1537. About the same time, he was ordained as an Anabaptist pastor and took a wife. Thereafter, branded a heretic in every nation, he lived the life of a fugitive. Men could be executed if

THE KINGDOM OF MÜNSTER

After Melchior Hoffman's imprisonment in Strasbourg, one of the few German cities to which his followers and other Anabaptists could safely retreat was Münster in Westphalia. The influential Lutheran preacher in the city, Bernhard Rothman (1495–1535), had Anabaptist leanings, and as a result of his teachings the city council became a majority Anabaptist assembly in 1533.

The radicals who came to Münster were led by two Dutch Anabaptists, Jan Mathijsz (d.1534) and John Beuckelszoon (d.1536) – better known as 'John of Leiden' – who declared the city the New Jerusalem and introduced adult baptism in January 1534. The next month, the radicals seized control of the city hall, appointed one of their own – Bernhard Knipperdolling (c.1495–1535) – as mayor, expelled many 'infidels', instituted a theocracy and began to proclaim their intention of conquering the world (with God's help, of course).

The region's prince bishop, Franz de Waldeck, laid siege to the rebellious city. In April, on Easter Sunday, Mathijsz prophesied that God would use him as an instrument of heavenly justice against the enemies of the New Jerusalem, and with a retinue of 30 men rode out against the besieging army. He and his men were all promptly killed. His body was decapitated and castrated, his head impaled on a pole outside the city walls, and his genitals nailed to the city gate.

Undeterred, John of Leiden declared Münster a 'kingdom of a thousand years' and the new 'Zion of God', proclaimed himself its king (after the order of King David), and instituted such 'Christian' ordinances as the dissolution of all private property, in favour of a community of goods, and polygamy. He himself took 16 wives (one of whom, however, he was obliged to behead with his own hands in the public square, on account of some transgression or other).

In June 1535, the city was taken by a combined force of Catholic and Lutheran soldiers. The following January, three of the Anabaptist leaders of the city – including King John of Leiden – were hideously tortured and put to death; their flayed bodies were then displayed in iron cages suspended from the steeple of St Lambert's Church, and left there until only bones remained.

convicted of sheltering him. In 1542, Emperor Charles V put a price on his head. And yet Menno continued to write and preach with a rare eloquence, and died of natural causes 25 years after his 'apostasy'.

The Catholic Reformation

In the 16th and 17th centuries, the Catholic Church instituted changes in Church discipline, undertook liturgical reforms, rooted out internal corruption and abuses, and promulgated a number of clarifications of its doctrines and practices. This movement for spiritual and institutional renewal is often spoken of as the 'Counter-Reformation', but this is a misleading term; for, though many of the Catholic doctrinal pronouncements of the time were responses to Protestant theological claims, the movement for reform in the Church antedated the schisms of the 16th century, and the advocates of reform within the Church had not disappeared as a result of those schisms. Many in the Catholic hierarchy and in the ranks of the educated laity deplored clerical malfeasances, 'superstitions', hypocrisies and spiritual sloth no less than the Protestant Reformers, but did not share the latter's theological convictions or understanding of the Church.

The Spanish theologian St Ignatius Loyola was an influential figure of the Catholic Reformation, founding the Society of Jesus (the Jesuits) in 1534. Education of the laity and the common clergy was one of the stated goals of the Society, together with total devotion to the pope as the only earthly authority to which it answered.

Men like the Dutch Catholic humanist Desiderius Erasmus (1469–1536) and his friend the English humanist and statesman Sir Thomas More (1477–1535) – both contemporaries of Luther – were strong champions of Church reform, but were equally strong opponents of schism and of the severe late Augustinianism of Luther's understanding of sin and grace. Erasmus was inspired especially by the writings of the Greek Church Fathers, and by their spiritual exegesis of scripture. He detested the corruption of the papacy, excessive clericalism, sectarian persecution, ecclesial peculation and the obscurantism of many established forms of Catholic piety, but he disliked fanaticism and division as well. He and Luther were early admirers of one another, but they disagreed fundamentally in their reading of St Paul and on the issue of the freedom of the fallen will. Thomas More – famously 'martyred' under King Henry VIII (1491–1547) – shared Erasmus' enthusiasm for biblical and patristic scholarship and for Church reform, but was far more censorious of Luther and his fellow 'schismatics'.

The work of Church reform, however, was largely the work not of humanists, but of monks and nuns. New religious orders and renewals of existing orders were the chief engines of a spiritual regeneration that spread throughout the Catholic world in the 16th century, producing men such as St Ignatius of Loyola (1491–1556) or the great Spanish Carmelite mystic (and Spain's greatest lyric poet) St John of the Cross (1542–91) or the Jesuit spiritual writer St Francis de Sales (1567–1622). And the great zeal for missions abroad inspired by this revival ultimately helped lead to the global ubiquity and immense demography of the modern Roman Catholic Church.

The great institutional renewal of the Roman Church, though, began when Pope Paul III (1468–1549) convoked the Council of Trent in 1545. This council continued (with occasional interruptions) under a number of popes until 1563. It instituted a massive reform and regularization of the Western liturgy, dealt systematically with a number of clerical abuses, forbade the sale of indulgences, prescribed the proper pastoral duties of bishops and priests, established definitively the canon of the Bible and dictated the sort of education to be provided for

The Council of Trent, the subject of this fresco painting, played a vital role in the Catholic Reformation. As well as issuing wide-ranging decrees on reform, it also clarified existing Catholic doctrine.

priests. The council also, however, reaffirmed many doctrines controverted by the Protestant reformers: Purgatory, Christ's real presence in the Eucharistic elements (by 'transubstantiation' rather than by 'consubstantiation'), the existence of seven sacraments, the supremacy of papal authority and so on. Most importantly, the council rejected Luther's teachings on justification, asserting the reality of human freedom in the work of redemption, the indispensability of good works and the need for the co-operation of the will set free by grace. Moreover, it did this with so thorough and plenteous an exposition from scripture that no Protestant theologian – however much he might disagree with the council's conclusions – could plausibly doubt the centrality of the Bible in its deliberations.

SCHISM AND WAR: EARLY MODERN EUROPE

The history of the Reformation is unintelligible if its political causes are not taken into account. The desire for ecclesial reform was quite sincere among many Catholics and Protestants, but it would have remained unrealized had the cause of reform not served the interests of princes. Protestant churches were, by their nature, national establishments, subordinate to local rulers, and beyond the influence of pope and emperor alike. In the case of England, in fact, reformation was the result – and not the cause – of schism from the Roman Church.

A statue at Trinity College, Cambridge of King Henry VIII, who founded the institution in 1546. Henry's rift with the Catholic Church was not occasioned by doctrinal differences, but by his paramount urge to secure the Tudor succession.

Moreover, Europe's early modern period was an age of extraordinary violence, during which the modern sovereign nation state was forged in the crucibles of war, civil strife and not a few massacres. It was inevitable that the new religious movements of the continent would be conscripted into those struggles, and the new religious divisions exploited by the powerful.

The Catholic Church in England

The Anglican Church was not born out of any great popular movement for reform in England; nor did it begin as a Protestant establishment. When King Henry VIII (1491–1547) had himself declared head of the Church in his dominions, he understood this to mean head of the Catholic Church in England. In breaking with the pope, he did not intend to adopt an Evangelical theology or Church discipline. He detested Martin Luther and took pride in his title 'Defender of the Faith', which the pope had granted him for writing an anti-Lutheran defence of Catholic sacramental theology entitled *Assertio Septem Sacramentorum* ('The Defence of the Seven Sacraments') in 1521.

Indeed, the hesitancy with which reform was embraced in England left its mark on the communion ever after: not only in its historical emphasis upon the need to preserve the 'Apostolic Succession' (the direct continuity of its bishops in a line of consecration going back to the Apostles), or in the existence today of Anglican monastic orders, but in the regularity with which 'High Church' movements have arisen that have been theologically, liturgically, and devotionally committed to the position that the Anglican Church is a Catholic communion.

Henry would not have broken with Rome at all had he been able to procure an annulment of his marriage to Catherine of Aragon (1485–1536) – supposedly on biblical grounds – so that he might marry the younger Anne Boleyn (*c.*1507–36) and so perhaps produce a male heir. The pope dared not grant such a request, however, since Catherine was the aunt of the Holy Roman emperor Charles V (1500–58). In 1531, after seven years of waiting, Henry separated from Catherine; a year and a half later, he married Anne; and five months after that, he had the

Thomas Cranmer, archbishop of Canterbury, won Henry VIII's favour by suggesting that the king circumvent papal authority in the matter of his annulment.

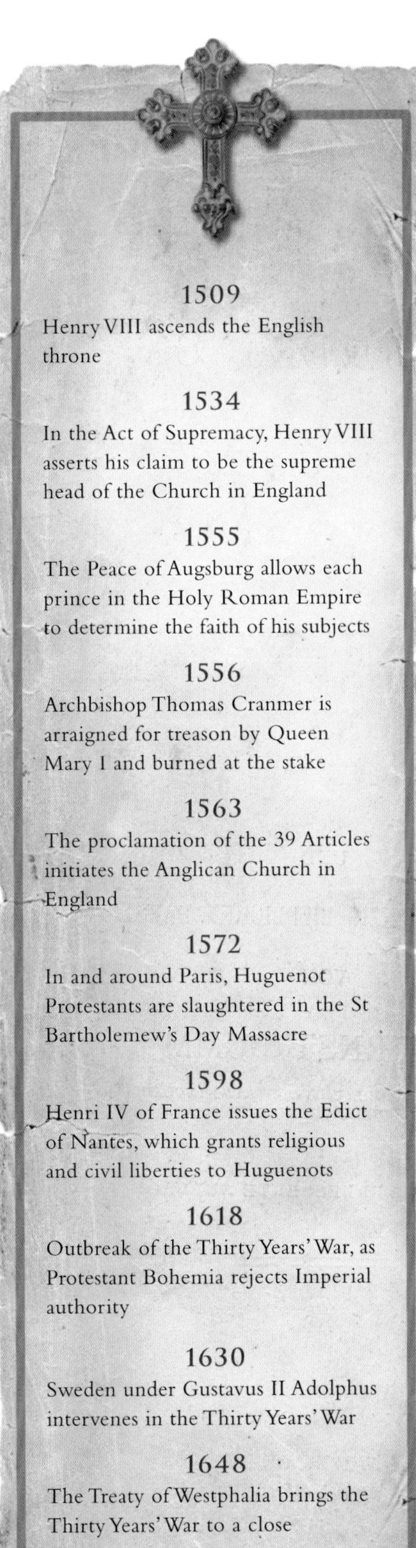

new archbishop of Canterbury, Thomas Cranmer (1489–1556) – Henry's own appointment in 1533 – officially declare the first marriage annulled.

1509
Henry VIII ascends the English throne
1534
In the Act of Supremacy, Henry VIII asserts his claim to be the supreme head of the Church in England
1555
The Peace of Augsburg allows each prince in the Holy Roman Empire to determine the faith of his subjects
1556
Archbishop Thomas Cranmer is arraigned for treason by Queen Mary I and burned at the stake
1563
The proclamation of the 39 Articles initiates the Anglican Church in England
1572
In and around Paris, Huguenot Protestants are slaughtered in the St Bartholemew's Day Massacre
1598
Henri IV of France issues the Edict of Nantes, which grants religious and civil liberties to Huguenots
1618
Outbreak of the Thirty Years' War, as Protestant Bohemia rejects Imperial authority
1630
Sweden under Gustavus II Adolphus intervenes in the Thirty Years' War
1648
The Treaty of Westphalia brings the Thirty Years' War to a close

The Monarch's Supremacy

Cranmer (who had Lutheran leanings) counselled Henry to note that, in scripture, it is kings – and not popes – who are God's anointed rulers over all spheres, spiritual no less than temporal. This suited both Henry's taste for the new, 'French' monarchical absolutism, and the political designs of Thomas Cromwell (*c.*1485–1540), the powerful head of the king's Privy Council, who in 1534 convinced Parliament to pass the 'Act of Supremacy', which declared the English monarch the sole head of the Church in England. Cromwell had few discernible convictions, but he favoured Reformation for reasons of state, and he was largely responsible for the dissolution of the English monasteries and seizure of their property by the crown. Henry, however, remained Catholic by conviction; he insisted upon a celibate priesthood, retained the sacramental theology of the Roman Church and steadfastly resisted 'Lutheran' reforms to the end.

Only after Henry's death did Cranmer begin to introduce Protestant forms of worship into the English Church, principally through his exquisitely beautiful Book of Common Prayer, the first version of which appeared in 1549. He paid the price for this, though, under the Roman Catholic Queen Mary I (1516–58), who had him burned at the stake. When, however, Elizabeth I (1533–1603) – Henry's daughter by Anne Boleyn – became queen, she made the English Church a Protestant establishment. Elizabeth was not much more enthusiastic for reform than her father had been, but she recognized the political utility of the Act of Supremacy; in religion, she was a moderate traditionalist, who believed in Christ's real presence in the Eucharist, but who felt equal distaste for the overly elaborate ritualism of high churchmen and for the undisciplined congregationalism of the English 'Puritan' party. And it was she who determined the shape the Church of England would assume: Catholic in hierarchical structure, Protestant in practice, and simultaneously Catholic and Protestant in constituency.

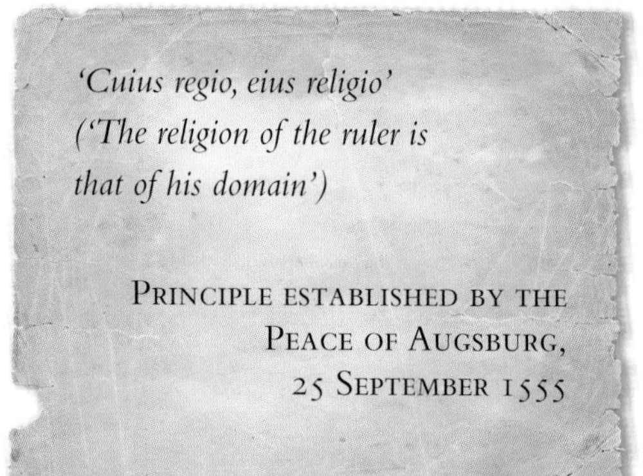

'Cuius regio, eius religio'
('The religion of the ruler is that of his domain')
PRINCIPLE ESTABLISHED BY THE PEACE OF AUGSBURG, 25 SEPTEMBER 1555

THE 'WARS OF RELIGION'

The term 'wars of religion' has traditionally been used as a general designation for the monstrously brutal conflicts fought between and within the nations of western Europe from the early 16th to the middle of the 17th centuries – which suggests that these were wars fought along confessional lines, prompted by religious passions, and waged for religious ends. Both the term and the impression it conveys are wildly inaccurate. These wars were, in fact, the birth-pangs of the modern European nation-state, and were fought for political power and national sovereignty, and though religious allegiances and hatreds were exploited by regional princes, they were at most incidental, and determined neither the alliances nor the aggressions of the time.

The earliest of these conflicts were those waged by the Habsburg Holy Roman Emperor Charles V (1500–58) — who was at war, from 1521 to 1522, with Catholic France and, in 1527, with the pope (that year his armies even sacked Rome). It is true that Charles objected to the spread of Lutheranism in his vassal states, but this was because he correctly recognized it as part of a movement of national independence. And though the German wars that began in 1547 ended in 1555 with the 'Peace of Augsburg' – which granted each prince the right to determine the religion of his own state – this was a charter of national, not religious, autonomy. The Catholic princes of Germany did not fight alongside Charles, for they too desired the settlement of Augsburg.

A print showing the slaughter that ensued following the long siege of Magdeburg in 1630–1. The Thirty Years' War visited terrible depredations upon the civilian population of central Europe.

As for the 'religious' wars fought in France during the latter half of the century, these were struggles for the crown of France among three noble houses during the last years of the Valois monarchy. Various factions may have associated their causes with Reformed or Catholic interests, when it served their purposes, but rarely with inflexible zeal. The Valois regent Catherine de Médicis was equally capable of issuing an edict of toleration of French Protestants in 1562 and of instigating the massacre of thousands of Huguenot Protestants in and around Paris in 1572, as the situation dictated. And those Catholic parties that favoured absolute monarchy and a subordinate 'Gallican' Catholic Church were often supporters of the Huguenot cause and enemies of the champions of a free Catholic Church and

Just ten years after the Edict of Toleration that granted France's Huguenot community freedom from persecution, bitter rivalry at the French court between political factions sparked the St Bartholomew's Day Massacre in August 1572.

a limited monarchy. When Philip II of Spain (1527–98), moreover, became involved in the struggle for succession, in league with the Catholic house of Guise, a brief alliance was forged between the Catholic French king Henri III (1551–89) and his Protestant heir, Henri de Bourbon (1553–1610), king of Navarre. And though, in 1593, this same Henri de Bourbon – King Henri IV of France since 1589 – became Catholic, this did not deter Philip.

The most protracted and devastating of these conflicts was the Thirty Years' War, which began in 1618, when King Ferdinand of Bohemia (1578–1637) – later Holy Roman emperor Ferdinand II – provoked a Protestant uprising in Bohemia by attempting to enforce religious uniformity in his dominions. But Ferdinand certainly had no objection to the aid provided by the Protestant Elector of Saxony in quelling the rebellion. And though, during the first half of the wars that ensued in the German states, foreign Protestant powers entered the fray on the side of the seditious princes, this was hardly a result of religious principle. Nor could religious motives plausibly account for the way in which these wars were absorbed into the struggle between the Catholic Habsburgs and the Catholic Bourbons during the last dozen years of the war (by far, the bloodiest phase of the

THE ST BARTHOLOMEW'S DAY MASSACRE

The most notorious atrocity committed during the French wars of succession in the late 16th century was the St Bartholomew's Day Massacre of 1572 – which actually lasted for two days (23–24 August) – in the course of which thousands of Huguenot Protestants were slaughtered in Paris and the surrounding countryside. Often cited as a prime instance of extreme religious intolerance, the massacre is better understood as one of European history's more horrifying examples of heartless political machination.

The occasion of the violence was the marriage of Henri de Bourbon (1553–1610), king of Navarre, to Princess Marguerite de Valois (1553–1615), sister of the French king Charles IX (1550–74). A great many Huguenots, both noble and common, had come from Navarre to celebrate the nuptials and were still in the city on 22 August, four days after the wedding, when an attempt was made to assassinate Gaspard II de Coligny, admiral of France, a Huguenot but also a close confidant of the king. The attempt failed, and the king promised an investigation.

The conspiracy against Coligny, however, was almost certainly concocted by the House of Guise and Charles' mother Catherine de Médicis. Both resented Coligny's influence on the king and both opposed his plan to send a combined Huguenot and French Catholic army against Spain in the Netherlands. Fearing discovery, Catherine apparently convinced her son that Coligny and the other Huguenot leaders were plotting against him; at least, the order to kill Coligny and the other Huguenot leaders probably came from Charles. But it was to Catherine's benefit that all the Huguenots in the city be killed, to make Coligny's death seem like one among many, and to hide her complicity in an ocean of blood.

Even so, religious hatred fed upon the tale. The royal court in Spain and the papal court in Rome reportedly rejoiced at the news of the slaughter — though, one should note, for political as much as for religious reasons.

'I was awakened about three hours after midnight by the sound of all the bells and the confused cries of the populace. Upon entering the street I was seized with horror at the sight of the furies, who rushed from all parts, bawling out, "Slaughter, slaughter, massacre the Hugeuenots".'

MAXIMILIEN DE BÉTHUNE, *MÉMOIRES*, August 1572

fighting), or for the subventions supplied in 1630 by Cardinal Richelieu (1585–1642) to the Lutheran king of Sweden Gustavus II Adolphus (1594–1632) – with the blessing of the pope – so that the latter could send troops into Germany, or for France's direct entry into the war in 1635 on the side of the Protestant powers.

This is not to deny that Catholics and Protestants often hated one another quite sincerely in the early modern period, but that hatred was impotent to move armies. Simply stated, the European wars of the early modern period were not in any meaningful sense 'wars of religion'.

COLONIES AND MISSIONS

From the time of the rise of the Islamic caliphate to the early modern period, Christendom was ever more strictly confined to Europe, and Christianity was largely a European faith, with a few isolated and often beleaguered outposts to the South and East. In the 16th and 17th centuries, however, Christianity became a truly global faith, spreading to the South, West and East. In part, this happened by way of colonization of the newly discovered Americas, and in part by way of missions. And among the Christian missionaries of the age, the most remarkable were the Jesuits.

The way to European settlement of the Americas was, of course, opened by the four transatlantic voyages of Christopher Columbus (1451–1506), from 1492 to 1504, and so Spain – which sponsored Columbus's venture – became the first European nation to profit from and establish itself in the New World. By 1497, however, England gained a foothold in the Americas by its sponsorship of another Italian explorer, Giovanni Caboto (*c.*1450–*c.*1499) – or John Cabot – the discoverer of Newfoundland. The 1500 voyage of the Portuguese explorer Pedro Álvarez Cabral (1467–1520) opened up Brazil. And, between 1523 and 1528, Giovanni da Verrazzano (1485–1528) – who ended up being eaten by cannibals in the Antilles – planted the French standard in North America and the 'West Indies'.

A Puritan missionary preaching to Native People at Martha's Vineyard, Massachusetts.

The New World

The nations that established colonies in the New World, needless to say, were interested primarily in the acquisition of territory and the gathering of spoils, not in the advance of Christianity into heathen lands. But where the new colonial empires spread, missionaries followed. And in some cases, as with the Jesuit missions to Latin America, these missionaries were the only allies the indigenous peoples had against governments that wished to enslave or displace them. A testament to the idealism and the talents of the Jesuits of Latin America were the 'Reductions' (reducciones) they established in Paraguay, Argentina and southern Brazil: these were autonomous Indian communities, with townships, schools, churches, libraries, public arts and native industries; from 1609 to 1768, many of these Reductions together constituted an independent republic, administered only by the Society of Jesus. Ultimately, though, Spain and Portugal invaded and destroyed the Reductions, seized the land, subjugated the Indians, and expelled the Jesuits.

The English settlements in North America were not organized imperial ventures, but independent colonies; and their religious configurations were determined by the conditions of their original charters, and in part by the vicissitudes of English religious history. It is imprecise, but not entirely inaccurate, to say (using the terms provided by the English Civil Wars of 1642 to 1651) that the colonies of the South – Virginia (1607), Maryland (1634) and Carolina (1670) – were 'Cavalier'

A sketch of a mission by Father Florian Paucke, a Swiss Jesuit who lived and worked with the Mocobi people of the Chaco region of Argentina.

country, while the colonies of the North were generally 'Roundhead' or 'Puritan'. During the reign (1625–49) of Charles I (1600–49), for instance, thousands of English Puritans fled persecution at home to the New England settlements; and during the years of the Commonwealth in England, many Cavaliers migrated to Virginia. Maryland was a special case, since it began as a haven for English Catholics. Its charter was granted by Charles I in 1632 to Cecil Calvert, Lord Baltimore (1605–75), who established the colony in 1634. In 1649, moreover, the Maryland General Assembly instituted the 'Act of Religious Toleration', which granted full freedom of worship to all Christian communions. In 1650, however, Puritans sheltering under that toleration overthrew the government and outlawed Catholicism and Anglicanism both. With their defeat in 1658, the Act of Toleration was re-instituted; but, after England's installation of the Protestant monarchs William III (1650–1702) and Mary II (1662–94), an Anglican establishment was imposed on Maryland and Catholicism was suppressed.

The Jesuit Missions in Ethiopia and India

From its beginning, the Society of Jesus was a missionary order, and the first mission for which Ignatius Loyola requested papal authorization was to Ethiopia, where Portugal had conducted various embassies since 1490. The mission was a failure, since most Ethiopians were already Christians, and so the purpose of any Catholic mission could be only to promote submission to Rome. The Jesuit Pedro Páez (1564–1622) – who came to Ethiopia in 1603 – did procure a profession of such submission from the emperor Malak Sagad III (1572–1632), who hoped thereby to attract Western military assistance; and the emperor did try to impose Roman Catholicism on his people. Páez's successor, Alfonso Mendez,

1505
The first Portuguese missionaries arrive in Ethiopia, but fail to spread Roman Catholicism there

1549
Jesuit missions to Japan begin

1560
Inquisition established in India to enforce the conformity of the St Thomas Christians

1583
Matteo Ricci arrives in Beijing as part of an embassy; however, the Jesuits succeed only in converting a few high-ranking Chinese officials

1587
Toyotomi Hideyoshi expels all Christian missionaries from Kyushu

1609
The first Jesuit missions are established in South America

1612–32
Systematic persecution of Christians in Japan under Ieyasu and Hidetada

1614
Tokugawa Ieyasu signs the Christian Expulsion Edict, banning Christianity and expelling all foreigners

1620
The Puritan Pilgrim colonists found the settlement of Plymouth on Cape Cod, Massachusetts

1768
The crowns of Spain and Portugal ban the Jesuits from their colonial territories (the Society of Jesus is outlawed five years later by Pope Clement XIV)

arrived in 1624 and, with the emperor's help, immediately set about suppressing all native Christian practices; when this provoked revolt, however, Mendez did not hesitate to have indigenous 'heretics' burned. The emperor was forced to abdicate in 1632 in favour of his son Fasilidas (d.1662), who promptly expelled all Catholic missionaries.

The missions to India were far more successful, though (again) the indigenous Christians were not well served by them. The Portuguese ruled in Goa, in the southwestern part of the subcontinent, and it was here that the Catholic missions arrived. The most famous of the Jesuit missionaries to preach in India was St Francis Xavier (1506–52), who won thousands of converts among the fishermen of the south. In 1560, however, an Inquisition was established, in large part to enforce conformity of the St Thomas Christians of India to Roman rule; over the next century, in the course of various insurrections, almost all of the ancient literature of the Indian Christians – and a few of the Christians themselves – were consigned to the flames. When the Dutch seized most of the Malabar region in the 1660s, the St Thomas community regained much of its liberty; but it was a divided community ever thereafter.

The Far East

Jesuit missions to Japan began in 1549, in the vanguard of Portugal's mercantile embassies. Francis Xavier was the first to arrive, and found the island empire extraordinarily fertile ground for the propagation of Christian beliefs. And, indeed, converts were made in every class; even certain powerful feudal lords embraced the new faith, along with many of their samurai and commoner subjects. Later in the century, though, Dominicans and Franciscans, sponsored by Spain, also began to arrive in the country, which led to a number of unseemly disputes among the different missionary orders. In the end, however, there was nothing for which to fight. In 1587, the prime imperial minister Toyotomi Hideyoshi (1536–98) outlawed Christianity among the aristocracy and instituted the first persecutions of Japanese Christians and foreign missionaries; in 1597, 26 Christians (20 of them native Japanese) were crucified in Nagasaki. And in 1614 the first Tokugawa shogun, Ieyasu (1543–1616), inaugurated the total ban on Catholicism that remained in place until 1873. During those centuries, though, a small number of Japanese 'Kirishitans' kept the faith in secret, without priests or catechists.

As a rule, Catholic missionaries to the East were better able consistently to exhibit Christ-like gentleness in lands where their missions could not become implicated in the politics of empire. The Tibetan missions of Jesuits such as António de Andrade (1580–1634) and Ippolito Desideri (1684–1733), for instance, were necessarily marked by humility and a certain intellectual generosity. And the Jesuit missions in China that

THE CHINESE RITES

Matteo Ricci believed that, if Christianity was to be made credible in the eyes of the Chinese people, it should not offend against their natural pieties and ceremonial forms. Many of the indigenous rites of the Chinese – such as offerings made in honour of the emperor, their ancestors, Confucius, or Shang-ti (the Heavenly Emperor, or God) – he regarded as perfectly admirable expressions of civilized reverence and entirely compatible with Christianity.

Early in the 17th century, however, the 'Chinese Rites Controversy' broke out between, on the one side, the Jesuits, who generally subscribed to Ricci's view, and, on the other, the Dominicans and Franciscans in China, who saw such rites as inherently heathen, idolatrous and even demonic in inspiration. The latter appealed to Rome, which forbade all such rites for Chinese Christians in 1645, only to reverse its decision in 1656 after a Jesuit appeal. Yet the controversy did not abate, and in 1704, 1715 and 1742, Rome issued decrees prohibiting the Chinese rites; the last of these, promulgated by Benedict XIV (1676–1758), even forbade any further discussion of the matter.

The papal bull of 1715 proved a grave misfortune for European missions in China. The Kangxi emperor (1654–1722) – the greatest of the Manchu Qing dynasty emperors, and perhaps the greatest ruler China ever possessed – had until then been quite well disposed to the Christians; he especially valued the scientific knowledge, scholarship and artistic skills of the Jesuits who served in the imperial court, and in 1692 issued a decree of toleration of Christian worship in China, particularly commending the peaceful nature of this 'venerable' faith.

When the Kangxi emperor read the papal bull in 1722, however – which not only banned all the traditional Chinese rites, but forbade Christians even to refer to God by such traditional Chinese names as Shang-ti or Tien (Heaven), or to mark their churches with the traditional temple sign 'Reverence for Heaven' – he reacted with a decree in which he berated the 'occidentals' for their pettiness, their ignorance and their bigotry (reminiscent, he said, of the bigotry of certain Buddhist or Taoist sects), and prohibited all further Christian evangelization in China.

began in 1582 were originally models of peaceful intellectual and cultural exchange, in large part because the most remarkable of the missionaries to China – Matteo Ricci (1552–1610) and Michele Ruggieri (1543–1607) – wished to aid in the creation of a genuinely Chinese Christianity, in harmony with native forms of piety and philosophy, and as untainted by 'Europeanism' as possible. Ricci was especially drawn to Confucianism (the dominant tradition among the rich and educated) through which he believed divine truth had made itself known to the Chinese from ancient times. Ruggieri, by contrast, was drawn to Taoism (which flourished more among persons of lower estate) and believed that it was principally under the form of the Tao that a knowledge of God's eternal *Logos* had entered China. This difference occasionally caused tension between the two men's converts; but both Ricci and Ruggieri passionately believed in the presence of a 'primordial revelation' in Chinese tradition, and that the philosophical and spiritual riches of that tradition might one day – as had once happened with the traditions of Greece and Rome – be assumed into a new Christian cultural synthesis.

THE CHURCH AND THE SCIENTISTS

One of those historical myths that enjoy popular currency, even though they cannot survive the scrutiny of serious historical study, is that, at the dawn of the Christian era, there was a thriving Hellenistic scientific culture that Christianity – through some supposed hostility to learning and reason – methodically destroyed; and that this Christian antagonism to science persisted into the early modern period – as is evident from Galileo's trial in Rome – until the power of the Church was at last broken, and secular faculties of science began to appear.

This story is impossible to reconcile with the historical evidence, ancient, Medieval, or modern. It misrepresents the characters both of Hellenistic science and of early Christianity, as well as that of Medieval intellectual culture; and it entirely belies the fascinating reality that, in the 16th and 17th centuries, Christian scientists educated in Christian universities and following a Christian tradition of scientific and mathematical speculation overturned a pagan cosmology and physics unchallenged since the days of Aristotle.

The geocentric view of the universe postulated by the brilliant mathematician and astronomer Ptolemy, as portrayed by the German mapmaker Andreas Cellarius in his celestial atlas of 1660, Harmonia Macrocosmica. *Ptolemy's system held sway until the modern development of new theories of motion.*

Ancient and Medieval Science

There never was a particularly advanced culture of Hellenistic 'science' – at least, not in the sense the word has now: a systematic and analytic use of experiment and observation to correct and refine hypotheses. Careful astronomical observation had led to the invention of the astrolabe, some of the remedies prescribed by medical 'science' were effective (or, at least, not harmful), some fine work in the geometry of optics was achieved by Ptolemy (*c.*100–*c.*170), and a few clever mechanical inventions had appeared by the end of the first century AD; but Greek science had never been much interested in concrete experiment, and as a whole had declined towards encyclopaedism and commentary before the Christian age. But research of a sort did persist in Alexandria, and was pursued during the Christian period as avidly by Christian scholars as by pagan.

Cosmology was at once the most elaborately developed and the most static area of scientific erudition. From antiquity through the late Middle Ages, almost all scientists – pagan, Christian or Muslim – accepted some version of the Aristotelian model of the universe, and some version of Ptolemy's attempt to describe a geocentric universe mathematically. According to the former, the stationary earth is surrounded by a series of revolving concentric crystalline planetary spheres, the lowest of which contains the moon; the 'sublunar' realm is the region of change and decay, of the elements of air and fire, earth and water; the 'superlunar' realm, however, is composed of the 'quintessence' or 'aether', and there all is changeless.

A statue of Nicolaus Copernicus in his home town of Torun, Poland.

Beyond the farthest planetary sphere lies the sphere of the fixed stars. And the whole machinery of the cosmos is driven by the outermost sphere of the 'prime mover'.

Ptolemy's exquisitely complex model of the heavens was an attempt to make this model of reality somehow consonant with the observable movements of heavenly objects – including the apparent 'retrograde' movement of certain planets – but this, in the end, was impossible. Ptolemy was forced to introduce such bizarre devices as 'eccentrics' (extraterrestrial axes for certain planetary orbits), 'equants' (imaginary secondary axes that allowed orbits to be measured as mathematically uniform) and 'epicycles' (small local orbital axes located within the planetary spheres) into his calculations. Nor did Ptolemy trouble overly much about empirical observation (one could disprove his description of the lunar cycle, for instance, simply by looking at the moon several nights in succession). None of his mathematical devices, moreover, was compatible with Aristotelian physics, but – while scientists occasionally attempted to improve upon the model thus produced – few ever thought to reject it outright.

One exception to this rule was the sixth-century Christian scientist John Philoponus, who speculated that heavenly bodies are in fact mutable, that above the atmosphere there was perhaps a vacuum, that the stars were not (as pagan scientists believed) spiritual intelligences, but merely masses of fire, and that the planets might move by an 'impressed' impetus. A few later Muslim astronomers addressed Philoponus' ideas, without adopting them, and by that route they entered into Western Christian scholastic science, where they were taken up and explored by men like Thomas Bradwardine (*c.*1290–1349), Richard Swineshead (*fl.* 1348), Jean Buridan (1300–58) and Nicholas Oresme (*c.*1320–82).

The Heliocentric Revolution

Nicolaus Copernicus (1473–1543) was a beneficiary of this tradition; but he was the first Christian theorist explicitly to argue for a heliocentric cosmos, in his treatise *De revolutionibus orbium coelestium* (published 1543). His argument was not particularly compelling, as it happens; his mathematical models were defective and almost as

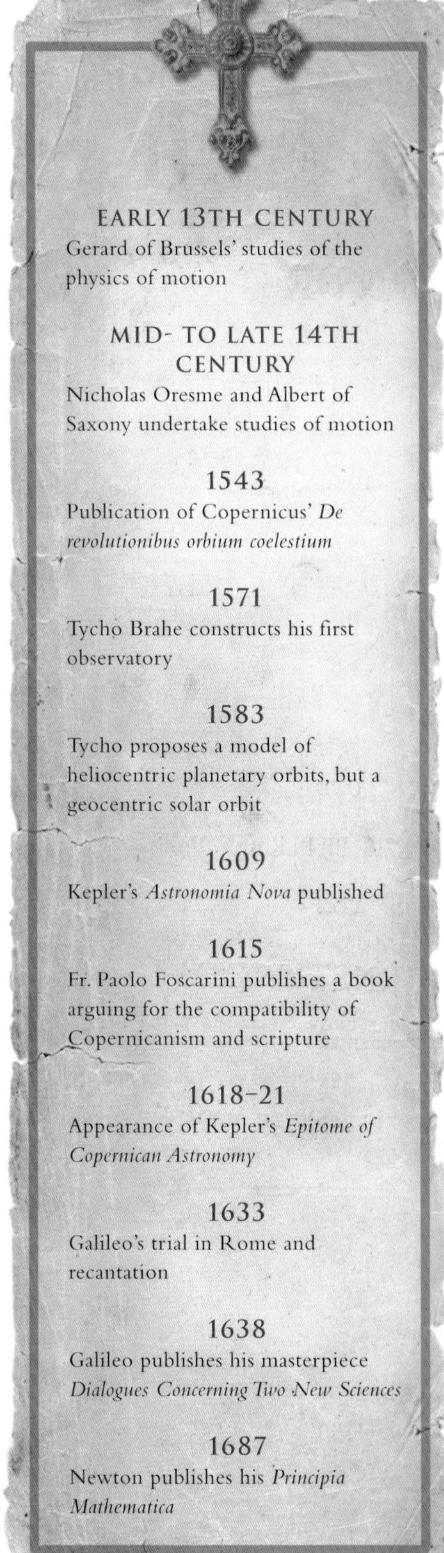

EARLY 13TH CENTURY
Gerard of Brussels' studies of the physics of motion

MID- TO LATE 14TH CENTURY
Nicholas Oresme and Albert of Saxony undertake studies of motion

1543
Publication of Copernicus' *De revolutionibus orbium coelestium*

1571
Tycho Brahe constructs his first observatory

1583
Tycho proposes a model of heliocentric planetary orbits, but a geocentric solar orbit

1609
Kepler's *Astronomia Nova* published

1615
Fr. Paolo Foscarini publishes a book arguing for the compatibility of Copernicanism and scripture

1618–21
Appearance of Kepler's *Epitome of Copernican Astronomy*

1633
Galileo's trial in Rome and recantation

1638
Galileo publishes his masterpiece *Dialogues Concerning Two New Sciences*

1687
Newton publishes his *Principia Mathematica*

COSMIC HARMONIES

Johannes Kepler (1571–1630) was a brilliant astronomer, natural scientist, theorist of optics and mathematician, but was also a metaphysician, an astrologer and something of a mystic; in his youth, he had intended to become a theologian, and to the end of his life he regarded his scientific endeavour as a sacred vocation, which allowed him to discover the sublime harmonies informing creation, and the ways in which the Trinity is reflected in them. In Copernicus' heliocentrism – which he encountered in the early 1590s – Kepler believed he had found (if only in intuitive form) a model of the cosmic order that adequately mirrored the divine governance of the universe: the sun's centrality being, as it were, a physical symbol of the Father, Son and Holy Spirit ruling over and guiding all things. And even in his discovery of the elliptical shape of planetary orbits (in which he was aided by Tycho Brahe's meticulously precise astronomical observations) he believed he could discern depths of geometric perfection in which the divine archetypes of all things shone forth.

Though a devout Lutheran, Kepler had no interest in sectarian disputes; he was on good terms with many Calvinists and Catholics (with many friends and protectors among the Jesuits). He was content to labour under Catholic or Lutheran princes; he was not, however, shown comparable tolerance. At one point, he was expelled from the Lutheran communion; at another, Catholic authorities confiscated his books and told him to send his children to mass.

Kepler, though, laboured on, inspired to the end by his vision of a cosmic order of intricate beauties and delicate concords. The work that probably best expresses his vision of reality is his *Harmonices Mundi* of 1619, in which he gave free rein to his Christian Platonist and semi-Pythagorean tendencies. He described there the structure of the cosmos in terms of a 'universal music', found in all the geometric ratios of the natural order, and especially in the subtle consonances – and spiritual influences – between heavenly bodies and the human soul.

complicated as Ptolemy's (and as fraught with 'epicycles'). His basic model did seem to explain why Mercury and Venus remain always near the sun, but so did the later system of Tycho Brahe (1546–1601) according to which all the planets above revolve around the sun, while only the sun revolves directly around the earth. By the time of the trial of the most famous defender of the Copernican theory, Galileo Galilei (1564–1642), many of the best astronomers (a great many of whom were Jesuits) had adopted the 'Tychonic' model.

When challenged by theologians, Galileo quite correctly appealed to the Church Fathers to defend the claim that the scriptures ought not to be mistaken for cosmological treatises. In the 17th century, though, under the pressure of Protestant criticism, the Catholic Church had become much more diffident in the latitude with which it read scripture, and had begun to incline towards greater literalism. That said, in the years leading up to his trial, Galileo had enjoyed the esteem of many prominent churchmen; several Jesuit astronomers helped to confirm many of his telescopic observations; and even when his Copernican sympathies became clear in 1613 he was not censured by ecclesial authority.

Galileo on trial in Rome. It is a myth that Galileo was tortured by the Roman Inquisition (though, in keeping with the unsavoury forensic procedures of the time, he was reminded that torture could be applied as a penalty for perjury). But he definitely was ordered to recant his Copernicanism, an instruction with which he complied.

Galileo's most important admirer and ally in the Church, in fact, was Cardinal Maffeo Barberini (1568–1644), who in 1623 became Pope Urban VIII – the very man who would ultimately command Galileo to recant.

Galileo, however, was a frequently unpleasant man, who often refused to give other scientists credit for their own discoveries, belittled those he saw as rivals (such as Johannes Kepler), and insisted on provoking disputes. His demands for unconditional acceptance of his theories led to an ecclesial consultation in 1616. When he failed to produce a single convincing proof for his position, the consultation admonished him against teaching Copernican theory as a fact. Even so, Urban himself encouraged Galileo to write the book that became the *Dialogue concerning the Two Chief World Systems, the Ptolemaic and Copernican* (1632), enjoining only that it include a statement to the effect that Copernican theory was only an unproven hypothesis. Galileo did include such a statement in his dialogue, but placed it on the lips of a clownishly obtuse character named Simplicio.

This seemed an unwarranted insult of a generous friend; Urban took offence and resolved upon a trial. Moreover, as it turned out, Urban was quite right about the unproven nature of the Copernican theory. For all his brilliance as a physicist, Galileo was an amateur astronomer at best, and seemed unaware how mathematically and empirically incoherent Copernicus' book was. The only evidence he provided for the Earth's movement was a theory about the tides that was completely irreconcilable with observable tidal sequences. He could have defended heliocentrism better if he had been willing to adopt Kepler's theory of elliptical planetary orbits – of which he was aware – but he was loath to do so.

The ultimate effect of Rome's authoritarian meddling was to make the Church hierarchy appear ridiculous. The case was, though, an aberration, and not a true indicator of the relation between the Catholic Church and the sciences. In fact, the Church was a generous patron of the sciences, while the Jesuits fostered many of the most original scientific minds of the age. But the embarrassment created for the Catholic Church by Urban's outraged pride has never entirely faded.

DEISM, ENLIGHTENMENT AND REVOLUTION

It was in the 17th and 18th centuries that Europe began clearly to become a 'post-Christian' civilization. It was a period not only during which the Church as an institution began to lose much of its political power and social influence, but during which many persons – educated and uneducated alike – began more openly to reject the Christian story and to adopt alternate narratives of reality.

In some cases, this shift of attitude meant the embrace of a 'rational' theism or 'Deism', shorn (so its adherents believed) of the absurd tangle of superstition and metaphysical obscurantism that made the old faith incredible to them. In other, rarer cases, however, it meant the total rejection of all faith in transcendent reality.

Deists and Metaphysical Optimists

Beginning as early as the mid-16th century, 'Deism' was a style of religious philosophy that enjoyed its greatest vogue from the early 17th to the late 18th centuries. It varied in form, but its content was fairly uniform: it was an attempt at a 'natural' or 'rational' religion, common to all nations and cultures, available to all reflective minds without recourse to childish mythologies, 'revealed' truth, miracles or abstruse metaphysical systems. The 'Bible of Deism' was *Christianity as Old as the Creation* (first edition 1730) by Matthew Tindal (1657–1733); but the 'father' of the movement was Edward, Lord Herbert of Cherbury (1583–1648), and it was he who first enunciated its general principles: belief in a supreme being who created the cosmos, who is a moral being, who is worthy of our reverence, who requires moral goodness of us all and who assigns rewards and punishments to human souls. Not all Deists retained Lord Herbert's belief in the immortal soul, but most did; and all shared his certainty that this sort of 'reasonable faith' was the true form of religion before its degeneration into cult, superstition and intolerance.

> *'God acts like the greatest geometer, who prefers the best constructions of problems.'*
>
> Gottfried Wilhelm Leibniz, *A Speculation of Discoveries about Marvellous Secrets of Nature in General*, c.1686

Deist writers tended to imagine God principally as the designer of nature, and sought evidences of his existence in the intricacy and regularity of nature's laws, and reserved a special antipathy for any form of religion that involved belief in God's miraculous interventions in the operation of those laws. One of the principal intellectual projects of developed Deism, in fact, was the elaboration of 'theodicy' – that is, the attempt to defend the justice of God in light of the sufferings of his creatures – meant to demonstrate the impossibility of a created order governed by uniform natural laws that does not involve chance, catastrophe, pain and moral evil; and hence to prove that ours is the best of all possible worlds. This sort of 'metaphysical optimism' was a tremendous fashion in the late 17th and early 18th centuries, and became the common intellectual currency even of many traditional Christians; it was given especially sophisticated metaphysical form, for instance, by the Lutheran philosopher G.W. Leibniz (1646–1716). Again, though,

Deism was not a single creed, and its elements varied. One could, for example, number among its French adherents the satirist and public philosopher Voltaire (1694–1778), than whom no one was more censorious of 'metaphysical optimism'.

By the latter half of the 18th century, Deism was perhaps the most respectable religious philosophy among the educated classes of England, Germany, France and North America; it was the system of belief favoured by – to choose a few notable examples – Thomas Paine (1737–1809), Benjamin Franklin (1706–90), and Thomas Jefferson (1743–1826). Soon, however, the fashion would fade, defeated in part by the devastating assaults upon the argument for God's existence from cosmic design mounted by David Hume (1711–76) and others, and in part by Deism's own inherent blandness; and what vestiges of Deism remained were swept away in the 19th century by the rise of Darwinism.

The philosopher Gotttfried Wilhelm Leibniz argued that, in creating the universe, God had ensured that a rational harmony reigns in the 'best of all possible worlds'. Voltaire satirized this position in Candide.

Atheists and Revolutionaries

The rise and fall of Deism was part of that larger cultural movement traditionally called the 'Enlightenment', the chief tenet of which was that human reason possesses the power not only to penetrate to the natural laws underlying the world, but to determine the nature of a just society, to advance the cause of human freedom, to discover the rational basis of morality and to instill moral behaviour in individuals and nations. And though there were many fairly orthodox Christians who shared the aims of the Enlightenment, the general tendency of those who held to the ideal implicit in this 'new awakening of reason' was either towards a more 'rational' religion, or towards an even more 'rational' irreligion.

The greatest thinker of the time to retain the idea of God – but then only as a deduction of reason – was Immanuel Kant (1724–1804), who argued forcefully against traditional metaphysics, but who believed that God and the soul were necessary postulates of the 'metaphysics of morals' (though, one must add, Kant's moral philosophy depends

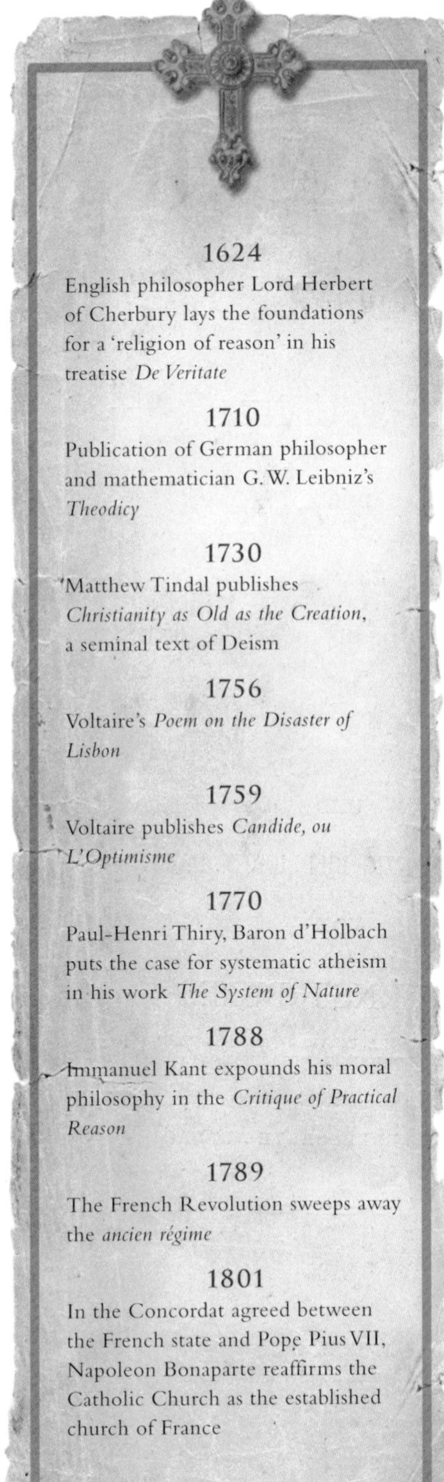

1624
English philosopher Lord Herbert of Cherbury lays the foundations for a 'religion of reason' in his treatise *De Veritate*

1710
Publication of German philosopher and mathematician G.W. Leibniz's *Theodicy*

1730
Matthew Tindal publishes *Christianity as Old as the Creation*, a seminal text of Deism

1756
Voltaire's *Poem on the Disaster of Lisbon*

1759
Voltaire publishes *Candide, ou L'Optimisme*

1770
Paul-Henri Thiry, Baron d'Holbach puts the case for systematic atheism in his work *The System of Nature*

1788
Immanuel Kant expounds his moral philosophy in the *Critique of Practical Reason*

1789
The French Revolution sweeps away the *ancien régime*

1801
In the Concordat agreed between the French state and Pope Pius VII, Napoleon Bonaparte reaffirms the Catholic Church as the established church of France

Secularization of a Church During the Revolution, *by the French painter Jacques François de Fontaine (1769–1823). Under the* ancien régime, *the Catholic Church had been the largest landowner in France, and now found itself dispossessed. The revolutionary regime sought to replace religion with the 'Cult of Reason'.*

upon no supernatural premises). Others, though, believed that true enlightenment was possible for mankind only if every concept of God was rejected, as an irrational superaddition to the evidences of experience, and only if all religion was repudiated, as a system of fanciful deceptions, invented principally by priests for their own benefit. Paul-Henri Thiry, Baron d'Holbach (1723–89), for instance – most especially in his 1770 book *The System of Nature* – argued that all religion is the work of ignorance and dread, exploited by tyranny, that reality consists in nothing more than matter in motion, and that the conventions of morality are simply that, and ought – where they interfere with the happiness of the individual – to be abandoned. Denis Diderot (1713–84), an equally fervent (and more brilliantly insightful) materialist, famously declared that 'Never shall man be free until the last king has been strangled with the entrails of the last priest'.

Such sentiments, if they are in any way amusing, remain so only until someone takes them literally; and among the more radical political champions of a 'progressive' or 'enlightened' social revolution there were many disposed to do just that. It was natural, of course, for the society that emerged from the French Revolution of 1789 and after to include a certain powerful tendency towards anti-clericalism, given how closely the Roman Catholic Church in France – for all intents and purposes, little more than a Gallican establishment – had been associated with the interests of the *ancien régime*. But the revolutionary government of 1793 to 1794, which instituted the 'Reign of Terror', and which was administered according to the 'ideals' of the radical Jacobin Club, not only closed the churches in Paris, and forbade most public worship and the display of the cross, but directly participated in the murder of hundreds or perhaps thousands of 'non-juring' priests (that is, priests who would not vow allegiance to the new

VOLTAIRE AND THE LISBON EARTHQUAKE

Voltaire's most passionate and most eloquent assault on the arguments of those (such as Leibniz) who thought this the best of all possible worlds was his great *Poem on the Disaster of Lisbon*, written soon after that city – the resplendent capital of the Portuguese empire – was devastated by a massive earthquake on All Saints' Day (1 November) 1755.

The quake struck just off shore, in three discrete shocks, with what is now estimated as a Richter force of 9.0. As it was Sunday morning, and a Feast Day, most people were in church. In a matter of moments, thousands were killed, crushed beneath collapsing buildings, or swallowed by the crevices that opened in the streets; soon thereafter, many more – including the invalid patients of the city's great hospital – perished in the fires that raged through the city; and many thousands more who had fled to the mouth of the River Tagus and to the shore to escape the catastrophe were killed by the enormous tsunamis that reached land half an hour later. At least 60,000 died in the city, and many thousands more were killed by the waters in North Africa, Spain and the Algarve.

Voltaire was a theist, but of a rather austere variety. He may not have been convinced by the Christian idea that creation has been corrupted by the fall of rational creatures, but he was quite certain that the cosmos does not reflect a morally or metaphysically necessary order. In his poem, he disdainfully dismisses the notion that the world is governed by a 'universal law' set in place to assure the greatest possible good for the greatest possible number of persons. He asks by what moral calculus we can reconcile ourselves to infants crushed upon their mothers' breasts, thousands devoured by the earth, thousands more slowly expiring in their broken bodies or buried alive beneath their fallen roofs, all crying out in torment. Was this, he asks, divine vengeance on the city's iniquities? Was Lisbon more wicked than other cities, were the children who died there guilty of some crime? And would the natural and moral order of the universe have somehow been worse had the city not been engulfed in this 'hellish abyss?' Does the cosmos become morally beautiful if we imagine that some sort of 'general happiness' is somehow mysteriously preserved by this 'fatal chaos of individual miseries?'

government), bishops and nuns. Massacres, rigged trials and summary executions were routine; and, throughout the country, the killing was often accompanied by one or another sadistic mockery of the beliefs of the victims – for instance, the rite of 'republican matrimony', which consisted in tying a naked priest to a naked nun and drowning them together in a lake or pool. Even after the Terror had subsided, the persecution of Catholic clergy continued, ending only when the revolutionary regime itself was replaced by the rule of Napoleon (1769–1821), who in 1801 signed a Concordat with Rome restoring (limited) liberties to the Church in France.

However, a pattern had been established that other 'utopian' revolutionary movements of later years would repeat, on an ever greater scale: a radical hostility to religion, emphasized by mass murder.

EASTERN ORTHODOXY IN THE EARLY MODERN PERIOD

After the Turkish conquest of what remained of the Eastern Roman world in the mid-15th century, the only Orthodox countries not under Islamic rule were those of the Slavic and Balkan north; and, among these, Russia soon emerged as the most powerful.

In many significant respects, Moscow became the chief city in the Eastern Christian world, and the Russian empire became the successor of the Byzantine – so much so, indeed, that it came to refer to itself as the 'Third Rome'. In 1547, on the occasion of his coronation, the grand prince of Moscow, Ivan IV 'the Terrible' (1530–84), even assumed the title of 'Tsar' – that is, 'Caesar'.

Tsar and Patriarch

Until 1448, the head of the Church in Russia wore the title of 'Metropolitan of Kiev' (though the metropolitanate had actually resided in Moscow for more than a century) and was under the nominal governance of the patriarch of Constantinople. In that year, however – in part, as a response to Constantinople's 'shameful' capitulation to Roman demands at the Council of Florence – the bishops of Russia appointed a Bishop Jonas (d.1461) as the 'metropolitan of Moscow', thereby declaring the Russian Church's 'autocephaly' (that is, self-government). In 1589, with Constantinople's approval, the title became 'Patriarch of Moscow.'

'The Tsar's authority must be subordinate to episcopal authority, to which Almighty God has entrusted the keys of the kingdom of heaven and given, on earth, the power to bind and to loose. Moreover, episcopal power is spiritual, while that given to the Tsar is of this world … the clergy is a more honoured and higher authority than the state itself.'

Patriarch Nikon, *A Refutation or Demolishment*, c.1663

Tensions between tsar and patriarch were often quite severe, though inevitably, when anything approaching an actual conflict arose, the tsar was the victor. When Metropolitan Philip II (1507–69) publicly reproached Ivan the Terrible (quite justly) for perpetrating massacres, he was deposed, imprisoned and strangled. The energetic, reforming Patriarch Nikon (1605–81) was perhaps the most powerful patriarch in Russian history; Tsar Alexei I (1629–76) was his ardent admirer; but when Nikon – an imperious character at the best of times – began to overshadow the tsar, he was deposed and reduced to a common monk. And, in 1721, Tsar Peter I 'the Great' (1672–1725) abolished the office of patriarch altogether, and – in imitation of the Lutheran establishments in Sweden and Protestant Germany – replaced it with a synod that functioned as an office of the state. There would not be another patriarch of Moscow until 1917.

The history of the Church in the Ukraine – old Kievan Russia – took a somewhat different course, especially after 1569, when much of the Ukraine belonged to Roman Catholic Poland. In 1596, the Union of Brest-Litovsk –

which placed the Kievan metropolitanate under Rome – was imposed on the Orthodox population. And though in 1620 an Orthodox metropolitanate was re-established, and in 1686 was placed under Moscow, Ukrainian Christianity remained divided thereafter between Orthodox and 'Eastern Rite' Catholic Churches.

The Love of Beauty

It is not an exaggeration to say that one of the most important events in the early modern history of the Eastern Orthodox Church was the publication in 1782 of a book called the *Philokalia*, which means 'the love of beauty'. It was an anthology of Eastern Christian mystical texts, from the fourth to the 14th centuries, assembled by two monks of Mount Athos: Nicodemus of the Holy Mountain (1748–1809) and Macarius of Corinth (1731–1805). The book was notable in part for its comprehensiveness, and in part for making available many texts never previously printed. It was significant, as well, for somewhat rehabilitating Evagrius Ponticus, whose condemnation as an Origenist had relegated his works to something very near oblivion for over a thousand years, but whose writings on the spiritual life were both too brilliant and too important for the Eastern contemplative tradition not to be included. And it is fair to say that the book established Hesychasm once and for all as the dominant form of Orthodox spirituality.

The cathedral of Saint Basil the Blessed on Moscow's Red Square was commissioned by Tsar Ivan IV ('the Terrible') and built between 1555 and 1561.

The true significance of the *Philokalia*, however, lay in the contribution it made to a movement of spiritual renewal throughout the Orthodox world. On its publication, many saw it as a uniquely powerful expression of the heart of Orthodoxy. It was especially influential in Russia and the greater Slavic world. In 1793, the Athonite monk Paissy Velichkovsky (1722–94) issued a Slavonic translation in St Petersburg; it was Paissy also who was largely responsible for introducing the Greek institution of spiritual 'elders' to the Slavic Church. An elder (*geron* in Greek, *staretz* in Russian) was a master of the spiritual life, responsible for the formation of young monks and acting as a confessor and guide to the laity; and these *startsi* (the plural of *staretz*) were a vital part of the renewal of the Orthodox monastic life.

1569
Martyrdom of Philip II, metropolitan of Moscow at the hands of Tsar Ivan the Terrible

1589
Autocephaly of the Church of Russia recognized

1596
At the Union of Brest-Litovsk, millions of Ukrainian and Belorussian Christians are forcibly placed under papal jurisdiction by their Polish rulers

1652–58
Patriarch Nikon revises liturgical books to bring them in line with the Greek liturgy and excommunicates dissenters ('Old Believers')

1721
Tsar Peter I abolishes the office of patriarch of the Russian Orthodox Church

1759
Birth of the ascetic St Seraphim of Sarov

1782
The *Philokalia* is first published

1794
Russian Orthodox missionaries arrive on Kodiak Island, Alaska

1811
Autocephaly of the Church of Georgia is revoked after Russia takes control of the region

1871
Russian Orthodox priest Nikolai Kasatkin establishes a mission in Japan

The Slavonic *Philokalia* – already immensely popular – was translated into Russian by Theophan the Recluse (1815–94), one of the most beloved of modern Russian saints. A perfect (if somewhat stylized) picture of the effect of the anthology on the devotional life of the laity can be found in two anonymous narratives written in the 19th century (possibly by an Athonite monk): *The Way of a Pilgrim* and its sequel *The Pilgrim Continues Upon His Way*, which tell the story of a wanderer who undertakes to practise the Hesychastic method of constant inward prayer.

Orthodox Missions

The 18th century was also the great age of Russian missions, not only into the wild interior of Siberia, the far north, and Central Asia, but even to North America. Among the most revered of the Russian missionaries was St Herman of Alaska (*c.*1758–1837), a devout and gentle Russian monk who in 1794 arrived on Kodiak Island – at that time a Russian possession – with six other monks to establish the first Orthodox mission in the New World. Herman not only ministered to the native Aleuts and made a great many converts; he soon found himself obliged to act as an advocate for and protector of the native peoples against the abuse they suffered at the hands of the Russian colonists. In 1808, Herman created a hermit's retreat for himself on Spruce Island, a little more than a mile away from Kodiak Island. He also had a school built on the island, as well as a chapel, and devoted much of the remainder of his life to caring for orphans and for the ill.

Of the next generation of Russian missionaries to the Aleuts, St Innocent of Alaska (1797–1879) perhaps accomplished the most. He was a married priest who, in 1824, arrived with his wife and family on Unalaska Island, where he promptly built a church and began to study the native languages of his parishioners: the native inhabitants not only of Unalaska, but of the Pribilof and Fox Islands. As his mastery of Aleutian dialects increased, he devised an Aleut alphabet and began translating the Bible into Unagan, the most important of them. In 1829, he undertook a mission to the coasts of the Bering Sea, and in 1834 moved to Sitka Island, where he learned the language of the native Tlingit people.

Innocent lost his wife in 1838, and was persuaded in 1840 to take the vows of a monk. That same year he was made a bishop with a diocese comprising the Aleutian Islands, the Kamchatka Peninsula and the Kurile Islands northeast of Japan. He did not cease, though, to work as a travelling missionary, a scholar of native North American tongues and a translator. He was elevated to the Moscow Synod in 1865, and became its head in 1868.

SAINT SERAPHIM

Of all the *startsi* who arose during the years of Russia's great spiritual renewal, none is remembered more fondly than St Seraphim of Sarov (1759–1833). Born Prohor Moshnin to a merchant family in Kursk, he was marked from an early age by a pious, mild and even somewhat mystical temper. In 1777 he entered the Sarov Monastery, taking his final vows and his monastic name Seraphim in 1786.

From the beginning of his novitiate to his death, he lived an ascetical life, never eating more than was required for bare sustenance, and spending most of his hours in prayer before the altar of the monastery church. He was made a hierodeacon in 1793, and soon after – with the blessing of his *staretz* – retreated into the forest to pray in solitude. There he was occasionally visited by monks and nuns seeking spiritual guidance, as well as by (if the stories are to be believed) the beasts of the forest; one nun witnessed him feeding a bear from his hand.

A nun lights candles during a celebration in 2003 to mark the 100th anniversary of the canonization of St Seraphim of Sarov.

He was set upon one day by brigands who mistakenly thought he had possessions they might steal; he had been cutting wood at the time, but made no attempt to defend himself, even when they began bludgeoning him with the handle of his own axe; they ceased beating him only when they thought him dead. The *staretz* recovered – though never entirely – and when the men were caught and brought to trial, Seraphim implored the judge to show them mercy.

Not long after his recovery, he embarked on 1000 nights of continuous prayer, standing on a rock with bare feet and his hands raised to God. Then, in 1815, supposedly in response to a vision of the Mother of God, he opened his hermitage to all who wished to come to him for spiritual counsel, and to learn from him how to 'acquire' the Holy Spirit through the practice of Christian love. Reports of his wisdom, his 'miraculous' power to see into his visitors' hearts and his great cheerfulness, charity and gentleness soon spread, and pilgrims came constantly.

The most famous account of such a visit is that of Nicholas Motovilov, who not only recorded many of Seraphim's teachings, but claimed to have been present when the elder was transfigured by the 'uncreated light'.

Seraphim died peacefully in 1833, while praying before an icon of the Mother of God.

THE NINETEENTH CENTURY: A TIME OF RADICAL DOUBT

By the end of the 19th century, the decline of Christianity in Western Europe that began in the early modern period seemed irreversible, and had come moreover to be regarded by many as representing the natural course of history, for all of humanity. The educated classes of the continent had more and more detached themselves from the faith of their ancestors, and atheism had even begun to acquire the kind of quiet respectability in some circles it had never enjoyed in any previous age.

To some, the decline of Christianity was a cause for rejoicing; to others, it was simply a cultural fact, probably to be rued. Whatever the case, a great many thought they could foresee a time when religion would vanish entirely.

Elegies for Faith

Throughout the 19th century, of course, the vast majority of Europeans were not only nominal Christians, but in all likelihood believers of some variety or another. In absolute numbers, sceptics and unbelievers constituted a distinct minority; but they were an increasingly public minority, and their explicit rejection of received beliefs was in many ways symptomatic of a more general loosening of traditional Christianity's hold over the imagination of Western culture.

The causes of this larger cultural movement are impossible to isolate with any certainty. No doubt some were material, some intellectual, some social and some more or less unquantifiable. In part, the rise of a literate middle class in an age of discovery had created a culture in which differing 'narratives of reality' naturally multiplied. In part, the early modern disintegration of Christendom into often irreconcilable versions of Christianity had served to make all dogmatic claims seem somewhat less credible. And, in part, a general (if not necessarily logical) sense that the modern scientific picture of the universe was somehow irreconcilable with Christian doctrine began to take hold. But the phenomenon of 'secularization' has no single explanation.

A print by the illustrator Gustave Doré shows St Paul's Cathedral amid the teeming metropolis of London in the 1870s. In the 19th century new social factors such as industrialization and the rapid growth of cities helped engender an increasingly materialist outlook whose corollary was secularization.

Many reflective observers of the time – even many who were themselves no longer believers – wrote of the new reality in distinctly elegiac tones, aware that with the departure of faith, much of what had in the past given form and meaning to existence, and had provided hope and solace to those most in need of these things, had also disappeared; and aware also that the moral nature of a society devoid of religious belief might not necessarily be something in which one could vest much confidence. The most famous expression of 'wistful unbelief' was

LONDON CHATHAM & DOVER RAILWAY
PARTINGTON & Co.
ONE PENNY
SALE OVER HALF A MILLION
ONE PENNY
DAILY NEWS
STANDARD

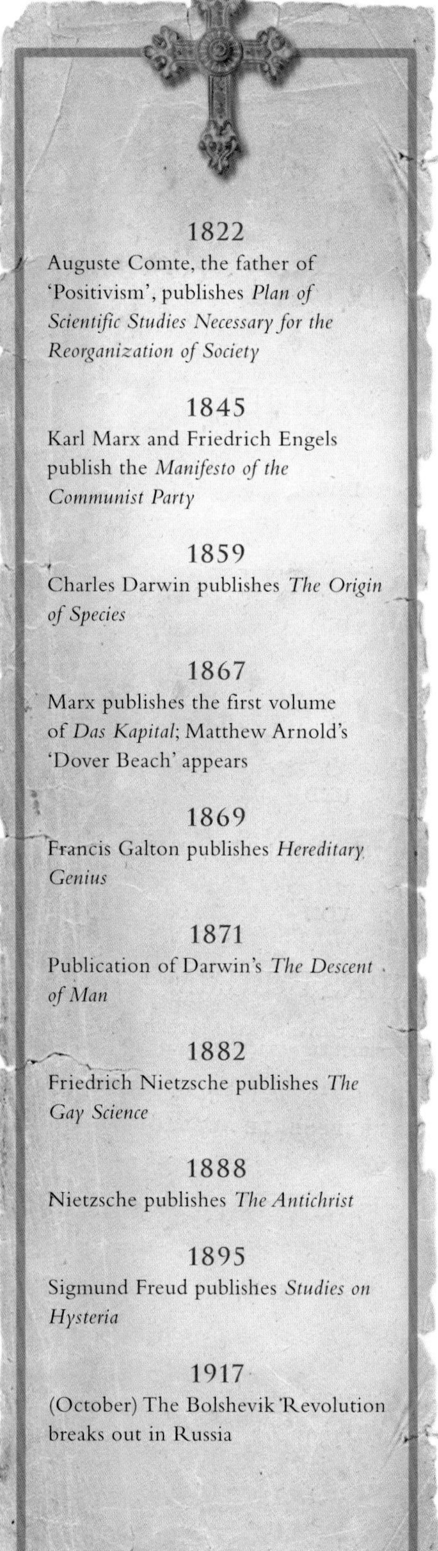

1822
Auguste Comte, the father of 'Positivism', publishes *Plan of Scientific Studies Necessary for the Reorganization of Society*

1845
Karl Marx and Friedrich Engels publish the *Manifesto of the Communist Party*

1859
Charles Darwin publishes *The Origin of Species*

1867
Marx publishes the first volume of *Das Kapital*; Matthew Arnold's 'Dover Beach' appears

1869
Francis Galton publishes *Hereditary Genius*

1871
Publication of Darwin's *The Descent of Man*

1882
Friedrich Nietzsche publishes *The Gay Science*

1888
Nietzsche publishes *The Antichrist*

1895
Sigmund Freud publishes *Studies on Hysteria*

1917
(October) The Bolshevik Revolution breaks out in Russia

'Dover Beach', the 1867 poem by Matthew Arnold (1822–88), with its imagery of the 'melancholy, long, withdrawing roar' of the 'sea of faith', and of a world devoid of joy, love, light, certitude, peace or help for pain, in which the poet descries only 'a darkling plain/ Swept with confused alarms of struggle and flight,/ Where ignorant armies clash by night'. Less known, however (deservedly, perhaps), is the poem 'God's Funeral' by Thomas Hardy (1840–1928), written around 1908, which describes a vision of a funeral cortege upon a 'twilit plain', bearing the 'mystic form' of the dead God away: a procession in which, as it progresses, more and more mourners join. The poet confesses his own sorrow over the loss of something he too once had prized, and speaks longingly of those times long past when one began the day 'with trustful prayer' and ended it in assurance of God's presence. Now 'who or what shall fill his place?' And, says Hardy, 'how to bear such loss I deemed/ The insistent question for each animate mind'.

Nature Red in Tooth and Claw

Without question, no greater blow was struck against conventional religious belief in the 19th century than the 1859 publication of *The Origin of Species*, in which Charles Darwin for the first time publicly unfolded the concept of special evolution, as something accomplished over vast periods of time by fortunate mutation and natural selection. Though Darwin did not there discuss the evolution of humanity, the implications of his thought were obvious; and those implications became explicit with the 1871 publication of *The Descent of Man*.

To the most literalist readers of scripture, of course, Darwin's ideas were scandalous simply because they contradicted the creation story of Genesis; but the ancient Christian practice of reading that story allegorically had never died out in Christian culture, and there were many 19th-century Christians who found the idea of special evolution entirely inoffensive. One of Darwin's earliest and most vigorous champions, the extremely accomplished American botanist Asa Gray (1810–88), was a devout Christian who saw such evolution as a manifestation of God's creative power in the fabric of nature. The true challenge Darwin's books posed to the Christian vision of reality was not so much one of logic as one of sensibility: it was not so much the idea of evolution as such, but that of the mechanism of natural selection, that seemed to exercise a corrosive effect upon

> *'The mystery of the beginning of all things is insoluble to us; and I for one must be content to remain an agnostic.'*
>
> CHARLES DARWIN, *AUTOBIOGRAPHY*, 1876

A caricature in a popular 19th-century French magazine lampoons Charles Darwin's theories of the descent of man from the higher apes by portraying him as a monkey swinging in a tree.

the power of the imagination to see the world in a Christian light. Darwin's argument summoned up before the mind of his society an image of the world as a reality governed at once by heartless necessity and mindless chance, shaped by countless epochs of death, and struggle, and blind striving. Could such a world have been created by the Christian God?

Masters of Suspicion

In truth, the 19th century gave birth to all the great schools of 'post-religious' or 'materialist' thought that have either explicitly or invisibly formed late modern culture at its deepest levels: the most notable of these being modern psychology and modern social theory. Sigmund Freud (1856–1939) was, of course, the most important figure for the development of the former, and though his reputation has perhaps declined somewhat in recent years, the 'mythos' of human consciousness created by him remains very much intact. For Freud, the self is – rather than a soul with an eternal nature – a complex amalgam of biological and social impulses, many of them quite 'Darwinian' in their primal mechanisms, and the conscious mind is only the surface of the 'unconscious', where hidden, largely irrational impulses, repressed desires, secret resentments, tacit memories and conflicting sexual urges reside. Freud, moreover, firmly believed that, as science advanced, and as the science of the mind progressively defeated supernatural thinking, the 'illusion' of religion – whose origin he ascribed in large measure to the human fear of death – would melt away.

Of all the theorists of 19th century Europe who attempted to construct a vision of the social or political good in unambiguously materialist terms, obviously none was more influential than Karl Marx (1818–83), the father of a somewhat heterodox form of revolutionary socialism. Marx's reputation has also suffered considerably over the past century; but, again, his vision of politics, culture and society as creations of a 'material dialectic', and of history as driven almost exclusively by class struggle and economic motives, profoundly affected the thought even of many of his detractors. And, if nothing else, the 20th century demonstrated the enormous power of his sort of atheist utopianism radically to transform (and often to destroy) whole societies.

Darwin's half-cousin Sir Francis Galton was the originator of the theory of eugenics, which posited an improvement of the human race by means of selective breeding.

Another school of social theory that attached itself to socialist economics and 'progressive' thought at the end of the 19th century – with worse than tragic consequences – was that of 'eugenics'. Its principles were first clearly enunciated in the 1860s by Sir Francis Galton (1822–1911), and its aims were shared by many of the most 'enlightened' minds of the late 19th and early 20th centuries including, it seems, Darwin himself. Many who embraced this movement believed they were simply drawing the conclusions dictated by Darwinian science: if, they reasoned, natural selection is the mechanism by which a species thrives and improves, then civilization should not be allowed to retard this process among human beings, and carriers of hereditary defects, as well as those who are racially, morally or mentally 'inferior,' should ideally be prevented from reproducing. Of course, logically speaking, to mistake Darwinian biology for a moral imperative is rather absurd; but the eugenic premise was widely accepted by liberal-minded individuals and states for decades. In the early 20th century, many of the traditionally Protestant countries of Europe, as well as the USA, Canada and Australia, admitted certain eugenic principles into law. And it was not unusual to read an idealistic socialist like H. G. Wells (1866–1946) calmly predicting a day when entire races would have to be exterminated for the good of the species.

Western society was on the verge of discovering that a radical materialism could breed horrors far greater than even the worst religious fanaticism.

THE PROPHET OF ANTICHRIST

In the writings of no other thinker of the 19th century did the voice of unbelief reach so pure and piercing a pitch as in those of Friedrich Nietzsche (1844–1900), the brilliant classicist, philologist and philosopher.

Nietzsche was the most coherent interpreter of faith's decline, the most uncompromising advocate of a post-religious ethos, and the most vehemently anti-Christian philosopher of his or any era. He believed that the triumph of Christianity had been a catastrophe for Western humanity, one that had elevated the slavish and resentful values of the weak and ill-constituted over the noble, life-affirming and healthy virtues of the strong and guileless. He also thought that Christian tales of heavenly reality had drained the earth of meaning, that the 'moral' distinction between good and evil was a perversion of human values, and that the gospel's concern for the frail and meek, and its cult of pity, had poisoned the wellsprings of human nature. He did not hesitate to speak of himself as an 'antichrist'.

Nietzsche's most famous dictum from The Gay Science *is 'God is dead! He remains dead! And we have killed him!'*

Nietzsche was not, however, entirely sanguine in his prognostications for a future without God. He feared that, in the absence of any higher aspiration, humanity might degenerate into those he called the 'Last Men' (*die letzten Menschen*), an insect-like race of vapid narcissists, sunk in petty satisfactions. But he hoped that humanity might rouse itself from the stupor induced by two millennia of Christianity to will 'that which is beyond the merely human': the 'Overman' (*der Übermensch*), that inspiring but indefinable hero or artist or leader to whose advent humanity might yet aspire, if it still had the strength to affirm earthly life rather than succumb to an ultimate nihilism.

In a famous passage from *The Gay Science* (1882) Nietzsche relates the fable of a madman who comes into a city to announce the 'death of God' – that is, the end of human faith in the transcendent; an event of such immense significance that the very horizons of our world have been 'sponged away'. But no one knows what to make of his words. Even those who have ceased to believe in God cannot understand how momentous his message is. So the madman leaves, knowing that it may be centuries before humanity grasps what the death of God has meant: what an utter revision of all values it must bring about, and how utterly it will transform all things human.

THE NINETEENTH CENTURY: A TIME OF FERVENT FAITH

The 19th century was not an age only of unbelief. As enormous as were the advances of various atheisms and scepticisms towards the centre of Western culture, an equally powerful (and numerically far stronger) tendency towards renewed religious devotion also arose in those years. It was a time of great expansion for many churches, and of consolidation and revival for others. It was, for the greater Christian world, a century of faith.

Perhaps the most enormous development in Protestant circles in the 19th century was the rapid growth of a kind of piety that had first appeared in England in the 18th century and that soon migrated to North America: evangelicalism. This was a movement associated with no specific denomination and not bound – after its first few decades, at least – to any standard theology. Its emphasis was upon the personal experience of conversion, repentance, redemption by God's grace and sanctification. Its typical expression was a certain type of worship marked by palpable fervour, and its chief emphasis was upon the cultivation of a life of prayer, a personal sense of assurance in Christ as one's saviour and evangelization.

John Wesley preaching, in a portrait of 1766 by Nathaniel Hone.

The most important early form of the evangelical movement (which was concurrent with other 'pietist' movements in Europe, Catholic and Protestant) was that of Methodism, which began within the Church of England under the leadership of John Wesley (1703–91), a learned and devout Anglican priest, and his brother Charles (1707–88), also an Anglican priest, as well as a poet and one of the great hymnodists of Christian history. The Wesleys, from early in their pastoral careers, were devoted to regular participation in the Eucharist, bible study and prison ministry; but in 1738 they both had conversion experiences. John was soon persuaded by another Anglican priest, George Whitefield (1714–70), to preach in public – whereby was invented what would become the evangelical revival meeting (though Wesley and Whitefield would later part over the latter's belief in predestination, which Wesley could not abide).

Whitefield was particularly important for introducing 'revivalism' to America, as well as for inspiring the first 'Great Awakening', the movement of religious pietism and enthusiast religion that swept through the American colonies from the 1720s through the 1740s. In the 1790s a second Great Awakening arose simultaneously in New England and Kentucky; in the former region, it was

of a soberer kind than the first Awakening, and in the latter it was of an even more 'enthusiast' and 'ecstatic' kind. And over the course of the century that followed, an evangelical form of Christianity – in which the experience of conversion, rather than baptism, came to be regarded as the way in which a person is 'born again' in Christ – gradually became one of the dominant forms of American Protestantism.

The Methodist preacher George Whitefield holds a revival meeting at Moorfields in London in 1742. Whitefield was also instrumental in bringing evangelicalism to the United States, making a total of 13 trips there from the late 1730s onwards.

Protestant Missions

The 19th century was also the period in which the Protestant churches began to make a concerted effort to carry the gospel to unconverted peoples. The Methodist Bishop Thomas Coke (1747–1814) brought his communion into the 'mission field', while the English Baptist minister William Carey (1761–1834) was the first of his confession to establish a mission in India. Anthony Norris Groves (1795–1853), one of the founders of the Plymouth Brethren, even served as a missionary in Baghdad before relocating to India.

A Catholic school in Beijing, China, from Work of the Propagation of the Faith, *published in 1882. The Society for the Propagation of the Faith is a Catholic organization founded in France in 1822 to promote missionary work around the globe.*

The most famous of the 19th-century Protestant missions was the 'China Inland Mission' led by Hudson Taylor (1832–1905), who lived for more than 50 years in China, founding many schools, converting thousands of Chinese by his own preaching, and attracting hundreds of missionaries to the country. Taylor, in fact, integrated himself entirely into Chinese society, adopting indigenous dress, many of the native customs and even the language as his own. And while few Protestant missionaries of later years imitated him in this, his example inspired many thousands to undertake missions in inland regions, not only in China, but in many remote parts of the globe.

Vatican I

During these years, Catholic missions also remained robust, and the Roman Church continued to grow in absolute numbers all around the world. But the most significant institutional developments of the period concerned the shifting situation of the papacy in Europe, as both a secular and a spiritual power. The end of the real independence of the Papal States, and Rome's integration into a unified Italy, was an inevitability after the 'revolutionary year' of 1848; and, after 1870, it was a *fait accompli*. This was the political situation with which Pope Pius IX (1792–1878) was forced to come to terms during his long pontificate (32 years). And the cultural situation was perhaps even direr: rising materialism, anti-clericalism and the obvious decay of the Church's moral authority in society at large.

All of these considerations contributed to the pope's decision to convoke the First Vatican Council, which he intended as an enormous project of dogmatic clarification and institutional reorganization. In fact, the council lasted only from December 1869 to October 1870, when Pius had to suspend it indefinitely because of the occupation of Rome by Piedmontese forces. Before its premature dissolution, however, the council did issue two doctrinal documents. The first, 'Dei Filius' (Son of God), which concerned the authority of the Church's magisterium (teaching office) in making all final determinations of the validity of theological and exegetical statements, and which attempted to define the essential harmony – and relative authority – of faith and reason.

The second document, 'Pastor Aeternus' (Eternal Shepherd), concerned the jurisdiction and dogmatic authority of the pope, and was the object of a vehement debate among the council's participants. The document affirmed that the pope, as Peter's successor, is the inheritor of a unique authority over the entire Church – including complete and irresistible jurisdiction over every diocese – and that his authority in matters of doctrine was absolute and literally 'infallible.' This last claim meant that, when he definitively enunciates a doctrinal teaching of the Church that does not contradict dogmatic tradition, he does so without possibility of error; and, moreover, that he has the power to define doctrine 'from himself, and not from the consensus of the Church', and so does not require a Church council to arrive at his doctrinal determinations.

Russian 'Religious Philosophy'

The most significant developments in Eastern Orthodox thought in the 19th century occurred in Russia. In the first half of the century, there arose a loose movement called 'Slavophilism' dedicated to the unification of all of Slavic culture and to a creative recovery of the Orthodox tradition as an alternative to the supposed authoritarianism, materialism and spiritual poverty of modern Western Europe. The Slavophiles were, as a rule, political liberals who advocated the emancipation of the serfs, the end of capital punishment and freedom of the press, and who wanted the tsar to become a constitutional monarch answerable to a

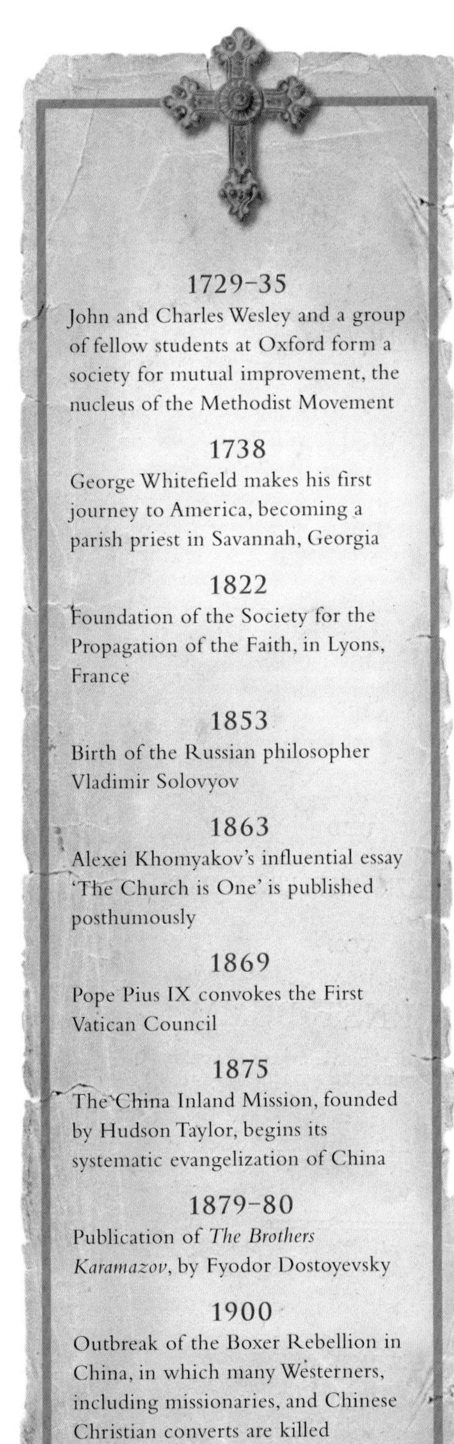

1729–35
John and Charles Wesley and a group of fellow students at Oxford form a society for mutual improvement, the nucleus of the Methodist Movement

1738
George Whitefield makes his first journey to America, becoming a parish priest in Savannah, Georgia

1822
Foundation of the Society for the Propagation of the Faith, in Lyons, France

1853
Birth of the Russian philosopher Vladimir Solovyov

1863
Alexei Khomyakov's influential essay 'The Church is One' is published posthumously

1869
Pope Pius IX convokes the First Vatican Council

1875
The China Inland Mission, founded by Hudson Taylor, begins its systematic evangelization of China

1879–80
Publication of *The Brothers Karamazov*, by Fyodor Dostoyevsky

1900
Outbreak of the Boxer Rebellion in China, in which many Westerners, including missionaries, and Chinese Christian converts are killed

parliament; but they also wished to inspire a renewal of the native spiritual and cultural traditions of the Slavic Christian peoples, and especially of the Christian spirit of old Kievan Russia.

The most impressive of these men was Alexei Khomyakov (1804–60), a poet, philosopher, political theorist and theologian, who was the first to expound the 'Slavic Christian' ideal of *Sobornost* – which might be translated as 'concordance', 'integralism' or 'harmony' – as both a spiritual and a political principle. Khomyakov was equally contemptuous of capitalism and socialism, which he saw as two sides of the same Western materialist heresy, and two forms of authoritarian social organization incompatible with human dignity. Equally devoted to this idea of *Sobornost* was Ivan Kireevsky (1806–56), who saw it as an alternative to both the individualism and the collectivism of Western modernity. Kireevsky was also profoundly important in bringing a fascination with German Idealist philosophy – and especially that of Friedrich Wilhelm Schelling (1775–1854) – into Russian Christian philosophy.

'The execrable doctrine called communism … is wholly contrary to natural law itself; nor could it establish itself without turning upside-down all rights, all interests, the essence of property, and society itself.'

POPE PIUS IX, 'QUI PLURIBUS' ENCYCLICAL, 9 NOVEMBER 1846

After an early flirtation with nihilism, Vladimir Solovyov returned to the bosom of the Orthodox Church and became one of Russian Christianity's most original thinkers.

The next generation of Russian Christian thinkers took up almost all of the ideas and ideals of the Slavophiles, though some did so with even more nativist passion and others with even more cosmopolitan openness. It is in the latter class that one would have to number the philosopher and poet Vladimir Solovyov (1853–1900), a towering figure in modern Russian thought. Though Orthodox, Solovyov was ardently ecumenical in outlook, and yearned for the ultimate reconciliation of all Christians; he shared the Slavophiles' disdain for capitalism and socialism, and their political liberalism, and he mastered the philosophical tradition of Europe – and German Idealism especially – as no previous Russian philosopher had. The centre of his thought was 'divine humanity', mankind's original and natural orientation towards divinization, and the 'God-man'. Christ, who brings this orientation to fruition and so joins all of creation to God. Solovyov is also accounted the father of 'Sophiology', a movement concerned with reflection on the Biblical figure of the divine Sophia or Wisdom, understood almost as a kind of 'sacred feminine' in nature in history: at once the indwelling presence of God in creation and also the deep spiritual openness of creation to union with God.

POET OF THE GOD-MAN

Fyodor Dostoyevsky (1821–81) is generally regarded as one of the greatest novelists of Western literary history, and almost certainly the greatest philosophical novelist ever. In later life, he was deeply impressed and influenced by the thought of 'the young philosopher' Solovyov, and most especially by Solovyov's opposition between the 'God-man' – Christ, humanity as perfected and divinized by God's grace – and the 'man-god' – a figure who represents the highest achievement of the fallen human will to dominate and triumph over material nature, and whom both Solvyov and Dostoyevsky portrayed in terms sometimes eerily similar to the *Übermensch* of Nietzsche (of whom neither in all likelihood had ever heard).

Dostoyevsky was a man of enormous contradictions, who in his youth had gone through phases of irreligion and political radicalism, and who as a result of the latter had even been subjected to the cruel ordeal of a mock execution and a period of Siberian exile, imprisonment and forced labour. He returned fully to Christian faith in maturity, and developed a fervent devotion both to Orthodoxy and to Russia (not always in that order), but he refused any kind of glib or easy faith. In his last and greatest novel, *The Brothers Karamazov* (1879–80), in a chapter entitled 'Rebellion', he set forth what many regard as one of the most powerful cases ever made against Christian faith.

As a novelist, Dostoyevsky was widely praised even in his day for the depth of his psychological insights, a talent that first became fully obvious in his novella *Notes from the Underground* (1864). The story was written in the first-person voice of perhaps the strangest, most complex and most impulsive fictional personality to have appeared in Western literature to that point: a petty, self-loathing and self-absorbed creature of post-Christian rationalism who is, nevertheless, tormented by his knowledge of the human will's perverse resistance to all rationalization, and haunted by his guilt – which he constantly and unconvincingly denies – over an act of cruelty he once committed.

Everything that Nietzsche saw regarding the withdrawal of Christian faith in the modern West, and regarding the crisis and uncertainty it would bring in its wake, Dostoyevsky also saw, though with a depth of humane subtlety that Nietzsche usually lacked. Unlike Nietzsche, though, Dostoyevsky believed the descent of modern humanity into nihilism (whose worst political and social consequences he foresaw with remarkable perspicacity) to be the result not of Christianity's corruption of the human will, but of the inability of modern men and women to bear the power of Christian freedom. And, as an answer to nihilism, Dostoyevsky proposed not the *Übermensch*, but the *staretz* Zosima (a character in *The Brothers Karamazov*): a monk able to look upon all of creation with fervent and self-outpouring charity.

THE TWENTIETH CENTURY IN AMERICA

By the end of the 20th century, more than two billion persons – one-third of the human race – were at least nominally Christian, and the gospel had reached every corner of the globe in one form or another. Considered in purely historical terms, it might well seem that nothing has ever come nearer to constituting a truly global faith. On the other hand, Christian adherence had never before come in so vast a variety of forms, some of them all but incomprehensible to one another. If Christianity is a global faith, it is not by any means a unified or uniform community.

An Italian family arriving at the immigration centre on Ellis Island in New York harbour in 1905. The number of Catholics that came to the United States in the late 19th and early 20th centuries was so great that the Catholic Church is now far and away the country's largest denomination.

Nowhere does this diversity of Christian confessions show itself more vividly than in North America, and in the United States in particular, where the always heterogeneous Christianity of the various original settlers was further fecundated by the great inpouring of immigrants in the late 19th and early 20th centuries.

Fundamentalism

The Evangelical Protestantism that took such firm hold in the United States in the 19th century was not, of course, a single church, nor was it even organized around a single unvarying theology. It admitted of innumerable variants, and in the second decade of the 20th century, a new variant arose called 'fundamentalism', so named because of a series of 12 books outlining its principles that appeared from 1909 to 1915 under the collective title *The Fundamentals*.

In principle, fundamentalism was a reaction to 'liberal theology', which is to say those forms of mainline Protestantism that were willing to allow for a certain latitude in their interpretation of the content of scripture (regarding, for instance, which aspects of its narratives were to be taken literally, and which symbolically). It was also, however, a reaction against many of the developments of modern society, religion and science that fundamentalists believed undermined Christian faith, such as Darwinism, spiritualism, Mormonism and materialism. The actual 'fundamentals' were a set of the five basic 'propositions' supposedly definitive of true Christianity: Christ's substitutionary atonement for sin, the reality of miracles, the virgin birth, Christ's bodily resurrection and the inerrancy of scripture (some versions of the list include Christ's divinity and the last judgment).

Of these, scriptural inerrancy was the only wholly novel principle. It went far beyond the traditional Christian belief in the divine inspiration and truthfulness in scripture; it meant that every single event reported in the Bible was historically factual, every word recorded therein literally true and every apparent contradiction unreal. Such a view of scripture might have been tacitly held by many Christians down the centuries; but, as an explicit dogma, it was contrary to almost all of Christian tradition, Protestant, Catholic or Orthodox.

Baptist worshippers in the 1930s. Baptist churches in America were generally 'holiness congregations,' which subscribed to an Evangelical theology.

Pentecostalism and the Charismatic Movement

Just as significant a development for American Evangelicalism – and ultimately more important in global terms – was the birth in the first decade of the century of the 'Pentecostal' movement, a variety of 'enthusiast' spirituality that involves belief in a second baptism 'by the Holy Spirit' (as distinct from that 'by water') that confers on the believer the spiritual 'charisms' or gifts experienced by the first-century Church: speaking in tongues, miraculous healings, prophecy, the power to cast out demons and so forth. Many Pentecostals believed that, in their time, the 'latter reign' of the Holy Spirit had begun, and dated its start to the Azusa Street Mission Revival of 1906–15, in Los Angeles – a revival disdained by its critics for both its mixture of races and its ecstatic worship.

Pentecostalism, moreover, did not remain confined to Evangelical communities; in the 1960s it began to migrate into the mainline Protestant, Catholic and even (in a very small way) Orthodox Churches in America. In 1960, it even made its way into the staid and respectable environs of the Episcopal Church, brought there by – among others – an Episcopal priest named Dennis Bennett (1917–91). In 1967, the Roman Catholic theology student (and later deacon) Kevin Ranaghan (b.1940), along with his wife, experienced a charismatic conversion, and it was largely because of him that a 'Charismatic renewal' began to spread through the Catholic Church, not only in America, but around the world.

As a rule, the denominations where the Charismatics appeared came to accept this style of spirituality as a legitimate and even admirable form of Christian life, grounded in Biblical tradition. It soon became

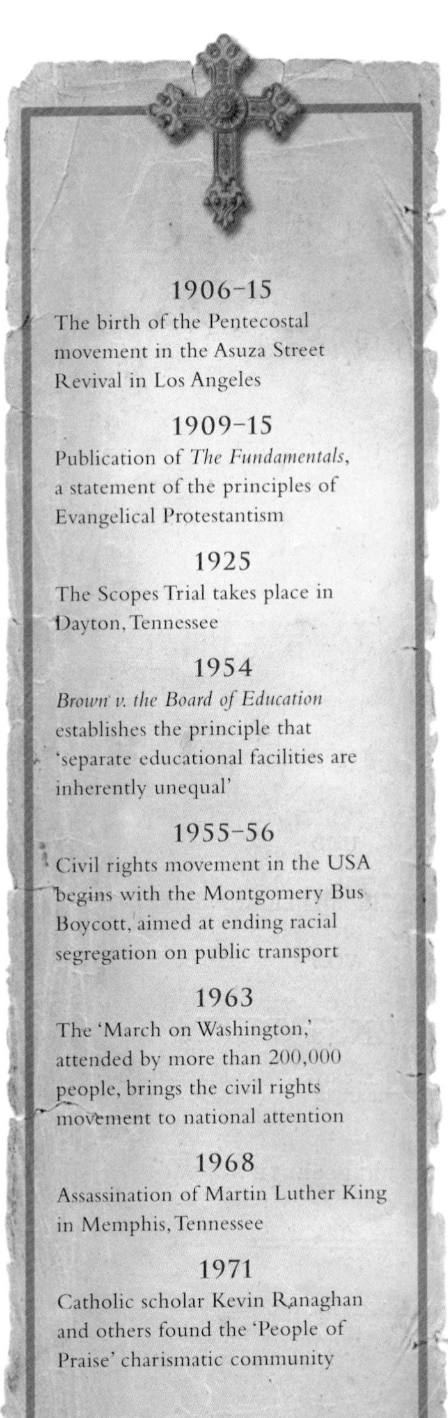

1906–15
The birth of the Pentecostal movement in the Asuza Street Revival in Los Angeles

1909–15
Publication of *The Fundamentals*, a statement of the principles of Evangelical Protestantism

1925
The Scopes Trial takes place in Dayton, Tennessee

1954
Brown v. the Board of Education establishes the principle that 'separate educational facilities are inherently unequal'

1955–56
Civil rights movement in the USA begins with the Montgomery Bus Boycott, aimed at ending racial segregation on public transport

1963
The 'March on Washington,' attended by more than 200,000 people, brings the civil rights movement to national attention

1968
Assassination of Martin Luther King in Memphis, Tennessee

1971
Catholic scholar Kevin Ranaghan and others found the 'People of Praise' charismatic community

'I have a dream that one day this nation will live out the true meaning of its creed: "We hold these truths to be self-evident; that all men are created equal." When we let freedom ring, when we let it ring for every village and hamlet, for every state and every city, we will be able to speed up that day when all of God's children ... will be able to join hands and sing in the words of the old Negro spiritual, "Free at last! Free at last! Thank God Almighty, we are free at last!"'

MARTIN LUTHER KING, SPEECH AT THE LINCOLN MEMORIAL, 28 AUGUST 1963

evident, for instance, that a belief in the gifts of the Spirit did not alienate Catholics from their Church, but often seemed to make them better Catholics. By the end of the century, the Catholic Charismatic movement had become not only a recognized form of Catholicism, but in some parts of the world (such as sub-Saharan Africa, the Philippines and Brazil) one of the dominant forms.

Civil Rights

The American civil rights movement that began after the 1954 Supreme Court decision in *Brown v. the Board of Education* (which desegregated public education) was in many very real respects a movement within the American churches. Peaceful protests were promoted and supported by local congregations and Christian organizations such as the Southern Christian Leadership Conference. In fact, one of the founders of that conference, the Baptist pastor T. J. Jemison (b.1918), set the pattern for such protests by leading a bus boycott in Baton Rouge, Louisiana in 1953. Another founder, the Rev. Fred Shuttleworth (b.1922) – whom the Ku Klux Klan attempted to assassinate in 1957 – was one of the chief organizers of the 'Freedom Rides' of 1961.

The most famous, revered and ultimately mourned of the civil rights movement's many ordained leaders was the Rev. Dr Martin Luther King Jr. (1929–68), the Baptist minister who – through his sheer eloquençe, unrelenting effort and personal courage – did perhaps more than anyone else to transform the

Dr Martin Luther King addressing the crowd before a civil rights march from Selma to Montgomery, Alabama, in 1965.

THE SCOPES TRIAL

Easily the most famous episode of conflict between American evangelical fundamentalism and modern 'materialist' ideas was the 'Scopes Trial' of 1925, in Dayton, Tennessee, in which two legendary figures in American law and politics – Clarence Darrow (1857–1938) and William Jennings Bryan (1860–1925) – fought a pitched court battle over the right of a public school instructor to teach evolution.

The instructor in question was one John Scopes (1900–70), who was accused of teaching from a text book (*Civic Biology* by George Hunter) that included a chapter on biological evolution; technically this violated Tennessee's 'Butler Act', passed earlier that year, which prohibited the teaching of any theory denying the biblical story of creation and suggesting human descent from lower beasts. Darrow, an agnostic and member of the American Civil Liberties Union, volunteered to join the defence team, while Bryan, who shared the beliefs of the fundamentalist movement, joined the prosecution. The moment in the trial that entered most deeply into national lore involved Bryan taking the stand, as an 'expert on the Bible', to be cross-examined by Darrow on the plausibility of the scriptural accounts of creation and of various miracles; this circular and aimless debate was ultimately expunged from the record. Scopes was found guilty, but was merely fined $100; on appeal, the conviction was nullified.

The trial has usually been remembered merely as a conflict between primitive religiosity and disinterested science, but the facts of the case are rather more complicated. Bryan was in his youth one of the most passionate and populist of 'progressive' politicians, a champion of labour and of the poor, an enemy of race theory, and a firm believer in democracy. In his day, evolutionary theory was inextricably associated with eugenics, and from early on he had denounced Darwinism as a philosophy of hatred and oppression, ardently believing that the Christian law of love was the only true basis of a just society. As yet, the rather obvious truth that evolutionary science need involve no social ideology whatsoever was not obvious even to Darwinian scientists.

Moreover, *Civic Biology* was a monstrously racist text, which ranked humanity in five categories of evolutionary development (with blacks at the bottom and whites at the top), advocated eugenic cleansing of the race, denounced intermarriage and the perpetuation of 'degenerate' stock and suggested 'humane' steps for the elimination of social 'parasites'. These were the ideas that Bryan had long believed would lead humanity into an age of war, murder and tyranny; and, given what came in the decades following the trial, it would be hard to argue that Bryan – whatever his faults – was simply an alarmist.

movement into a national cause. And his unwavering commitment to peaceful protest made the violence of the movement's opponents – violence, incidentally, that was often even worse in northern cities such as Chicago than in the south – that much more vividly repellent in the eyes of many millions who saw and heard it reported in the media. The national scope of the movement became clear in 1963, with the 'March on Washington'. No event did more to force the moral demands of the movement into the consciousness of the nation – with the exception, perhaps, of King's assassination in 1968, in Memphis, Tennessee.

THE MOST VIOLENT CENTURY IN HISTORY

At the high meridian of the 'Enlightenment', the hope of many was that a world freed from the burden of 'superstition' and 'priestcraft' would evolve into a rational society, capable of ordering itself peacefully, harmoniously and wisely. Even in the 19th century, when unbelief was often prompted by a somewhat darker view of human nature, the 'progressive' view was still that a secular society, purged of the pernicious influences of religion by the cleansing gales of scientific reason, would by its nature prove to be more just, peaceful and humane than the 'Age of Faith' had been.

A call to arms from post-revolutionary Russia; this recruitment poster dating from 1917 urges: 'Still not a member of the Co-operative – sign up immediately!'

And yet, by the end of the 20th century, wars had been waged on a scale never before imagined, and a number of Utopian, strictly secularist ideologies – each in its own way the inheritor both of the Enlightenment project to remake society on a more rational model and of the late 19th-century project to 'correct' human nature through the mechanisms of a provident state – had together managed to kill perhaps 150 million persons. Over three centuries, the worst abuse of ecclesial authority in Christian history – the Spanish Crown's Inquisitions – caused the deaths of maybe 30,000, and even then only after a legal process that produced far more acquittals than convictions; the Soviet Union or the People's Republic of China, by contrast, often killed that many of its own citizens in three days, without any trial at all. By century's end, all certainties had been shattered: the power of 'organized religion' in the West had been largely subdued, but organized irreligion had proved a far more despotic, capricious and murderous historical force.

The People's Revolution

Russia's pre-eminence among Orthodox countries after the 15th century had been a consequence principally of its freedom from foreign rule; among Orthodox peoples, only the Slavs were not subjects of non-Christian nations, and among the Slavic nations, Russia was the largest and most powerful. But, by the last decades of the 19th century, several radically atheist political movements had spread through Russia, many of them inspired by the ideals of 'scientific socialism' and committed to the overthrow of such 'bourgeois' institutions as the monarchy and the Church. By the 1870s, to prescient observers of the Russian scene, the question was not whether the revolution would come, but when.

After the Bolshevik seizure of power in November 1917, the new Soviet government instituted a systematic persecution of the Church, which consisted not only in the seizure of ecclesiastical properties, but in the imprisonment, torture and murder of a great many bishops, priests and religious – a pattern that would be imitated, with greater or lesser ferocity, by other Eastern European 'revolutionary' regimes later in the century. In 1927, the revered and learned

Metropolitan Sergius (1867–1944), who would later become patriarch of Moscow (the patriarchate having been restored a few months before the Bolshevik coup), attempted to purchase some relief for his Church by publicly professing loyalty to the Soviet government; but only in 1943 did a period of greater toleration begin, lasting until about 1959, when Nikita Khrushchev (1894–1971) reinstituted persecutions. Only in the late 1980s, when the Soviet system itself was on the verge of collapse, did the repressive measures abate.

A poster issued in 1933, the year of Hitler's appointment as chancellor of Germany, shows a podium flanked by a First World War soldier and a Brownshirt storm-trooper, and reads: 'To the New Germany'.

One of the most famous of Orthodox priests to be murdered during the early decades of the Soviet regime was the extraordinary Pavel Florensky (1882–1937) who, as well as being a theologian and philosopher (and writer of considerable skill), was an electrical engineer and mathematician. He was an admirer of Vladimir Solovyov, whose 'sophiology' he adopted and developed, and whose social ideas he had attempted in his youth to make the principles of a Christian revolutionary movement. In 1924, he published his magnum opus, *The Pillar and Ground of Truth*, a long treatise on the Christian metaphysics of love. Had it not been for his expertise in electrodynamic theory and electric engineering, he probably would have been executed not long after the revolution. As it was, the new government had need of his services in the grand project of the 'electrification of Russia'. Florensky served, but refused to abandon the traditional cassock, uncropped hair and beard of an Orthodox priest. In 1933, he was sentenced to ten years' hard labour in a gulag, and in 1937 was sentenced to death by a secret tribunal and killed some time soon thereafter.

Blood, Soil and Destiny

The sort of 'internationalist' socialism favoured by the communists of eastern Europe, though, was as a rule concerned with class rather than with race, and with the reorganization of society rather than with the refinement of the species. When they killed, it was generally in the name of a social, political or economic principle. But the other stream of 'progressive' socialist thought – race theory, eugenics, euthanasia of 'defectives' and forced sterilization – was taken up by the 'nationalist' socialists of Germany in the 1930s, where it was combined with native racial and social 'philosophies' to produce the genocidal policies of the Third Reich. The six million or so Jews murdered by the Nazis – as well as the millions from other communities and nations – were the victims principally of an ideology of racial and

1914–18
The First World War claims more than 19 million lives

1917
Riots in Russia in March result in the abdication of Tsar Nicholas II; the Bolsheviks seize power on 7 November. Persecution of Church and clergy by the Soviet state

1924
Pavel Florensky publishes *The Pillar and Ground of Truth*

1927
Metropolitan Sergius declares support for the Soviet government; a period of religious toleration ensues

1933
The anti-Semitic National Socialist German Workers' Party controls the German Reichstag, and Adolf Hitler becomes chancellor of Germany; the 'Protestant Reich Church' is formed

1934
Birth of the 'Confessing Church' movement in Germany

1937
Florensky is sentenced to death

1944
An assassination attempt on Hitler is made by members of the Confessing Church and military collaborators

1959
Further persecution of the Russian Church under Nikita Khrushchev

1968
The Council of Latin American Bishops in Colombia gives rise to the Liberation Theology movement

national destiny that claimed for itself both the mystical authority of a kind of Germanic neo-paganism and the pedigree of 'scientific' socialism.

The generally invertebrate and even subservient response of many of the churches in Germany to the rise of the Nazis, however, was in part the result of centuries of European anti-Semitism, and in even larger part the result of cowardice. The National Socialist Workers' Party was clearly a post-Christian political movement, intent ultimately on superseding the Gospel's 'Jewish corruption' of 'Aryan' culture and racial consciousness; but it also seemed quite content to leave most established institutions intact as it undertook its project of national transformation. In 1933, though, as part of the Reich's policy of *Gleichschaltung* ('enforced uniformity'), all Protestant congregations in Germany were amalgamated into a single 'Protestant Reich Church', committed to purifying Christianity of its Jewish alloys (such as the Old Testament).

Martyrdom

The Reich Church quickly proved a failure, but it did give rise in 1934 to the Christian resistance movement called the 'Confessing Church', led by a number of prominent Lutheran pastors and theologians, and organized around the 'Barmen Declaration', a document written chiefly by the great Swiss theologian Karl Barth (1886–1968). As an underground organization, the Confessing Church had very little effect on the culture at large, and those among its numbers who spoke out publicly on behalf of the Jews were often moved to lament the movement's frequent timidity. That said, bolder members of the Confessing Church did engage in subversive activities, including hiding Jews, and certain of the more prominent leaders of the movement paid dearly for their involvement.

> *'When the Nazis came for the Communists, I remained silent because I wasn't a Communist. When they locked up the Social Democrats, I remained silent because I wasn't a Social Democrat. When they came for the trade unionists, I didn't speak out because I wasn't a trade unionist. When they came for me, there was no one left to speak out.'*
>
> Martin Niemöller, Lutheran theologian imprisoned by the Nazis, 1955

Among these, a particularly honoured place belongs to Dietrich Bonhoeffer (1906–45), a Lutheran theologian and pastor who was one of the founders of the Confessing Church. His vociferous opposition to the new regime in the early and middle 1930s, both in Germany and abroad, and his constant calls for Christian solidarity with the Jews

A THEOLOGY OF LIBERATION

Perhaps it was as a result of the general decline in the political power of the Church that the 20th century was a period so rich in 'political theologies'. Among the most controversial of these was the Latin American movement called 'Liberation Theology', usually thought to have begun in 1968 at a convocation of the Council of Latin American Bishops in Medellín, Colombia. The assembled bishops crafted a statement protesting those policies of rich nations that they believed perpetuated poverty in the developing world, and calling for a new commitment by the Church and governments to justice for the poor.

Liberation Theology, however, soon evolved a more distinct set of general principles. In its developed form, the movement revolved around reading the Bible in light of God's special 'preference' for the poor. According to proponents of Liberation Theology, fidelity to the Gospel demands that Christians lend themselves to the social and political struggles of the oppressed, even (many would say) when this might involve forms of revolutionary action. God's saving activity towards humanity, they say, is not merely 'spiritual' – or, rather, spiritual redemption cannot be separated from the prophetic law of justice and mercy proclaimed by Christ, the prophets and the apostles.

It is not in the power of humans to bring about the Kingdom of God, according to this theology; but one cannot serve Christ unless one seeks to live towards the Kingdom, which inevitably must involve the attempt to create conditions that manifest in concrete social, political and economic forms the justice of God's reign. The evils that God condemns on the cross include not only personal moral faults, but those 'structural evils' that alienate human societies from God.

The controversial aspect of Liberation Theology was obviously not its advocacy for the poor, or the *communidades* – local Bible study and social assistance associations – it encouraged, but the tendency of many of its proponents to adopt Marxist analyses of economic and social history, and occasionally to associate themselves with Marxist revolutionary organizations. This led the Vatican in the 1980s to rein the movement in, principally through the appointment of bishops unsympathetic to its more suspect elements. In the nations of Latin America, however, it remains an extremely popular theological movement.

against the Nazis, soon made him an object of Gestapo attention, and he was forbidden to teach, preach or speak in public. Though a firm believer in the Christian's duty to practise peace, he also believed that there were evils against which the Christian conscience demands struggle by any means necessary; and in 1939 he joined a conspiracy – which included his brother and his two brothers-in-law, as well as a number of high-ranking military officers – to assassinate Hitler. In April 1943, though, before the attempt had been made, he was discovered to have supplied money to aid Jews in escaping to Switzerland and was imprisoned.

When the attempt to kill Hitler was finally made, in July 1944, and failed, the investigation soon uncovered the names of the conspirators, and all were executed. Bonhoeffer was hanged at dawn on 9 April 1945, at the concentration camp in Flossenbürg, three weeks before the city was captured by the Allies.

THE 20TH TO THE 21ST CENTURY: THE RISE OF A NEW CHRISTENDOM

Christianity was born in the East, and in its earliest centuries was as much – or more – a part of the Near Eastern and North African world as the European; and, well into the Middle Ages, Syrian Christian outposts extended to 'far Cathay'. It was only as a result of a number of historical forces – chief among them, the rise of powerful Islamic empires in the seventh century and after – that Christianity came to be regarded almost exclusively as a European religion, that it was Europe alone where an exclusively Christian civilization took form, and that it was from early modern Europe that Christianity ventured farthest out into the larger world.

Now, though, at the beginning of the 21st century, Christianity is truly a global religion. While most Europeans remain nominally Christian, the number of active Christians – those, that is, who attend church – is a minuscule minority of the population; and, with the exception of the United States, all modern industrial nations have experienced a steep decline in active religious adherence over the past 50 years.

And yet Christianity is also spreading more rapidly today than at any previous point in its history; it already takes into its embrace roughly a third of the human race – more than two billion persons, if the generally accepted estimates are correct. The 'balance of power' within the Church – demographically and culturally, at any rate – has definitely begun to shift.

Restorations and Renewals

That said, the old Christendom did not vanish at the end of the 20th century. The post-war years were a time of immense transition for many Christian communions, in some cases of arguably epochal significance, and – if a capacity to adapt to current conditions is a sign of life – many of the oldest Christian Churches gave plenteous evidence of continued vitality. For one thing, those years were marked by a genuine movement among all the major Christian denominations towards ecumenism: that is, dialogue among confessions, conducted in hope of an eventual reconciliation among the divided communions, as well as initiatives undertaken jointly by separated Churches. 1948, for instance, saw the formation of the World Council of Churches (WCC), the single largest ecumenical body, which began as an association of mainline Protestant communions, but which came soon to include Eastern Orthodox and Oriental Orthodox Churches as well; and, while the Roman Catholic Church does not

A meeting of Pope John XXIII's ecumenical council in St Peter's Basilica in Vatican City. This meeting in 1962 of worldwide Catholic clergy was popularly known as the Second Vatican Council.

belong to the organization, it has often worked in concert with the WCC on any number of projects.

Ecumenical dialogues were also established between the Eastern Orthodox and many of the Oriental Churches, as well as between the Oriental Churches and Rome. Even more remarkably, perhaps – at least in terms of historical significance – were the relations that formed between Pope Paul VI (1897–1978), a pontiff profoundly committed to the reunion of the Churches, and the largely like-minded patriarch of Constantinople, Athenagoras I (1886–1972). The two met in person in Jerusalem in 1964, and the fruit of this unprecedented embassy was a joint statement of 1965 that, among other things, rescinded the excommunications of 1054 on both sides (without, however, re-establishing communion).

For his part, the pope's gesture was in keeping with the tenor of his entire pontificate, which was singularly devoted to the cause of Catholic renewal and Christian reconciliation, and with the ideals of the Second Vatican Council, which – having been convoked in 1962 by his predecessor John XXIII (1881–1963) – was already in session at the time of his elevation to the papacy in 1963. That council was, certainly, the single most enormous and transformative event in modern Catholic history. In part, it was the culmination of decades of a theological return *ad fontes* ('to the sources') by Catholic scholars who sought a patristic and early Medieval alternative to the rather arid late 'neo-scholasticism' that had dominated Catholic theology from the 17th century on; in larger part, though, it was a radical institutional revision of the liturgy (now to be celebrated in the vernacular rather than in Latin and with greater lay participation), of church administration (restoring an emphasis on the dignity and authority of local bishops), of Catholic exegetical methods (affirming modern biblical scholarship) and of Rome's relations with other Christians and even with other faiths.

Inside the Catholic church of Shangyanjing village in southwest China's Tibet Autonomous Region. As the sole Catholic church in Tibet, it has become a place of worship for some 600 Tibetan believers.

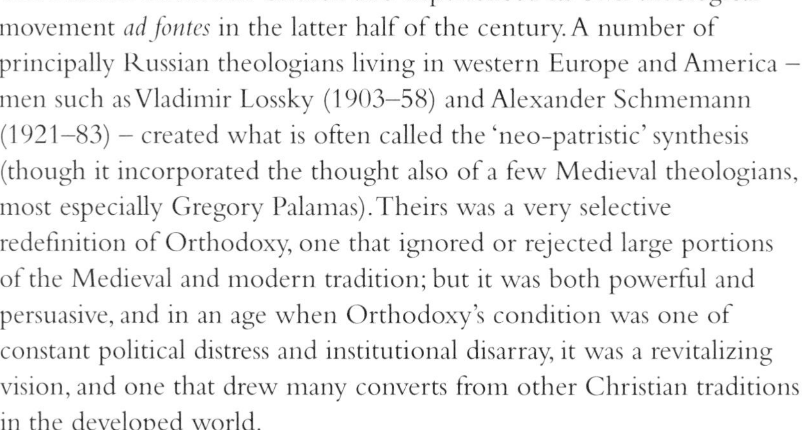

The Eastern Orthodox Church also experienced its own theological movement *ad fontes* in the latter half of the century. A number of principally Russian theologians living in western Europe and America – men such as Vladimir Lossky (1903–58) and Alexander Schmemann (1921–83) – created what is often called the 'neo-patristic' synthesis (though it incorporated the thought also of a few Medieval theologians, most especially Gregory Palamas). Theirs was a very selective redefinition of Orthodoxy, one that ignored or rejected large portions of the Medieval and modern tradition; but it was both powerful and persuasive, and in an age when Orthodoxy's condition was one of constant political distress and institutional disarray, it was a revitalizing vision, and one that drew many converts from other Christian traditions in the developed world.

The Global South and Far East

Whatever vitality native European and American Christianity may still possess, however, the most enormous changes the Christian world as a whole will experience as the 21st century advances – barring entirely unforeseen and unimaginable events – will be those wrought by the rise of a 'new Christendom' in the Global South and East Asia. For while the forms of Christianity that have been exported to the far reaches of the earth are European and North American in provenance and substance, the manner of their reception in cultures profoundly different from those of the prosperous and traditionally Christian West ensures that

THE CHURCH OF SAINTS AND MARTYRS

If Christianity today is the religion growing most rapidly and most widely throughout the world, it is also – not coincidentally – the most persecuted religion in the world. In Africa, the Middle East and Asia, in countries as diverse as Sudan, India, Turkey, Pakistan and China, the Church endures various degrees of oppression: in some places, chronic legal and extra-legal harassment; in others, sporadic episodes of popular violence; in others, enslavement; and, in still others, imprisonment, torture and death. The nation, though, where conditions perhaps most nearly resemble those of the early Church would almost certainly be China: where Christianity is growing among all classes, but especially among urban populations; where official policy is largely hostile to the faith, but inconsistent and somewhat capricious in its use of violence and intimidation; and where the majority of Christians worship in secret, in private houses.

Such parallels, of course, are never more than general. Ancient Rome possessed nothing like the state apparatus of the People's Republic, nor did it ever experience anything like the radical social and economic transformations occurring in China today. But, if the Church should ever prove victorious in China, it will be able – like the Church of the fourth century – to look back upon its own age of martyrs.

One such martyr, already particularly revered among Chinese Christians, was the man perhaps most responsible for founding the network of Protestant house churches in China, both before and after the revolution: Watchman Nee (1903–72), a free church Evangelical, much influenced by the congregationalist Plymouth Brethren of England.

Born Nee Shu-Tsu, he assumed the name Tuo-Sheng (Watchman) after his conversion in 1920, and became thereafter an indefatigable evangelist, founding churches wherever he went, and helping to establish the Chinese Local Church (an Evangelical communion committed to the proposition that there should be only one church in any city). He also became a prolific writer, producing books of scriptural interpretation and spiritual instruction – writings that placed a profound and distinctive emphasis upon the soul's union with and glorification in Christ, and upon the demands and delights of spiritual charity.

When the communists seized power, Watchman Nee did not desist from preaching and writing. After various harassments – including a deportation from Shanghai – Nee was finally arrested in 1952 and imprisoned, under the harshest conditions; and he was still in prison 20 years later when he died.

c.1925
Rise of the Chinese Local Church movement

1932–68
Karl Barth writes and publishes *Church Dogmatics*

1946
Henri de Lubac publishes *Surnaturel*

1948
Formation of the World Council of Churches

1956
Founding of the Brazil for Christ Pentecostal Church

1957
Vladimir Lossky publishes *The Mystical Theology of the Eastern Church*

1962
Pope John XXIII convokes the Second Vatican Council

1965
Pope Paul VI and Patriarch Athenagoras I rescind the excommunications of 1054

1972
Death of Watchman Nee in prison

1978
Karol Wojtyla becomes Pope John Paul II

1988
Public celebrations of the millennium of the Orthodox Church in Russia

2005
Joseph Ratzinger becomes Pope Benedict XVI

they will come increasingly to reflect the 'cultural ecologies' into which they have been transplanted, and that other, native forms of Christianity will continue to evolve in their shadows. In the nations of sub-Saharan Africa, for instance, traditional communions – such as the Catholic Church – almost inevitably assume characteristics congenial to the spiritual expectations of Africans. And in many ways these expectations more closely resemble those of the world in which the Gospel was first preached than those of the modern West. Peoples who believe firmly in the reality of spiritual warfare are naturally hospitable to 'Charismatic' or 'Pentecostal' worship; hence a Catholic service may have all the appearances of a revival meeting, and include exorcisms, healing, prophecy and speaking in tongues, in addition to the Eucharistic celebration.

> *'Good is stronger than evil; love is stronger than hate; light is stronger than darkness; life is stronger than death. Victory is ours, through him who loves us.'*
>
> DESMOND TUTU, ANGLICAN ARCHBISHOP OF CAPE TOWN, SOUTH AFRICA, *AN AFRICAN PRAYER BOOK*, 1995

Given the speed with which Christian conversions are occurring in the Global South, moreover, it would be somewhat absurd to speak of such practices as either anomalous or eccentric; they are rapidly becoming – in statistical terms – dominant expressions of Christian faith. At the beginning of the 19th century, in all of Africa there were perhaps no more than ten million Christians; today the number is around 390 million, and tens of thousands are added to that number every month. In Latin America – as a result of fairly robust birthrates, as well as of the success of Catholic renewal movements (many of them Charismatic) and of Evangelical and Pentecostal missions – there are over 500 million. And in Asia, there are perhaps 350 million.

This last number is somewhat uncertain, though: it encompasses not only, say, the historically Catholic nation of the Philippines, or democratic South Korea, where Christianity has proven immensely successful, but countries where the faith is discouraged or even persecuted. It is especially difficult to calculate the number of China's Christians with much exactitude, because of the odd oscillations of government policy between limited toleration and brutal repression.

The officially recognized Church in China boasts more than 20 million adherents; but the unofficial Christian communities – the underground Catholic Church and the Protestant household churches – are spiritual home to a great many more Christians, and estimates of the total Christian population of the country range between 45 and 90 million. However elusive the real number may be, though, few doubt that it is growing – fairly rapidly. It is also one of the distinctive traits of Chinese Christianity that its constituency is in very large measure drawn from the most educated class of society; it is even said that a considerable number of those in the ruling party are secretly Christians.

The Story of Christianity

Christianity has now entered its third millennium, and no-one – obviously – can foresee what shapes it will assume in the centuries ahead, what renewals it may or may not know, what divisions or reconciliations it may experience. What is certainly the case, however, is that the sage and confident predictions of the faith's imminent demise that were such a vogue in the late 19th and early 20th centuries, and that one still occasionally hears ventured by inattentive observers today, will not be proved correct. In both absolute and relative numbers, the world's community of Christians is far larger than it has ever been; and its rate of expansion is as nothing it has ever known in the past. It may very well be the case that now, after 2000 years, the story of Christianity is still only beginning.

A priest leads a service in a village in Zimbabwe, where the people are praying for the end of a drought. Some 25 percent of Zimbabwe's population today are Christian.

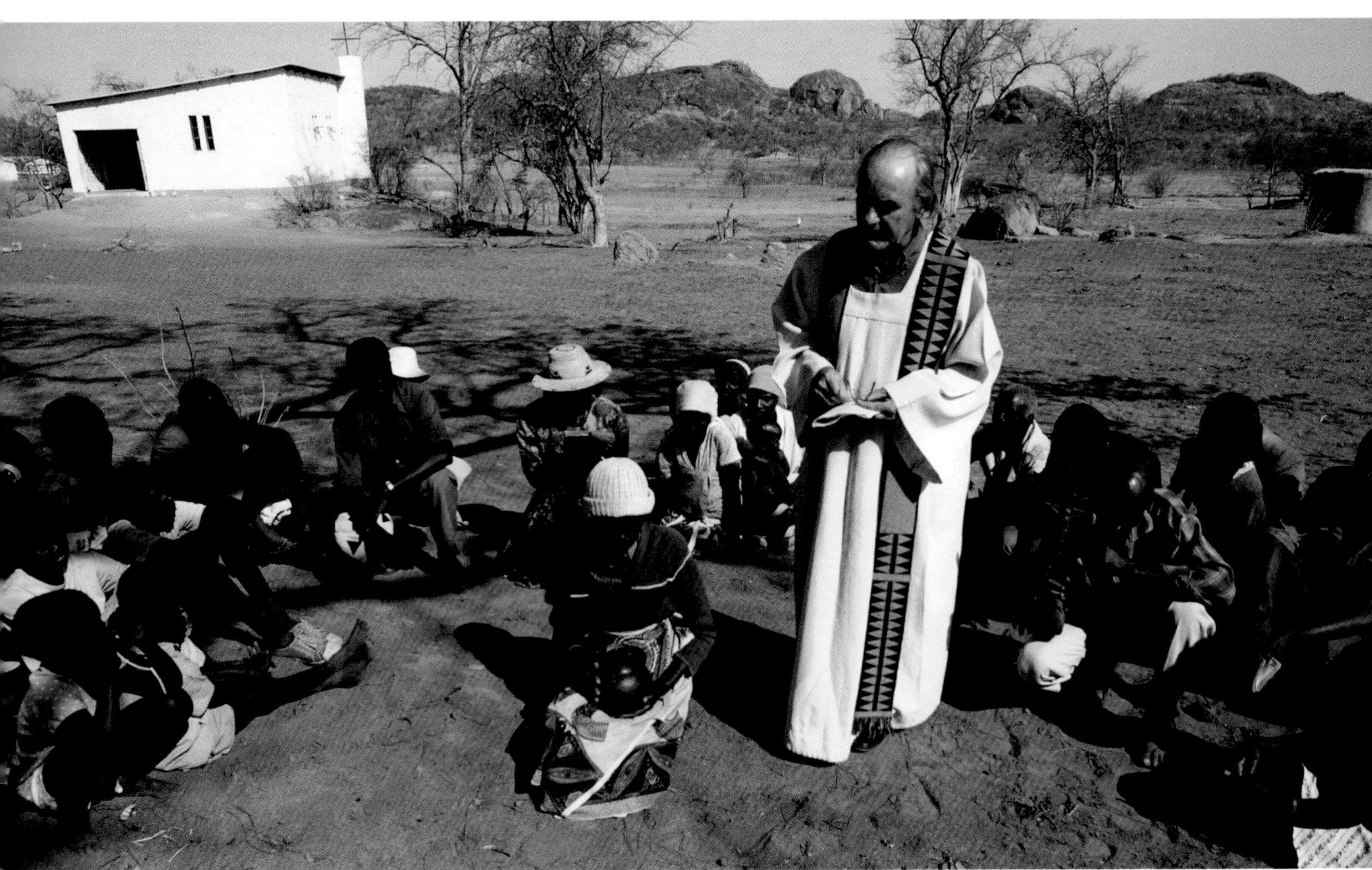

GLOSSARY

A

Apostasy Repudiation or abandonment of one's faith.

Apostolic church The church in the days of Christ's Apostles; the church as governed by the Apostles and their immediate successors.

Ascetic A person who practises asceticism: that is, who lives a life of austerity in order to 'mortify' or 'purify' his or her will, in order to make himself or herself better able to pray and pursue spiritual virtue.

Asceticism The practice of self-abnegation through discipline of the flesh, will and mind; the way of the hermit, monk or nun.

B

Bodhisattva In Mahayana Buddhism, a saviour; one who, having attained enlightenment, could enter into Nirvana, but decides instead to defer his own salvation in order to devote himself to the salvation of others.

Bull, papal An edict issued bearing the seal and authority of the pope.

Byzantine Of or pertaining to the Eastern Roman empire centred in Constantinople (Byzantium) and its civilization; of or pertaining to the theology, arts or culture of the Eastern Orthodox Church.

C

***c.* (circa)** around or in the vicinity of a certain date.

Caliphate In Islam, the order of the legitimate successors (caliphs) of the Prophet Muhammad as ruler and legislator of the Islamic world; the empire of Islam.

Canon The officially recognized books of the Bible; a rule or law of the church.

Catechist A teacher of Christian doctrine.

Catholic literally, 'universal'; a community belonging to or directly descending from the ancient Christian church; or claiming to the Eastern Orthodox, Roman Catholic, Coptic, Armenian, Assyrian, Malankara, and perhaps Anglican churches.

Charism A spiritual power or gift conferred by God.

Christology The theological study of Christ and of the relation of the divine and the human within him.

Church, Eastern The church of the Eastern Roman world, both before and after the great schism of 1054; the Greek, Syrian and Slavic church; the Eastern Orthodox Church.

Church, Western The church of the Western Roman world, both before and after the great schism of 1054; the Latin church; the Roman Catholic Church.

Coenobitic monasticism Communal monasticism, as opposed to the monastic discipline of hermits; a discipline involving communal life, prayer and work and governed by a common rule.

Confucianism The Chinese school of thought devoted to the teachings and principles of Confucius (551–479 BC) and to a number of traditional rituals.

Creed An official statement of the tenets of a faith; a system of beliefs.

D

d. (died).

Demiurge literally 'world maker'.

Diaspora The dispersed communities of a given people; the Jews living in countries outside of the Holy Land in the centuries after the Babylonian captivity.

Druids The order of priests in pre-Christian Celtic society.

E

Ecclesial Of or pertaining to the church (Ecclesia).

Episcopacy The church's order of bishops (Episkopoi).

Eschatological Of or pertaining to the last things or end of time; concerning the Final Judgement, the Kingdom of God and the destiny of souls; from the Greek word *exchatos*, meaning 'last' or 'final'.

Eucharist The Christian sacrament of holy communion, in which bread and wine are consumed as the body and blood of Christ.

Evangel literally, 'Good News' or 'Gospel'.

Exarchate In Byzantine political terms, an area governed by a provincial governor.

Exegesis The interpretation of texts, in particular scriptural texts.

Exegete One who practises exegesis.

Exegetical Of or pertaining to the discipline of exegesis.

F

fl. (flourished).

G

Gentiles Non-Jewish peoples; the non-Jewish nations; from the Latin *gens,* meaning 'nation', 'clan'or 'race'.

Gesso A plaster used as a base surface for painting, sometimes made with an admixture of alabaster or marble dust.

Gnostics Persons belonging to any of a number of schools of religious speculation (many of which claimed to be Christian) that flourished in the second and third centuries, and that taught a doctrine of salvation through spiritual 'knowledge' (*gnosis* in Greek).

H

Hellenistic Of or pertaining to the international Greek civilization created by the conquests of Alexander the Great and his successors.

Hermeticism Esoteric philosophy, often incorporating elements of alchemy, magic and occult wisdoms, loosely associated with a corpus of writings ascribed to the mythical Hermes Trismegistus (Hermes the Thrice-Great).

Hesychasm A Byzantine school of mysticism that from the 14th century onward became the dominant mystical school of the Eastern Orthodox Church.

Humanist In late Medieval and early modern Byzantine and (later) Western European tradition, a person who pursues the study of classical languages, philosophy and literature.

Hymnode A writer or composer of hymns.

Hypostasis A Greek term meaning 'substance' that came, in Christian theology, to designate a Person of the Trinity; a Person of the Trinity (Father, Son or Spirit) as distinct from the common 'ousia' or essence of the Trinity.

I

Icon A sacred image used in worship and private devotion; in the Eastern Christian world, an image of Christ or of a saint or saints.

Iconoclasm The destruction of icons; hostility to icons on religious grounds.

Iconoclast One who indulges in iconoclasm.

Iconodule One who venerates (but does not worship) icons.

Iconolatry The worship of icons, historically condemned by all schools of theology.

L

Latin Church The church of the Western Roman world, both before and after the great schism of 1054; the Roman Catholic Church.

Logos A Greek word almost impossible to translate fully: It can mean 'word', 'discourse', 'mind', 'principle', 'idea', 'spirit', 'scheme' or many other things; in Stoicism, the spiritual and intellectual reality pervading, animating and holding all things together; in Hellenistic Judaism of a certain kind, an emanation or lesser personal manifestation of God mediating between God Most High and creation; in Christian thought, the Second Person of the Trinity or Son of God, through whom all things were created, and who became incarnate as Jesus of Nazareth.

Lustrations Ritual ablutions or purifying acts of sacrifice.

M

Metaphysical Of or pertaining to metaphysics; transcending the physical.

Metaphysics The study or investigation of that which lies beyond physical reality, or of the principles underlying reality.

Monophysites Those who maintain that the incarnate Son of God possesses a single nature (physis), which is divine; a term misleadingly applied to Coptic and other Christians who, due to the different connotations of the word physis in their intellectual traditions, did not subscribe to the doctrine of Christ's two natures (divine and human) as proclaimed by the Council of Chalcedon in AD 451; Christians of the Coptic, Ethiopian and Armenian Churches.

N

Necromancy Magical consort with and use of the spirits of the dead or of the powers of the underworld.

Nestorians In accordance with the teachings ascribed to Nestorius, those who maintain that the incarnate Son of God possesses not only two natures, but two persons; a term misleadingly applied to East Syrian and Persian Christians who, due to the different connotations attached to the Syriac word for 'person', did not subscribe to the doctrine of Christ's two natures (divine and human) as proclaimed by the Council of Chalcedon in AD 451; Christians of the East Syrian (or Assyrian or Chaldean) Church of the East.

Nihilism The idea that there is no transcendent source of reality, no higher meaning to existence, no metaphysical or spiritual realm and no higher truth in whose light the world should be understood or judged.

O

Ophite A kind of gnostic who venerated the serpent (in Greek, *ophis*) who enlightened Adam and Eve and helped to free them from the delusions imposed upon them by the demiurge.

Orthodox Church The Eastern Orthodox Church or Eastern Church; also used to designate the Coptic, Armenian and Ethiopian churches.

P

Pagan(s) Non-Christian Gentiles; worshippers of the pre-Christian Gods, or practitioners of non-Christian and non-Jewish European or Indian religion or philosophy; from the Latin *paganus,* meaning 'man of the countryside', 'peasant' or 'rustic'; heathens.

Papal States The area of central Italy historically under the political rule of the pope.

Patristic Of or pertaining to the church fathers (patres).

Pendentives The concave triangular areas between a dome and the piers of its base.

Platonism The philosophical tradition derived from the teachings of Plato: a philosophical tendency with Pagan, Jewish, Christian and Muslim expressions.

Polytheism Belief in and worship of a plurality of gods.

Protestant Of or pertaining to those churches and Christian communities of the Western Christian world that broke with the Church of Rome in the 16th century and after; originally, one who protested a 1529 condemnation of the Reformation by the Holy Roman Emperor Charles V.

Puritan An English Christian of the Elizabethan period and after who wished to 'purify' the Anglican church of its Catholic elements; a Protestant who favors a congregationalist church organization (that is, without bishops and priests), and simple and unadorned worship, and who places an emphasis upon moral rectitude and restraint.

R

r. (reigned).

S

See The seat or throne of a bishop; a bishop's diocese.

Simony To sell or buy an ecclesiastical office or benefice; from Simon Magus, who attempted to purchase spiritual charisms from the Apostles Peter and John.

SS (saints).

Syncretism The practice of combining elements from various religions or philosophies.

Syncretistic Of or pertaining to syncretism.

Synoptic Affording a synopsis or general perspective; in Christian tradition, the Gospels of Matthew, Mark and Luke, each of which provides a synopsis of the life of Christ.

T

Taoism The Chinese philosophical school derived from the teachings of the legendary or semi-legendary sage Lao-Tzu (traditionally said to have been born in 604 BC); a mystical philosophy concerned with the 'Way' ('Tao'), the ubiquitous and mysterious power of life pervading all things, historically associated with alchemical and magical practices, and concerned with gods and spirits.

Theosophy A spiritual philosophy supposedly comprising a spiritual wisdom ('sophia') imparted directly by God; an occult or hermetic religious philosophy propounded by individuals claiming to possess such wisdom and even perhaps miraculous powers.

U

Universalism 1 The belief that all rational beings, even devils, will ultimately be saved, and that Hell is temporary and for the sake of purification. **2** The belief that Christ came for the salvation of all nations and that the divisions between Jew and Gentile had been abolished in him.

V

Vatican Home and temporal domain of the pope, sited within Rome, but recognized as independent from all other countries, including Italy.

Vicar of Christ A title for the pope, appearing perhaps as early as the eighth century, and gradually coming in the later Middle Ages to signify the papacy's claim of total jurisdiction over the church.

FURTHER REFERENCES

Brown, P. *The Rise of Western Christendom: Triumph and Diversity 200–1000 AD* (Blackwell, Oxford, UK, 2002)

Clement, O. *The Roots of Christian Mysticism: Texts from the Patristic Era with Commentary* (New City Press, New York, NY, 1996)

Jenkins, P. *The Next Christendom: The Coming of Global Christianity* (Oxford University Press, New York, NY, 2007)

Kamen, H. *The Spanish Inquisition: A Historical Revision* (Yale University Press, New Haven, CT, 1999)

Lane-Fox, R. *Pagans and Christians* (Penguin, Harmondsworth, UK, 2006)

McGinn, B. *Presence of God: A History of Western Christian Mysticism, Volume 1: The Foundations of Mysticism* (Herder and Herder, New York, NY, 1994)

McGinn, B. *Presence of God: A History of Western Christian Mysticism, Volume 2: The Growth of Mysticism* (Herder and Herder, New York, NY, 1996)

McGinn, B. *Presence of God: A History of Western Christian Mysticism, Volume 3: The Flowering of Mysticism* (Herder and Herder, New York, NY, 1998)

McGinn, B. *Presence of God: A History of Western Christian Mysticism, Volume 4: The Harvesting of Mysticism in Medieval Germany* (Herder and Herder, New York, NY, 2005)

Meyendorff, J. *Byzantine Theology: Historical Trends and Doctrinal Themes* (Fordham University Press, New York, NY, 1987)

Ostrogorsky, G. *History of the Byzantine State* (Rutgers University Press, New Brunswick, NJ, 1984)

Pelikan, J. *The Christian Tradition: A History of the Development of Doctrine, Volume 1: The Emergence of the Catholic Tradition (100–600)* (University of Chicago Press, Chicago, IL, 1973)

Pelikan, J. *The Christian Tradition: A History of the Development of Doctrine, Volume 2: The Spirit of Eastern Christendom (600–1700)* (University of Chicago Press, Chicago, IL, 1977)

Pelikan, J. *The Christian Tradition: A History of the Development of Doctrine, Volume 3: The Growth of Medieval Theology (600–1300)* (University of Chicago Press, Chicago, IL, 1980)

Pelikan, J. *The Christian Tradition: A History of the Development of Doctrine, Volume 4: Reformation of Church and Dogma (1300–1700)* (University of Chicago Press, Chicago, IL, 1985)

Pelikan, J. *The Christian Tradition: A History of the Development of Doctrine, Volume 5: Christian Doctrine and Modern Culture (since 1700)* (University of Chicago Press, Chicago, IL, 1991)

Runciman, S. *A History of the Crusades Vol. 1: The First Crusade and the Foundations of the Kingdom of Jerusalem* (Cambridge University Press, Cambridge, UK, 1987)

Runciman, S. *A History of the Crusades Vol. 2: The Kingdom of Jerusalem and the Frankish East* (Cambridge University Press, Cambridge, UK, 1987)

Runciman, S. A *History of the Crusades Vol. 3: The Kingdom of Acre and the Later Crusades* (Cambridge University Press, Cambridge, UK, 1987)

Wilken, R. *The Christians as the Romans Saw Them* (Yale University Press, New Haven, CT, 2003)

INDEX

Page numbers in *italic* refer to illustrations; numbers in brackets indicate a feature box

PICTURE ACKNOWLEDGEMENTS

2 Shutterstock/Bartlomiej K. Kwieciszewski; 4 (top) Shutterstock/Robert Young; 4 (bottom) Shutterstock/Vova Pomortzeff; 5 (top) Shutterstock/Roberto Caucino; 5 (bottom) Shutterstock/Yare Marketing; 8 Corbis/© Ted Spiegel/Corbis; 9 Corbis/© Burstein Collection/Corbis; 11 Shutterstock; 12 Shutterstock/Clara Natoli; 13 Corbis/© Araldo de Luca/ Corbis; 15 Corbis/© Ali Meyer/Corbis; 16 Shutterstock/ Jacqueline Abromeit; 17 Corbis/© The Gallery Collection/ Corbis; 19 Corbis/© Francis G. Mayer/Corbis; 20 Shutterstock/ Robert Young; 21 Corbis/© Arte & Immagini srl/Corbis; 22 Corbis/© Archivo Iconografico, S.A./Corbis; 25 Shutterstock/ Bartlomiej K. Kwieciszewski; 27 Corbis/© Christie's Images/ Corbis; 28–29 Corbis/© Francis G. Mayer/Corbis; 31 Corbis/ © Arte & Immagini srl/Corbis; 32 Shutterstock/Tawfik Dajani; 35 Corbis/© Chris Hellier/Corbis; 36–37 Corbis/© Bettmann/ Corbis; 39 Corbis/© Gianni Dagli Orti/Corbis; 40 British Library/HIP/Topfoto; 41 Corbis/© Philadelphia Museum of Art/Corbis; 45 Corbis/© Archivo Iconografico, S.A./Corbis; 46 Corbis/© Bettmann/Corbis; 49 Corbis/© Araldo de Luca/ Corbis; 51 Shutterstock/Vova Pomortzeff; 52 Corbis/© Philadelphia Museum of Art/Corbis; 54 Corbis/© Vanni Archive/Corbis; 56–57 Corbis/© Roger Wood/Corbis; 58 Corbis/© Christie's Images/Corbis; 61 Corbis/The Art Archive; 64 Shutterstock/Suzanne Long; 65 Corbis/© Corbis Sygma; 67 Corbis/© Corbis Sygma; 69 Shutterstock/Liudmila Gridina; 71 Corbis/© Chris Hellier/Corbis; 73 Corbis/© Bettmann/ Corbis; 74 Corbis/© Michael Nicholson/Corbis; 76 Corbis/© The Art Archive/Corbis; 78 Shutterstock/iofoto; 79 Corbis/© Bettmann/Corbis; 81 Corbis/© Bettmann/Corbis; 83 Corbis/ © Ali Meyer/Corbis; 85 Corbis/© National Gallery Collection, by kind permission of the Trustees of the National Gallery, London/Corbis; 86 Corbis/© Arte & Immagini srl/Corbis; 87 Corbis/© Ali Meyer/Corbis; 88 Corbis/© Archivo Iconografico, S.A./Corbis; 89 Corbis/© The Art Archive/ Corbis; 91 Shutterstock/Yare Marketing; 93 Corbis/© The Art Archive/Corbis; 95 Shutterstock/Albert Barr; 97 Corbis/© Bettmann/Corbis; 98 Corbis/© Historical Picture Archive/ Corbis; 99 Corbis/© Archivo Iconografico, S.A./Corbis; 100 Corbis/© Araldo de Luca/Corbis; 102 Shutterstock/Svetlana Tikhonova; 104–105 Corbis/© Roger Wood/Corbis; 107 Shutterstock/Tan Kian Khoon; 109 Shutterstock/David McKee; 113 Corbis/© Stapleton Collection/Corbis; 114 Shutterstock/Evelyn Dilworth; 115 Corbis/© Michael Nicholson/Corbis; 117 Corbis/© Archivo Iconografico, S.A./ Corbis; 119 Shutterstock/Vova Pomortzeff; 121 Shutterstock; 123 Shutterstock/Vova Pomortzeff; 125 Corbis/© Stefano Bianchetti/Corbis; 127 Corbis/© Bettmann/Corbis; 129 Corbis/© José F. Poblete/Corbis; 131 Shutterstock/Vova Pomortzeff; 133 Corbis/© The State Russian Museum/Corbis; 134 Corbis/© Bettmann/Corbis; 135 Corbis/© Wolfgang Kaehler/Corbis; 137 Corbis/© Christel Gerstenberg/Corbis; 139 Corbis/© Archivo Iconografico, S.A./Corbis; 140 Corbis/ © Archivo Iconografico, S.A./Corbis; 141 Corbis/© Archivo Iconografico, S.A./Corbis; 143 Corbis/© Bettmann/Corbis; 147 Corbis/© Bettmann/Corbis; 151 Corbis/© Gianni Dagli Orti/ Corbis; 153 Shutterstock/Mauro Bighin; 154 Corbis/© Gianni Dagli Orti/Corbis; 156 Corbis/© David Lees/Corbis; 159 Corbis/© Philadelphia Museum of Art/Corbis; 160 Corbis/© National Gallery Collection, by kind permission of the Trustees of the National Gallery, London/Corbis; 163 Corbis/© Bettmann/Corbis; 165 Corbis/© Bob Krist/Corbis; 167 Corbis/ © Roger Wood/Corbis; 168 Corbis/© Gavin Hellier/JAI/ Corbis; 171 Corbis/© The Art Archive/Corbis; 172 Corbis/© Alexander Burkatovski/Corbis; 174 Corbis/© Christie's Images/Corbis; 175 Corbis/© The Art Archive/Corbis; 176 Corbis/© National Gallery Collection, by kind permission of the Trustees of the National Gallery, London/Corbis; 179 Corbis/© Archivo Iconografico, S.A./Corbis; 180 Corbis/© Archivo Iconografico, S.A./Corbis; 181 Corbis/© Tibor Bognar/Corbis; 183 Corbis/© The Art Archive/Corbis; 184 Corbis/© Leonard de Selva/Corbis; 187 Corbis/© Fine Art Photographic Library/Corbis; 188 Corbis/© Bettmann/Corbis; 191 Corbis/© James L. Amos/Corbis; 192 Corbis/© Stefano Bianchetti/Corbis; 193 TopFoto© World History Archive/ TopFoto; 194 Corbis/© Bettmann/Corbis; 195 TopFoto © Print Collector/HIP/TopFoto; 196 Corbis/© Bettmann/Corbis; 198 Corbis/© Leonard de Selva/Corbis; 199 Corbis/© David Lees/ Corbis; 200 Shutterstock/discodave2000; 201 Corbis/© Bettmann/Corbis; 203 Corbis/© Bettmann/Corbis; 204 Corbis/© Krause, Johansen/Archivo Iconografico, S.A./Corbis; 206 Corbis/© Bettmann/Corbis; 207 Corbis/© Bojan Brecelj/ Corbis; 210 Corbis/© Enzo & Paolo Ragazzini/Corbis; 211 Shutterstock/Monster; 213 Corbis/© Stefano Bianchetti/ Corbis; 215 Corbis/© Bettmann/Corbis; 216 Corbis/© The Art Archive/Corbis; 219 Shutterstock/ Gilmanshin; 221 Corbis/© Reuters/Corbis; 223 Corbis/© Stapleton Collection/Corbis; 225 Corbis/© Archivo Iconografico, S.A./Corbis; 226 Corbis/ © Bettmann/Corbis; 227 Corbis/© Bettmann/Corbis; 228 Corbis/© Bettmann/Corbis; 229 Corbis/© Bettmann/Corbis; 230 Corbis/© Archivo Iconografico, S.A./Corbis; 232 Corbis/ © Michael Nicholson/Corbis; 234 Corbis/© Bettmann/Corbis; 235 Corbis/© Bettmann/Corbis; 236 Corbis/© Flip Schulke/ Corbis; 238 Corbis/© Bettmann/Corbis; 239 Corbis/© Christel Gerstenberg/Corbis; 243 Corbis/© David Lees/Corbis; 244 Corbis/© Wang Changshan/Xinhua Press/Corbis; 247 Corbis/© Gideon Mendel/Corbis

Quercus Publishing has made every effort to trace copyright holders of the pictures used in this book. Anyone having claims to ownership not identified above is invited to contact Quercus Publishing.

First published in Great Britain in 2007 by

Quercus
21 Bloomsbury Square
London
WC1A 2NS

A CIP catalogue record for this book is available from the British Library

ISBN-10 1 84724 140 9
ISBN-13 978 1 84724 140 5

Printed and bound in China

10 9 8 7 6 5 4 3 2 1

Designed and edited by BCS Publishing Limited, Oxford.